Confederate States of America

Regulations for the army of the Confederate States

Confederate States of America

Regulations for the army of the Confederate States

ISBN/EAN: 9783337184872

Printed in Europe, USA, Canada, Australia, Japan

Cover: Foto ©Andreas Hilbeck / pixelio.de

More available books at **www.hansebooks.com**

REGULATIONS

FOR THE

ARMY OF THE CONFEDERATE STATES,

1862.

RICHMOND, VA.
WEST & JOHNSTON, 145 MAIN STREET.
1862.

Macfarlane & Fergusson, Printers, Richmond, Va.

WAR DEPARTMENT,

RICHMOND, *November 1st*, 1862.

The following *Regulations for the Army* of the Confederate States are published by direction of the President, for the government of all concerned. They will accordingly be strictly obeyed, and nothing contrary to them will be enjoined or permitted in any portion of the forces of the Confederate States by the officers thereof.

GEO. W. RANDOLPH, *Secretary of War.*

INDEX.

Note.—The numbering in this Index is of the *paragraph*. Where the *page* or Article is referred to, it is specially stated.

A.

H.

I.

REGULATIONS FOR THE ARMY.

ARTICLE I.

MILITARY DISCIPLINE.

1. All inferiors are required to obey strictly, and to execute with alacrity and good faith, the lawful orders of the superiors appointed over them.

2. Military authority is to be exercised with firmness, but with kindness and justice to inferiors. Punishments shall be strictly conformable to military law.

3. Superiors of every grade are forbid to injure those under them by tyrannical or capricious conduct, or by abusive language.

ARTICLE II.

RANK AND COMMAND.

4. Rank of officers and non-commissioned officers:

1st. General.
2d. Major-General.
3d. Brigadier-General.
4th. Colonel.
5th. Lieut Colonel.
6th. Major.
7th. Captain.
8th. First Lieutenant.
9th. Second Lieutenant.
10th. Cadet.
11th. Sergeant-Major.
12th. Quartermaster-Sergeant of a Regiment.
13th. Ordnanee Sergeant and Hospital Steward.
14th. First Sergeant.
15th. Sergeant.
16th. Corporal.

And each grade by date of commission or appointment.

5. When commissions are of the same date, the rank is to be decided between officers of the same regiment or corps by the order of appointment; between officers of different regiments or corps: 1st, by rank in actual service when appointed; 2d, by former rank and service in the army or marine corps; 3d, by lottery among such as have not been in the military service of the Confederate States. In case of equality of ranks by virtue of a brevet commission, reference is had to commissions not brevet.

6. Officers having brevets or commissions of a prior date to those of the corps in which they serve, will take place on courts-martial or of inquiry, and on boards detailed for military purposes, when composed of different corps, according to the ranks given them in their brevets or former commissions; but in the regiment, corps, or company to which such officers belongs, they shall do duty and take rank, both in courts and on boards as aforesaid, which shall be composed of their own corps, according to the commissions by which they are there mustered.

7. If, upon marches, guards, or in quarters, different corps shall happen to join, or do duty together, the officer highest in rank, according to the commission by which he is mustered in the army, navy, marine corps, or militia, there on duty by orders from competent authority, shall command the whole, and give orders for what is needful for the service, unless otherwise directed by the President of the Confederate States, in orders of special assignment providing for the case.

8. An officer not having orders from competent authority, cannot put himself *on duty* by virtue of his commission alone.

9. Brevet rank takes effect only in the following cases: 1st, by special assignment of the President in commands composed of different corps; 2d, on courts-martial or of inquiry, and on boards detailed for military purposes, when composed of different corps. Troops are on *detachment* only when sent out temporarily to perform a special service.

10. In regularly constituted commands, as garrisons, posts, departments, companies, battalions, regiments, corps, brigades, divisions, army corps, or the army itself, brevet rank cannot be exercised except by special assignment.

11. The officers of engineers are not to assume nor to be ordered on any duty beyond the line of their immediate profession, except by the special order of the President.

12. An officer of the Medical Department cannot exercise command except in his own department, or over enlisted men, as a commissioned officer.

13. Officers of the Quartermasters or Subsistence Departments, though eligible to command according to the rank they hold in the army of the Confederate States, not subject to the orders of a junior officer, shall not assume the command of troops unless put on duty under orders which specially so direct by authority of the President.

ARTICLE III.

SUCCESSION IN COMMAND OR DUTY.

14. The functions assigned to any officer in these regulations by title of office devolve on the officer acting in his place, except as specially excepted.

15. During the absence of the Quartermaster-General, or the Chief of any Military Bureau of the War Department, his duties in the bureau prescribed by law or regulations, devolve on the officer of his department empowered by the president to perform them, in such absence.

16. An officer who succeeds to any command or duty stands in regard to his duties in the same situation as his predecessor. The officer relieved, shall turn over to his successor all orders in force at the time, and all the public property and funds pertaining to his command or duty, and shall receive therefor duplicate receipts, showing the condition of each article.

17. An officer in a temporary command shall not, except in urgent cases, alter or annul the standing orders of the regular or permanent commander, without authority from the next higher commander.

ARTICLE IV.

APPOINTMENT AND PROMOTION OF COMMISSIONED OFFICERS.

18. All vacancies in established regiments and corps to the rank of Colonel, shall be filled by promotion according to seniority, except in cases of disability or other incompetency.

19. Promotions to the rank of Colonel shall be made regimentally, according to the arm, as infantry, cavalry, &c.; and in the Staff Departments, and in the Engineers and other corps, according to corps.

20. Appointments above the rank of Colonel will be made by selection from the army.

21. Cadets appointed under Confederate law, shall be assigned to such duties, governed by exigencies of the service, as will best promote their military experience and improvement, until a military school shall be established by the Government for their instruction.

22. Whenever the public service may require the appointment of any citizen to the army, a board of officers will be instituted, before which the applicant will appear for examination into his physical ability, moral character, attainments and general fitness for the service. If the board report in favor of the applicant, he will be deemed eligible for a commission in the army.

ARTICLE V.

RESIGNATION OF OFFICERS

23. No officer will be considered out of service on the tender of his resignation, until it shall have been duly accepted by the proper authority.

24. Resignations will be forwarded by the commanding officer to the Adjutant and Inspector-General of the army for decision at the War Department.

25. Resignations tendered under charges, when forwarded by any commander, will always be accompanied by a copy of the charges; or, in the absence of written charges, by a report of the case, for the information of the Secretary of War.

26. Before presenting the resignation of any officer, the Adjutant and Inspector-General will ascertain and report to the War Department the state of such officer's accounts of money, as well as of public property, for which he may have been responsible.

27. In time of war, or with an army in the field, resignations shall take effect within thirty days from the date of the order of acceptance.

28. Leaves of absence will not be granted by commanding officers to officers on tendering their resignation, unless the resignation be unconditional and immediate.

ARTICLE VI.

EXCHANGE OR TRANSFER OF OFFICERS.

29. The transfer of officers from one regiment or corps to another, will be made only by the War Department, on the mutual application of the parties desiring the exchange.

30. An officer shall not be transferred from one regiment or corps to

another, with prejudice to the rank of any officer of the regiment or corps to which he is transferred.

ARTICLE VII.

APPOINTMENTS ON THE STAFF.

31. General Officers appoint their own Aides-de-camp.

32. Officers on duty as Brigadier and Major General, by virtue of Brevet Commissions, may, with the special sanction of the War Department, be allowed the Aids de-Camp of the grades corresponding to their brevets; but without such sanction, the number and rate of pay of the Aids will be regulated according to the lineal grade of the General.

33. An officer of a mounted corps shall not be separated from his regiment, except for duty connected with his particular arm.

34. The senior Lieutenant present, holding the appointment of Assistant Commissary of Subsistence, is entitled to perform the duties.

ARTICLE VIII.

DISTRIBUTION OF THE TROOPS.

35. The military geographical departments will be established by the War Department. In time of peace, brigades or divisions will not be formed, nor the stations of the troops changed, without authority from the War Department.

ARTICLE IX.

CARE OF FORTIFICATIONS.

36. No person shall be permitted to walk upon any of the slopes of a fortification, except the ramps and glacis. If, in any case, it be necessary to provide for crossing them, it should be done by placing wooden steps or stairs against the slopes. The *occasional* walking of persons on a parapet will do no harm, provided it be not allowed to cut the surface into paths.

37. No cattle, horses, or other animal shall ever be permitted to go upon the slopes, the ramparts, or the parapets, nor upon the glacis, except within fenced limits, which should not approach the crest nearer than 30 feet.

38. All grassed surfaces, excepting the glacis, will be carefully and frequently mowed, (except in dry weather,) and the oftener the better, while growing rapidly—the grass being never allowed to be more than a few inches high. In order to cut the grass even and close, upon small slopes, a light one-handed scythe should be used; and in mowing the steep slopes, the mower should stand on a light ladder resting against the slope, and not upon the grass. Crops of hay may be cut on the glacis; or, if fenced, it may be used as pasture, otherwise it should be treated as other slopes of the fortification. On all the slopes, spots of dead grass will be cut out and replaced by fresh sod. All weeds will be eradicated.

39. The burning of grass upon any portion of a fortification is strictly forbidden.

40. Particular attention is required to prevent the formation of gullies in the parade, terreplein, and ramps, and especially in slopes where grass is not well established.

41. Earth, sand or ashes, must not be placed against wood work; a

free ventilation must be preserved around it; and all wooden floors, platforms, bridges, &c., will be kept clean swept.

42. The machinery of draw bridges, gates, and posterns must be kept in good working order by proper cleaning and oiling of the parts; the bridges will be raised, and the gates and posterns opened as often as once a week.

43. The terrepleins of forts, the floors of casemates, caponniers, store-rooms, barracks, galleries, posterns, magazines, &c., and the side-walks in front of quarters, as well as other walks, are sometimes paved with brick or stones, or formed of concrete. These surfaces must be preserved from injury with great care. In transporting guns and carriages, and in mounting them, strong way-planks will be used, and neither the wheels nor any other part of the carriages, nor any machinery, such as shears, gins, &c., nor any handspike or other implements, will be allowed to touch those surfaces. Unless protected in a similar manner, no wheel-barrow, or vehicle, or barrel, shall be rolled on said surfaces. No violent work will be done, nor any heavy weight suffered, to fall upon them. In using machines, as gins, &c., in casemates, care must be taken not to injure the arch, or ceiling, or floors. Neglect of these precautions may cause injuries apparently slight, but serious in effect, from leaking of water into masonry, casemates, &c.

44. The doors and windows of all store rooms and occupied casemates, quarters, barracks, &c., will be opened several times a week for thorough ventilation.

45. Masonry shot-furnaces will be heated only on the approach of an enemy. For ordinary practice with hot shot, iron furnaces are provided.

46. The foregoing matters involve but little expense; the labor is within the means of every garrison, and no technical knowledge is required beyond what will be found among soldiers. Other repairs requiring small disbursements, such as repainting exposed wood or iron work, can be also executed by the garrison; but reports, estimates, and requisitions, may be necessary to obtain the materials.

47. No alteration will be made in any fortification, or in any building whatever belonging to it, nor in any building or work of any kind; nor will any building or work of earth, masonry, or timber, be erected within the fortification, or on its exterior, within half a mile, except under the superintendence of the Engineer Department, and by authority of the Secretary of War.

ARTICLE X.

CARE OF ARMAMENT OF FORTIFICATIONS.

48. At each permanent post with a fixed battery, and garrisoned by not more than one company, there will be kept mounted for purposes of instruction and target practice, *three* heavy guns; and at posts garrisoned by more than one company, at the rate of *two* for each of the companies composing its garrison. The other guns dismounted will be properly placed within their own traverse circles, and the carriages preserved from the weather.

49. All guns should be sponged clean, and their vents examined to see that they are clear. The chassis should be traversed and left in a different position, the top carriage moved backward and forward, and

left alternately over the front and rear transoms of the chassis; the elevating screws or machines wiped clean, worked and oiled if required, and the nuts of all bolts screwed up tight. This should all be done regularly once in every week.

50. When tarpaulins, or pent houses, are placed over the guns, they should be removed once a week when the weather is fair, the carriages and guns brushed off, and if damp, allowed to dry.

51. An old sponge staff and head, should be used for drill. The new sponges should never be used unless the gun is fired. The implements should be kept in stores, under cover, and be examined, wiped clean, or brushed at least once a month. In case of leather equipments, due care should be taken for their preservation, by the use of oil, but never using varnish.

52. Magazines should be frequently examined to see that the powder is well preserved. They should be opened every other day, when the air is dry and clear. Barrels of powder should be turned and rolled occasionally. Under ordinary circumstances, only a few cartridges should be kept filled. If the paper body of the cartridge becomes soft, or loses its sizing, it is certain that the magazine is very damp, and means should be found to improve the ventilation. Cartridge bags may be kept in the magazine ready for filling; also port-fires, fuses, tubes, and primers. Stands of grape, cannister, and wads, for barbette guns, should be kept in store with the implements. In casemate guns, wads may be hung in bundles, and grape and cannister near the guns. Shot, well lacquered and clean, may be placed in piles near the guns.

ARTICLE XI.

ARTILLERY PRACTICE.

53. At all posts with fixed batteries, the position of every gun, mounted or to be mounted, will have its number, and this number be placed on the gun when in position.

54. For every such work a post-book of record will be kept, under the direction of the commander of the post, in which will be duly entered the number of each mounted gun, its calibre, weight, names of founder, and its inspector, and other marks: the description of its carriage and date of reception at the post; where from, and the greatest field of fire of the gun in its position.

55. Every commander of a fort, or other fixed battery, will, before entering on artillery practice, carefully reconnoitre, and cause to be sketched for his record book, the water channels, with their soundings and other approaches to the work. Buoys or marks will be placed at the extreme and intermediate ranges of the guns, and these marks be numerically noted on the sketch. A buoy at every five hundred yards may suffice.

56. At the time of practice a distinct and careful note will be made for the record-book, of every shot or shell that may be thrown, designating the guns fired by their numbers, the charges of powder used, the time of flight of shots and shells, the ranges and ricochets, and the positions of guns in respect to the horizontal and vertical lines.

57. The time of flight of a shell may be noted with sufficient accuracy by a stop-watch, or by counting the beats (previously ascertaining their

value) of other watches, and the range may sometimes be computed by the time of flight. Other modes ascertaining the range will readily occur to officers of science.

58. When charged shells with fuze are thrown, the time of bursting will be noted. If they are intended to fall on land, only a blowing charge will be given to the shells, so that they may be picked up for further use.

59. On filling from the barrel, the proof range of powder will be marked on the cartridges.

60. The general objects of this practice are, to give to officers and men the ready and effective use of batteries; to preserve on record the more important results for the benefit of the same, or future commanders, and to ascertain the efficiency of guns and carriages.

61. The commanders of field artillery will also keep registers of their practice, so that not a shot or shell shall be thrown in the army, for instruction, without distinct objects, such as range, accuracy of aim, number of ricochets, time of bursting in the case of shells, &c.

62. The issue of blank cartridges for the drill and instruction of the light artillery companies will be authorized in such quantities as may be necessary, on requisitions duly approved by the proper department.

63. For artillery there will be three annual periods of practice in firing, viz: in April, June and October. At the termination of each period the commanding officers of posts will transmit to the Adjutant-General full reports of the results.

64. To determine accuracy in firing shot and shell, butts or targets will be used. If no natural butt presents itself, targets will be erected.

65. As practice in gunnery is a heavy expense, commanders of companies, and their immediate superiors, are charged with the strict execution of the foregoing details; and all officers on inspection duty will report, through the proper channels, upon such execution.

ARTICLE XII.

REGIMENTS.

66. On the organization of a regiment, companies receive a permanent designation by letters beginning with A, and the officers are assigned to companies; afterward, company officers succeed to companies, as promoted to fill vacancies. Companies take place in the battalion according to the rank of their captains.

67. Captains must serve with their companies. Though subject to the temporary details of service, as for courts-martial, military boards, &c., they shall not be detailed for any duty which may separate them for any considerable time from their companies.

68. The commander of a regiment will appoint the adjutant from the subalterns of the regiment. He will nominate the regimental quartermaster to the Secretary of War for appointment, if approved. He will appoint the non-commissioned staff of the regiment; and, upon the recommendation of the company commander, the sergeants and corporals of companies.

69. In cases of vacancy, and till a decision can be had from regimental headquarters, the company commanders may make temporary appointments of non-commissioned officers.

70. Commanders of regiments are enjoined to avail themselves of every opportunity of instructing both officers and men in the exercise and management of field artillery; and all commanders ought to encourage useful occupations, and manly exercises, and diversions among their men, and to repress dissipation and immorality.

71. It is enjoined upon all officers to be cautious in reproving non-commissioned officers in the presence or hearing of privates, lest their authority be weakened; and non-commissioned officers are not to be sent to the guard-room and mixed with privates during confinement, but be considered as placed in arrest, except in aggravated cases, where escape may be apprehended.

72. Non-commissioned officers may be reduced to the ranks by the sentence of a court-martial, or by order of the commander of the regiment on the application of the company commander. If reduced to the ranks by garrison courts, at posts not the headquarters of the regiment, the company commander will immediately forward a transcript of the order to the regimental commander.

73. Every non-commissioned officer shall be furnished with a certificate or warrant of his rank, signed by the colonel and countersigned by the adjutant. Blank warrants are furnished from the Adjutant-General's office. The first, or orderly sergeant, will be selected by the captain from the sergeants.

74. When it is desired to have bands of music for regiments, there will be allowed for each, sixteen privates to act as musicians, in addition to the chief musicians authorized by law, provided, the total number of privates in the regiment, including the band, does not exceed the legal standard.

75. The musicians of the band will, for the time being, be dropped from the company muster-rolls, but they will be instructed as soldiers, and liable to serve in the ranks on any occasion. They will be mustered in a separate squad under the chief musician, with the non-commissioned staff, and be included in the aggregate in all regimental returns.

76. When a regiment occupies several stations, the band will be kept at the headquarters, *provided* troops (one or more companies) be serving there. The field music belonging to companies not stationed at regimental headquarters, will not be separated from their respective companies.

77. No man, unless he be a carpenter, joiner, carriage maker, blacksmith, saddler, or harness maker, will be mustered as an "artificer."

78. Every article, excepting arms and accoutrements, belonging to the regiment, is to be marked with the number and name of the regiment.

79. Such articles as belong to companies are to be marked with the letter of the company, and number and name of the regiment; and such as belong to men, with their individual numbers, and the letter of the company.

80. The books for each regiment shall be as follows:

1. Original copies of general orders will be tied together in book form, and properly indexed as they are received, and at length bound in volumes of convenient size.
2. *Regimental Order Book*, of three quires of paper, 16 inches by 10½ inches, to contain regimental orders, with an index.

3. *Letter Book*, of three quires of paper, 16 inches by 10½ inches, to contain the correspondence of the commanding officer on regimental subjects, with an index.
4. An index of letters required to be kept on file, in the following form:

No.	NAME OF WRITER.	DATE.	SUBJECT.
1	Captain A. B., .	July 15, 1856.	Appoin't Non-Com. Officers.
2	Adj't General R. J.,	Sept. 4, 1846.	Recruiting Service.
3	Captain F. G, .	Oct. 14, 1846.	Error in Company Return.
4	Lieutenant C. D.,	Nov. 2, 1846.	Application for Leave.

The date of receipt should be endorsed on all letters. They should be numbered to correspond with the index, and filed in regular order, for easy reference.
5. *Descriptive Book*, of five quires of paper, 16 inches by 10½ inches, to contain a list of the officers of the regiment, with their rank, and dates of appointment and promotion; transfers, leaves of absence, and places and date of birth. To contain, also, the names of all enlisted soldiers entered according to priority of enlistments, giving their description, the dates and periods of their enlistments; and under the head of remarks, the cause of discharge, character, death, desertion, transfer—in short, everything relating to their military history. This book to be indexed.
One copy of the monthly returns to be filed.

POST BOOKS.

81. The following books will be kept at each post: A Morning Report Book, a Guard Report Book, an Order Book, a Letter Book, each two quires foolscap; also, copies of the monthly post returns.

ARTICLE XIII.

COMPANIES.

82. The captain will cause the men of the company to be numbered, in a regular series, including the non-commissioned officers, and divided into four squads, each to be put under the charge of a non-commissioned officer.
83. Each subaltern officer will be charged with a squad for the supervision of its order and cleanliness; and captains will require their lieutenants to assist them in the performance of *all* company duties.
84. As far as practicable, the men of each squadron will be quartered together.
85. The utmost attention will be paid by commanders of companies to the cleanliness of their men, as to their persons, clothing, arms, accoutrements and equipments, and also as to their quarters or tents.
86. The name of each soldier will be labeled on his bunk, and his company number will be placed against his arms and accoutrements.
87. The arms will be placed in the arm-racks, the stoppers in the muzzles, the cocks let down, and their bayonets in their scabbards; the accoutrements suspended over the arms, and the swords hung up by the belts on pegs.

88. The knapsack of each man will be placed on the lower shelf of his bunk, at its foot, packed with his effects, and ready to be slung; the great-coat on the same shelf, rolled and strapped; the coat, folded inside out, and placed under the knapsack; the cap on the second or upper shelf; and the boots well cleaned.

89. Dirty clothes will be kept in an appropriate part of the knapsack; no article of any kind to be put under the bedding.

90. Cooking utensils and table equipage will be cleaned and arranged in closets or recesses; blacking and brushes out of view; the fuel in boxes.

91. Ordinarily the cleaning will be on Saturdays. The chiefs of squads will cause bunks and beddings to be overhauled; floors dry rubbed; tables and benches scoured; arms cleaned; accoutrements whitened and polished; and everything put in order.

92. Where conveniences for bathing are to be had, the men should bathe once a week. The feet to be washed at least twice a week. The hair *kept short*, and beard neatly trimmed.

93. Non-commissioned officers, in command of squads, will be held more immediately responsible that their men observe what is prescribed above; that they wash their hands and faces daily; that they brush or comb their heads; that those who are to go on duty put their arms, accoutrements, dress, &c., in the best order, and that such as have permission to pass the chain of sentinels, are in the dress that may be ordered.

94. Commanders of companies and squads will see that the arms and accoutrements in possession of the men are always kept in good order, and that proper care be taken in cleaning them.

95. When belts are given to a soldier, the captain will see that they are properly fitted to the body; and it is forbidden to cut any belt without his sanction.

96. Cartridge-boxes and bayonet-scabbards will be polished with blacking; varnish is injurious to the leather, and will not be used.

97. All arms in the hands of the troops, whether browned or bright, will be kept in the state in which they are issued by the Ordnance Department. Arms will not be taken to pieces without permission of a commissioned officer. Bright barrels will be kept clean and free from rust without polishing them; care should be taken in rubbing not to bruise or bend the barrel. After firing, wash out the bore; wipe it dry, and then pass a bit of cloth, slightly greased, to the bottom. In these operations, a rod of wood, with a loop in one end, is to be used instead of the rammer. The barrel, when not in use, will be closed with a stopper. For exercise, each soldier should keep himself provided with a piece of sole-leather to fit the cup or countersink of the hammer.

98. Arms shall not be left loaded in quarters or in tents, or when the men are off duty, except by special orders.

99. Ammunition issued will be inspected frequently. Each man will be made to pay for the rounds expended without orders, or not in the way of duty, or which may be damaged or lost by his neglect.

100. Ammunition will be frequently exposed to the dry air, or sunned.

101. Special care shall be taken to ascertain that no ball-cartridges are mixed with the blank cartridges issued to the men.

102. All knapsacks are to be painted black. Those for the artillery will be marked in the centre of the cover with the number of the regiment only, in figures of one and a half inches in length, of the character called full-face, with yellow paint. Those for the infantry will be marked in the same way, in white paint. The knapsack straps will be black.

103. The knapsacks will also be marked upon the inner side with the letter of the company and the number of the soldier, on such part as may be readily observed at inspections.

104. Haversacks will be marked upon the flap with the number and name of the regiment, the letter of the company, and number of the soldier, in black letters and figures. And each soldier must, at all times, be provided with a haversack and canteen, and will exhibit them at all inspections. It will be worn on the left side on marches, guard, and when paraded for detached service—the canteen outside the haversack.

105. The front of the drums will be painted with the arms of the Confederate States, on a blue field for the infantry, and on a red field for the artillery. The letter of the company and the number of the regiment, under the arms, in a scroll.

106. Officers at their stations, in camp or in garrison, will always wear their proper uniform.

107. Soldiers will wear the prescribed uniform in camp or garrison, and will not be permitted to keep in their possession any other clothing. When on fatigue parties, they will wear the proper fatigue dress.

108. In camp or barracks, the company officers must visit the kitchen daily, and inspect the kettles, and at all times carefully attend to the messing and economy of their respective companies. The commanding officer of the post or regiment will make frequent inspections of the kitchens and messes.

109. The bread must be thoroughly baked, and not eaten until it is cold. The soup must be boiled at least five hours, and the vegetables always cooked sufficiently to be perfectly soft and digestible.

110. Messes will be prepared by privates of squads, including private musicians, each taking his tour. The greatest care will be observed in washing and scouring the cooking utensils; those made of brass and copper should be lined with tin.

111. The messes of prisoners will be sent to them by the cooks.

112. No persons will be allowed to visit or remain in the kitchen, except such as may come on duty, or be occupied as cooks.

113. Those detailed for duty in the kitchens will also be required to keep the furniture of the mess-room in order.

114. On marches and in the field, the only mess furniture of the soldier will be one tin plate, one tin cup, one knife, fork and spoon, to each man, to be carried by himself on the march.

115. If a soldier be required to assist his first sergeant in the writing of the company, to excuse him from a tour of military duty, the captain will previously obtain the sanction of his own commander, if he have one present; and whether there be a superior present or not, the captain will be responsible that the man so employed does not miss two successive tours of guard duty by reason of such employment.

116. Tradesmen may be relieved from ordinary military duty, to make, to alter, or to mend soldiers' clothing, &c. Company commanders will fix the rates at which work shall be done, and cause the men, for whose benefit it is done, to pay for it at the next pay day.

117. Each company officer, serving with his company, may take from it one soldier as waiter, with his consent and the consent of his captain. No other officers shall take a soldier as a waiter. Every soldier so employed shall be so reported and mustered.

118. Soldiers taken as officers' waiters shall be acquainted with their military duty, and at all times be completely armed and clothed, and in every respect equipped according to the rules of the service, and have all their necessaries complete and in good order. They are to fall in with their respective companies at all reviews and inspections, and are liable to such drills as the commanding officer shall judge necessary to fit them for service in the ranks.

119. Non-commissioned officers will, in no case, be permitted to act as waiters; nor are they, or private soldiers, not waiters, to be employed in any menial office, or made to perform any service not military, for the private benefit of any officer or mess of officers.

COMPANY BOOKS.

120. The following books are allowed to each company: one descriptive book, one clothing book, one order book, one morning report book, each one quire, sixteen inches by ten. One page of the descriptive book will be appropriated to the list of officers; two to the non-commissioned officers; two to the register of men transferred; four to the register of men discharged; two to register of deaths; four to register of deserters—the rest to the company description list.

LAUNDRESS.

121. Four women will be allowed to each company as washer-women, and will receive one ration per day each.

122. The price of washing soldiers' clothing, by the month, or by the piece, will be determined by the Council Administration.

123. Debts due the laundress by soldiers, for washing, will be paid, or collected at the pay-table, under the direction of the captain.

ARTICLE XIV.

ORDNANCE SERGEANTS.

124. The Secretary of War selects from the sergeants of the line of the army, who may have faithfully served, as many ordnance sergeants as the service may require.

125. Captains will report to their Colonels such sergeants as by their conduct and service merit such appointments, setting forth the description, length of service of the sergeant, the portion of his service he was a non-commissioned officer, his general character as to fidelity, and sobriety, his qualifications as a clerk, and his fitness for the duties to be performed by an ordnance sergeant. These reports will be forwarded to the Adjutant and Inspector General, to be laid before the Secretary of War, with an application in the following form:

Headquarters, &c.

To the Adjutant and Inspector General:

SIR—I forward for the consideration of the proper authority, an application for the appointment of ordnance sergeant.

Name and Regim'nt.	Letter of Company.	Length of Service.				Remarks.
		As non-commissioned Officer.		In the Army.		
		YEARS.	MONTHS.	YEARS.	MONTHS.	

Inclosed herewith you will receive the report of ——, the officer commanding the company in which the sergeant has been serving, to which I add the following remarks:

——— ———, Commanding —— Regiment.

126. When a company is detached from the headquarters of the regiment, the reports of the commanding officer in this matter, will pass to the regimental headquarters through the commanding officer of the post or detachment, and be accompanied by his opinion as to the fitness of the candidate.

127. Ordnance Sergeants will be assigned to posts when appointed, and are not to be transferred to other stations except by orders from the Adjutant and Inspector General's office.

128. At the expiration of their term of service, ordnance sergeants may be re-enlisted, provided they shall have conducted themselves in a becoming manner, and performed their duties to the satisfaction of the commanding officer. If the commanding officer, however, shall not think proper to re-enlist the ordnance sergeant of his post, he will not discharge him at the expiration of his service, unless it shall be the wish of the sergeant, but will communicate to the Adjutant and Inspector General his reasons for declining to re-enlist him, to be submitted to the War Department.

129. The officers interested must be aware, from the nature of the duties assigned to ordnance sergeants, that the judicious selection of them is of no small importance to the interests of the service; and that while the law contemplates, in the appointment of these non-commissioned officers, the better preservation of the ordnance and ordnance

stores in deposit in the several forts, there is the further motive of offering a reward to those faithful and well-tried sergeants who have long served their country, and of thus giving encouragement to the soldier in the ranks to emulate them in conduct, and thereby secure substantial promotion. Colonels and Captains can not, therefore, be too particular in investigating the characters of the candidates, and in giving their testimony as to their merits.

130. The appointment and removal of ordnance sergeants, stationed at military posts, in pursuance of the above provisions of law, shall be reported by the Adjutant and Inspector General to the Chief of the Ordnance Department.

131. When a non-commissioned officer receives the appointment of ordnance sergeant, he shall be dropped from the rolls of the regiment or company in which he may be serving at the time.

132. The duty of ordnance sergeants relates to the care of the ordnance, arms, ammunition, and other military stores at the post to which they may be attached, under the direction of the commanding officer, and according to the regulations of the Ordnance Department.

133. If a post be evacuated, the ordnance sergeant shall remain on duty at the station, under the direction of the Chief of the Ordnance Department, in charge of the ordnance and ordnance stores, and of such other public property as is not in charge of some officer or agent of other Departments; for which ordnance stores and other property he will account to the chiefs of the proper departments until otherwise directed.

134. An ordnance sergeant in charge of ordnance stores at a post where there is no commissioned officer, shall be held responsible for the safe keeping of the property, and he shall be governed by the regulations of the Ordnance Department in making issues of the same, and in preparing and furnishing the requisite returns. If the means at his disposal are not sufficient for the preservation of the property, he shall report the circumstances to the Chief of the Ordnance Department.

135. Ordnance sergeants are to be considered as belonging to the non-commissianed staff of the post, under the orders of the commanding officer. They are to wear the uniform, with the distinctive badges prescribed for the non-commissioned staff, of regiments of artillery; and they are to appear under arms with the troops at all reviews and inspections, monthly and weekly.

136. When serving at any post which may be the headquarters of a regiment, ordnance sergeants shall be reported by name on the post returns, and mustered with the non-commissioned staff of the regiment; and at all other posts they shall be mustered and reported in some company stationed at the post at which they serve; be paid on the muster-roll, and be charged with the clothing and all other supplies previously received from any officer, or subsequently issued to them by the commanding officer of the company for the time being. Whenever the company may be ordered from the post, the ordnance sergeant will be transferred to the rolls of any remaining company, by the order of the commanding officer of the post.

137. In the event of the troops being all withdrawn from a post at which there is an ordnance sergeant, he shall be furnished with his descriptive roll and account of clothing and pay, signed by the proper officer last in command, accompanied by the remarks necessary for his

military history; and on his exhibiting such papers to any Quartermaster, with a letter from the ordnance office acknowledging the receipt of his returns, and that they are satisfactory, he will be paid on a separate account the amount which may be due him at the date of the receipt of the return mentioned in such letter, together with commutation of rations, according to the regulations of the Subsistence Department. A certified statement of his pay account will be furnished the Ordnance sergeant by the Quartermaster by whom he may be last paid. When there are no troops at the post, the ordnance sergeant will report to the Adjutant and Inspector General's office by letter, on the last day of every month.

ARTICLE XV.

TRANSFER OF SOLDIERS.

138. No non-commissioned officer or soldier will be transferred from one regiment to another without the authority of the commanding General.

139. The Colonel may, upon the application of the Captains, transfer a non-commissioned officer, or soldier from one company to another of his regiment—with consent of the department commander in case of change of post; but in no case from one regiment to another where serving in different departments without approval of department commanders, and then at expense of parties transferred, except where transfer is required by interests of public service.

140. When soldiers are authorized to be transferred, the transfer will take place on the first of a month, with a view to the more convenient settlement of their accounts.

141. In all cases of transfer, a complete descriptive roll will accompany the soldier transferred, which roll will embrace an account of his pay, clothing, and other allowances; also, all stoppages to be made on account of the Government, and debts due the laundress, as well as such other facts as may be necessary to show his character and military history.

ARTICLE XVI.

DECEASED OFFICERS.

142. Whenever an officer dies, or is killed at any military post or station, or in the vicinity of the same, it will be the duty of the commanding officer to report the fact direct to the Adjutant and Inspector General, with the date, and any other information proper to be communicated. If an officer die at a distance from a military post, any officer having intelligence of the same will in like manner communicate it, specifying the day of his decease; a duplicate of the report will be sent to department headquarters.

143. Inventories of the effects of deceased officers, required by the 94th article of war, will be transmitted to the Adjutant and Inspector General.

144. If a legal administrator or family connection be present, and take charge of the effects, it will be so stated to the Adjutant and Inspector General.

ARTICLE XVII.

DECEASED SOLDIERS.

145. Inventories of the effects of deceased non-commissioned officers

and soldiers, required by the 95th article of war, will be forwarded to the Adjutant and Inspector General, by the commander of the company to which the deceased belonged, and a duplicate of the same to the Colonel of the regiment. Final statements of pay, clothing, &c., will be sent with the inventories. When a soldier dies at a post or station absent from his company, it will be the duty of his immediate commander to furnish the required inventory, and, at the same time, to forward to the commanding officer of the company to which the soldier belonged, a report of his death, specifying the date, place, and cause; to what time he was last paid, and the money or other effects in his possession at the time of his decease; which report will be noted on the next muster roll of the company to which the man belonged. Each inventory will be endorsed, "Inventory of the effects of ———, late of company (—) —— regiment of ——, who died at ———, the —— day of ———, 186—." If a legal representative receive the effects, it will be stated in the report. If the soldier leave no effects, the fact will be reported.

146. Should the effects of a deceased non-commissioned officer or soldier not be administered upon within a short period after his decease, they shall be disposed of by a Council of Administration, under the authority of the commanding officer of the post, and the proceeds deposited with the Quartermaster, to the credit of the Confederate States, until they shall be claimed by the legal representatives of the deceased.

147. In all such cases of sales by the Council of Administration, a statement in detail, or account of the proceeds, duly certified by the Council and commanding officer, accompanied by the Quartermaster's receipt for the proceeds, will be forwarded by the commanding officer to the Adjutant and Inspector General. The statement will be indorsed, "Report of the proceeds of the effects of ———, late of company (—) —— regiment of ———, who died at ———, the —— day of ———, 186—."

ARTICLE XVIII.

DESERTERS.

148. If a soldier desert from, or a deserter be received at, any post other than the station of the company or detachment to which he belonged, he shall be promptly reported by the commanding officer of such post, to the commander of his company or detachment. The time of desertion, apprehension and delivery will be stated. If the man be a recruit, unattached, the required report will be made to the Adjutant and Inspector General. When a report is received of the apprehension or surrender of a deserter at any post other than the station of the company or detachment to which he belonged, the commander of such company or detachment shall immediately forward his description and account of clothing to the officer making the report.

149. A reward of thirty dollars will be paid for the apprehension and delivery of a deserter to an officer of the Army at the most convenient post or recruiting station. Rewards thus paid will be promptly reported by the disbursing officer to the officer commanding the company in which the deserter is mustered, and to the authority competent to order his trial. The reward of thirty dollars will include the remuneration for all expenses incurred for apprehending, securing and delivering a deserter.

150. When non-commissioned officers or soldiers are sent in pursuit of a deserter, the expenses necessarily incurred will be paid whether he be apprehended or not, and reported as in case of rewards paid.

151. Deserters shall make good the time lost by desertion, unless discharged by competent authority.

152. No deserter shall be restored to duty without trial, except by the authority competent to order the trial.

153. Rewards and expenses paid for apprehending a deserter, will be set against his pay, when adjudged by a court-martial, or when he is restored to duty without trial on such condition.

154. In reckoning the time of service, and the pay and allowances of a deserter, he is to be considered in service when delivered up as a deserter to the proper authority.

155. An apprehended deserter, or one who surrenders himself, shall receive no pay while waiting trial, and only such clothing as may be actually necessary for him.

ARTICLE XIX.

DISCHARGES.

156. No enlisted man shall be discharged before the expiration of his term of enlistment without authority of the War Department, except by sentence of a general court-martial, or by the commander of the department, or of an army in the field, on certificate of disability, or on application of the soldier after twenty years' service.

157. When an enlisted man is to be discharged, his company commander shall furnish him certificates of his account, according to form 4, Pay Department.

158. Blank discharges will be furnished from the Adjutant and Inspector-General's office. No discharge shall be made in duplicate, nor shall any certificate be given in lieu of a discharge, except by order of the War Department.

159. The cause of dicharge will be stated in the body of the discharge, and the space at foot for character cut off, unless a recommendation is given.

160. When a non-commissioned officer or soldier shall be unfit for military service in consequence of wounds, disease or infirmity, his captain shall forward to the commandant of the Department, or of the army in the field, through the commander of the regiment or post, a statement of the case, with "certificates of disability," signed by the senior surgeon of the regiment or post, according to the form prescribed in the medical regulations. If the recommendation for the discharge of the invalid be approved, the authority therefor will be endorsed on the "certificates of disability," which will be sent back to be completed, and signed by the commanding officer of the regiment or command to which the invalid's company belongs, who will also sign the discharge, and cause the final statements to be made out, and forward the certificates of disability to the Adjutant and Inspector General.

161. When a non-commissioned officer or soldier is absent from his regiment or company, in hospital, and shall be unfit for military service, for the reasons set forth in the preceding paragraph, the senior surgeon of the hospital will make out "certificates of disability," and forward them, through the commander of the company or regiment, to the com-

mander of the department or of the army in the field, whose approval being given, the commanding officer will complete and forward the certificates of disability to the Adjutant and Inspector General, and send the papers of discharge to the surgeon. But when access to commanders is difficult, and attended with great delay, the certificates of disability may, in urgent cases, be forwarded by the surgeon to the surgeon general for approval; which being given, the discharge will be authorized from the Adjutant and Inspector General's office; and the surgeon will make out final statements.

162. The date, place, and cause of discharge of a soldier absent from his company, will be reported by the commander of the post to his company commander.

163. Company commanders are required to keep the blank discharges and certificates carefully in their own custody.

ARTICLE XX.

TRAVELING ON DUTY.

164. Whenever an officer, traveling under orders, arrives at his post, he will submit to the commanding officer a report in writing, of the time occupied in the travel, with a copy of the orders under which the journey was performed, and an explanation of any delay in the execution of the orders; which report the commanding officer shall transmit, with his opinion on it, to department headquarters. If the officer be superior in rank to the commander, the required report will be made by the senior himself.

165. Orders detaching an officer for a special duty, imply, unless otherwise stated, that he is thereafter to join his proper station.

ARTICLE XXI.

LEAVES OF ABSENCE TO OFFICERS.

166. In no case will leaves of asence be granted, so that a company be left without one of its *commissioned officers*, or that a garrisoned post be left without two commissioned officers and competent medical attendance; nor shall leave of absence be granted to an officer during the season of active operations, except on urgent necessity, and then as follows: The commander of a post may grant seven days leave—the commander of an army thirty.

167. When not otherwise specified, leaves of absence will be considered as commencing on the day that the officer is relieved from duty at his post. He will report himself monthly, giving his address for the next thirty days, to the commander of his post, and of his regiment or corps, and to the Adjutant and Inspector-General; and in his first report state the day when his leave of absence commenced; at the expiration of his leave he will join his station.

168. Applications for leave of absence for more than thirty days, must be referred to the Adjutant and Inspector-General for the decision of the Secretary of War. In giving a permission to apply for the extension of a leave of absence, the term of the extension should be stated.

169. The immediate commander of the officer applying for leave of absence, and all intermediate commanders, will endorse their opinion on the application before forwarding it.

170. The commander of a post may take leave of absence not to ex-

ceed seven days at one time, or in the same month, reporting the fact to his next superior.

171. Leaves of absence on account of sickness will not be granted to go beyond the limits of the Military Department within which they are stationed, unless the certificate of the medical officer shall explicitly state that a greater change is necessary to save life, or prevent permanent disability. Nor will sick leaves to go beyond the Department limits be given in any case, except of immediate urgency, without the previous sanction of the War Department.

172. On the expiration of a leave of absence given on account of sickness, if the officer be able to travel, he will forthwith proceed to his post, although his disability may not have been removed. Exceptions to this general rule must be made in each case by the War Department, on full and explicit medical certificates setting forth the reasons for delay, and the length of time delay is considered necessary.

173. An application for leave of absence on account of sickness, must be accompanied by a certificate of the senior medical officer present, in the following form:

———, of the regiment of ———, having applied for a certificate on which to ground an application for leave of absence, I do hereby certify that I have carefully examined this officer, and find that—[*Here the nature of the disease, wound, or disability, is to be fully stated, and the period during which the officer has suffered under its effects.*] And that in consequence thereof, he is, in my opinion, unfit for duty. I further declare my belief that he will not be able to resume his duties in a less period than ———. [*Here state candidly and explicitly the opinion as to the period which will probably elapse before the officer will be able to resume his duties. When there is no reason to expect a recovery, or when the prospect of recovery is distant and uncertain, or when a change of climate is recommended, it must be so stated.*] Dated at ——, this —— day of ——. *Signature of the Medical Officer.*

174. In all reports of absence, or application for leave of absence on account of sickness, the officer shall state how long he has been absent already on that account, and by whose permission.

ARTICLE XXII.

FURLOUGHS TO ENLISTED MEN.

175. Furloughs will be granted only by the commanding officer of the post or the commanding officer of the regiment actually quartered with it. Furloughs may be prohibited at the discretion of the officer in command.

176. Soldiers on furlough shall not take with them their arms or accoutrements, but in all cases of long expected absence, should be furnished with descriptive and clothing accounts, by their Captains, to enable them to draw their pay.

177. Form of furlough:

TO ALL WHOM IT MAY CONCERN.

The bearer hereof, —— ——, a sergeant (corporal, or private, as the case may be) of Captain —— —— company, — regiment of ——, aged — year, — feet — inches high, —— complexion, —— eyes,

—— hair, and by profession a —— ——, born in the —— of ——, and enlisted at ——, in the —— of ——, on the —— day of ——, eighteen hundred and ——, to serve for the period of ——, is hereby permitted to go to ——, in the county of ——, State of ——, he having received a furlough from the — day of ——, to the — day of ——, at which period he will rejoin his company or regiment at ——, or wherever it then may be, or be considered a deserter.

Subsistence has been furnished to said —— ——, to the —— day of ——, and pay to the —— day of ——, both inclusive.

Given under my hand, at ——, this —— day of ——, 18—.

Signature of the officer giving the furlough. }

ARTICLE XXIII.

COUNCILS OF ADMINISTRATION.

178. The commanding officer of every post shall, at least once in every two months, convene a *Post Council of Administration*, to consist of *three* regimental or company officers next in rank to himself; or, if there be but two, then the *two* next; if but one, the *one* next; and if there be none other than himself, then he himself shall act.

179. The junior member will record the proceedings of the council in a book, and submit the same to the commanding officer. If he disapprove the proceedings, and the council, after a reconsideration, adhere to its decision, a copy of the whole shall be sent by the officer commanding to the next higher commander, whose decision shall be final, and entered in the council book, and the whole be published in orders for the information and government of all concerned.

180. The proceedings of Councils of Administration shall be signed by the president and recorder, and the recorder of each meeting, after entering the whole proceedings, together with the final order thereon, shall deposit the book with the commanding officer. In like manner, the approval or objections of the officer ordering the council will be signed with his own hand.

181. The Post Council shall prescribe the quantity and kind of clothing, small equipments, and soldiers' necessaries, groceries, and all articles which the sutlers may be required to keep on hand; examine the sutler's books and papers, and fix the tariff of prices of the said goods or commodities; inspect the sutler's weights and measures; fix the laundress charges, and make the regulations for the post school.

182. Pursuant to the 30th Article of War, commanding officers reviewing the proceedings of the Council of Administration will scrutinize the tariff of prices proposed by them, and take care that the stores actually furnished by the sutler correspond to the quality prescribed.

POST FUND.

183. A post fund shall be raised at each post by a tax on the sutler of 10 cents a month for every officer and soldier of the command, according to the average in each month to be ascertained by the council, and from the saving on the flour ration, ordinarily 33 per cent., by baking the soldiers' bread at a post bakery: Provided, that when want of vegetables or other reasons make it necessary, the commanding officer may order the flour saved, or any part of it, issued to the men, after paying expenses of baking.

184. The commanding officer shall designate an officer to be post treasurer, who shall keep the account of the fund, subject to the inspection of the council and commanding officer, and disburse the fund on the warrants of the commanding officer, drawn in pursuance of specific resolves of the council.

185. At every settlement of the post fund by the Council of Administration, the amount of the sutler's tax since the preceding settlement will be apportioned to the regiments represented at the post in the ratio of the number of companies of each present; and the results communicated by the Council to the Adjutant of the regiments affected and to the headquarters of the department in which the regimental headquarters are stationed. The tax will enter into the post-treasurer's accounts, and will be transmitted by him to the Regimental Treasurers in accordance with the apportionment of the post-council.

186. In each regiment the fund accruing to it as above, or as much of it as may be necessary, will be appropriated to the maintenance of the band. It will be administered by the regimental commander, the Adjutant as treasurer, and a regimental council, and be accounted for to department headquarters, on the same plan as that prescribed by regulations for the post-fund.

187. The following are the objects of expenditure of the post fund: 1st, expenses of the bake-house; 2d, expenses of the soldiers' children at the post school.

188. On the last day of April, August and December, and when relieved from the duty, the treasurer shall make out his account with the fund since his last account, and submit it, with his vouchers, to the Council of Administration, to be examined by them, and recorded in the council book, and then forwarded by the commanding officer to department headquarters.

189. At each settlement of the treasurer's account, the council shall distribute the unexpended balance of the post fund to the several companies and other troops in the ratio of their average force during the period.

190. When a company leaves the post, it shall then receive its distributive share of the accrued fund.

191. The regulations in regard to a post-fund will, as far as practicable, be applied in the field to a regimental fund, to be raised, administered, expended, and distributed in like manner, by the regimental command and a regimental council.

COMPANY FUND.

192. The distributions from the post or regimental fund, and the savings from the company rations, constitute the Company fund, to be disbursed by the captain for the benefit of the enlisted men of the company, pursuant to resolves of the Company Council, consisting of all the company officers present. In case of a tie vote in the Council, the commander of the post shall decide. The Council shall be convened once in two months by the captain, and whenever he may think proper.

193. Their proceedings shall be recorded in a book, signed by all the Council, and open at all times to the inspection of the commander of the post. Every four months, and whenever another officer takes command of the company, and when the company leaves the post, the account of

the company fund shall be made up, audited by the Council, recorded in the Council book, and submitted, with a duplicate, to the post commander, who shall examine it and forward the duplicate to department headquarters.

194. The supervision of the company fund by the post commander herein directed, shall, in the field, devolve on the commander of the regiment.

ARTICLE XXIV.

CHAPLAINS.

195. The posts at, and regiments with, which Chaplains may be employed, will be announced by the War Department, upon recommendations made by the commanding officer of posts or regiments, and the pay of a Chaplain will be $50 per month.

ARTICLE XXV.

SUTLERS.

196. Every military post may have one sutler, to be appointed by the Secretary of War on the recommendation of the Council of Administration, approved by the commanding officer.

197. A sutler shall hold his office for a term of three years, unless sooner removed; but the commanding officer may, for cause, suspend a sutler's privilege until a decision of the War Department is received in the case.

198. In case of vacancy, a temporary appointment may be made by the commanding officer upon the nomination of the Council of Administration.

199. Troops in campaign, on detachment, or on distant service, will be allowed sutlers, at the rate of one for every regiment, corps, or separate detachment; to be appointed by the commanding officer of such regiment, corps, or detachment, upon the recommendation of the Council of Administration, subject to the approval of the general or other officer in command.

200. No tax or burden in any shape, other than the authorized assessment for the post fund, will be imposed on the sutler. If there be a spare building, the use of it may be allowed him, he being responsible that it is kept in repair. If there be no such building, he may be allowed to erect one; but this article gives the sutler no claim to quarters, transportation for himself or goods, or to any military allowance whatever.

201. The tariff of prices fixed by the Council of Administration shall be exposed in a conspicuous place in the sutler's store. No difference of prices will be allowed on cash or credit sales.

202. Sutlers are not allowed to keep ardent spirits or other intoxicating drinks, under penalty of losing their situations.

203. Sutlers shall not farm out or underlet the business and privileges granted by their appointment.

204. No sutler shall sell to an enlisted man, on credit, to a sum exceeding one-third of his monthly pay within the same month, without the written sanction of the company commander, or the commanding officer of the post or station, if the man does not belong to a company; and not exceeding one-half the monthly pay with such permission.

205. Three days before the last of every month, the sutler shall render for verification, to the company commander, or to the commanding officer, as the case may be, according to the meaning of the preceding paragraph, a written and separate account in each case, of any charges he may have against enlisted men for collection, and the officer shall submit the accounts to the soldier for acknowledgment and signature, and witness the same. In the case of a soldier's death, desertion, or removal from the post, the account will be rendered immediately. If the soldier dispute the account, and the sutler insist, and in case of death and desertion, the sutler will be required to establish the account by affidavit endorsed on it, before any officer authorised to administer an oath. Such verification will establish the debt unless disproved, and the amount may be collected at the pay table where the soldier is present, otherwise provided for in succeeding paragraph.

206. All accounts of sutlers against enlisted men, which are not collected at the pay table—as of those who have died, deserted, or been removed beyond the reach of the sutler—after being duly audited as above, will be entered on the next succeeding muster-roll, or on the descriptive roll, or certificate of discharge, as the case may be, and the same shall be retained from any balances due the soldier, after deducting forfeitures and stoppages for the Government and laundress, and be paid to the sutler, on application to the second auditor of the treasury, through the Quartermaster-General.

ARTICLE XXVI.

MILITARY DISCUSSIONS AND PUBLICATIONS.

207. Deliberations or discussions among any class of military men, having the object of conveying praise, or censure, or any mark of approbation toward their superiors or others in the military service; and all publications relative to transactions between officers of a private or personal nature, whether newspaper, pamphlet or hand-bill, are strictly prohibited.

ARTICLE XXVII.

ARRESTS AND CONFINEMENTS.

208. None but commanding officers have power to place officers under arrest, except for offences expressly designated in the 27th article of war.

209. Officers are not to be put in arrest for light offences. For these the censure of the commanding officer will, in most cases, answer the purpose of discipline.

210. An officer in arrest may, at the discretion of his commanding officer, have larger limits assigned him than his tent or quarters, on written application to that effect. Close confinement is not to be resorted to unless under circumstances of an aggravated character.

211. In ordinary cases, and where inconvenience to the service would result from it, a medical officer will not be put in arrest until the court-martial for his trial convenes.

212. The arrest of an officer, or confinement of a soldier, will, as soon as practicable, be notified to his immediate commander.

213. All prisoners under guard, without written charges, will be released by the officer of the day at guard-mounting, unless orders to the contrary be given by the commanding officer.

214. On a march, company officers and non-commissioned officers in

arrest will follow in the rear of their respective companies, unless otherwise particularly ordered.

215. Field officers, commissioned and non-commissioned staff officers, under the same circumstances, will follow in the rear of their respective regiments.

216. An officer under arrest will not wear a sword, or visit officially his commanding or other superior officer, unless sent for; and in case of business, he will make known his object in writing.

ARTICLE XXVIII.

HOURS OF SERVICE AND ROLL CALL.

217. In garrison, *reveille* will be at day-break; retreat at sunset; the *troop, surgeon's call, signals* for breakfast and dinner at the hours prescribed by the commanding officer, according to climate and season. In the cavalry, *stable calls* immediately after reveille, and an hour and a half before retreat; *water-calls* at the hours directed by the commanding officer.

218. In camp, the commanding officer prescribes the hours of reveille, reports, roll-calls, guard-mounting, meals, stable-calls, issues, fatigues, &c.

SIGNALS.

219.
1. To go for fuel—*poing-stroke and ten stroke roll.*
2. To go for water—*two strokes and a flam.*
3. For fatigue party—*pioneer's march.*
4. Adjutant's call—*first part of the troop.*
5. First sergeant's call—*one roll and four taps.*
6. Sergeant's call—*one roll and three taps.*
7. Corporal's call—*one roll and two taps.*
8. For the drummers—*the drummer's call.*

220. The *drummers call* shall be beat by the drums of the police-guard five minutes before the time of beating the stated calls, when the drummers will assemble before the colors of their respective regiments, and as soon as the beat begins on the right, it will be immediately taken up along the line.

ROLL-CALLS.

221. There shall be, daily, at least three stated roll-calls, viz: at *reveille, retreat, and tattoo.* They will be made on the company parades by the first sergeants, *superintended by a commissioned officer* of the company. The captains will report the absentees without leave to the colonel or commanding officer.

222. Immediately after *reveille* roll-call, (after stable duty in the cavalry,) the tents or quarters, and the space around them, will be put in order by the men of the companies, superintended by the chiefs of squads, and the guard-house or guard tent by the guard or prisoners.

223. The morning reports of companies, signed by the Captains and First Sergeants, will be handed to the Adjutant before eight o'clock in the morning, and will be consolidated by the Adjutant within the next hour, for the information of the Colonel; and if the consolidation is to be sent to higher authority, it will be signed by the Colonel and the Adjutant.

ARTICLE XXIX.

HONORS TO BE PAID BY THE TROOPS.

224. The *President* or *Vice-President* is to be saluted with the highest

honors—all standards and colors dropping, officers and troops saluting, drums beating and trumpets sounding.

225. *A General* is to be received—by cavalry, with sabres presented, trumpets sounding the march, and all the officers saluting, standards dropping; by infantry, with drums beating the march, colors dropping, officers saluting, and arms presented.

226. *A Major-General* is to be received—by cavalry, with sabres presented, trumpets sounding twice the trumpet flourish, and officers saluting; by infantry, with three ruffles, colors dropping, officers saluting, and arms presented.

227. *A Brigadier-General* is to be received—by cavalry, with sabres presented, trumpets sounding once the trumpet flourish, and officers saluting; by infantry, with two ruffles, colors dropping, officers saluting, and arms presented.

228. *An Adjutant-General* or *Inspector-General*, if under the rank of a General officer, is to be received at a review or inspection of the troops under arms—by cavalry, with sabres presented, officers saluting; by arms presented. The same honors to be paid to any field-officer, authorized to review and inspect the troops. When the inspecting officer is junior to the officer commanding the parade, no compliments will be paid; he will be received only with swords drawn and arms shouldered.

229. All guards are to turn out and present arms to *General officers* as often as they pass them, except the personal guards of General officers, which turn out only to the Generals whose guards they are, and to officers of superior rank.

230. To commanders of regiments, garrisons, or camps, their own guards turn out, and present arms once a day; after which, they turn out with shouldered arms.

231. *To the members of the Cabinet; to the Chief Justice, the President of the Congress of the Confederate States; and to Governors within their respective States and Territories*—the same honors will be paid as to a General.

232. *Officers of a foreign service* may be complimented with the honors due to their rank.

233. *American and Foreign Envoys or Ministers* will be received with the compliments due to a Major-General.

234. The colors of a regiment passing a guard are to be saluted, the trumpets sounding, and the drums beating a march.

235. When General officers or persons entitled to salute, pass in the rear of a guard, the officer is only to make his men stand shouldered, and not to face his guard about, or beat his drum.

236. When General officers, or persons entitled to a salute, pass guards while in the act of relieving, both guards are to salute, receiving the word of command from the senior officer of the whole.

237. All guards are to be under arms when armed parties approach their posts; and to parties commanded by commissioned officers, they are to present their arms, drums beating a march, and officers saluting.

238. No compliments by guards or sentinels will be paid between *retreat* and *reveille*, except as prescribed for *grand rounds*.

239. All guards and sentinels are to pay the same compliments to the officers of the navy, marines, and militia, in the service of the Confede-

rate States, as are directed to be paid to the officers of the army, according to their relative ranks.

240. It is equally the duty of non-commissioned officers and soldiers, *at all times*, and *in all situations*, to pay the proper compliments to officers of the navy and marines, and to officers of other regiments, when in uniform, as to officers of their own particular regiments and corps.

241. Courtesy among military men is indispensable to discipline. Respect to superiors will not be confined to obedience on duty, but will be extended to all occasions. It is always the duty of the inferior to accost or to offer first the customary salutation, and of the superior to return such complimentary notice.

242. Sergeants, with swords drawn, will salute by bringing them to a present—with muskets, by bringing the left hand across the body, so as to strike the musket near the right shoulder. Corporals out of the ranks, and privates not sentries, will carry their muskets at a shoulder as sergeant, and salute in like manner.

243. When a soldier without arms, or with side-arms only, meets an officer, he is to raise his hand to the right side of the visor of his cap, palm to the front, elbow raised as high as the shoulder, looking at the same time in a respectful and soldier-like manner at the officer, who will return the compliment thus offered.

244. A non-commissioned officer or soldier being seated, and without particular occupation, will rise on the approach of an officer, and make the customary salutation. If standing, he will turn toward the officer for the same purpose. If the parties remain in the same place or on the same ground, such compliments need not be repeated.

SALUTES.

245. The national salute is determined by the number of States composing the Confederacy, at the rate of one gun for each State.

246. The *President of the Confederate States* alone is to receive a national salute.

247. The *Vice-President* is to receive a salute of two guns less than a national salute.

248. The *Heads of the great Executive Departments of the National Government*; the *Generals*; the *Governors of States and Territories*, within their respective jurisdictions, two guns less than Vice-President.

249. A *Major-General*, one gun less than General.

250. A *Brigadier-General*, one gun less than Major-General.

251. *Foreign ships of war* will be saluted in return for a similar compliment, gun for gun, on notice being officially received of such intention. If there be several posts in sight of, or within six miles of each other, the principal only shall reciprocate compliments with ships passing.

252. *Officers of the Navy* will be saluted according to relative rank.

253. *Foreign officers* invited to visit a fort or post, may be saluted according to their relative rank.

254. *Envoys and Ministers* of the Confederate States and foreign powers are to be saluted with 7 guns.

255. A General officer will be saluted but once in a year at each post, and only when notice of his intention to visit the post has been given.

256. Salutes to individuals are to be fired on their arrival only.

257. A national salute will be fired at meridian on the anniversary of the adoption of the Provisional Constitution, 8th February, 1861, at each military post and camp provided with artillery and ammunition.

ESCORTS OF HONOR.

258. Escorts of honor may be composed of cavalry or infantry, or both, according to circumstances. They are guards of honor for the purpose of receiving and escorting personages of high rank, civil or military. The troops for this purpose will be selected for their soldierly appearance and superior discipline.

259. The escort will be drawn up in line, the centre opposite to the place where the personage presents himself, with an interval between the wings to receive him and his retinue. On his appearance, he will be received with the honors due to his rank. When he has taken his place in the line, the whole will be wheeled into platoons or companies, as the case may be, and take up the march. The same ceremony will be observed, and the same honors paid, on his leaving the escort.

260. When the position of the escort is at a considerable distance from the point where he is expected to be received, as, for instance, where a court yard or wharf intervenes, a double line of sentinels will be posted from that point to the escort, facing inward, and the sentinels will successively salute as he passes.

261. An officer will be appointed to attend him, to bear such communications as he may have to make to the commander of the escort.

FUNERAL HONORS.

262. On the receipt of official intelligence of the death of the *President of the Confederate States*, at any post or camp, the commanding officer shall, on the following day, cause a gun to be fired at every half hour, beginning at sunrise and ending at sunset. When posts are contiguous, the firing will take place at the post only commanded by the superior officer.

263. On the day of interment of a *General commanding-in chief*, a gun will be fired at every half hour, until the procession moves, beginning at sunrise.

264. The funeral escort of a *General* shall consist of a regiment of infantry, a squadron of cavalry, and six pieces of artillery.

265. That of a *Major-General*, a regiment of infantry, a squadron of cavalry, and four pieces of artillery.

266. That of a *Brigadier-General*, a regiment of infantry, one company of cavalry, and two pieces of artillery.

267. That of a *Colonel*, a regiment.

268. That of a *Lieutenant-Colonel*, six companies.

269. That of a *Major*, four companies.

270. That of a *Captain*, one company.

271. That of a *Subaltern*, half a company.

272. The funeral escort shall always be commanded by an officer of the same rank with the deceased; or, if none such be present, by one of the next inferior grade.

273. The funeral escort of a non-commissioned staff officer shall consist of sixteen rank and file, commanded by a Sergeant.

274. That of a Sergeant, of fourteen rank and file, commanded by a Sergeant.

275. That of a Corporal, of twelve rank and file, commanded by a Corporal; and

276. That of a Private, of eight rank and file, commanded by a Corporal.

277. The escort will be formed in two ranks, opposite to the quarters or tent of the deceased, with shouldered arms and bayonets unfixed, the artillery and cavalry on the right of the infantry.

278. On the appearance of the corpse, the officer commanding the escort will command,

Present ARMS!

when the honors due to the deceased will be paid by the drums and trumpets. The music will then play an appropriate air, and the coffin will then be taken to the right, where it will be halted. The commander will next order,

1. *Shoulder* ARMS. 2. *By company, (or platoon) left wheel.* 3. MARCH. 4. *Reverse* ARMS. 5. *Column, forward.* 6. *Guide right.* 7. MARCH.

The arms will be reversed at the order by bringing the fire-lock under the left arm, butt to the front, barrel downward, left hand sustaining the lock, the right steadying the fire-lock behind the back; swords are reversed in a similar manner under the right arm.

279. The column will be marched in slow time to solemn music, and on reaching the grave, will take a direction so as that the guides shall be next to the grave. When the centre of the column is opposite the grave, the commander will order,

1. *Column.* 2. HALT. 3. *Right, into line wheel.* 4. MARCH.

The coffin is then brought along the front, to the opposite side of the grave, and the commander then orders,

1. *Shoulder* ARMS. 2. *Present* ARMS.

And when the coffin reaches the grave, he adds:

1. *Shoulder* ARMS. 2. *Rest on* ARMS.

The rest on arms is done by placing the muzzle on the left foot, both hands on the butt, the head on the hands or bowed, right knee bent.

280. After the funeral service is performed, and the coffin is lowered into the grave, the commander will order,

1. *Attention!* 2. *Shoulder* ARMS. 3. *Load at will.* 4. LOAD.

When three rounds of small arms will be fired by the escort, taking care to elevate the pieces.

281. This being done, the commander will order,

1. *By company, (or platoon) right wheel.* 2. MARCH. 3. *Column, forward.* 4. *Guide left.* 5. *Quick* MARCH.

The music will not begin to play until the escort is clear of the enclosure.

282. When the distance to the place of interment is considerable, the escort may march in common time, and in column of route, after leaving the camp or garrison, and till it approaches the burial ground.

283. The pall bearers, six in number, will be selected from the grade of the deceased, or from the grade or grades next above or below it.

284. At the funeral of an officer, as many in commission of the army, division, brigade, or regiment, according to the rank of the deceased, as can conveniently be spared from other duties, will join in procession, in uniform and with side-arms. The funeral of a non-commissioned officer or private will be attended, in like manner, by the non-commissioned officers or privates of the regiment or company, according to the rank of the deceased, with side-arms only.

285. Persons joining in the procession, follow the coffin in the inverse order of their rank.

286. The usual badge of military mourning is a piece of black crape around the left arm, above the elbow, and also upon the sword hilt, and will be worn when in full or in undress.

287. As family mourning, crape will be worn by officers (when in uniform) only around the left arm.

288. The drums of a funeral escort will be covered with black crape, or thin black serge.

289. Funeral honors will be paid to deceased officers without military rank according to their assimilated grades.

ARTICLE XXX.

INSPECTIONS OF THE TROOPS.

290. The inspection of troops, as a division, regiment, or other body composing a garrison or command, not less than a company will generally be preceded by a review.

291. There will be certain periodical inspections, to wit:

1. The commanders of regiments and posts will make an inspection of their commands on the last day of every month.
2. Captains will inspect their companies every Sunday morning. No soldier will be excused from Sunday inspection except the guard, the sick, and the necessary attendants in the hospital.
3. Medical officers having charge of hospitals will also make a thorough inspection of them every Sunday morning.
4. Inspection when troops are mustered for payment.

292. Besides these inspections, frequent visits will be made by the commanding officer, company and medical officers, during the month, to the men's quarters, the hospital guard-house, &c.

FORM OF INSPECTION.

293. The present example embraces a battalion of infantry. The inspecting officer and the field and staff officers will be on foot.

294. The battalion being in the order of battle, the Colonel will cause it to break into open column of companies, right in front. He will next order the ranks to be opened, when the color-rank and color guard, under the direction of the Adjutant, will take post ten paces in front, and the band ten paces in rear of the column.

295. The Colonel, seeing the ranks aligned, will command,

1. *Officers and Sergeants, to the front of your companies.* 2. MARCH.

The officers will form themselves in one rank, eight paces, and the non-commissioned officers in one rank, six paces in advance, along the whole fronts of their respective companies, from right to left; in the order of seniority; the pioneers and music of each company, in one rank, two paces behind the non-commissioned officers.

296. The Colonel will next command,

Field and Staff to the front, MARCH.

The commissioned officers thus designated will form themselves in one rank, on a line equal to the front of the column, six paces in front of the colors, from right to left, in the order of seniority; and the non-commissioned staff, in a similar manner, two paces in rear of the preceding rank. The Colonel, seeing the movement executed, will take post on the right of the Lieutenant-Colonel, and wait the approach of the inspecting officer. But such of the field officers as may be superior in rank to the Inspector, will not take post in front of the battalion.

297. The Inspector will commence in front. After inspecting the dress and general appearance of the field and commissioned staff under arms, the Inspector, accompanied by these officers, will pass down the open column, looking at every rank in front and rear.

298. The Colonel will now command,

1. *Order arms*. 2. REST.

When the Inspector will proceed to make a minute inspection of the several ranks or divisions, in succession, commencing in front.

299. As the Inspector approaches the non-commissioned staff, color-rank, the color-guard, and the band, the Adjutant will give the necessary orders for the inspection of arms, boxes, and knapsacks. The colors will be planted firm in the ground, to enable the color-bearers to display the contents of their knapsacks. The non-commissioned staff may be dismissed as soon as inspected; but the color-rank and color-guard will remain until the colors are to be escorted to the place from which they were taken.

300. As the Inspector successively approaches the companies, the Captains will command,

1. *Attention*. 2. *Company*. 3. *Inspection*—ARMS.

The inspecting officer will then go through the whole company, and minutely inspect the arms, accoutrements, and dress of each soldier. After this is done, the Captain command,

Open—BOXES.

When the ammunition and the boxes will be examined.

301. The Captain will then command,

1. *Shoulder*—ARMS.
2. *Close order*.
3. MARCH.
4. *Order*—ARMS.
5. *Stack*—ARMS.
6. *To the rear, open order*.
7. MARCH.
8. *Front rank, About*—FACE.
9. *Unsling Knapsacks*.
10. *Open*—*Knapsacks*.

302. The Sergeants will face inward at the 2d command, and close upon the centre of the 3d, and stack their arms at the 5th command; at the 6th command they face outward, and resume their positions at

the 7th. When the ranks are closed, preparatory to *take arms*, the Sergeants will also close upon the centre, and at the word, take their arms and resume their places.

303. The knapsacks will be placed at the feet of the men, the flaps from them, with the great coats on the flaps, and the knapsacks leaning on the great coats. In this position the Inspector will examine their contents, or so many of them as he may think necessary, commencing with the non-commissioned officers, the men standing at attention.

304. When the Inspector has passed through the company, the Captain will command,

Re-pack—Knapsacks,

when each soldier will re-pack and buckle up his knapsack, leaving it on the ground, the number upward, turned from him, and then stand at rest.

305. The Captain will then command,

1. *Attention.* 2. *Company.* 3. *Sling—Knapsacks.*

At the word *sling*, each soldier will take his knapsack, holding it by the inner straps, and stand erect; at the last word he will replace it on his back. The Captain will continue,

4. *Front rank, About*—FACE.
5. *Close order.*
6. MARCH.
7. *Take*—ARMS.
8. *Shoulder*—ARMS.
9. *Officers and Sergeants, to your posts.*
10. MARCH,

and will cause the company to file off to their tents and quarters, except the company that is to re-escort the colors, which will await the further orders of the Colonel.

306. In an extensive column, some of the rearmost companies may, after the inspection of dress and general appearance, be permitted to *stack arms* until just before the Inspector approaches them, when they will be directed to *take arms* and resume their position.

307. The inspection of the troops being ended, the field and staff will next accompany the Inspector to the hospital, magazine, arsenal, quarters, sutler's shop, guard-house, and such other places as he may think proper to inspect. The Captains and subalterns repair to their companies and sections to await the Inspector.

308. The hospital being at all times an object of particular interest, it will be critically and minutely inspected.

309. The men will be formed in the company quarters in front of their respective bunks, and on the entrance of the Inspector, the word *Attention!* will be given by the senior non-commissioned officer present, when the whole will salute with the hand, without uncovering.

310. The Inspector attended by the company officers, will examine the general arrangement of the interior of the quarters, the bunks, bedding, cooking, and table utensils, and such other objects as may present themselves; and afterwards the exterior.

311. The Adjutant shall exhibit to the Inspector the regimental books and papers, including those relating to the transactions of the council of administration. The company books and papers will also be exhibited, the whole together, generally at the Adjutant's office, and in the presence of the officers not otherwise particularly engaged.

312. The Inspector will examine critically the books and accounts of the administrative and disbursing officers of the command, and the money and property in their keeping.

313. The inspection of cavalry and artillery will conform to the principles laid down in the foregoing paragraphs, regard being had to the system of instruction for those arms of service respectively.

ARTICLE XXXI.

MUSTERS.

314. The musters will be made by an Inspector-General, if present, otherwise by an officer specially designated by the commander of the army, division, or department; and in absence of either an Inspector-General, or officer specially designated, the muster will be made by the commander of the post at the end of every month.

315. When one inspecting officer cannot muster all the troops himself on the day specified, the commanding officer will designate such other competent officer as may be necessary to assist him.

316. All stated musters of the troops shall be preceded by a minute and careful *inspection* in the prescribed mode; and if the command be more than a company, by a *review*, before inspection.

317. The mustering officer having inspected the companies in succession, beginning on the right, returns to the first company to muster it. The company being at *ordered arms*, with open ranks, as when inspected, the Captain will, as the mustering officer approaches, command,

1. *Attention*. 2. *Company*. 3. *Shoulder*—ARMS. 4. *Support*—ARMS.

The mustering officer will then call over the names on the roll, and each man, as his name is called, will distinctly answer, *Here!* and bring his piece to a *carry* and to an *order*.

318. After each company is mustered, the Captain will order it to be marched to the company parade, and there dismissed to quarters to await the Inspector's visit.

319. After mustering the companies, the mustering officer, attended by the company commanders, will visit the guard hospital, to verify the presence of the men reported there.

320. The muster and pay-rolls will be made on the printed forms furnished from the Adjutant and Inspector-General's office, and according to the directions given on them. On the muster-rolls companies are designated by the name of the Captain, whether present or absent. The pay-roll is left blank, to be filled by the Quartermaster.

321. One copy of each muster-roll will be transmitted by the mustering officer to the Adjutant and Inspector-General's office, in the War Department, within three days after the muster.

ARTICLE XXXII.

FORMS OF PARADE.

322. On all parades of ceremony, such as reviews, guard-mounting, at *Troop* or *Retreat* parades, instead of the word "*Rest*," which allows the men to move or change the position of their bodies, the command will be, "*Parade*—REST." At the last word of this command, the sol-

dier will carry the right foot six inches in the rear of the left heel, the left knee slightly bent, the body upright upon the right leg; the musket resting against the hollow of the right shoulder, the hands crossed in front, the backs of them outward, and the left hand uppermost. At the word "*Attention!*" the soldier will resume the correct position at order arms. In the position here indicated, the soldier will remain silent and motionless; and it is particularly enjoined upon all officers to cause the commands above given, on the part of the soldier, to be executed with great briskness and spirit.

323. Officers on all duties under arms are to have their swords drawn, without waiting for any words of command for that purpose.

I. DRESS PARADE.

324. There shall be daily one dress parade, at *Troop* or *Retreat*, as the commanding officer may direct.

325. A signal will be beat or sounded half an hour before *Troop* or *Retreat*, for the music to assemble on the regimental parade, and each company to turn out under arms on its own parade, for roll-call and inspection by its own officers.

326. Ten minutes after that signal, the *Adjutant's call* will be given, when the Captains will march their companies (the band playing) to the regimental parade, where they take their positions in the order of battle. When the line is formed, the Captain of the first company, on notice from the Adjutant, steps one pace to the front, and gives to his company the command, "*Order*—ARMS, *Parade*—REST," which is repeated by each Captain in succession to the left. The Adjutant takes post two paces on the right of the line; the Sergeant-Major two paces on the left. The music will be formed in two ranks on the right of the Adjutant. The senior officer present will take the command of the parade, and will take post at a suitable distance in front, opposite the centre, facing the line.

327. When the companies have ordered arms, the Adjutant will order the music to *beat off*, when it will commence on the right, beat in front of the line to the left, and back to its place on the right.

328. When the music has ceased, the Adjutant will step two paces to the front, face to the left, and command,

1. *Attention*. 2. *Battalion*. 3. *Shoulder*—ARMS. 4. *Prepare to open ranks*. 5. *To the rear, open order*. 6. MARCH.

At the sixth command, the ranks will be opened according to the system laid down in the Infantry Tactics, the commissioned officers marching to the front, the company officers four paces, filed officers six paces, opposite to their positions in the order of battle, where they will halt and dress. The Adjutant, seeing the ranks aligned, will command,

FRONT!

and march along the front to the centre, face to the right, and pass the line of company officers eight or ten paces, where he will come to the right about, and command,

Present—ARMS!

when arms will be presented, officers saluting.

329. Seeing this executed, he will face about to the commanding officer, salute, and report, "*Sir, the parade is formed.*" The Adjutant will then, on intimation to that effect, take his station three paces on the left of the commanding officer, one pace retired, passing round his rear.

330. The commanding officer having acknowledged the salute of the line by touching his hat, will, after the Adjutant has taken his post, draw his sword and command,

1. *Battalion.* 2. *Shoulder*—ARMS!

and add such exercises as he may think proper, concluding with

Order—ARMS!

then return his sword, and direct the Adjutant to receive the reports.

331. The Adjutant will now pass round the right of the commanding officer, advance upon the line, halt midway between him and the line of company officers, and command,

1. *First Sergeants, to the front and centre.* 2. MARCH.

At the first command, they will *shoulder arms* as Sergeants, march two paces to the front, and face inward. At the second command, they will march to the centre and halt. The Adjutant will then order,

1. *Front*—FACE. 2. *Report.*

At the last word, each in succession, beginning on the right, will salute by bringing the left hand smartly across the breast to the right shoulder, and report the result of the roll-call previously made on the company parade.

332. The Adjutant again commands,

1. *First Sergeants, outward*—FACE! 2. *To your posts*—MARCH!

when they will resume their places, and order arms. The Adjutant will now face to the commanding officer, salute, report absent officers, and give the result of the First Sergeants' reports. The commanding officer will next direct the orders to be read, when the Adjutant will face about, and announce,

Attention to Orders.

He will then read the orders.

333. The orders having been read, the Adjutant will face to the commanding officer, salute, and report; when, on an intimation from the commander, he will face again to the line, and announce,

Parade is dismissed.

All the officers will now return their swords, face inward and close on the Adjutant, he having taken position in their line, the field officers on the flanks. The Adjutant commands,

1. *Front*—FACE! 2. *Forward*—MARCH!

when they will march forward, dressing on the centre, the music playing; and when within six paces of the commander, the Adjutant will give the word,

Halt!

The officers will then salute the commanding officer by raising the hand to the cap, and there remain until he shall have communicated to them such instructions as he may have to give, or intimates that the ceremony is finished. As the officers disperse, the First Sergeants will close the ranks of their respective companies, and march them to the company parades, where they will be dismissed, the band continuing to play until the companies clear the regimental parade.

334. All field and company officers and men will be present at *dress parades*, unless especially excused, or on some duty incompatible with such attendance.

335. A dress parade once a day will not be dispensed with, except on extraordinary and urgent occasions.

II. REVIEW OF A BATTALION OF INFANTRY.

336. Preparatory to a review, the Adjutant will cause a camp color to be placed 80 or 100 paces, or more, according to the length of the line, in front of, and opposite to, where the centre of the battalion will rest, where the reviewing officer is supposed to take his station; and, although he may choose to quit that position, still the color is to be considered as the point to which all the movements and formations are relative.

337. The Adjutant will also cause points to be marked, at suitable distances, for the wheelings of the divisions, so that their right flanks, in marching past, shall only be about four paces from the camp color, where it is supposed the reviewing officer places himself to receive the salute.

338. The battalion being formed in the order of battle at *shouldered arms*, the Colonel will command,

1. *Battalion, prepare for review*. 2. *To the rear, open order*. 3. MARCH

At the word MARCH, the field and staff officers dismount; the company officers and the color rank advance four paces in front of the front rank, and place themselves opposite to their respective places in the order of battle. The color-guard replace the color-rank. The staff officers place themselves, according to rank, three paces on the right of the rank of company officers, and one pace from each other; the music takes post as at parade. The non-commissioned staff take post one pace from each other, and three paces on the right of the front rank of the battalion.

339. When the ranks are aligned, the Colonel will command,

FRONT!

and place himself eight paces, and the Lieutenant-Colonel and Major will place themselves two paces, in front of the rank of company officers, and opposite to their respective places in the order of battle, all facing to the front.

340. When the reviewing officer presents himself before the centre, and is fifty or sixty paces distant, the Colonel will face about, and command,

Present—ARMS!

and resume his front. The men present arms, and the officers salute, so as to drop their swords with the last motion of the fire-lock. The non-commissioned staff salute by bringing the sword to a *poise*, the hilt resting on the breast, the blade in front of the face, inclining a little outward. The music will play, and all the drums beat, according to the rank of the reviewing officer The colors only salute such persons as, from their rank, and by regulation, (see Article XXIX.) are entitled to that honor. If the reviewing officer be junior in rank to the commandant of the parade, no compliment will be paid to him, but he will be received with arms carried, and the officers will not salute as the column passes in review.

341. The reviewing officer having halted, and acknowledged the salute of the line by touching or raising his cap or hat, the Colonel will face about, and command,

Shoulder—ARMS!

when the men shoulder their pieces; the officers and non-commissioned staff recover their swords with the last motion, and the Colonel faces to the front.

342. The reviewing officer will then go toward the right, the whole remaining perfectly steady, without paying any further compliment, while he passes along the front of the battalion, and proceeds round the left flank, and along the rear of the file-closers, to the right. While the reviewing officer is going round the battalion, the band will play, and will cease when he has returned to the right flank of the troops.

343. When the reviewing officer turns off, to place himself by the camp color in front, the Colonel will face to the line and command,

1. *Close Order.* 2. MARCH!

At the first command, the field and company officers will face to the right-about, and at the second command all persons, except the Colonel, will resume their places in the order of battle; the field and staff officers mount.

344. The reviewing officer having taken his position near the camp color, the Colonel will command,

1. *By company, right wheel.* 2. *Quick*—MARCH! 3. *Pass in review,*
4. *Column, forward.* 5. *Guide right.* 6. MARCH!

The battalion, in column of companies, right in front, will then, in common time, and at *shouldered arms*, be put in motion; the Colonel four paces in front of the Captain of the leading company: the Lieutenant-Colonel on a line with the leading company; the Major on a line with the rear company; the Adjutant on a line with the second company; the Sergeant-Major on a line with the company next preceding the rear—each six paces from the flank (left) opposite to the reviewing officer; the staff officers in one rank, according to the order of precedency, from the right, four paces in rear of the column; the music, preceded by the principal musician, six paces before the Colonel; the pioneers, preceded by a Corporal, four paces before the principal musician; and the Quartermaster-Sergeant two paces from the side opposite to the guides, and in line with the pioneers.

345. All other officers and non-commissioned officers will march past in the places prescribed for them in the march of an open column. The guides and soldiers will keep their heads steady to the front in passing in review.

346. The color-bearer will remain in the ranks while passing and saluting.

347. The music will begin to play at the command to march, and after passing the reviewing officer, wheel to the left out of the column, and take a position opposite and facing him, and will continue to play until the rear of the column shall have passed him, when it will cease, and follow in the rear of the battalion, unless the battalion is to pass in *quick time*, also, in which case it will keep its position.

348. The officers will salute the reviewing officer when they arrive within six paces of him, and recover their swords when six paces past him. All officers, in saluting, will cast their eyes toward the reviewing officer.

349. The Colonel, when he has saluted at the head of the battalion, will place himself near the reviewing officer, and will remain there until the rear has passed, when he will rejoin the battalion.

350. The colors will salute the reviewing officer, if entitled to it, when within six paces of him, and be raised when they have passed by him an equal distance. The drums will beat a march, or ruffle, according to the rank of the reviewing officer, at the same time that the colors salute.

351. When the column has passed the reviewing officer, the Colonel will direct it to the ground it marched from, and command,

Guide left.

in time for the guides to cover. The column having arrived on its ground, the Colonel will command,

1. *Column.* 2. HALT!

form it in order of battle, and cause the ranks to be opened, as in paragraph 341. The review will terminate by the whole saluting as at the beginning.

352. If, however, instructions have been previously given to march the troops past in *quick* time, also, the Colonel will, instead of changing the guides, halting the column and wheeling it into line, as above directed, give the command,

1. *Quick time.* 2. MARCH.

In passing the reviewing officer again, no salute will be offered by either officer or men. The music will have kept its position opposite the reviewing officer, and at the last command will commence playing, and as the column approaches, will place itself in front of, and march off with the column, and continue to play until the battalion is halted on its original ground of formation. The review will terminate in the same manner as prescribed above.

353. The Colonel will afterwards cause the troops to perform such exercises and manœuvres as the reviewing officer may direct.

354. When two or more battalions are to be reviewed, they will be formed in parade order, with the proper intervals, and will also perform the same movements that are laid down for a single battalion, observing the additional directions that are given for such movements when applied to the line. The Brigadier-General and his staff, on foot, will place themselves opposite the centre of the brigade; the Brigadier-

General two paces in front of the rank of Colonels, his aid two paces on his right, and one retired; and the other brigade staff officers, those having the rank of field officers, in the rank of Lieutenant-Colonels and Majors and those below that rank, in the rank of company officers.

355. In passing in review, a Major-General will be four paces in front of the Colonel of the leading battalion of his division, and the Brigadier-General will be on the right of the Colonels of the leading battalions of their brigades; staff officers on the left of their Generals.

356. When the line exceeds two battalions, the reviewing officer may cause them to march past in quick time only. In such cases, the mounted officers only will salute.

357. A number of companies less than a battalion will be reviewed as a battalion, and a single company as if it were with the battalion. In the latter case, the company may pass in column or platoons.

358. If several brigades are to be reviewed together, or in one line, this further difference will be observed: the reviewing personage, joined by the General of the division, on the right of his division, will proceed down the line, parallel to its front, and when near the Brigadier-Generals respectively, will be saluted by their brigades in succession. The music of each, after the prescribed salute, will play while the reviewing personage is in front, or in rear of it, and only then.

359. In marching in review, with several battalions in common time, the music of each succeeding battalion will commence to play when the music of the preceding one has ceased, in order to follow its battalion. When marching in quick time, the music will begin to play when the rear company of the preceding battalion has passed the reviewing officer.

360. The reviewing officer or personage will acknowledge the salute by raising, or taking off his cap or hat, when the commander of the troops salutes him; and also when the colors pass. The remainder of the time occupied by the passage of the troops he will be covered.

361. The review of cavalry and artillery will be conducted on similar principles, and according to the systems of instruction for those arms of the service.

III. GUARD-MOUNTING.

362. Camp and garrison guards will be relieved every twenty-four hours. The guards at outposts will ordinarily be relieved in the same manner; but this must depend on their distance from camp, or other circumstances, which may sometimes require their continuing on duty several days. In such cases they must be previously warned to provide themselves accordingly.

363. At the first call for guard-mounting, the men warned for duty turn out on their company parades for inspection by the First Sergeants; and at the second call, repair to the regimental or garrison parade, conducted by the First Sergeants. Each detachment, as it arrives, will, under the direction of the Adjutant, take post on the left of the one that preceded it, in open order, arms shouldered and bayonets fixed; the supernumeraries five paces in the rear of the men of their respective companies; the First Sergeants in the rear of them. The Sergeant-Major will dress the ranks, count the files, verify the details,

and when the guard is formed, report to the Adjutant, and take post two paces on the left of the front rank.

364. The Adjutant then commands *Front*, when the officer of the guard takes post twelve paces in front of the centre, the Sergeants in one rank, four paces in the rear of the officers; and the Corporals in one rank, four paces in the rear of the Sergeants—all facing to the front. The Adjutant then assigns their places in the guard.

365. The Adjutant will then command,

1. *Officer, and non-commissioned officers.* 2. *About*—FACE! 3. *Inspect your guards*—MARCH!

The non-commissioned officers then take their posts. The commander of the guard then commands,

1. *Order*—ARMS! 2. *Inspection*—ARMS!

and inspects his guard. When there is no commissioned officer on the guard, the Adjutant will inspect it. During inspection, the band will play.

366. The inspection ended, the officer of the guard takes post as though the guard were a company of a battalion, in open order, under review; at the same time, also, the officers of the day will take post in front of the centre of the guard; the old officers of the day three paces on the right of the new officer of the day, one pace retired.

367. The Adjutant will now command,

1. *Parade*—REST! *Troop—Beat off!*

when the music, beginning on the right, will beat down the line in front of the officer of the guard to the left, and back to its place on the right, where it will cease to play.

368. The Adjutant then commands,

1. *Attention!* 2. *Shoulder*—ARMS! 3. *Close order*—MARCH!

At the word "close order," the officer will face about; at "march," resume his post in line. The Adjutant then commands,

Present—ARMS!

at which he will face to the new officer of the day, salute, and report, "*Sir, the guard is formed.*" The new officer of the day, after acknowledging the salute, will direct the Adjutant to march the guard in review, or by flank to its post. But if the Adjutant be senior to the officer of the day, he will report without saluting with the sword then, or when marching the guard in review.

369. In review, the guard march past the officer of the day, according to the order of review, conducted by the Adjutant, marching on the left of the first division; the Sergeant-Major on the left of the last division.

370. When the column has passed the officer of the day, the officer of the guard marches it to its post, the Adjutant and Sergeant-Major retiring. The music, which has wheeled out of the column, and taken post opposite the officer of the day, will cease, and the old officer of the day salute, and give the old or standing orders to the new officer of the day. The supernumeraries, at the same time, will be marched by the First Sergeants to their respective company parades, and dismissed.

371. In bad weather, or at night, or after fatiguing marches, the ceremony of turning off may be dispensed with, but not the inspection.

372. Grand guards, and other brigade guards, are organized and mounted on the brigade parade by the staff officer of the parade, under the direction of the field officer of the day of the brigade, according to the principles here prescribed for the police guard of a regiment. The detail of each regiment is assembled on the regimental parade, verified by the Adjutant, and marched to the brigade parade by the senior officer of the detail. After inspection and review, the officer of the day directs the several guards to their respective posts.

373. The officer of the old guard having his guard paraded, on the approach of the new guard, commands,

Present—Arms!

374. The new guard will march, in quick time, past the old guard, at *shoulder arms*, officers saluting, and take post four paces on its right, where, being aligned with it, its commander will order,

Present—Arms!

The two officers will then approach each other and salute. They will then return to their respective guards, and command,

1. *Shoulder*—Arms! 2. *Order*—Arms.

375. The officer of the new guard will now direct the detail for the advanced guard to be formed and marched to its post, the list of the guard made and divided into three reliefs, experienced soldiers placed over the arms of the guard and at the remote and responsible posts, and the young soldiers in posts near the guard for instruction in their duties, and will himself proceed to take possession of the guard-house or guard-tent, and the articles and prisoners in charge of the guard.

376. During the time of relieving the sentinels and of calling in the small posts, the old commander will give the new all the information and instructions relating to his post.

377. The first relief having been designated and ordered two paces to the front, the Corporal of the new guard will take charge of it, and go to relieve the sentinels, accompanied by the Corporal of the old guard, who will take command of the old sentinels, when the whole are relieved.

378. If the sentinels are numerous, the Sergeants are to be employed, as well as Corporals, in relieving them.

379. The relief, with arms at a support, in two ranks, will march by flank, conducted by the Corporal on the side of the leading front-rank man; and the men will be numbered alternately in the front and rear rank, the man on the right of the front rank being No. 1. Should an officer approach, the Corporal will command *carry arms*, and resume the *support arms* when the officer is passed.

380. The sentinels at the guard-house or guard-tent will be the first relieved and left behind; the others are relieved in succession.

381. When a sentinel sees the relief approaching, he will halt and face to it, with his arms at a shoulder. At six paces, the Corporal will command,

1. *Relief*. 2. Halt!

when the relief will halt and carry arms. The Corporal will then add, "No. 1," or "No. 2," or "No. 3," according to the number of the post,

Arms—Port!

The two sentinels will, with arms at *port*, then approach each other, when the old sentinel, under the correction of the Corporal, will whisper the instructions to the new sentinel. This done, the two sentinels will shoulder arms, and the old sentinel will pass, in quick time, to his place in rear of the relief. The Corporal will then command,

1. *Support*—Arms! 2. *Forward.* 3. March!

and the relief proceeds in the same manner until the whole are relieved.

382. The detachments and sentinels from the old guard having come in, it will be marched, at *shoulder arms*, along the front of the new guard, in quick time, the new guard standing at *present arms;* officers saluting, and the music of both guards beating, except at the outposts.

383. On arriving at the regimental or garrison parade, the commander of the old guard will send the detachments composing it, under charge of the non-commissioned officers, to their respective regiments. Before the men are dismissed, their pieces will be drawn or discharged at a target. On rejoining their companions, the chiefs of squads will examine the arms, &c., of their men, and cause the whole to be put away in good order.

384. When the old guard has marched off fifty paces, the officer of the new guard will order his men to stack their arms, or place them in the arm racks.

385. The commander of the guard will then make himself acquainted with all the instructions for his post, visit the sentinels, and question them and the non-commissioned officers relative to the instructions they may have received from other persons of the old guard.

ARTICLE XXXIII.

GUARDS.

386. Sentinels will be relieved every two hours, unless the state of the weather, or other causes, should make it necessary or proper that it be done at shorter or longer intervals.

387. Each relief, before mounting, is inspected by the commander of the guard or of its post. The Corporal reports to him, and presents the old relief on its return.

388. The *countersign*, or watchword, is given to such persons as are entitled to pass during the night, and to officers, non-commissioned officers, and sentinels of the guard. Interior guards receive the countersign only when ordered by the commander of the troops.

389. The *parole* is imparted to such officers only as have a right to visit the guards, and to make the grand rounds; and to officers commanding guards.

390. As soon as the new guard has been marched off, the officer of the day will repair to the office of the commanding officer and report for orders.

391. The officer of the day must see that the officer of the guard is furnished with the parole and countersign before *retreat*.

392. The officer of the day visits the guards during the day at such times as he may deem necessary, and makes his rounds at night at least once after 12 o'clock.

393. Upon being relieved, the officer of the day will make such remarks in the report of the officer of the guard as circumstances require, and present the same at headquarters.

394. Commanders of guards leaving their posts to visit their sentinels, or on other duty, are to mention their intention, and the probable time of their absence, to the next in command.

395. The officers are to remain constantly at their guards, except while visiting their sentinels, or necessarily engaged elsewhere on their proper duty.

396. Neither officers nor soldiers are to take off their clothing or accoutrements while they are on guard.

397. The officer of the guard must see that the countersign is duly communicated to the sentinels a little before twilight.

398. When a fire breaks out, or any alarm is raised in a garrison, all guards are to be immediately under arms.

399. Inexperienced officers are put on guard as supernumeraries, for the purpose of instruction.

400. Sentinels will not take orders or allow themselves to be relieved, except by an officer or non-commissioned officer of their guard or party, the officer of the day, or the commanding officer; in which case the orders will be immediately notified to the commander of the guard by the officer giving them.

401. Sentinels will report every breach of orders or regulations they are instructed to enforce.

402. Sentinels must keep themselves on the alert, observing every thing that takes place within sight and hearing of their post. They will carry their arms habitually at support, or on either shoulder, but will never quit them. In wet weather, if there be no sentry-box, they will secure arms.

403. No sentinel shall quit his post or hold conversation not necessary to the proper discharge of his duty.

404. All persons, of whatever rank in the service, are required to observe respect toward sentinels.

405. In case of disorder, a sentinel must call out *the guard;* and if a fire take place, he must cry—"*Fire!*" adding the number of his post. If in either case the danger be great, he must discharge his firelock before calling out.

406. It is the duty of a sentinel to repeat all calls made from posts more distant from the main body of the guard than his own, and no sentinel will be posted so distant as not to be heard by the guard, either directly or through other sentinels.

407. Sentinels will present arms to general and field officers, to the officer of the day, and to the commanding officer of the post. To all other officers they will carry arms.

408. When a sentinel in his sentry-box sees an officer approaching, he will stand at *attention*, and as the officer passes will salute him, by

bringing the left hand briskly to the musket, as high as the right shoulder.

409. The sentinel at any post of the guard, when he sees any body of troops, or an officer entitled to compliment, approach, must call "*Turn out the guard!*" and announce who approaches.

410. Guards do not turn out as a matter of compliment after sunset; but sentinels will, when officers in uniform approach, pay them proper attention, by facing to the proper front, and standing steady at *shouldered arms.* This will be observed until the evening is so far advanced that the sentinels begin challenging.

411. After retreat (or the hour appointed by the commanding officer), until broad daylight, a sentinel challenges every person who approaches him, taking, at the same times the position of *arms port.* He will suffer no person to come nearer than within reach of his bayonet, until the person has given the countersign.

412. A sentinel, in challenging, will call out—"*Who comes there?*" If answered—"*Friend, with the countersign,*" and he be instructed to pass persons with the countersign, he will reply "Advance friend, with the countersign!" If answered—"*Friends!*" he will reply, "*Halt friends! Advance one, with the countersign!*" If answered—"*Relief,*" "*Patrol,* or "*Grand rounds,*" he will reply—"*Halt! Advance, Sergeant* (*or Corporal*) *with the countersign!*" and satisfy himself that the party is what it represents itself to be. If he have no authority to pass persons with the countersign, if the wrong countersign be given, or if the persons have not the countersign, he will cause them to stand, and call, "*Corporal of the Guard!*"

413. In the daytime, when the sentinel before the guard sees the officer of the day approach, he will call—"*Turn out the guard! Officer of the day.*" The guard will be paraded, and salute with presented arms.

414. When any person approaches a post of the guard at night, the sentinel before the post, after challenging, causes him to halt until examined by a non-commissioned officer of the guard. If it be the officer of the day, or any other officer entitled to inspect the guard and to make the rounds, the non-commissioned officer will call—"*Turn out the guard!*" when the guard will be paraded at shouldered arms, and the officer of the guard, if he thinks necessary, may demand the countersign and parole.

415. The officer of the day, wishing to make the rounds, will take an escort of a non-commissioned officer and two men. When the rounds are challenged by a sentinel, the Sergeant will answer—"*Grand rounds!*" and the sentinel will reply—"*Halt, grand rounds! Advance, Sergeant, with the countersign!*" Upon which the Sergeant advances and gives the countersign. The sentinel will then cry—"*Advance rounds!*" and stand at a shoulder till they have passed.

416. When the sentinel before the guard challenges, and is answered—"*Grand rounds!*" he will reply—"*Halt, grand rounds! Turn out the guard: grand rounds!*" Upon which the guard will be drawn up at shouldered arms. The officer commanding the guard will then order a Sergeant and two men to advance; when within ten paces, the Sergeant challenges. The Sergeant of the grand round answers—"*Grand rounds!*" The Sergeant of the guard replies—"*Advance, Sergeant,*

FORM OF GUARD REPORT.

Report of Guard mounted at ——, on the ——, and relieved on the ——.

	Lieutenants.	Sergeants.	Corporals.	Musicians.	Privates.	Total.	Aggregate.	Articles in charge.				Received the foregoing articles. A. B——, Lieutenant 1st. Infantry.
Parole.												
Countersign.												
Detail												

LIST OF THE GUARD.

No.	Reliefs, and when posted. 1st Relief. From — to —, and — to —. Name.	Co.	Rt.	2d Relief. From — to —, and — to —. Name.	Co.	Rt.	3d Relief. From — to —, and — to —. Name.	Co.	Rt.	Where posted.	Remarks.
1	C. D.	A.	1st	I. J.	D.	3d	O. P.	G.	8th	Guard house.	
2	E. F.	B.	4th	K. L.	E.	2d	Q. R.	H.	9th	Magazine.	
3	G. H.	C.	6th	M. N.	F.	5th	S. T.	I.	10th	Quarm'r store.	
1	Sergeant W. V., Co. A, 1st Artillery.									Serg't guard.	
2	Corporal W. X., Co. B, 1st Infantry.									Corp'l "	
3	Corporal Y. Z., Co. C, 3d infantry.									" "	

LIST OF PRISONERS.

No.	Names.	Company.	Regiment.	Confined: When.	Confined: By whom.	Charges.	Sentences.	Remarks
1								
2								
3								
4								
5								

A. B. C,

Lieut. —— Regiment ——,
Commanding the Guard.

with the countersign!" The Sergeant of the round advances alone, gives the countersign, and returns to his round. The Sergeant of the guard calls to his officer—"*The countersign is right!"* on which the officer of the guard calls—"*Advance, rounds!"* The officer of the rounds then advances alone, the guard standing at shouldered arms. The officer of the rounds passes along the front of the guard to the officer, who keeps his post on the right, and gives him the parole. He then examines the guard, orders back his escort, and, taking a new one, proceeds in the same manner to other guards.

417. All material instructions given to a sentinel on post by persons entitled to make grand rounds, ought to be promptly notified to the commander of the guard.

418. Any General officer, or the commander of a post or garrison, may visit the guards of his command, and go to the grand rounds, and be received in the same manner as prescribed for the officer of the day.

ARTICLE XXXIV.

ORDERS AND CORRESPONDENCE.

419. The orders of commanders of armies, divisions, brigades, regiments, are denominated orders of such army, division, &c., and are either general or special. Orders are numbered, general and special, in separate series, each beginning with the year.

420. General orders announce the time and place of issues and payments, hours for roll calls and duties; the number and kind of orderlies, and the time when they shall be relieved; police regulations, and the prohibitions required by circumstances and localities; returns to be made, and their forms; laws and regulations for the army; promotions and appointments; eulogies or censures to corps or individuals, and generally, whatever it may be important to make known to the whole command.

421. Special orders are such as do not concern the troops generally, and need not be published to the whole command; such as relate to the march of some particular corps, the establishment of some post, the detaching of individuals, the granting requests, &c., &c.

422. A general order, and an important special order, must be read and approved by the officer whose order it is, before it is issued by the staff officer.

423. An order will state at the head, the source, place and date, and at the foot, the name of the commander who gives it; as for example:

Headquarters of the First Brigade, Second Division.

Camp at ———, *1st June, 186*—.

GENERAL ORDERS,
No. ——.

By command of Brigadier-General A. B.
C. D., Assistant Adjutant-General.

424. Orders may be put in the form of letters, but generally in the strict military form, through the office of the Adjutant or Adjutant and Inspector-General of the command.

425. Orders are transmitted through all the intermediate commanders in the order of rank. When an intermediate commander is omitted,

the officer who gives the order shall inform him, and he who receives it shall report it to his immediate superior.

426. Orders for any body of troops will be addressed to the commander, and will be opened and executed by the commander present, and published or distributed by him when necessary; printed orders, however, are generally distributed direct to posts from the headquarters where issued.

427. Orders assigning the stations of officers of engineers, ordnance, and of the staff departments, except as provided in the regulations for troops in the campaign, will be given by the Secretary of War, through the Adjutant and Inspector-General's office, or by commanders of geographical departments, under the special authority of the War Department. The commander of a department, who, in consequence of the movement of troops or other necessity of the service, removes an officer from the station assigned to him by the Secretary of War, shall promptly report the case to the Adjutant and Inspector-General.

428. A file of the printed orders will be kept with the headquarters of each regiment, with each company, and at each military post, and will be regularly turned over by the commander, when relieved, to his successor.

429. If general orders are not received in regular succession, commanding officers will report the missing numbers to the proper headquarters.

430. The orderly hours being fixed at each headquarters, the staff officers and chiefs of the special services either attend in person, or send their assistants to obtain the orders of the day; and the First Sergeants of companies repair for that purpose to the regimental or garrison headquarters.

431. During marches and active operations, and when the regular orderly hours cannot be observed, all orders will be either sent direct to the troops, or the respective commanders of regiments or corps will be informed when to send to headquarters for them. Under the same circumstances, orders will be read to the troops during a halt, without waiting for the regular parades.

432. Orders to any officer to make a tour of travel on duty, as for the inspection or payment of troops, &c., shall designate the troops and posts he shall visit, and the order in which he shall visit them, and the route of travel.

433. Every commander who gives an order involving an expenditure of public money, shall send a copy, without delay, to the bureau of the War Department to which the expenditure appertains; and if such commander be serving in a military department, he shall send a copy of the order to the headquarters of the Department.

434. If a military commander shall give to a disbursing officer any order in conflict with orders received by him from the officer in charge of his department, at any superior headquarters, such commander shall forthwith transmit the order to such headquarters, with explanation of the necessity which justifies it.

435. Copies of all orders of the commanders of armies, departments, divisions, and detached brigades, and of the superintendent of the recruiting service, will be forwarded at their dates, or as soon thereafter

as practicable, in separate series, on full sheets of letter paper, or as printed, to the Adjutant and Inspector-General's office.

436. Written communications from a commander to those under his command may be made by his staff officer. In all other cases, by the officer himself.

437. In signing an official communication, the writer shall annex to his name his rank and corps. When he writes by order, he shall state by whose order. All communications requiring answers must indicate the Post-Office to which they should be sent.

438. Communications to a commander from those under his command are addressed to the proper officer of his staff; to the chief of the Adjutant and Inspector-General's Department, in what relates specially to his bureau, or to the service generally; to the chief of any other departments of the staff, in what relates specially to his branch of the service. Communications to the Secretary of War will be made through the Adjutant and Inspector-General's office of the War Department, unless it be a case of claim, allowance, or other business specially appertaining to some other bureau; for example—claims of pay or for mileage, or quarters, will be transmitted through the Quartermaster-General. All communications, except rolls and stated returns, and accounts, are to be passed through the intermediate commanders. The same rule governs in verbal applications; for example—a Lieutenant seeking an indulgence must apply through his Captain. Communication from officers of the staff and administrative services to their own chiefs do not pass through the military commanders under whom they serve, except estimates for funds or supplies.

439. Copies of all important communications from the bureaus of the War Department to disbursing officers, relating to the service in a military department, shall be sent from the bureau to the department commander.

440. Rolls and returns will be accompanied by a letter of transmittal, enumerating them, and referring to no other subject.

441. Generally, officers who forward communications, indorse on them their remarks or opinion, without other letters of transmittal.

442. Official letters should generally refer to one matter only. In regard to an enlisted man, the company and regiment must be stated.

443. Letters on letter paper will be folded in three folds, parallel with the writing.

444. All communications on public service are to be marked on the cover, "*Official business,*" and to receive attention, *must* conform to the requirements of paragraph 438.

ARTICLE XXXV.

RETURNS AND REPORTS.

MONTHLY RETURNS.

445. Commanders of Army corps, regiments and battalions, will make to the Adjutant and Inspector-General's office of the War Department, monthly returns of their respective corps, regiments and battalions, on the forms furnished from that office, and according to the directions expressed on them.

In like manner, Captains make monthly company returns to regimental headquarters. All monthly returns will be forwarded on the first day of the next month, except regimental returns, which are forwarded as soon as all the company returns are received.

446. If any company be so far from regimental headquarters as to delay the transmittal of the monthly return to the 10th of the month, the Colonel will not wait for the return of such company, but leave space for it to be entered at the Adjutant and Inspector-General's office; for which purpose the Captain will transmit a copy of the return *direct* to the Adjutant and Inspector-General, as well as to regimental headquarters.

447. In campaign, monthly returns of divisions and detached brigades will be made to the Adjutant and Inspector-General's office. They will exhibit separately the several regiments, and detachments, and staff corps, and the strength of each garrison within the command. These returns, and those of regiments, corps, and posts, in campaign, will, unless otherwise ordered, be transmitted through the intermediate commanders.

448. The established *printed* forms and blanks of all returns required from the commanders of divisions, brigades, regiments, corps, companies, and posts, will be furnished from the Adjutant and Inspector-General's office on their *requisitions* annually made, or oftener, if necessary. The receipt of these forms and blanks will be immediately acknowledged, and afterward accounted for on the next monthly returns.

449. Manuscript returns, rolls, certificates, and other documents, are prohibited, unless the proper *printed* forms have not been received in time. Regimental returns must be made out in the name of the Colonel, whether he be present or absent.

ANNUAL RETURNS—CASUALITIES.

450. This return will exhibit the various changes and alterations which may have taken place in the regiment during the preceding twelve months; that is to say—a statement of the number of resignations, transfers, deaths, &c., of commissioned officers; the number of men joined by enlistment, transferred and discharged; the number tried by courts-martial or by the civil law, and the nature of their offences; the number of discharges, deaths, dismissals, and desertions; number joined from desertion, pardoned, &c.

RETURN OF DECEASED SOLDIERS.

451. To be forwarded to the Adjutant and Inspector-General, by the Colonels of regiments, *quarterly*. Also, a duplicate to the Second Auditor of the Treasury.

FIELD RETURNS.

452. Besides the stated returns of the troops, such other *field returns* and reports will be made as may be necessary to keep the government informed of the condition and strength of the forces.

453. After an action or affair, a return of the killed, wounded, and missing will be made, in which the name, rank, and regiment of each officer and soldier will be specified, with such remarks and explanations as may be requisite for the records of the Department of War, or be necessary to establish the just claims of any individual who may have

been wounded, or of the heirs and representatives of any killed in action (taking care to specify the *nature of the wound*, the *time* and *place* of its occurrence, the company, regiment, or corps, and the name of the Captain, Colonel, or other commanding officer.)

REPORTS.

454. The date of appointment, of detail, and of removal of all staff officers, or of officers selected for duty in staff departments, which may entitle them to receive additional pay, will be immediately reported by the officer making such appointment, detail, or removal, to the Adjutant and Inspector-General, and to the Quartermaster of the department or command to which such officers belong.

455. Whenever any change takes place in the position or location of troops, the fact will be immediately reported by the commanding officer to general, division, and department-head-quarters, specifying the date of departure of the whole or any part of the troops, or of the arrival of any detachment; as well as all other circumstances connected with such changes in the command. These special reports will always be accompanied by an exact *return* of the troops according to the established printed forms. A similar report will be noted on the next monthly return of the post or station. If a new post or position be established, its situation, and the nearest post-office and proper route to it, should be reported.

456. Officers on detached duty, will report monthly to the commanders of their posts, of their regiments or corps, and to the Adjutant and Inspector-General—such reports will give the officer's station, the nature of his duty, and the authority placing him thereon. Those visiting the seat of government will register their names at the office of the Adjutant and Inspector-General.

PRISONERS OF WAR—CAPTURED PROPERTY.

457. A return of prisoners, and a report of the number and description of the killed and wounded of the enemy, will be forwarded to the Adjutant and Inspector General's office, Richmond, Va.

458. A return of all property captured will be made by the commanding officer of the troops by whom such capture was made, to the Adjutant and Inspector-General, at Richmond, in order that it may be disposed of according to the orders of the War Department.

INSPECTION REPORTS.

459. Inspection reports will show the discipline of the troops; their instruction in all military exercises and duties; the state of their arms, clothing, equipments, and accoutrements of all kinds; of their kitchens and messes; of the barracks and quarters at the post; of the guard-house, prisons, hospital, bake-house, magazine, store-houses, and stores of every description; of the stables and horses; the condition of the post school; the management and application of the post and company funds; the state of the post, and regimental, and company books, papers, and files; the zeal and ability of the officers in command of troops; the capacity of the officers conducting the administrative and staff services, the fidelity and economy of their disbursements; the condition of all public property, and the amount of money in the hands of each dis-

bursing officer; the regularity of issues and payments; the mode of enforcing discipline by courts-martial, and by the authority of the officers; the propriety and legality of all punishments inflicted; and any information whatsoever, concerning the service in any matter or particular that may merit notice, or aid to correct defects or introduce improveme ts.

460. Inspectors are required particularly to report if any officer is of intemperate habits, or unfit for active service by infirmity or any other cause.

ARTICLE XXXVI.

TROOPS IN CAMPAIGN.

ORGANIZATION OF AN ARMY IN THE FIELD.

461. The formation by divisions is the basis of the organization and administration of armies in the field.

462. A division consists usually of two or three brigades, either of infantry or cavalry, and troops of other corps in the necessary proportion.

463. A brigade is formed of two or more regiments. The first number takes the right.

464. Mixed brigades are sometimes formed of infantry and light cavalry, especially for the advance guards.

465. As the troops arrive at the rendezvous, the general commanding-in-chief will organize them into brigades and divisions.

466. The light cavalry is employed as flankers and partizans, and generally for all service out of the line.

467. Heavy cavalry belongs to the reserve, and is covered, when necessary, in marches, camps, or bivouacs, by light troops, or infantry of the line.

468. The arrangement of the troops on parade and in order of battle is—1st, the light infantry; 2d, infantry of the line; 3d, light cavalry; 4th, cavalry of the line; 5th, heavy cavalry. The troops of the artillery and engineers are in the centre of the brigades, divisions, or corps to which they are attached; marines take the left of other infantry; volunteers and militia take the left of regular troops of the same arm, and among themselves, regiments of volunteers or militia of the same arm take place by lot. This arrangement is varied by the general commanding-in-chief, as the circumstances of war render expedient.

469. Brigades in divisions, and divisions in the army, are numbered from right to left; but in reports of military operations, brigades and divisións are designated by the name of the general commanding them.

470. The order of regiments in brigades and of brigades in divisions may be changed by the commander of the division for important reasons, such as the weakness of some corps, or to relieve one from marching too long at the rear of the column. Such changes must be reported to the general commanding-in-chief.

471. The general commanding-in-chief assigns the generals of divisions and of brigades to their respective commands, when the assignment is not made by the Department of War.

472. The general of brigade inspects his troops in detail, by companies, when he takes the command and at the opening of the campaign,

and as often as may be necessary to ascertain exactly their condition. The general of division makes similar inspections when he thinks proper. At these inspections the generals examine the arms, clothing, equipments, harness, horses, &c.; direct the necessary repairs, and designate the men and horses to remain in depot, or march with the train.

473. Reports of inspections are made by the general of brigade to the general of division, and by the general of division to the general commanding in-chief.

474. During marches and all active operations, generals of brigades keep themselves exactly informed, by reports of corps and by their inspections, of the actual strength of the regiments, so as always, and especially after an engagement, to make accurate returns to the general of division.

475. Staff officers and officers of engineers, and artillery, according to the nature of the service, are assigned to the head-quarters of armies and divisions, and detached brigades, by order of the general commanding-in-chief, when the distribution of these officers has not been regulated by the War Department. The necessary staff will be assigned to commanders of brigades.

476. When an Engineer or other officer is charged with directing an expedition or making a reconnoisance, without having command of the escort, the commander of the escort shall consult him on all the arrangements necessary to secure the success of the operation.

477. Staff officers, and commanders of engineers, and artillery, report to their immediate commanders the state of the supplies and whatever concerns the service under their direction, and receive their orders, and communicate to them those they receive from their superiors in their own corps.

478. The senior officer of engineers, of artillery, and the departments of the general staff serving at the chief head-quarters in the field, will transmit to the bureau of his department at Richmond, at the close of the campaign, and such other times as the commander in the field may approve, a full report of the operations of his department, and whatever information to improve its service he may be able to furnish.

The report of the officer of engineers will embrace plans of military works executed during the campaign, and, in case of siege, a journal of the attack or defence.

CONTRIBUTIONS.

479. When the wants of the army absolutely require it, and in other cases, under special instructions from the War Department, the general commanding the army may levy contributions in money or kind on the enemy's country occupied by the troops. No other commander can levy such contributions without written authority from the general commanding-in-chief.

ORDERLIES.

480. At the opening of a campaign, the commander of an army determines and announces in orders the number of orderlies, mounted or foot, for the Generals, and the corps or regiments by which they are to be supplied, and the periods at which they shall be relieved.

481. In marches, the mounted orderlies follow the Generals, and

perform the duty of escorts, or march with orderlies on foot at the head of the division or brigade.

482. The staff officer who distributes the orderlies to their posts sends with them a note of the time and place of departure; those relieved receive a like note from the staff officer at head quarters.

483. Mounted soldiers are to be employed to carry dispatches only in special and urgent cases.

484. The precise time when the dispatch is sent off, and the rate at which it is to be conveyed, are to be written clearly on the covers of all letters transmitted by a mounted orderly, and the necessary instructions to him, and the rate of travel going and returning, are to be distinctly explained to him.

DEPOTS.

485. The grand depots of an army are established where the military operations would not expose them to be broken up. Smaller depots are organized for the divisions and the several arms. They are commanded by officers temporarily disabled for field service, or by other officers when necessary, and comprise, as much as possible, the hospitals and depots for convalescents. When conveniently placed, they serve as points for the halting and assembling of detachments. They receive the disabled from the corps on the march; and the officers in command of the depots send with the detachments to the army those at the depots who have become fit for service.

CAMPS.

486. Camp is the place where troops are established in tents, in huts, or in bivouac. Cantonments are the inhabited places which troops occupy for shelter when not put in barracks. The camping-party is a detachment detailed to prepare a camp.

487. Reconnoissances should precede the establishment of the camp. For a camp of troops on the march, it is only necessary to look to the health and comfort of the troops, the facility of the communications, the convenience of wood and water, and the resources in provisions and forage. The ground for an intrenched camp, or a camp to cover a country, or one designed to deceive the enemy as to the strength of the army, must be selected, and the camp arranged for the object in view.

488. The camping-party of a regiment consists of the regimental Quartermaster and Quartermaster-Sergeant, and a Corporal and two men per company. The General decides whether the regiments camp separately or together, and whether the police guard shall accompany the camping-party, or a larger escort shall be sent.

489. Neither baggage nor led horses are permitted to move with the camping-party.

490. When the General can send in advance to prepare the camp, he gives his instructions to the chief of the Quartermaster's Department, who calls on the regiments for their camping-parties, and is accompanied, if necessary, by an Engineer, to propose the defences and communications.

491. The watering-places are examined, and signals placed at those

that are dangerous. Any work required to make them of easier access is done by the police guard or Quartermaster's men. Sentinels, to be relieved by the guards of the regiment when they come up, are placed by the camping-party over the water if it is scarce, and over the houses and stores of provisions and forage in the vicinity.

492. If the camping-party does not precede the regiment, the Quartermaster attends to these things as soon as the regiment reaches the camp.

493. On reaching the ground, the infantry form on the color front; the cavalry in rear of its camp.

494. The Generals establish the troops in camp as rapidly as possible, particularly after long, fatiguing marches.

495. The number of men to be furnished for guards, pickets, and orderlies; the fatigue parties to be sent for supplies; the work to be done, and the strength of the working parties; the time and place for issues; the hour of marching, &c., are then announced by the Brigadier-Generals to the Colonels, and by them to the field officers—the Adjutant and Captains formed in front of the regiment, the First Sergeants taking post behind their Captains. The Adjutant then makes the details, and the First Sergeants warn the men. The regimental officer of the day forms the picket, and sends the guards to their posts. The colors are then planted in the centre of the color line, and the arms are stacked on the line; the fatigue parties to procure supplies, and the working parties form in rear of the arms; the men not on detail pitch the tents.

496. If the camp is near the enemy, the picket remains under arms until the return of the fatigue parties, and, if necesssary, is reinforced by details from each company.

497. In the cavalry, each troop moves a little in rear of the point at which its horses are to be secured, and forms in one rank; the men then dismount; a detail is made to hold the horses; the rest stack their arms and fix the picket rope; after the horses are attended to, the tents are pitched, and each horseman places his carbine at the side from the weather, and hangs his sabre and bridle on it.

498. The standard is then carried to the tent of the Colonel.

499. The terms front, flank, right, left, file, and rank, have the same meaning when applied to camps as to the order of battle.

500. The front of the camp is usually equal to the front of the troops. The tents are arranged in ranks and files. The number of ranks varies with the strength of the companies and the size of the tents.

501. No officer will be allowed to occupy a house, although vacant and on the ground of his camp, except by permission of the commander of the brigade, who shall report it to the commander of the division.

502. The staff officer charged with establishing the camp will designate the place for the shambles. The offal will be buried.

CAMP OF INFANTRY.

503. Each company has its tents in two files, facing on a street perpendicular to the color line. The width of the street depends on the front of the camp, but should not be less than five paces. The interval between the ranks of tents is two paces; between the files of tents of adjacent companies, two paces; between regiments, twenty-two paces.

504. The color line is ten paces in front of the front rank of tents. The kitchens are twenty paces behind the rear rank of company tents; the non-commissioned staff and sutler, twenty paces in rear of the kitchen; the company officers, twenty paces farther in rear; and the field and staff, twenty paces in rear of the company officers.

505. The company officers are in rear of their respective companies; the Captains on the right.

506. The Colonel and Lieutenant Colonel are near the centre of the line of field and staff; the Adjutant, a Major and Surgeon, on the right; the Quartermaster, a Major and Assistant Surgeon, on the left.

507. The police guard is at the centre of the line of the non-commissioned staff, the tents facing to the front, the stacks of arms on the left.

508. The advanced post of the police guard is about 200 paces in front of the color line, and opposite the centre of the regiment, or on the best ground; the prisoners' tent are about four paces in rear. In a regiment of the second line, the advanced post of the police guard is 200 paces in rear of the line of its field and staff.

509. The horses of the staff officers and of the baggage train are twenty-five paces in rear of the tents of the field and staff; the wagons are parked on the same line, and the men of the train camped near them.

510. The sinks of the men are 150 paces in front of the color line—those of the officers 100 paces in rear of the train. Both are concealed by bushes. When convenient, the sinks of the men may be placed in the rear or on the flank. A portion of the earth dug out for sinks to be thrown back occasionally.

511. The front of the camp of a regiment of 1000 men in two ranks will be 400 paces, or one-fifth less paces than the number of files, if the camp is to have the same front as the troops in order of battle. But the front may be reduced to 190 paces by narrowing the company streets to five paces; and if it be desirable to reduce the front still more, the tents of companies may be pitched in single file—those of a division facing on the same street.

CAMP OF CAVALRY.

512. In the cavalry, each company has one file of tents—the tents opening on the street facing the left of the camp.

513. The horses of each company are placed in a single file, facing the opening of the tents, and are fastened to pickets planted firmly in the ground, from three to six paces from the tents of the troops.

514. The interval between the file of tents should be such that, the regiment being broken into column of companies, each company should be on the extension of the line on which the horses are to be picketed.

515. The streets separating the squadrons are wider than those between the companies by the interval separating squadrons in line; these intervals are kept free from any obstruction throughout the camp.

516. The horses of the rear rank are placed on the left of those of their file leaders.

517. The horses of the Lieutenants are placed on the right of their platoons; those of the Captains on the right of the company.

518. Each horse occupies a space of about two paces. The number

Camp of a Regiment of Infantry.

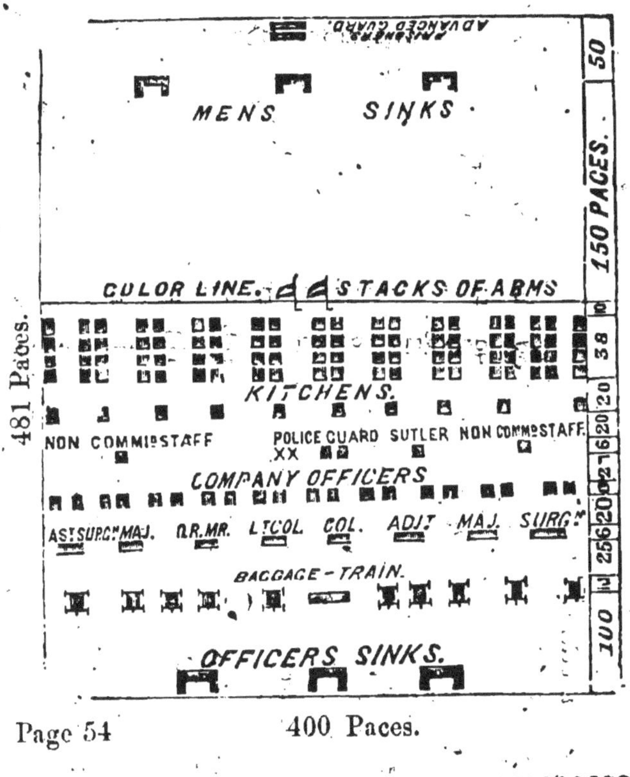

Page 54

Camp of a Regiment of five Squadrons of Cavalry.

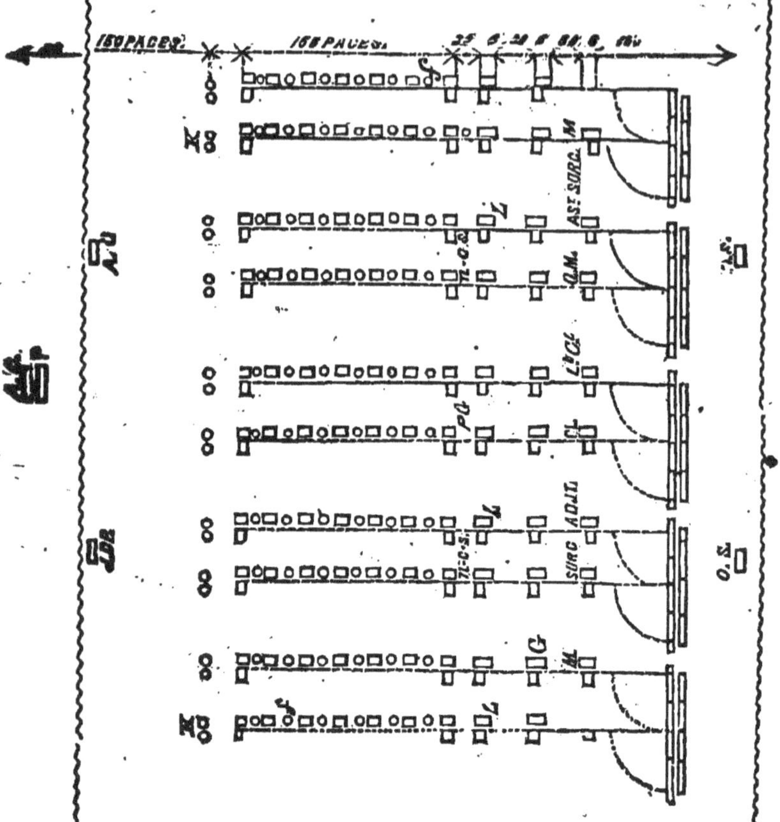

Cl.—*Colonel.*
Lt.—*Lieut. Colonel.*
M.—*Major.*
Surg.—*Surgeon.*
Ast. Surg.—*Assistant Surgeon.*
Adjt.—*Adjutant.*
Q. M.—*Quarter Master.*
C.—*Captain.*
L.—*Lieutenant.*
A. G.—*Advanced Guard.*
P. G.—*Police Guard.*
m. s.—*Men's Sinks.*
o. s.—*Officers' Sinks.*
k.—*Kitchens.*
f.—*Forage.*
n. c. s.—*Non. Com. Staff.*
P.—*Prisoners.*

of horses in the company fixes the depth of the camp and the distance between the files of tents; the forage is placed between the tents.

519. The kitchens are twenty paces in front of each file of tents.

520. The non-commissioned officers are in the tents of the front rank. Camp followers, teamsters, &c., are in the rear rank. The police guard in the rear rank, near the centre of the regiment.

521. The tents of the Lieutenants are 30 paces in rear of the file of their company; the tents of the Captains 30 paces in rear of the Lieutenants.

522. The Colonel's tent 30 paces in the rear of the Captains', near the centre of the regiment; the Lieutenant-Colonel on his right; the Adjutant on his left; the Majors on the same line, opposite the second company on the right and left; the Surgeon on the left of the Adjutant.

523. The field and staff have their horses on the left of their tents, on the same line with the company horses; sick horses are placed in one line on the right or left of the camp. The men who attend them have a separate file of tents; the forges and wagons in rear of this file. The horses of the train and of camp-followers are in one or more files extending to the rear, behind the right or left squadron. The advanced post of the police guard is 200 paces in front, opposite the centre of the regiment; the horses in one or two files.

524. The sinks for the men are 150 paces in front—those for officers, 100 paces in the rear of the camp.

CAMP OF ARTILLERY.

525. The artillery is encamped near the troops to which it is attached, so as to be protected from attack, and to contribute to the defence of the camp. Sentinels for the park are furnished by the artillery, and, when necessary, by the other troops.

526. For a battery of six pieces, the tents are in three files—one for each section; distance between the ranks of tents, 15 paces; tents opening to the front. The horses of each section are picketed in one file, 10 paces to the left of the file of tents. In the horse artillery, or if the number of horses makes it necessary, the horses are in two files, on the right and left of the file of tents. The kitchens are 25 paces in front of the front rank of tents. The tents of the officers are in the outside files of company tents, 25 paces in the rear of the rear rank—the Captain on the right, the Lieutenants on the left.

527. The park is opposite the centre of the camp, 40 paces in rear of the officers' tents. The carriages in files four paces apart; distance between ranks of carriages sufficient for the horses when harnessed to them; the park guard is 25 paces in rear of the park. The sinks for the men, 150 paces in front; for the officers, 100 paces in the rear. The harness is in the tents of the men.

BIVOUACS.

528. A regiment of cavalry being in order of battle, in rear of the ground to be occupied, the Colonel breaks it by platoons to the right. The horses of each platoon are placed in a single row, and fastened as prescribed for camps; near the enemy, they remain saddled all night, with slackened girths. The arms are at first stacked in rear of each row of horses; the sabres, with the bridles hung on them are placed against the stacks.

529. The forage is placed on the right of each row of horses. Two stable-guards for each platoon watch the horses.

530. A fire for each platoon is made near the color line, 20 paces to the left of the row of horses. A shelter is made for the men around the fire, if possible, and each man then stands his arms and bridle against the shelter.

531. The fires and shelter for the officers are placed in rear of the line of those for the men.

532. The intervals between the squadrons must be without obstruction throughout the whole depth of the bivouac.

533. The interval between the shelters should be such that the platoons can take up a line of battle freely to the front or rear.

534. The distance from the enemy decides the manner in which the horses are to be fed and led to water. When it is permitted to unsaddle, the saddles are placed in the rear of the horses.

535. In infantry, the fires are made in rear of the *color line*, on the ground that would be occupied by the tents in camp. The companies are placed around them, and, if possible, construct shelters. When liable to surprise, the infantry should stand to arms at daybreak, and the cavalry mount until the return of the reconnoitering parties. If the arms are to be taken apart to clean, it must be done by detachments, successively.

CANTONMENTS.

536. The cavalry should be placed under shelter whenever the distance from the enemy, and from the ground where the troops are to form for battle, permit it. Taverns and farm-houses, with large stables and free access, are selected for quartering them.

537. The Colonel indicates the place of assembling in case of alarm. It should generally be outside the cantonment; the egress from it should be free, the retreat upon the other positions secure, and roads leading to it on the side of the enemy obstructed.

538. The necessary orders being given, as in establishing a camp, the picket and grand guards are posted. A sentinel may be placed on a steeple or high house, and then the troops are marched to the quarters. The men sleep in the stables, if it is thought necessary.

539. The above applies in the main to infantry. Near the enemy, companies or platoons should be collected, as much as possible, in the same houses. If companies must be separated, they should be divided by platoons or squads. All take arms at daybreak.

540. When cavalry and infantry canton together, the latter furnish the guards by night, and the former by day.

541. Troops cantoned in presence of the enemy, should be covered by advanced guards and natural or artificial obstacles. Cantonments taken during a cessation of hostilities, should be established in rear of a line of defence, and in front of the point on which the troops would concentrate to receive an attack. The General commanding-in-chief assigns the limits of their cantonments to the divisions, the commanders of divisions to brigades, and the commanders of brigades post their regiments. The position for each corps in case of attack is carefully pointed out by the Generals.

HEADQUARTERS.

542. Generals take post at the centre of their commands, on the main channels to communication. If troops bivouac in presence of the enemy, the Generals bivouac with them.

MILITARY EXERCISES.

543. When troops remain in camp or cantonment many days, the Colonels require them to be exercised in the school of the battalion and squadron. Regiments and brigades encamped by division are not united for drills without the permission of the General of division. The troops must not be exercised at the firings without the authority of the General commanding-in-chief. The practice of the drums must never begin with the "general," or the "march of the regiment;" nor the trumpets with the sound "to horse." The hour for practice is always announced.

ORDERS.

544. In the field, verbal orders and important sealed orders are carried by officers, and, if possible, by staff officers. When orders are carried by orderlies, the place and time of departure will be marked on them, and place and time of delivery on the receipt.

DISPATCHES.

545. Dispatches, particularly for distant corps, should be entrusted only to officers to whom their contents can be confided. In a country occupied by the enemy, the bearer of dispatches should be accompanied by at least two of the best mounted men; should avoid towns and villages, and the main roads; rest as little as possible, and only at out-of-the-way places. Where there is danger, he should send one of the men in advance, and be always ready to destroy his dispatches. He should be adroit in answering questions about the army, and not be intimidated by threats.

WATCHWORDS.

546. The parole and countersign are issued daily from the principal headquarters of the command. The countersign is given to the sentinels and non-commissioned officers of the guards; the parole to the commissioned officers of guards. The parole is usually the name of a General; the countersign of a battle.

547. When the parole and countersign cannot be communicated daily to a post or detachment which ought to use the same as the main body, a series of words may be sent for some days in advance.

548. If the countersign is lost, or one of the guard deserts with it, the commander on the spot will substitute another, and report the case at once to the proper superior, that immediate notice may be given to headquarters.

ISSUES.

549. At what time and for what period issues are made, must depend on circumstances, and be regulated in orders. When an army is not moving, rations are generally issued for four days at a time. Issues to the companies of a regiment, and the fatigues to receive them, are su-

perintended by an officer detailed from the regiment. Issues are made from one end of the line to the other, beginning on the right and left alternately. An issue commenced on one regiment will not be interrupted for another entitled to precedence if it had been in place.

THE ROSTER, OR DETAILS FOR SERVICE.

550. The duties performed by detail are of three classes. The *first class* comprises, 1st, grand guards and outposts; 2d, interior guards, as of magazine, hospital, &c.; 3d, orderlies; 4th, police guards.

The *second class* comprises, 1st, detachments to protect laborers on military works, as field-works, communications, &c.; 2d, working parties on such works; 3d, detachments to protect fatigues.

The *third class* are all fatigues, without arms, in or out of camp.

In the cavalry, stable-guards form a separate roster, and count before fatigue.

551. The rosters are distinct for each class. Officers are named on them in the order of rank. The details are taken in succession in the order of the roster, beginning at the head.

552. Lieutenants form one roster, and First and Second Lieutenants are entered on it alternately. The senior First Lieutenant is the first on the roster; the senior Second Lieutenant is the second, &c. The Captains form one roster, and are exempt from fatigues, except to superintend issues. A Captain commanding a battalion temporarily is exempt from detail, and duty falling to him passes. Lieutenant-Colonels and Majors are on one roster. They may be detailed for duties of the first and second classes, when the importance of the guards and detachments requires it. Their roster is kept at division and brigade headquarters. In the company, Sergeants, Corporals and privates form distinct rosters.

553. Officers, non-commissioned officers, and soldiers take duties of the first class in the order stated, viz: the first for the detail, takes the grand guards; the next, the interior guards; the last, the police guards; and the same rule in regard to the details and duties of the second class. In the details for the third class, the senior officer takes the largest party. The party first for detail takes the service out of camp.

554. When the officer whose tour it is, is not able to take it, or is not present at the hour of marching, the next after him takes it. When a guard has passed the chain of sentinels, or an interior guard has reached its post, the officer whose tour it was cannot then take it. He takes the tour of the officer who has taken his. When an officer is prevented by sickness from taking his tour, it passes. These rules apply equally to non-commissioned officers and soldiers.

555. Duties of the first and second classes are credited on the roster when the guards or detachments have passed the chain of sentinels, or an interior guard has reached its post; fatigue duties when the parties have passed the chain or begun the duties in camp.

556. Every officer, non-commissioned officer, or soldier on duty of the first class, or who is of the next detail for such duty, takes, when relieved, the duty of the second or third class that has fallen to him during that time, unless he has marched for detachment of more than twenty-four hours.

557. Soldiers march with knapsacks on all duties of the first class;

and with arms and equipments complete on all working parties out of the camp, unless otherwise ordered. In the cavalry, horses are packed for all mounted service.

558. In the cavalry, dismounted men, and those whose horses are not in order, are preferred for the detail for dismounted service. Those who are mounted are never employed on those services, if the number of the other class are sufficient.

559. Every non-commissiond officer and soldier in the cavalry detailed for dismounted service must, before he marches, take to the First Sergeant of the troop, or Sergeant of his squad, his horse equipments and his valise ready packed. In case of alarm, the First Sergeant sees that the horses of these men are equipped and led to the rendezvous.

560. These rules in regard to the roster apply also to service in garrison.

POLICE GUARD.

561. In each regiment a police guard is detailed every day, consisting of two Sergeants, three Corporals, two drummers, and men enough to furnish the required sentinels and patrols. The men are taken from all the companies, from each in proportion to its strength. The guard is commanded by a Lieutenant, under the supervision of a Captain, as regimental officer of the day. It furnishes ten sentinels at the camp; one over the arms of the guard; one at the Colonel's tent; three on the color front—one of them over the colors; three, fifty paces in rear of the field officers' tents; and one on each flank, between it and the next regiment. If it is a flank regiment, one more sentinel is posted on the outer flank.

562. An advanced post is detached from the police guard, composed of a Sergeant, a Corporal, a drummer, and nine men to furnish sentinels and the guard over the prisoners. The men are first of the guard roster from each company. The men of the advanced post must not leave it under any pretext. Their meals are sent to the post. The advanced post furnishes three sentinels; two a few paces in front of the post, opposite the right and left wing of the regiment, posted so as to see as far as possible to the front, and one over the arms.

563. In the cavalry, dismounted men are employed in preference on the police guard. The mounted men on guard are sent in succession, apart at a time, to groom their horses. The advanced post is always formed of mounted men.

564. In each company, a Corporal has charge of the stable-guard. His tour begins at retreat, and ends at morning stable-call. The stable-guard is large enough to relieve the men on post every two hours. They sleep in their tents, and are called by the Corporal when wanted. At retreat he closes the streets of the camp with cords, or uses other precautions to prevent the escape of loose horses.

565. The officer of the day is charged with the order and cleanliness of the camp; a fatigue is furnished to him when the number of prisoners is insufficient to clean the camp. He has the calls beaten by the drummer of the guard.

566. The police guard and the advanced post pay the same honors as other guards. They take arms when an armed body approaches.

567. The sentinel over the colors has orders not to permit them to

be moved, except in presence of an escort; to let no one touch them but the color-bearer, or the Sergeant of the police guard when he is accompanied by two armed men.

568. The sentinels on the color front permit no soldier to take arms from the stacks, except by order of some officer, or a non-commissioned officer of the guard. The sentinel at the Colonel's tent has orders to warn him, day or night, of any unusual movement in or about the camp.

569. The sentinels on the front, flanks, and rear, see that no soldier leaves camp with horse or arms, unless conducted by a non-commissioned officer. They prevent non-commissioned officers and soldiers from passing out at night, except to go to the sinks, and mark if they return. They arrest, at any time, suspicious persons prowling about the camp; and at night, every one who attempts to enter, even the soldiers of other corps. Arrested persons are sent to the officer of the guard, who sends them, if necessary, to the officer of the day.

570. The sentinels on the front of the advanced post have orders to permit neither non-commissioned officers or soldiers to pass the line, without reporting at the advanced post; to warn the advanced post of the approach of any armed body, and to arrest all suspicious persons. The Sergeant sends persons so arrested to the officer of the guard, and warns him of the approach of any armed body.

571. The sentinel over the arms at the advanced post guards the prisoners and keeps sight of them, and suffers no one to converse with them without permission. They are only permitted to go to the sinks one at a time, and under a sentinel.

572. If any one is to be passed out of camp at night, the officer of the guard sends him under escort to the advanced post, and the Sergeant of the post has him passed over the chain.

573. At retreat, the officer of the guard has the roll of his guard called, and inspect arms, to see that they are loaded and in order; and visits the advanced post for the same purpose. The Sergeant of the police guard, accompanied by two armed soldiers, folds the colors and lays them on the trestle in the rear of the arms. He sees that the sutler's stores are closed, and the men leave them, and that the kitchen fires are put out at the appointed hour.

574. The officer of the day satisfies himself frequently during the night of the vigilance of the police guard and advanced post. He prescribes patrols and rounds to be made by the officer and non-commissioned officers of the guard. The officer of the guard orders them when he thinks necessary. He visits the sentinels frequently.

575. At reveille, the police guard takes arms; the officer of the guard inspects it and the advanced post. The Sergeant re-plants the colors in place. At retreat and reveille the advanced post takes arms; the Sergeant makes his report to the officer of the guard when he visits the post.

576. When necessary, the camp is covered at night with small outposts, forming a double chain of sentinels. These posts are under the orders of the commander of the police guard, and are visited by his patrols and rounds.

577. The officer of the guard makes his report of his tour of service, including the advanced post, and sends it, after the guard is marched off, to the officer of the day.

578. When the regiment marches, the men of the police guard return to their companies, except those of the advanced post. In the cavalry, at the sound "boot and saddle," the officer of the guard sends one-half the men to saddle and pack; when the regiment assembles, all the men join it.

579. When the camping party precedes the regiment, and the new police guard marches with the camping party, the guard, on reaching the camp, forms a line thirty paces in front of the centre of the ground marked for the regiment. The officer of the guard furnishes the sentinels required by the commander of the camping party.

The advanced post takes its station.

580. The advanced post of the old police guard takes charge of the prisoners on the march, and marches, bayonets fixed, at the centre of the regiment. On reaching the camp, it turns over the prisoners to the new advanced post.

581. The detail for the picket is made daily, after the details for duty of first class, and from the next for detail on the roster of that class. It is designed to furnish detachments and guards unexpectedly called for in the twenty-four hours; it counts as a tour of the first class to those who have marched on detachment or guard, or who have passed the night in bivouac.

582. The officers, non-commissioned officers, and soldiers of the picket are at all times dressed and equipped; the horses are saddled, and knapsacks and valises ready to be put on.

583. Detachments and guards from the picket are taken from the head of the picket roll in each company, and, if possible, equally from each company. The picket of a regiment is composed of a Lieutenant, two Sergeants, four Corporals, a drummer, and about forty privates. For a smaller force, the picket is in proportion to the strength of the detachment.

584. Officers and men of the picket who march on detachment or guard before retreat, will be replaced.

585. The picket is assembled by the Adjutant at guard-mounting; it is posted twelve paces in the rear of the guard, and is inspected by its own commander. When the guard has marched in review, the commandant of the picket marches it to the left of the police guard, where it stacks its arms, and is dismissed; the arms are under charge of the sentinel of the police guard.

586. The picket is only assembled by the orders of the Colonel or officer of the day. It forms on the left of the police guard.

587. The officer of the day requires the roll of the picket to be called frequently during the day; the call is sounded from the police guard. At roll-calls and inspections, infantry pickets assemble with knapsacks on; cavalry on foot. The picket is assembled at retreat; the officer has the roll called, and inspects the arms. The pickets sleep in their tents, but without undressing.

588. The picket does not assemble at night except in cases of alarm, or when the whole or a part is to march; then the officer of the day calls the officers, the latter the non-commissioned officers, and these the men, for which purpose each ascertains the tents of those he is to call; they are assembled without beat of drum or other noise. At night cavalry pickets assemble mounted.

589. Pickets rejoin their companies whenever the regiment is under arms for review, drill, march, or battle.

GRAND GUARDS AND OTHER OUTPOSTS.

590. Grand guards are the advanced posts of a camp or cantonment, and should cover the approaches to it. Their number, strength, and position are regulated by the commanders of brigades; in detached corps, by the commanding officer. When it can be, the grand guards of cavalry and infantry are combined, the cavalry furnishing the advanced sentinels. When the cavalry is weak, the grand guards are infantry, but furnished with a few cavalry soldiers, to get and carry intelligence of the enemy.

591. The strength of a grand guard of a brigade will depend on its object and the strength of the regiments, the nature of the country, the position of the enemy, and the disposition of the inhabitants. It is usually commanded by a Captain.

592. Under the supervisions of the Generals of Division and Brigade, the grand guards are specially under the direction of a field officer of the day in each brigade. In case of necessity, Captains may be added to the roster of Lieutenant-Colonels and Majors for this detail.

593. Staff officers sent from division headquarters to inspect the posts of grand guards, give them orders only in urgent cases, and in the absence of the field officer of the day of the brigade

594. Grand guards usually mount at the same time as the other guards, but may mount before daybreak if the General of Brigade thinks it necessary to double the outposts at that time. In this case they assemble and march without noise, and during their march throw out scouts; this precaution should always be taken in the first posting of a grand guard. The doubling of guards weakens the corps and fatigues the men, and should seldom be resorted to, and never when preparing to march or fight.

595. A grand guard is conducted to its post, in the first instance, by the field officer of the day, guided by a staff officer who accompanied the General in his reconnoissance. After the post has been established, the commander sends to the field officer of the day, when necessary, a soldier of the guard to guide the relieving guard to the post. He also sends to him in the evening a Corporal or trusty man of the guard for the note containing the parole and countersign, and sends them before dark to the detached posts. He will not suffer his guard to be relieved except by a guard of the brigade, or by special orders.

596. If there is no pass to be observed or defended, the grand guards are placed near the centre of the ground they are to observe, on sheltered, and, if possible, high ground, the better to conceal their strength and observe the enemy; they ought not to be placed near the edge of a wood. When, during the day, they are placed very near or in sight of the enemy, they fall back at night on posts selected farther to the rear.

597. In broken or in mountainous countries, and particularly if the inhabitants are ill-disposed, intermediate posts must be established when it is necessary to post the grand guard distant from the camp.

598. Grand guards are chiefly to watch the enemy in front; their flanks are protected by each other, and the camps must furnish posts to protect their rear and secure their retreat.

599. Grand guards are seldom intrenched, and never without the orders of the General, except by a barricade or ditch when exposed in a plain to attacks of cavalry.

600. The General of Division, if he thinks proper, changes the stations and orders of these guards, and establishes posts to connect the brigades or protect the exterior flanks.

601. After a grand guard is posted, the first care of the commander and of the field officer of the day is to get news of the enemy; then to reconnoitre his position, and the roads, bridges, fords, and defiles. This reconnoisance determines the force and position of the small posts and their sentinels day and night. These posts, according to their importance, are commanded by officers or non-commissioned officers; the cavalry posts may be relieved every four or eight hours.

602. The commander of a grand guard receives detailed instructions from the General and field officer of the day of the brigade, and instructs the commanders of the small posts as to their duties and the arrangements for the defence or retreat. The commanders of grand guards may, in urgent cases, change the positions of the small posts. If the small posts are to change their positions at night, they wait until the grand guard have got into position and darkness hides their movements from the enemy; then march silently and rapidly under the charge of an officer.

603. In detached corps, small posts of picked men are at night sent forward on the roads by which the enemy may attack or turn the position. They watch the forks of the roads, keep silence, conceal themselves, light no fires, and often change place. They announce the approach of the enemy by signals agreed upon, and retreat, by routes examined during the day, to places selected, and rejoin the guard at daybreak.

604. Grand guards have special orders in each case, and the following in all cases: to inform the nearest posts and the field officer of the day, or the General of Brigade, of the march and movements of the enemy, and of the attacks they receive or fear; to examine every person passing near the post, particularly those coming from without; to arrest suspicious persons, and all soldiers and camp followers who try to pass out without permission, and to send to the General, unless otherwise directed, all country people who come in.

605. All out-guards stand to arms at night on the approach of patrols, rounds, or other parties; the sentinel over the arms has orders to call them out.

606. Advanced posts will not take arms for inspection or ceremony when it would expose them to the view of the enemy.

607. Grand guards are often charged with the care and working of telegraphic signals.

608. The sentinels and videttes are placed on points from which they can see farthest, taking care not to break their connection with each other or with their posts. They are concealed from the enemy as much as possible by walls, or trees, or elevated ground. It is generally even of more advantage not to be seen than to see far. They should not be placed near covers, where the enemy may capture them.

609. A sentinel should always be ready to fire, videttes carry their pistols or carbines in their hands. A sentinel must be sure of the

presence of an enemy before he fires; once satisfied of that, he must fire, though all defence on his part be useless, as the safety of the post may depend on it. Sentinels fire on all persons deserting to the enemy.

610. If the post must be where a sentinel on it can not communicate with the guard, a corporal and three men are detached for it, or the sentinels are doubled, that one may communicate with the guard. During the day the communication may be made by signals, such as raising a cap or handkerchief. At night sentinels are placed on low ground, the better to see objects against the sky.

611. To lessen the duty of rounds, and keep more men on the alert at night, sentinels are relieved every hour. To prevent sentinels from being surprised, it is sometimes well to precede the countersign by signals, such as striking the musket with the hand, striking the hands together, &c.

612. On the approach of any one at night, the sentinel orders—"*Halt!*" If the order is not obeyed after once repeated, he fires. If obeyed, he calls—"*Who goes there?*" If answered—"*Rounds*" or "*Patrol*," he says—"*Advance with the countersign.*" If more than one advance at the same time, or the person who advances fails to give the countersign or signal agreed on, the sentinel fires, and falls back on his guard. The sentinel over the arms, as soon as his hail is answered, turns out the guard, and the Corporal goes to reconnoitre. When it is desirable to hide the position of the sentinel from the enemy, the hail is replaced by signals; the sentinel gives the signal, and those approaching the counter signal.

613. With raw troops, or when the light troops of the enemy are numerous or active, and when the country is broken or wooded, the night stormy or dark, sentinels should be doubled. In this case, while one watches, the other called a flying sentinel, moves about, examining the paths and hollows.

614. The commandants of grand guards visit the sentinels often; change their positions when necessary; make them repeat their orders; teach them under what circumstances and at what signals to retire, and particularly not to fall back directly on their guard if pursued, but to lead the enemy in a circuit.

615. At night, half the men of the grand guard off post watch under arms, while the rest lie down, arms by their side. The horses are always bridled; the horsemen hold the reins, and must not sleep.

616. When a grand guard of cavalry is so placed as not to be liable to a sudden attack from the enemy, the General may permit the horses to be fed during the night, unbridled for this purpose a few at a time—the horsemen being vigilant to prevent them from escaping.

617. An hour before break of day, infantry grand guards stand to arms, and cavalry mount. At the advanced posts, some of the infantry are all night under arms, some of the cavalry on horseback.

618. The commander of a grand guard regulates the numbers, the hours, and the march of patrols and rounds, according to the strength of his troop and the necessity for precaution; and, accompanied by those who are to command the patrols and rounds during the night, he will reconnoitre all the routes they are to follow.

619. Patrols and rounds march slowly, in silence, and with great precaution; halt frequently to listen, and examine the ground. The

rounds consist of an officer or non-commissioned officer and two or three men.

620. Toward the break of day the patrols ought to be more frequent, and sent to greater distances. They examine the hollow-ways, and ground likely to conceal an enemy, but with great caution, to avoid being cut off, or engaged in an unequal combat; if they meet the enemy, they fire and attempt to stop his march. While the patrols are out the posts are under arms.

621. Cavalry patrols should examine the country to a greater distance than infantry, and report to the infantry guard every thing they observe. The morning patrols and scouts do not return until broad daylight; and when they return, the night sentinels are withdrawn, and the posts for the day resumed.

622. When patrols are sent beyond the advanced posts, the posts and sentinels should be warned.

623. On their return, commanders of patrols report in regard to the ground and every thing they have observed of the movements of the enemy, or of his posts, and the commandant of the grand guard reports to the field officer of the day.

624. The fires of the grand guards should be hidden by a wall, or ditch or other screen. To deceive the enemy, fires are sometimes made on ground not occupied. Fires are not permitted at small posts liable to surprise.

625. The horses of cavalry guards are watered or fed by detachments; during which the rest are ready to mount.

626. If a body of troops attempt to enter the camp at night, unless their arrival has been announced, or the commander is known to, or is the bearer of a written order to the commander of the grand guards, he stops them, and sends the commander under escort to the field officer of the day, and warns the post near him.

627. Bearers of flags are not permitted to pass the outer chain of sentinels; their faces are turned from the post of army; if necessary their eyes are bandaged; a non-commissioned officer stays with them to prevent indiscretion of the sentinels.

628. The commandant of the grand guard receipts for dispatches, and sends them to the field officer of the day or General of Brigade, and dismisses the bearer; but if he has discovered what ought to be concealed from the enemy, he is detained as long as necessary.

629. Deserters are disarmed at the advanced posts, and sent to the commander of the grand guard, who gets from them all the information he can concerning his post. If many come at night they are received *cautiously, a few at a time.* They are sent in the morning to the field officer of the day, or to the nearest post or camp, to be conducted to the General of the brigade. All suspected persons are searched by commanders of the posts.

630. When an enemy advances to an attack, unless he is in too great force, or the grand guard is to defend an intrenched post or a defile, it will take positions and execute the movements to check the enemy, acting as skirmishers, or fighting in close or open order, as may be best. The guard joins its corps when in line, or when a sufficient number of troops have reached the ground it defends.

INTRENCHED POSTS.

631. Unless the army be acting on the defensive, no post should be intenched, except to cover the weak parts of the line, or at points which the enemy cannot avoid, or in mountain warfare, or to the close of a defile, or to cover winter quarters.

632. Posts connected with the operations of an army are intrenched only by order of the General commanding-in-chief or a General of Division.

633. Any intrenchment that requires artillery is considered as a post, and a guard or garrison and commander are assigned to it.

634. The General who establishes an intrenched post gives to its commander detailed instructions in regard to its defence, and the circumstances under which the defence should cease.

635. The commander reconnoiters his post; distributes the troops; posts the officers and non-commissioned officers; forms a reserve; gives orders for all contingencies he can foresee; supposes an attack, and arranges his troops for defence, so as to prepare them for an attack, day or night.

636. In dark weather he redoubles his vigilance, and changes the hours and direction of the rounds and patrols. He permits no flags of truce, deserters or strangers to enter. If a flag ought to pass his post, he bandages his eyes. He refuses admittance to a relief or any other party until he has carefully examined them. In case of an attack, he does not wait for orders or hold a council. Having defended his post to the last extremity, or till the purpose of the defence, according to his instructions, is answered, he may then spike his guns and rejoin the army under cover of night, or by cutting his way through the enemy.

DETACHMENTS.

637. When a detachment is to be formed from the different regiments of a brigade, the Assistant Adjutant-General of the brigade assembles it, and turns it over to the commander.

638. When a detachment is to be formed from different brigades, the Assistant Adjutant-General in each, forms the contingent of the brigade, and sends it to the place of assembling.

639. Detachments are generally formed by taking battalions, squadrons, companies, platoons in turn, according to the roster for such detail.

640. When the detachment is to consist of men from every company or troop, the first on the roster for guard are taken.

641. Officers, non-commissioned officers, and soldiers, whose tour it is to go on detachment, if employed otherwise at the time, are relieved from the duty they are on, if they can reach the camp in time to march with the detachment.

642. When detachments meet, the command is regulated while they serve together as if they formed one detachment. But the senior officers cannot prevent the commander of any detachment from moving, when he thinks proper, to execute the orders he has received.

643. On the return of a detachment, the commander reports to the headquarters from which he received his orders.

RECONNOISANCES.

644. Near the enemy, daily reconnoisances are made to observe the ground in front, and to discover whether the advanced guards of the enemy have been increased or put in motion, or any other sign of his preparation for march or action.

645. They are made by small parties of cavalry and infantry, from the brigade, under direction of the General of Division or the General of a separate brigade, and to less distance by the pastoral of the grand guard, and are not repeated at the same hour or by the same route. On the plain, reconnoisances are made by cavalry; among mountains, by infantry, with a few horsemen to carry intelligence.

646. Reconnoitering parties observe the following precautions: to leave small posts, or sentinels at intervals, to transmit intelligence to the advanced posts of an army, unless the return is to be by a different route; to march with caution, to avoid fighting; and see, if possible, without being seen; to keep an advanced guard; to send well mounted men ahead of the advanced guard; and on the flank of the party; to instruct the scouts that no two should enter a defile or mount a hill together, but to go one at a time, while one watches to carry the news if the other is taken.

647. Before daybreak the advanced guard and scouts are drawn closer; the party then march slowly and silently, stop frequently to listen, and keep the horses that neigh in the rear. The party should enter no wood, defile, village, or inclosure, until it has been fully examined by the scouts.

648. Special reconnoisances are made under the instruction of the General in command, by such officers and with such force as he may direct.

649. Offensive or forced reconnoisances are to ascertain with certainty points in the enemy's position, or his strength. They are sometimes preludes to real actions, and sometimes only demonstrations. They drive in his outposts, and sometimes engage special corps of his line. They are only made by order of the General commanding-in chief, or the commander of an isolated corps.

650. In all reports of reconnoisances, the officer making them shall distinguish expressly what he has seen from the accounts he has not been able to verify personally.

651. In special and offensive reconnoisances, the report must be accompanied by a field-sketch of the localities, the dispositions and defences of the enemy.

PARTISANS AND FLANKERS.

652. The operations of partisan corps depend on the nature and theatre of the war; they enter into the general plan of operations, and are conducted under the orders of the General commanding-in-chief.

653. The composition and strength of partisan corps and detachment of flankers depend on the object, the difficulties, the distance, and the probable time of the expedition.

654. The purpose of these isolated corps is to reconnoitre at a distance on the flanks of the army, to protect its operations, to deceive the enemy, to interrupt his communications, to intercept his couriers and his correspondence, to threaten or destroy his magazines, to carry off

his posts and his convoys, or at all events, to retard his march by making him detach largely for their protection.

655. While these corps fatigue the enemy and embarrass his operations, they endeavor to inspire confidence and secure the good will of the inhabitants in a friendly country, and to hold them in check in an enemy's country.

656. They move actively, appear unexpectedly on different points, in such a manner as to make it impossible to estimate their force, or to tell whether they are irregular forces or an advanced guard.

657. These operations require vigilance, secresy, energy, and promptness. The partisan commander must frequently supply by stratagem and audacity what he wants in numbers.

658. These detachments are sometimes composed of different arms, but the service belongs more particularly to the light cavalry, which can move to a distance by rapid marches, surprise the enemy, attack unexpectedly, and retire as promptly.

659. Stormy weather, fogs, extreme heat, and the night above all, are favorable to the success of ambuscades; when the enemy are careless, the break of day is the best time. A partisan commander should communicate to his second in command, his secret orders, the direction and object of the expedition, and the different points of junction with the army.

660. Guides of the country and spies are often necessary to the partisan. They are examined separately, and confronted if their accounts differ. When there is but one guide, he marches with the advanced guard, guarded by two men, and bound if necessary. Peddlers and smugglers are specially suitable for spies.

661. A fit time to attack a convoy is at a halt, or when they begin to park, or when they are watering, passing a wood or a defile; at a bend of the road, a bridge or steep ascent.

662. The attacking party may be principally cavalry, with some infantry. The first object is to disperse the escort. A part of the detachment attacks the main body of the escort, another the wagons, and a third is in reserve; skirmishers line the road, and try to cut the traces, and to seize the front and rear wagons, and turn them across the road, to prevent the train from advancing or retreating.

663. If the convoy is parked, the cavalry surrounds it, assails the escort, and tries to draw it away from the train. The infantry then engage the troops remaining at the park, slip under the wagons, and get into the park. When the cavalry is alone and the enemy are shaken, they dismount a portion of the men to supply the want of infantry.

664. If it is a large convoy, the principal attack is made on the centre; the most valuable wagons are also selected and additional horses are put to them if the attack is successful. Those that cannot be carried off are burned.

MARCHES.

665. The object of the movement and the nature of the ground determine the order of march, the kind of troops in each column, and the number of columns.

666. The force is divided into as many columns as circumstances permit, without weakening any one too much. They ought to preserve

their communications, and be within supporting distance of each other. The commander of each column ought to know the strength and direction of the others.

667. The advance and rear guards are usually light troops; their strength and composition depend on the nature of the ground and the position of the enemy. They serve to cover the movements of the army, and to hold the enemy in check until the General has time to make his arrangements.

668. The advance guard is not always at the head of the column; in a march to a flank, it takes such positions as cover the movement. Sappers are attached to the advanced guard if required.

669. The "*general*," sounded one hour before the time of marching, is the signal to strike tents, to load the wagons, and pack horses, and send them to the place of assembling. The fires are then put out, and care taken to avoid burning straw, &c., or giving to the enemy any other indication of the movement.

670. The "march" will be beat in the infantry, and the "advance" sounded in the cavalry, in succession, as each is to take its place in the column.

671. When the army should form suddenly to meet the enemy, the "*long roll*" is beat, and "*to horse*" sounded. The troops form rapidly in front of their camp.

672. Batteries of artillery and their caissons move with the corps to which they are attached; the field train and ambulances march at the rear of the column; and the baggage with the rear guard.

673. Cavalry and infantry do not march together, unless the proximity of the enemy makes it necessary.

674. In cavalry marches, when distant from the enemy, each regiment, and, if possible, each squadron, forms a separate column, in order to keep up the same gait from front to rear, and to trot, when desirable, on good ground. In such cases, the cavalry may leave camp later, and can give more rest to the horses, and more attention to the shoeing and harness. Horses are not bridled until the time to start.

675. When necessary, the orders specify the rations the men are to carry in their haversacks. The field officers and Captains make inspections frequently during the march; at halts they examine the knapsacks, valises and haversacks, and throw away all articles not authorized. The officers and non-commissioned officers of cavalry companies attend personally to the packs and girths.

676. When it can be avoided, troops should not be assembled on high roads or other places where they interrupt the communication.

677. Generals of Division and commanders of detached corps send a staff officer to the rendezvous, in advance, to receive the troops, who, on arriving, take their place in the order of battle, and form in close column, unless otherwise ordered. Artillery, or trains halted on the roads, form in file on one side.

678. The execution of marching orders must not be delayed. If the commander is not at the head of his troops when they are to march, the next in rank puts the column in motion.

679. If possible, each column is preceded by a detachment of sappers, to remove obstacles to the march, aided, when necessary, by infantry, or the people of the country. The detachment is divided into two sec-

tions; one stops to remove the first obstacle, the other moves on to the next.

680. In night marches, and at bad places, and at cross-roads, when necessary, intelligent non-commissioned officers are posted to show the way, and are relieved by the regiments as they come up.

681. On the march, no one shall fire a gun, or cry "*halt*," or "*march*," without orders.

682. Soldiers are not to stop for water; the canteens should be filled before starting.

683. It is better to avoid villages; but if the route lies through them, officers and non-commissioned officers are to be vigilant to prevent straggling. Halts should not take place at villages.

684. Besides the rear guard, the General sometimes takes a detachment from the last regiment, and adds to it non-commissioned officers from each regiment, to examine villages and all hiding-places on the route, to bring up stragglers and seize marauders.

685. In night marches, the Sergeant-Major of each regiment remains at the rear with a drummer, to give notice when darkness or difficulty stops the march. In cavalry, a trumpet is placed in rear of each squadron, and the signal repeated to the head of the regiment.

686. The General and field officers frequently stop, or send officers to the rear, to see that the troops march in the prescribed order, and keep their distances. To quicken the march, the General warns the Colonels, and may order a signal to be beat. It is repeated in all the regiments.

687. In approaching a defile, the Colonels are warned; they close their regiments as they come up; each regiment passes separately, at an accelerated pace, and in as close order as possible. The leading regiment having passed, and left room enough for the whole column in close order, then halts, and moves again as soon as the last regiment is through. In the cavalry, each squadron, before quickening the pace to rejoin the column, takes its original order of march.

688. When the distance from the enemy permits, each regiment, after closing up in front and rear of the defile, stacks arms.

689. Halts to rest and re-form the troops are frequent during the day, depending on the object and length of the march. They are made in preference after the passage of defiles.

690. No honors are paid by troops on the march or at halts

691. The sick march with the wagons.

692. Led horses of officers, and the horses of dismounted men, follow their regiment. The baggage wagons never march in the column. When the General orders the field train and ambulances to take place in the column, he designates the position they shall take.

693. If two corps meet on the same road, they pass to the right, and both continue their march, if the road is wide enough; if it is not, the first in the order of battle takes the road, the other halts.

694. A corps in march must not be cut by another. If two corps meet at cross-roads, that which arrives last halts if the other is in motion. A corps in march passes a corps at a halt, if it has precedence in the order of battle, or if the halted corps is not ready to move at once.

695. A column that halts to let another column pass resumes the

march in advance of the train of this column. If a column has to pass a train, the train must halt, if necessary, till the column passes. The column which has precedence must yield it if the commander, on seeing the orders of the other, finds it for the interest of the service.

BATTLES.

696. Dispositions for battle depend on the number, kind, and quality of the troops opposed, on the ground, and on the objects of the war; but the following rules are to be observed generally:

697. In attacking, the advanced guard endeavors to capture the enemy's outposts, or cut them off from the main body. Having done so, or driven them in, it occupies, in advancing, all the points that can cover or facilitate the march of the army, or secure its retreat, such as bridges, defiles, woods, and heights; it then makes attacks, to occupy the enemy, without risking too much, and to deceive them as to the march and projects of the army.

698. When the enemy is hidden by a curtain of advanced troops, the commandant of the advanced guard sends scouts, under intelligent officers, to the right and left, to ascertain his position and movements. If he does not succeed in this way, he tries to unmask the enemy by demonstrations; threatens to cut the advance from the main body; makes false attacks; partial and impetuous charges in echelon; and if all fail, he makes a real attack to accomplish the object.

699. Detachments left by the advanced guard to hold points in the rear, rejoin it when other troops come up. If the army takes a position, and the advanced guard is separated from it by defiles or heights, the communication is secured by troops drawn from the main body.

700. At proper distance from the enemy, the troops are formed for the attack in several lines; if only two can be formed, some battalions in column are placed behind the wings of the second line. The lines may be formed of troops in column or in order of battle, according to the ground and plan of attack.

701. The advanced guard may be put in the line or on the wings, or other position, to aid the pursuit or cover the retreat.

702. The reserve is formed of the best troops of foot and horse, to complete a victory or make good a retreat. It is placed in the rear of the centre, or chief point of attack or defence.

703. The cavalry should be distributed in echelon on the wings and at the centre, on favorable ground.

704. It should be instructed not to take the gallop until within charging distance; never to receive a charge at a halt, but to meet it, or, if not strong enough, to retire manœuvring; and in order to be ready for the pursuit, and prepared against a reverse, or the attacks of the reserve, not to engage all its squadrons at once, but to reserve one third, in column or in echelon, abreast of or in the rear of one of the wings; this arrangement is better than a second line with intervals.

705. In the attack, the artillery is employed to silence the batteries that protect the position. In the defence, it is better to direct its fire on the advancing troops. In either case, as many pieces are united as possible, the fire of artillery being formidable in proportion to its concentration.

706. In battles and military operations it is better to assume the

offensive, and put the enemy on the defensive; but to be safe in doing so requires a larger force than the enemy, or better troops, and favorable ground. When obliged to act on the defensive, the advantage of position and of making the attack may sometimes be secured by forming in rear of the ground on which we are to fight, and advancing at the moment of action. In mountain warfare, the assailant has always the disadvantage; and even in offensive warfare, in the open field, it may frequently be very important, when the artillery is well posted, and any advantage of the ground may be secured, to await the enemy and compel him to attack.

707. The attack should be made with a superior force on the defensive point of the enemy's position, by masking this by false attacks and demonstrations on other points, and by concealing the troops intended for it by the ground or by other troops in the front.

708. Besides the arrangements which depend on the supposed plan of the enemy, the wings must be protected by the ground, or supported by troops in echelon; if the attack of the enemy is repulsed, the offensive must at once be taken, to inspire the troops; to disconcert the enemy, and often to decide the action. In thus taking the offensive, a close column should be pushed rapidly on the wing or flank of the enemy. The divisions of this column form in the line of battle successively, and each division moves to the front as soon as formed, in order, by a rapid attack in echelon, to prevent the enemy from changing front or bringing up his reserves. In all arrangements, especially in those for attacks, it is most important to conceal the design until the moment of execution, and then to execute it with the greatest rapidity. The night, therefore, is preferred for the movement of troops on the flank or rear of the enemy, otherwise it is necessary to mask their march by a grand movement in front, or by taking a wide circuit.

709. In making an attack, the communications to the rear and for retreat must be secured, and the General must give beforehand all necessary orders to provide for that event.

710. When a success is gained, the light troops should pursue the enemy promptly and rapidly. The other troops will restore order in their columns, then advance from position to position, always prepared for an attack or to support the troops engaged.

711. Before the action, the Generals indicate the places where they will be; if they change position, they give notice of it, or leave a staff officer to show where they have gone.

712. During the fight the officers and non-commissioned officers keep the men in the ranks, and enforce obedience if necessary. Soldiers must not be permitted to leave the ranks to strip or rob the dead, nor to assist the wounded, unless by express permission, which is only to be given after the action is decided. The highest interest and duty is to win the victory, which only can insure proper care of the wounded.

713. Before the action, the Quartermaster of the division makes all the necessary arrangements for the transportation of the wounded. He establishes the ambulance depots in the rear, and gives his assistants the necessary instruction for the service of the ambulance wagons and other means of removing the wounded.

714. The ambulance depot, to which the wounded are carried or directed for immediate treatment, is generally established at the most

convenient building nearest the field of battle. A *red flag* marks its place, or the way to it, to the conductors of the ambulances and to the wounded who can walk.

715. The active ambulances follow the troops engaged to succor the wounded and remove them to the depots; for this purpose the conductors should always have the necessary assistants, that the soldiers may have no excuse to leave the ranks for that object.

716. The medical director of the division, after consultation with the Quartermaster-General, distributes the medical officers and hospital attendants at his disposal, to the depots and active ambulances. He will send officers and attendants when practicable, to the active ambulances, to relieve the wounded who require treatment before being removed from the ground. He will see that the depots and ambulances are provided with the necessary apparatus, medicines and stores. He will take post and render his professional services at the principal depot.

717. If the enemy endanger the depot, the Quartermaster takes the orders of the General to remove it or strengthen its guard.

718. The wounded in the depots and the sick are removed as soon as possible to the hospitals that have been established by the Quartermaster-General of the army on the flanks or rear of the army.

719. After an action, the officers on ordnance duty collect the munitions of war left on the field, and make a return of them to the General. The Quartermaster's Department collects the rest of the public property, captured, and makes the returns to headquarters.

720. Written reports for the General commanding-in-chief are made by commandants of regiments, batteries, and separate squadrons, and by all commanders of a higher grade, each in what concerns his own command, and to his immediate commander.

721. When an officer or soldier deserves mention for conduct in action, a special report shall be made in his case, and the General commanding-in-chief decides whether to mention him in his report to the government and in his orders But he shall not be mentioned in the report until he has been mentioned in the orders to the army. These special reports are examined with care by the intermediate commanders, to verify the facts, and secure commendation and rewards to the meritorious only.

722. The report of battles, which must frequently be made before these special reports of persons are scrutinized, is confined to general praise or blame, and an account of the operations.

PRISONERS OF WAR.

723. Prisoners of war will be disarmed and sent to the rear, and reported as soon as practicable to the headquarters. The return of prisoners from the headquarters of the Army to the War Department will specify the number, rank, and corps.

724. The private property of prisoners will be duly respected, and each shall be treated with the regard due to his rank. They are to obey the necessary orders given them. They receive for subsistence one ration each, without regard to rank; and the wounded are to be treated with the same care as the wounded of the army. Other allow-

ances to them will depend on conventions with the enemy. Prisoner's horses will be taken for the army.

725. Exchanges of prisoners and release of officers on parole depend on the orders of the General commanding-in-chief, under the instructions of government.

CONVOYS AND THEIR ESCORTS.

726. The strength and composition of the escort of a convoy depend on the country, the nature and value of the convoy, and the dangers it may incur. A larger escort is required for a convoy of powder, that the defence may not be near the train.

727. Cavalry is employed in escorts chiefly to reconnoitre; the proportion is larger as the country is more open.

728. Pioneers or working parties are attached to convoys to mend roads, remove obstacles, and erect defences. The convoys should always be provided with spare wheels, poles, axles, &c.

729. The commandant of the escort should receive detailed instructions in writing.

730. As far as the defence permits, the commander of the escort shall refer to the officer in charge of the convoy for the hours of departure, the halts, the parking and order of the train, and the precautions against accidents.

731. Officers who accompany the convoy, but do not belong to the escort, shall exercise no authority in it except by consent of the commander. If these officers are junior to the commander, he may assign them to duty if the defence requires it.

732. Large convoys are formed into divisions, each with a conductor. The distance between the wagons is four paces. A small party of infantry is attached to each division.

733. Generally, munitions of war are at the head of the convoy, subsistence next, and then other military stores; the sutler last. But always that part of the convoy which is most important to the army shall be where it is most secure from danger.

734. The commandant should send out reconnoitering parties, and never put the convoy in motion until their reports have been received. He always forms an advance and rear guard, and keeps the main body under his immediate order at the most important point, with small guards or posts at other points.

735. In an open country the main body marches by the side of the road, opposite the centre of the convoy; in other cases at the head or rear of the column, as the one or the other is more exposed.

736. The advance guard precedes the convoy far enough to remove all obstacles to its advance. It examines the woods, defiles, and villages, and by mounted men gives information to the commander, and receives his orders. It reconnoitres places for halts and parks.

737. If the head of the column is threatened, the advanced guard seizes the defiles and places which the enemy might occupy, and holds them until the main body advances to the front and relieves it; the main body holds the positions until the head of the convoy arrives, and then leaves detachments, which are relieved by the parties marching with the divisions; the posts are not abandoned until the whole convoy has passed and the position is no longer important.

738. When the rear is threatened, like measures are taken; the rear guard defends the grounds and retards the enemy by breaking the bridges and blocking the road.

739. If the flanks are threatened, and the ground is broken, and many defiles are to be passed, the defence of the convoy becomes more difficult; the advance and rear guards must be reduced, the flanks strengthened, and positions which will cover the march of the convoy must be occupied by the main body of the troops before the head of the convoy reaches them, and until it has passed.

740. If the convoy is large and has to pass places that the force and position of the enemy make dangerous, the loss of the whole convoy must not be risked; it must pass by divisions, which reunite after the passage. In this case the greater part of the troops guard the first division; they seize the important points, and cover them with light troops, or, if necessary, with small posts, and hold them until all the divisions have passed.

741. If there is artillery in the convoy, the commander of the escort uses it for the defence.

742. To move faster and make the defence easier, the wagons move in double file whenever the road allows it. If a wagon breaks, it is at once removed from the road; when repaired, it takes the rear; when it cannot be repaired, its load and horses are distributed to some of the other wagons kept in the rear for that purpose.

743. Convoys by water are escorted on the same principles. Each boat has a small infantry guard; one portion of the escort precedes or follows the convoy in boats. The cavalry march opposite the convoy; the advance and rear guard move by land, and all are connected by flankers with the convoy. Where a river runs through a narrow valley, the body of the infantry moves by land to prevent the enemy from occupying the heights and disturbing the convoy.

744. Convoys halt every hour to let the horses take breath and the wagons close up. Long halts are made but seldom, and only in places that have been reconnoitered and found favorable for defence. At night the park is arranged for defence, and in preference at a distance from inhabited places, if in an enemy's country.

745. The wagons are usually parked in ranks, axle against axle, the poles in the same direction, and with sufficient space between the ranks for the horses. If an attack is feared, they are parked in square, the hind wheels outside, and the horses inside.

746. On the appearance of the enemy during the march, the commander closes up the wagons and continues his march in order; he avoids fighting; but if the enemy seizes a position that commands his road, he attacks vigorously with the mass of his force, but is not to continue the pursuit far from the convoy. The convoy halts, and resumes the march when the position is carried.

747. When the enemy is too strong to be attacked, the convoy is parked in square if there is room; if not closed up in double file; at the front and rear the road is blocked by wagons across it. The drivers are dismounted at the heads of the horses. They are not permitted to make their escape. The light troops keep the enemy at a distance as long as possible, and are supported when necessary, but prudently, as the troops must be kept in hand to resist the main attack.

748. If a wagon takes fire in the park, remove it if possible; if not, remove first the ammunition wagons, then those to leeward of the fire.

749. When a whole convoy cannot be saved, the most valuable part may sometimes be by abandoning the rest. If all efforts fail, and there is no hope of succor, the convoy must be set on fire and the horses killed that cannot be saved; the escort may then cut its way through.

750. If the convoy is of prisoners of war, every effort should be made to reach a village or strong building where they may be confined; if forced to fight in the field, the prisoners must be secured and made to lie down until the action is over.

BAGGAGE TRAINS.

751. The baggage train of general headquarters and the trains of the several divisions are each under the charge of an officer of the Quartermaster's Department. These officers command and conduct the trains under the orders they receive from their respective headquarters. When the trains of different divisions march together, or the train of a division marches with the train of general headquarters, the senior Quartermaster directs the whole.

752. The regimental Quartermaster has charge of the wagons, horses, equipments, and all means of transport employed in the service of the regiment. Under the orders of the Colonel, he assembles them for the march, and maintains the order and police of the train in park on the march. On marches, the regimental trains are under the orders of the Quartermaster of the division. When the march is by brigade, the senior Regimental Quartermaster in the brigade, or the Quartermaster of the brigade has the direction of the whole. The necessary wagon-masters, or non-commissioned officers to act as such, are employed with the several trains.

753. None but the authorized wagons are allowed to march with the train. The wagons of the several headquarters, the regimental wagons, and the wagons of sutlers authorized by orders from headquarters to march with the train, are all to be conspicuously marked.

754. When the train of headquarters is to have a guard, the strength of the guard is regulated by the General. Generals of Brigade guard their trains by the men attached to the train of the first regiment of their brigades. The regimental trains are loaded, unloaded, and guarded, as far as practicable, by convalescents and men not effective in the ranks; in the cavalry, by dismounted men. When the guard of a train is the escort for its defence, the regulations in regard to convoys and escorts take effect.

755. Habitually each division is followed by its train, the regimental trains, uniting at the brigade rendezvous. When otherwise, the order for the movement of the divisions, brigades, and regiments contains the necessary directions in regard to the assembling and marching of the respective trains. The several trains march in an order analogous to the rank of the generals, and the order of battle of the troops to which they belong. Trains are not allowed in any case to be in the midst of the troops, or to impede the march of the troops.

756. The wagon-masters, under the orders of the officers of the Quartermaster's Department, exercise the necessary restraints over the teamsters and servants who leave their teams, or do not properly con-

duct them; or who ill-treat their horses, or who attempt to pillage, or run away in case of attack.

757. The General commanding the army, and the Generals of Division will not permit any general or staff officer, or regiment under their orders, or any person whatsoever, attached to their command, to have more than the authorized amount or means of transportation. For this purpose they will themselves make, and cause to be made, frequent reviews and inspections of the trains. They will see that no trooper is employed to lead a private horse, no soldier to drive a private vehicle, and that no trooper is put on foot to lend his horse to an officer. They will not permit the wagons of the artillery or of the train to be loaded with anything foreign to their proper service, nor any public horse, for any occasion, to be harnessed to a private carriage.

758. The officers of the Quartermaster's Department, the wagon masters, and all conductors of trains, are charged with watching that the regulations respecting transportation allowances are strictly observed.

GENERAL POLICE.

759. When necessary, the General-in-chief, or General of Division, may appoint a provost martial to take charge of prisoners, with a suitable guard, or other police force.

760. Private servants, not soldiers, will not be allowed to wear the uniform of any corps of the army; but each will be required to carry with him a certificate from the officer who employs him, verified, for regimental officers, by the signature of the Colonel; for other officers under the rank of Colonel, by the chief of their corps or department.

761. Laundresses permitted to follow the army will be furnished with certificates, signed as in the preceding paragraph, and no woman of bad character will be allowed to follow the army. Other persons with the army, not officers or soldiers, such as guides of the country, interpreters, &c., will carry about them similar certificates from the head-quarters that employs them.

762. Deserters from the enemy, after being examined, will be secured for some days, as they may be spies in disguise; as opportunities offer, they will be sent to the rear; after which, if they are found lurking about the army, or attempting to return to the enemy, they will be treated with severity.

763. The arms and accoutrements of deserters will be turned over to the Ordnance Department, and their horses to the corps in want of them, after being branded with the letters "C. S." The compensation to be accorded to deserters, for such objects, will be according to appraisement, made under the direction of the Quartermaster's Department. The enlistment of deserters, without express permission from General head-quarters, is prohibited.

764. It is forbidden to purchase horses without ascertaining the right of the party to sell. Stolen horses shall be restored. Estrays, in the enemy's country, when the owner is not discovered, are taken for the army.

765. Plundering and marauding, at all times disgraceful to soldiers, when committed on the persons or property of those whom it is the duty of the army to protect, become crimes of such enormity as to ad-

mit of no remission of the awful punishment which the military law awards against offences of this nature.

SAFEGUARDS.

766. Safeguards are protections granted to persons or property in foreign parts by the commanding general, or by other commanders within the limits of their command.

767. Safeguards are usually given to protect hospitals, public establishments, establishments of religion, charity, or instruction, museums, depositories of the arts, mills, post-offices, and other institutions of public benefit; also to individuals whom it may be the interest of the army to respect.

768. A safeguard may consist of one or more men of fidelity and firmness, generally non-effective non-commissioned officers, furnished with a paper setting out clearly the protection and exemptions it is intended to secure, signed by the commander giving it, and his staff officer; or it may consist of such a paper, delivered to the party whose person, family, house and property it is designed to protect. These safeguards must be numbered and registered.

769. The men left as safeguards by one corps may be replaced by another. They are withdrawn when the country is evacuated; but if not, they have orders to await the arrival of the enemy's troops, and apply to the commander for a safe-conduct to the outposts.

770. Form of a safeguard:

By authority of —— ——,

A safeguard is hereby granted to [A. B——, or the house and family of A. B——, or the college, mills, or property, stating precisely the place, nature and description of the person, property or buildings.] All officers and soldiers belonging to the army of the Confederate States are therefore commanded to respect this safeguard, and to afford, if necessary, protection to [the person, family, or property of ——, as the case may be.]

Given at Headquarters, the —— day of ——.

A. B——, Major-General commanding-in-chief.

By command of the General.

C. D——, Adjutant-General.

55th Article of the Rules and Articles of War.

"Whosoever belonging to the armies of the Confederate States, employed in foreign parts, shall force a safeguard, shall suffer death."

SIEGES.

771. In the following regulations the besieging force is supposed to be two divisions of infantry and a brigade of cavalry. The same principles govern in other cases.

772. The Brigadier-Generals of infantry serve, in turn, as Generals of the trenches; one or more of them are detailed daily, according to the front and number of attacks; they superintend the operations, and dispose the guards of the trenches to repulse sorties and protect the works. Officers of the general staff are assigned to them to transmit their orders and attend to the details of service.

773. The Colonels and Lieutenant-Colonels of infantry alternate for duty in the trenches; one or more are detailed daily; they superintend the service of the guards and workmen in the part of the work to which the general of the trenches assigns them, being posted with troops of their own regiments in preference. The commandant of the siege may place the Colonels on the roster with the Brigadier-Generals.

774. The commandants of engineers and artillery accompany the first troops before the place to examine the works and the approaches. When the engineers have completed the reconnoissance of the works, and of each front as far as practicable, the commandant of engineers makes a plan of the works as exact and detailed as possible, and under the instructions of the General commanding the siege, draws up the general plan of the siege, and discusses it with the commandant of artillery in regard to the best employment of that arm. These officers then submit their joint or separate opinions to the General who decides on the plan of the siege, and gives the orders for the execution. The commandant of engineers directs the construction of all the works of the siege, under the authority of the General, and lays before him every day a report of his operations, and a plan showing the progress of the attack. The commandant of artillery also makes daily reports to the General of all that relates to his branch of the service.

775. The Quartermaster General establishes the hospitals, and organizes the means for transporting the wounded to them.

776. The commanding General appoints a field officer of the trenches, who is aided by one or two Captains or Lieutenants.

777. The field officer of the trenches is charged with all the details relative to the assembling of the guards and the workmen. He distributes the guards on the different points of the attack agreeably to the orders of the General of the trenches, and forms the detachments of workmen for the engineers and artillery; that he may be prepared for this distribution, he receives every day from the Adjutant-General a statement of the details for the next day.

778. On the arrival of the General of the trenches, the field officer of the trenches gives him all the information necessary to enable him to station the troops, attends him in his visit of the trenches, and takes his orders on the changes to make in the position of the troops. The execution is intrusted to the commandants of the troops.

779. The field officer of the trenches sees that men and litters are always ready to bring off the wounded. One or more companies of the guards of the trenches are put under his immediate orders for the preservation of order and police in the trenches.

780. The divisions, brigades, regiments, and battalions, are encamped during the siege in the order of battle. The service of camp is conducted as heretofore prescribed.

781. The infantry has two kinds of siege service—the guard of the trenches and the work of the trenches.

782. The guards of the trenches mount every day by battalions, in such order of detail that all the troops may take an equal share, and no part of the line to be left too weak. If only one battalion is required, each division furnishes it alternately; if two are required, each division gives one; if three, one division furnishes two, the other one, al-

ternately. The two battalions of the same divisions are not taken from the same brigade.

783. The detail for work of the trenches is by company, from all the regiments at one time, or in turn, and continues generally twelve hours. The detail from any regiment should never be less than a company. If only half a company would be needed from all the regiments at a time, every other regiment furnishes a full company alternately.

784. The battalions for guard are detailed at least twelve hours in advance; they furnish no other details during this tour. If the whole regiment is called out, it leaves a sufficient police guard in camp.

785. Twenty-four hours, or twelve at least, before mounting guard in the trenches, the battalions detailed for guard do not furnish workmen; and the companies of these battalions whose tour it would have been to work in the trenches do not go there for twenty-four hours after guard, if possible, or at the least twelve.

786. The workmen who are required for other work than that of the trenches, are taken from the roster for fatigue from the battalions and companies not employed in the trenches.

787. The battalions first for detail for guard of the trenches, and the companies first for detail for work in the trenches, furnish no other details, and are held on picket, ready to march at the call of the field officer of the trenches.

788. Materials for the siege, such as fascines, gabions, hurdles, pickets, &c., are furnished by the different corps, in the proportion ordered by the General.

789. Guards and workmen going to the trenches, march without beat of drum or music.

790. At all times, and especially on the day the trenches are opened, everything is avoided likely to attract the attention of the enemy. With this view, the General may vary the hour of relieving guards.

791. The chiefs of engineers and artillery make requisitions for workmen in advance, that the details may be made in time to prevent any delay in the work. They should exceed the number strictly required, that there may be a reserve for unforeseen wants. If this reserve is found insufficient, the General directs the field officer of the trenches to call on the picket.

792. Before the guards and workmen march, the field officer of the trenches arranges them so that each detachment can reach its ground without confusion. The troops are posted in the trenches according to the position of their regiments in the order of battle, and, as far as possible, the companies of workmen in like order. The reserves of workmen are placed at the depot of the trenches, or the nearest suitable place to the works.

793. The workmen leave their knapsacks and swords in camp, and march with their fire-arms and cartridge-boxes, which they place near them while at work. They always carry their overcoats, to cover them in resting or when wounded.

794. The guards always enter the trenches with arms *trailed*, and the workmen also, unless they carry materials or tools, when the arms are in the sling.

795. The guards and detachments of workmen send a Corporal to the

openings of the trenches to guide the relief. They march out of the trenches by the flank, with trailed arms.

796. Sand bags, forming loop-holes, are placed at intervals on the parapet to protect the sentinels; they are more numerous than the sentinels, so that the enemy may not know where the sentinels are placed.

797. When detachments are placed at night in advance of the trenches, to cover the workmen, the men sit or lie down, with their fire-arms in their hands, to hide themselves better from the enemy; the sentinels put their ears to the ground frequently, that they may hear troops coming out of the place. To prevent mistakes, the workmen are told what troops cover them.

798. No honors are paid in the trenches. When the General commanding the siege visits them, the guards place themselves in rear of the banquette, and rests on their arms. The colors are never carried to the trenches unless the whole regiment marches to repulse a sortie or make an assault. Even in this case, they are not displayed until the General commanding the siege gives a formal order.

799. The materials of the siege of all kinds, together with the tools, are collected in part at the depots of the trenches, and in part at the opening of the trenches, or in such other place as has been appointed for the convenience of the service by the field officers of the trenches, on the advice of the chiefs of artillery and engineers. They are in charge of officers of engineers and artillery, with guards or non-commissioned officers of both corps. But if these corps cannot furnish them, the chiefs apply for assistance from the infantry.

800. The workmen, in going to the trenches, carry such tools and materials as are required by the artillery and engineers. In this case, the field officer of the trenches has notice and superintends it.

801. The soldiers sent to the trenches go with their cartridge-boxes filled. Cartridges, when needed, are sent to the trenches on the requisition of commanders of battalions, approved by the General of the trenches.

802. In the case of a sortie, the guards move rapidly to the places that have been designated by the General of the trenches, and which afford the best defence for the head of the works, the batteries, the communications, or the flanks, or best enable them to take the sortie itself in flank or reverse. Having lined the banquette to fire on the enemy, the troops form on the reverse of the trench to receive him. The workmen take arms, retain their positions, or retire with their tools, as ordered. The officers commanding the detachments of workmen see that their movements are made promptly and in good order, so as to avoid all confusion in the communications.

803. The troops that advance beyond the trenches to repulse the sortie, must not follow in pursuit. The General takes care that they return to the trenches before the retreat of the sortie allows the artillery of the place to open on them. When the workmen return, the officers and non-commissioned officers of the detachments call the roll without interrupting the work, which is immediately resumed.

804. When it is necessary to dismount cavalry and send them to the trenches, they should be employed as near their camp as possible, and posted between the detachments of infantry.

805. Men belonging to the cavalry may, in assaults, be employed in carrying fascines and other materials to fill ditches and make passages.

806. The general officers of cavalry are more particularly employed in the service of posts and detachments placed in observation to protect the siege. They and the field officers of this arm are employed in the command of escorts to convoys, of whatever arms the escorts may be composed. When these duties are not sufficient to employ them, they take their share of the duty of the trenches.

807. The officers of engineers and artillery of the trenches make to the General of the trenches a return of all losses in their troops, and such other reports on the work as he requires, in addition to the reports direct to their respective chiefs on the details of the service.

808. At the end of each tour, the field officer of the trenches draws up a report for the twenty-four hours to the General of the trenches. The General of the trenches reports to the General commanding the siege.

809. The commanders of the several corps in the trenches report, when relieved, to their respective headquarters the losses during the tour, and the conduct of the officers and men.

810. However practicable the breach may appear, or however ruined the work in rear of it, the heads of columns must always be supplied with ladders to get over unexpected obstacles.

811. The General commanding the siege designates picked companies to protect property and persons, and prevent pillage and violence, from the moment the place is carried. The officers exert themselves to restrain the men.

812. The General designates the places requiring particular protection, such as churches, asylums, hospitals, colleges, schools and magazines. The order of their protection should remind the soldiers, at the time, of the penalty of disobeying it.

813. Whether the place be taken by assault or by capitulation, the provisions and the military stores, and the public funds, are reserved for the use of the army.

814. The commander of engineers will keep a journal of the siege, showing the operations of each day in detail, the force employed on the work, the kind and quantity of materials used in them, &c. He will also mark on a plan of the ground the daily progress of the works, and make the necessary drawings explanatory of their construction.

815. The commander of the artillery will keep a daily journal of the operations under his direction, showing the number and kind of pieces in battery, the force employed in serving them, the kind and quantity of ammunition expended, the number of rounds fired from each piece of ordnance, the effect of the fire, and all other particulars relative to his branch of the service.

816. These journals and drawings will be sent after the siege, with the report of the General, to the War Department.

DEFENCE OF FORTIFIED PLACES.

817. In war, every commander of a fortified place shall always hold himself prepared with his plan of defence, as if at any time liable to attack. He arranges this plan according to the probable mode of attack; determines the posts of the troops in the several parts of the

works, the reliefs, the reserves, and the details of service in all the corps. He draws up instructions for a case of attack, and exercises the garrison according to his plan of defence. In sea-coast works he provides the instructions for the different batteries on the approach of ships.

818. In framing his plan, he studies the works and the exterior within the radius of attack and investment, the strength of the garrison, the artillery, the munitions of war, subsistence and supplies of all kinds, and takes immediate measures to procure whatever is deficient of troops or supplies, either by requisition on the Government, or from the means put at his disposal.

819. On the approach of an enemy, he removes all houses and other objects, within or without the place, that cover the approaches, or interrupt the fire of the guns or the movements of the troops. He assures himself personally that all posterns, outlets, or embrasures, &c., are in proper state of security.

820. He shall be furnished by the Department of War with a plan of the works, showing all the details of the fortifications and of the exterior within the radius of attack; with a map of the environs within the radius of investment, with a map of the vicinity, including the neighboring works, roads, water-channels, coasts, &c.; with a memoir explaining the situation and defence of the place, and the relations and bearings of the several works on each other, and on the approaches by land and water—all of which he carefully preserves, and communicates only to the council of defence.

821. He consults his next in rank, and the senior officer of the engineers and of the artillery, either separately, or as a council of defence. In the latter case, he designates an officer to act as secretary to the council, and to record their proceedings and their joint or separate opinions, which are to be kept secret during the siege. The members may record their opinions under their own signature. In all cases, the commander decides on his own responsibility.

822. The commander of the place, and the chiefs of engineers and of artillery, shall keep journals of the defence, in which shall be entered, in order of date, without blank or interlineation, the orders given or received, the manner in which they are executed, their results, and every event and circumstance of importance in the progress of the defence. These journals, and the proceedings of the council of defence, shall be sent, after the siege, to the Department of War.

823. There shall be kept in the office of the commandant of the place, to be sent after the siege to the Department of War, a map of the environs, a plan of the fortifications, and a special plan of the front of attack, on which the chief engineer will trace, in succession, the positions occupied, and the works executed by the enemy from the investment; and also the works of counter approach of defence, and the successive positions of the artillery and other troops of the garrison during the progress of the siege.

824. The commander shall defend in succession the advanced works, the covered way and outworks, the body of the work, and the interior entrenchments. He will not be content with clearing away the foot of the breaches, and defending them by abattis, mines, and all the means used in sieges; but he shall begin in good time, behind the bastions or

front of attack, the necessary entrenchments to resist assaults on the main work.

825. He shall use his means of defence in such manner as always to have a reserve of fresh troops, chosen from his best soldiers, to resist assaults, re-take the outworks, and especially to resist assaults on the body of the place; and a reserve of provisions for the last period of the siege, and of ammunition for the last attacks.

826. He must, in every case, compel the besieging force to approach by the slow and successive works of siege, and must sustain at least one assault on a practicable breach in the body of the place.

827. When the commander thinks that the end of the defence has come, he shall still consult the council of defence on the means that may remain to prolong the siege. But in all cases he alone will decide on the time, manner, and terms of the surrender. In the capitulation, he shall not seek or accept better terms for himself than for the garrison, but shall share their fate, and exert his best endeavors for the care of the troops, and especially of the sick and wounded.

828. No commander in the field shall withdraw troops or supplies from any fortified place, or exercise any authority over its commandant, unless it has been put subject to his orders by competent authority.

ARTICLE XXXVII.

TROOPS ON BOARD OF TRANSPORTS.

829. Military commanders charged with the embarkation of troops, and officers of the Quartermaster's Department intrusted with the selection of the transports, will take care that the vessels are entirely seaworthy and proper for such service, and suitable arrangements are made in them for the health and comfort of the troops.

830. If, in the opinion of the officer commanding the troops to be embarked, the vessel is not proper or suitably arranged, the officer charged with the embarkation shall cause her to be inspected by competent and experienced persons.

831. Immediately after embarking, the men will be assigned to quarters, equal parties on both sides of the ship, and no man will be allowed to loiter or sleep on the opposite side. As far as practicable, the men of each company will be assigned to the same part of the vessel, and the squads, in the same manner, to contiguous berths.

832. Arms will be so placed, if there be no racks, as to be secure from injury, and enable the men to handle them promptly; bayonets unfixed and in scabbard.

833. Ammunition in cartridge-boxes to be placed as to be entirely secure from fire; reserve ammunition to be reported to the master of the transport, with request that he designate a safe place of deposit. Frequent inspections will be made of the service ammunition, to insure its safety and good condition.

834. No officer is to sleep out of his ship, or to quit his ship, without the sanction of the officer commanding on board.

835. The guard will be proportioned to the number of sentinels required. At sea, the guard will mount with side arms only. The officer of the guard will be the officer of the day.

836. Sentinels will be kept over the fires, with buckets of water at

hand, promptly to extinguish fires. Smoking is prohibited *between decks or in the cabins*, at all times; nor shall any lights be allowed between decks except such ship lanterns as the master of the transport may direct, or those carried by the officer of the day in the execution of his duty.

837. Regulations will be adopted to enable companies or messes to cook in turn; no others than those whose turn it is will be allowed to loiter round or approach the galleys or other cooking places.

838. The commanding officer will make arrangements, in concert with the master of the vessel, for calling the troops to quarters, so that in case of alarm, by storm, or fire, or the approach of the enemy, every man may repair promptly to his station. But he will take care not to crowd the deck. The troops not wanted at the guns, or to assist the sailors, and those who cannot be advantageously employed with small arms, will be formed as a reserve between decks.

839. All the troops will turn out at —— A. M., without arms or uniform, and (in warm weather) without shoes or stockings; when every individual will be clean, his hands, face and feet washed, and his hair combed. The same personal inspection will be repeated thirty minutes before sunset. The cooks alone will be exempted from *one* of these inspections per day, if necessary.

840. Recruits or awkward men will be exercised in the morning and evening in the use of arms, an hour each time, when the weather will permit.

841. Officers will enforce cleanliness as indispensable to health. When the weather will permit, bedding will be brought on deck every morning for airing. Tubs may be fixed on the forecastle for bathing, or the men may be placed in the chains and have buckets of water thrown over them.

842. *Between decks* will not be washed oftener than once a week, and only when the weather is fine. The boards of the lower berths will be removed once or twice a week to change the straw. Under the direction of the Surgeon and the officer of the day, frequent fumigations will be performed between decks. The materials required are—common salt, four ounces; powdered oxide of manganese, one ounce; sulphuric acid, one ounce, diluted with two ounces of water. The diluted acid is poured over the other ingredients in a basin placed in a hot sand bath. Solutions of chloride of lime and chloride of zinc are excellent disinfecting agents.

843. During voyages in hot weather, the master of the vessel will be desired to provide wind-sails, which will be kept constantly hung up, and frequently examined, to see that they draw well and are not obstructed.

844. During cooking hours, the officers of companies visit the caboose, and see that the messes are well prepared. The coppers and other cooking utensils are to be regularly and well washed, both *before* and *after* use.

845. The bedding will be replaced in the berths at sunset, or at an earlier hour when there is a prospect of bad weather; and at *tattoo* every man not on duty will be in his berth. To insure the execution of this regulation, the officer of the day, with a lantern, will make a tour between decks.

846. Lights will be extinguished at *tattoo*, except such as are placed under sentinels. The officer of the day will see to it, and report to the commanding officer. The officers' lights will be extinguished at 10 o'clock, unless special permission be given to continue them for a longer time, as in case of sickness or other emergency.

847. For the sake of exercise, the troops will be occasionally called to quarters by the beat *to arms*. Those appointed to the guns will be frequently exercised in the use of them. The arms and accoutrements will be frequently inspected. The metalic parts of the former will be often wiped and greased again.

848. The men will not be allowed to sleep on deck in hot weather or in the sun; they will be encouraged and required to take exercise on deck, in squads by succession, when necessary.

849. At morning and evening parades, the Surgeon will examine the men, to observe whether there be any appearance of disease.

850. The sick will, as far as practicable, be separated from the healthy men. On the first appearance of malignant contagion, a signal will be made for the hospital vessel (if there be one in company,) and the diseased men removed to her.

851. A good supply of hospital stores and medicines will be taken on each vessel, and used only for the sick and convalescent.

852. The Surgeon will guard the men against costiveness on approaching a hot climate. In passing through the West Indies to the Southern coast, for instance, and for some weeks after landing in those latitudes, great care is required in the use of fruit, as strangers would not be competent to judge of it, and most kinds, after long voyages, are prejudicial.

853. In harbor, where there is no danger from sharks, the men may bathe; but not more than ten at a time, and attended by a boat.

854. In fitting up a vessel for the transportation of horses, care is to be taken that the requisite arrangements are made for conveniently feeding and cleaning them, and to secure them from injury in rough weather by ropes attached to breast-straps and breeching, or by other suitable means; and especially that proper ventilation is provided by openings in the upper deck, wind-sails, &c. The ventilation of steamers may be assisted by using the engine for that purpose.

855. Horses should not be put on board after severe exercise or when heated. In hoisting them on board, the slings should be made fast to a hook at the end of the fall, or the knot tied by an expert seaman, so that it may be well secured and easily loosened. The horse should be run up quickly to prevent him from plunging, and should be steadied by guide ropes. A halter is placed on him before he is lifted from the ground.

856. On board, care is to be taken that the horses are not over-fed; bran should form part of their ration. The face, eyes, and nostrils of each horse are to be washed at the usual stable hours; and occasionally, the manges should be washed and the nostrilsof the horse sponged with vinegar and water.

857. In loading vessels with stores for a military expedition, the cargo of each should be composed of an assortment of such stores as may be available for service in case of the non-arrival of others, and they should be placed on board in such a manner that they may be easily

reached, in the order in which they are required for service. Each store-ship should be marked, at the bow and stern, on both sides, in large characters, with a distinctive letter and number. A list is to be made of the stores on board of each vessel, and of the place where they are to be found in it; a copy of this list to be sent to the chief officer of the proper department in the expedition, or at the place of destination.

ARTICLE XXXVIII.

COURT-MARTIAL.

858. In appointing a general court-martial, as many members will be detailed, from five to thirteen inclusive, as can be assembled without manifest injury to the service.

859. The decision of the officer appointing the court, as to the number that can be assembled without manifest injury to the service, is conclusive.

860. A President of the court will not be appointed. The officer highest in rank present will be President.

861. Form of order appointing court-martial, the last paragraph omitted when the court can be kept up with thirteen members:

Headquarters, ——— &c.

A general court-martial is hereby appointed to meet at ———, on the ——— day of ———, or as soon thereafter as practicable, for the trial of ———, and such other prisoners as may be brought before it.

Detail for the Court:

1.	8. ....
2.	9. ....
3.	10. ....
4.	11. ....
5.	12. ....
6.	13. ....
7.	

——— ———, Judge Advocate.

No other officers than those named can be assembled without manifest injury to the service.

By order of ———. ———, commanding ———.

——— ———, Assistant Adjutant-General.

862. In the detail the members will be named, and they will take place in the court, in the order of their rank. A decision of the proper authority in regard to the rank of the members cannot be reversed by the court.

863. The place of holding a court is appointed by the authority convening it.

864. Application for delay or postponement of trial must, when practicable, be made to the authority convening the court. When made to the court, it must be before plea, and will then, if in the opinion of the court well founded, be referred to the authority convening the court, to decide whether the court shall be adjourned or dissolved, and the charges reserved for another court.

865. Upon application by the accused for postponement on the ground of absence of witness, it ought distinctly to appear on his oath, 1st, that

the witness is material, and how; 2d, that the accused has used due diligence to procure his attendance, and 3d, that he has reasonable ground to believe, and does believe, that he will be able to procure such attendance within a reasonable time stated.

866. The President of a court-martial, besides his duties and privileges as member, is the organ of the court, to keep order and conduct its business. He speaks and acts for the court in each case where the rule has been prescribed by law, regulation, or its own resolution. In all their deliberations the law secures the equality of the members.

867. The 76th Article of War does not confer on a court-martial the power to punish its own members. For disorderly conduct, a member is liable as in other offences against military discipline; improper words are to be taken down, and any disorderly conduct of a member reported to the authority convening the court.

868. The Judge Advocate shall summon the necessary witnesses for the trial; but he shall not summon any witness at the expense of the Confederate States, nor any officer of the army, without the order of the court, unless satisfied that his testimony is material and necessary to the ends of justice.

869. Every court-martial shall keep a complete and accurate record of its proceedings, to be authenticated by the signatures of the President and Judge Advocate, who shall also certify, in like manner, the sentence pronounced by the court in each case. The record must show that the court was organized as the law requires; that the court and Judge Advocate were duly sworn in the presence of the prisoner; that he was previously asked whether he had objection to any member, and his answer thereto. A copy of the order appointing the court will be entered on the record in each case.

870. Whenever the same court-martial tries more prisoners than one, and they are arraigned on separate and distinct charges, the court is to be sworn at the commencement of each trial, and the proceedings in each case will be made up separately.

871. The record shall be clearly and legibly written; as far as practicable, without erasures or interlineations, the pages to be numbered, with a margin of one inch on the left side of each page, and at the top of the odd and bottom of the even pages; through this last margin the sheets to be stitched together; the documents accompanying the proceedings to be noted and marked in such a manner as to afford an easy reference.

872. No recommendation will be embraced in the body of the sentence. Those members only who concur in the recommendation will sign it.

873. The legal punishments for soldiers by sentence of a court-martial according to the offence, and the jurisdiction of the court, are—death; corporeal punishment by flogging; confinement; confinement on bread and water diet; solitary confinement; hard labor; ball and chain; forfeiture of pay and allowances: discharges from service; and reprimands. Solitary confinement, or confinement on bread and water, shall not exceed fourteen days at a time, with intervals between the periods of such confinement not less than such periods, and not exceeding eighty-four days in one year.

874. A court-martial cannot assign and make over the pay of a sol-

dier to any other person, and the receipt of such person will not be a sufficient voucher for the disbursing officer. Nor can a soldier be required to receipt for money paid without his consent to another person. The law prohibits any receipt or voucher in accounts of public money, unless the full amount of the receipt is paid to the party who signed it.

875. The jurisdiction and authority of courts-martial are the same with reference to Ordnance Sergeants and Hospital Stewards as in the cases of other enlisted men. When, however, an Ordnance Sergeant or Hospital Steward is sentenced by an inferior court to be reduced to the ranks, such sentence, though it may be approved by the reviewing officer, will not be carried into effect until the case has been referred to the Secretary of War for final action. In these cases of reduction, the application of the man for discharge from service, though not recognized as a right, will generally be regarded with favor, if his offence has not been of too serious a nature, and especially where he has not been recently promoted from the ranks.

876. The Judge Advocate shall transmit the proceedings, without delay, to the officer having authority to confirm the sentence, who shall state, at the end of the proceedings in each case, his decision and orders thereon.

877. The original proceedings of all general courts-martial, after the decision on them of the reviewing authority, and all proceedings that require the decision of the President under the 65th and 89th Articles of War, and copies of all orders confirming or disproving, or remitting the sentences of courts-martial, and all official communications for the Judge Advocate of the army, will be addressed to "*The Adjutant and Inspector-General of the Army, War Department,*" marked on the cover, "*Judge Advocate.*"

878. The proceedings of garrison and regimental courts-martial will be transmitted without delay, by the garrison or regimental commander, to the department headquarters for the supervision of the department commander.

879. The power to pardon or mitigate the punishment ordered by a court-martial, is vested in the authority confirming the proceedings, and in the President of the Confederate States. A superior military commander to the officer confirming the proceedings may suspend the execution of the sentence when, in his judgment, it is void upon the face of the proceedings, or when he sees a fit case for executive clemency. In such cases, the record, with his order prohibiting the execution, shall be transmitted for the final orders of the President.

880. When a court-martial or court of inquiry adjourns without day, the members will return to their respective posts and duties, unless otherwise ordered.

881. When a court adjourns for three days, the Judge Advocate shall report the fact to the commander of the post or troops, and the members belonging to the command will be liable to duty during the time.

ARTICLE XXXIX.

WORKING PARTIES.

882. When it is necessary to employ the army at work on fortifications, in surveys, in cutting roads, and other constant labor of not less

than ten days, the non-commissioned officers and soldiers so employed are enrolled as extra-duty men, and are allowed twenty-five cents a day when employed as laborers and teamsters, and forty cents a day when employed as mechanics, at all stations east of the Rocky Mountains, and thirty-five and fifty cents per day, respectively, at all stations west of those mountains.

883. Enlisted men of the Ordnance and Engineer Departments, and artificers of artillery, are not entitled to this allowance when employed in their appropriate work.

884. Soldiers will not be employed as extra-duty men for any labor in camp or garrison which can properly be performed by fatigue-parties.

885. No extra-duty men, except those required for the ordinary service of the Quartermaster, Commissary, and Medical Departments, and saddlers in mounted companies, will be employed without previous authority from department headquarters, except in case of necessity, which shall be promptly reported to the department commander.

886. Extra-duty pay of a saddler in a mounted company will be charged on the company muster-roll, to be paid by the Quartermaster and refunded by the Ordnance Department. Extra-duty pay of cooks and nurses in the hospital service will be paid by the Quartermaster, in the absence of a medical disbursing officer, and refunded by the Medical Department. The extra pay of cooks and nurses will be charged on hospital muster-rolls.

887. The officer commanding a working party will conform to the directions and plans of the engineer or other officer directing the work, without regard to rank.

888. A day's work shall not exceed ten hours in summer, nor eight in winter. Soldiers are paid in proportion for any greater number of hours they are employed each day. Summer is considered to commence on the 1st of April, and winter on the 1st of October.

889. Although the necessities of the service may require soldiers to be ordered on working parties as a duty, commanding officers are to bear in mind that fitness for military service by instruction and discipline is the object for which the army is kept on foot, and that they are not to employ the troops when not in the field, and especially the mounted troops, in labors that interfere with their military duties and exercises, except in cases of immediate necessity, which shall be forthwith reported for the orders of the War Department.

ARTICLE XL.

PUBLIC PROPERTY, MONEY, AND ACCOUNTS.

890. All officers of the Commissary and Quartermaster's Departments, and military store-keepers, shall, previous to their entering on the duties of their respective offices, give good and sufficient bonds to the Confederate States fully to account for all monies and public property which they may receive, in such sums as the Secretary of War shall direct; and the officers aforesaid shall renew their bonds every four years, and oftener if the Secretary of War shall so require, and whenever they receive a new commission or appointment.

891. The sureties to the bond shall be bound jointly and severally for

the whole amount of the bond, and shall satisfy the Secretary of War that they are worth jointly double the amount of the bond, by the affidavit of each surety, stating that he is worth, over and above his debts and liabilities, the amount of the bond, or such other sum as he may specify, and each surety shall state his place of residence.

892. The chiefs of disbursing departments who submit requisitions for money to be remitted to disbursing officers, shall take care that no more money than is actually needed is in the hands of any officer.

893. The Treasury Department having provided, by arrangement with the Assistant Treasurers at various points, secure depositories for funds in the hands of disbursing officers, all disbursing officers are required to avail themselves, as far as possible, of this arrangement, by depositing with the Assistant Treasurers such funds as are not wanted for immediate use, and drawing the same in convenient sums as wanted.

894. No public funds shall be exchanged except for gold and silver. When the funds furnished are gold and silver, all payments shall be in gold and silver. When the funds furnished are drafts, they shall be presented at the place of payment, and paid according to law; and payments shall be made in the funds so received for the drafts, unless said funds or said drafts can be exchanged for gold and silver at par. If any disbursing officer shall violate any of these provisions, he shall be suspended by the Secretary of War, and reported to the President, and promptly removed from office or restored to his trust and duties, as to the President may seem just and proper.

895. No disbursing officer shall accept, or receive, or transmit to the Treasury to be allowed in his favor, any receipt or voucher from a creditor of the Confederate States without having paid to such creditor, in such funds as he received for disbursement, or such other funds as he is authorized by the preceding article to take in exchange, the full amount specified in such receipt or voucher; and every such act shall be deemed to be a conversion to his own use of the amount specified in such receipt or voucher. And no officer in the military service charged with the safe-keeping, transfer, or disbursement of public money, shall convert to his own use, or invest in any kind of merchandise or property, or loan with or without interest, or deposit in any bank, or exchange for other funds, except as allowed in the preceding article, any public money entrusted to him; and every such act shall be deemed to be a felony and an embezzlement of so much money as may be so taken, converted, invested, used, loaned, deposited, or exchanged.

896. Any officer who shall directly or indirectly sell or dispose of, for a premium, any treasury note, draft, warrant, or other public security in his hands for disbursement, or sell or dispose of the proceeds or avails thereof without making returns of such premium and accounting therefor by charging it in his accounts to the credit of the Confederate States, will forthwith be dismissed by the President.

897. If any disbursing officer shall bet at cards or any game of hazard, his commanding officer shall suspend his functions, and require him to turn over all the public funds in his keeping, and shall immediately report the case to the proper bureau of the War Department.

898. All officers are forbid to give or take any receipt in blank for public money or property; but in all cases the voucher shall be made

out in full, and the true date, place, and exact amount of money, in words, shall be written out in the receipt before it is signed.

899. When a signature is not written by the hand of the party, it must be witnessed.

900. No advance of public money shall be made, except advances to disbursing officers, and advances by order of the War Department to officers on distant stations, where they can not receive their pay and emoluments regularly; but in cases of contracts for the performance of any service, or the delivery of articles of any description, payment shall not exceed the value of the service rendered, or of the article delivered, previously to payment.

901. No officer disbursing or directing the disbursement of money for the military service shall be concerned, directly or indirectly, in the purchase or sale, for commercial purposes, of any article intended for, making a part of, or appertaining to the department of the public service in which he is engaged, nor shall take or apply to his own use any gain or emolument for negotiating or transacting any public business other than what is or may be allowed by law.

902. No wagon-master or forage-master shall be interested or concerned, directly or indirectly, in any wagon or other means of transport employed by the Confederate States, nor in the purchase or sale of any property procured for or belonging to the Confederate States, except as the agent of the Confederate States.

903. No officer or agent in the military service shall purchase from any other person in the military service, or make any contract with any such person to furnish supplies or services, or make any purchase or contract in which such person shall be admitted to any share or part, or to any benefit to arise therefrom.

904. No person in the military service whose salary, pay, or emoluments is or are fixed by law or regulations, shall receive any additional pay, extra allowance, or compensation in any form whatever, for the disbursement of public money, or any other service or duty whatsoever, unless the same shall be authorized by law, and explicitly set out in the appropriation.

905. All accounts of expenditures shall set out a sufficient explanation of the object, necessity and propriety of the expenditure.

906. The facts on which an account depends must be stated and vouched by the certificate of an officer, or other sufficient evidence.

907. If any account paid on the certificate of an officer to the facts is afterwards disallowed for error of fact in the certificate, it shall pass to the credit of the disbursing officer, and be charged to the officer who gave the certificate.

908. An officer shall have credit for an expenditure of money or property made in obedience to the order of his commanding officer. If the expenditure is disallowed, it shall be charged to the officer who ordered it.

909. Disbursing officers, when they have the money, shall pay cash and not open an account. Heads of bureaus shall take care, by timely remittances, to obviate the necessity of any purchases on credit.

910. When a disbursing officer is relieved, he shall certify the outstanding debts to his successor, and transmit an account of the same to the head of the bureau, and turn over his public money and property

appertaining to the service from which he is relieved to his successor, unless otherwise ordered.

911. The chief of each military bureau of the War Department shall, under the direction of the Secretary of War, regulate, as far as practicable, the employment of hired persons required for the administrative service of his department.

912. When practicable, persons hired in the military service shall be paid at the end of the calendar month, and when discharged. Separate pay-rolls shall be made for each month.

913. When a hired person is discharged and not paid, a certified statement of his account shall be given him.

914. Property, paid for or not, must be taken up on the return, and accounted for when received.

915. No officer has authority to insure public property or money.

916. Disbursing officers are not authorized to settle with heirs, executors, or administrators, except by instructions from the proper bureau of the War Department upon accounts duly audited and certified by the proper accounting officers of the Treasury.

917. Public horses, mules, oxen, tools, and implements shall be branded conspicuously C. S. before being used in service, and all other public property that it may be useful to mark; and all public property having the brand of the C. S. when sold or condemned, shall be branded with the letter C.

918. No public property shall be used, nor labor hired for the public be employed, for any private use whatsoever not authorized by the regulations of the service.

919. When public property becomes damaged, except by fair wear and tear, the officer accountable for the property shall report the case to the commanding officer, who shall appoint a board of survey of two or more officers to examine the property and ascertain the cause and amount of damage, and whether by any fault of any person in the military service, and report the facts and their opinion to him; which report, with his opinion thereon, he shall transmit to the chief of the department to which the property appertains, and give a copy to the officer accountable for the property and to the person chargeable for the damage.

920. If any article of public property be lost or damaged by neglect or fault of any officer or soldier, or person hired in the public service, he shall pay the value of such article, or amount of damage, or cost of repairs, in either case at such rates as a Board of Survey, with the approval of the commanding officer, may assess, according to the place and circumstances of the loss or damage.

921. Charges against a soldier shall be set against his pay on the muster-roll. Charges against an officer to be set against his pay shall be promptly reported to the Secretary of War.*

922. If any article of public property be embezzled, or by neglect lost or damaged, by any person hired in the public service, the value or

---

*If the pay of an officer or soldier is wrongfully withheld for arrears or liabilities to the Confederate States, a civil remedy is provided by law.

damage shall be charged to him, and set against any pay or money due him, to be deducted on pay-roll next following.

923. Public property lost or destroyed in the military service must be accounted for by affidavit, or the certificate of a commissioned officer, or other satisfactory evidence.

924. Affidavits or depositions may be taken before any officer in the list, as follows, when recourse can not be had to any before named on said list, which fact shall be certified by the officer offering the evidence: 1st. a civil magistrate competent to administer oaths; 2d. a judge advocate; 3d. the recorder of a garrison or regimental court-martial: 4th. the Adjutant of a regiment; 5th. a commissioned officer.

925. When military stores or other army supplies are unsuitable to the service, the officer in charge thereof shall report the case to the commanding officer, who shall refer the report, with his opinion thereon, to the bureau of the department to which the property appertains, for the order in the case of the Secretary of War. But if, from the nature or condition of the property or exigency of the service, it be necessary to act without the delay of such reference, in such case of necessity the commanding officer shall appoint a board of survey, composed of two or more competent officers, to examine the property and report to him, subject to his approval, what disposition the public interest requires to be made of it; which he shall cause to be made, and report the case to the proper bureau of the War Department for the information of the the Secretary of War. These cases of necessity arise when the property is of a perishable nature, and can not be kept, or when the expense of keeping it is too great in proportion to its value, or when the troops, in movement, would be compelled to abandon it. Horses incurably unfit for any public service may also constitute a case of necessity, but shall be put to death only in case of an incurable wound or contagious disorder.

926. When military stores or other army supplies are reported to the War Department as unsuitable to the service, a proper inspection or survey of them shall be made by an Inspector General, or such suitable officer or officers as the Secretary of War may appoint for that purpose. Separate inventories of the stores, according to the disposition to be made of them, shall accompany the inspection report: as of articles to be repaired, to be broken up, to be sold, of no use or value, and to be dropped, &c., &c. The inspection report and inventories shall show the exact condition of the different articles.

927. Military stores and other army supplies found unsuitable to the public service, after inspection by an Inspector General, or such special inspection as may have been directed in the case, and ordered for sale, shall be sold for cash at auction, on due public notice, and in such market as the public interest may require. The officer making the sale will bid in and suspend the sale when, in his opinion, better prices may be got. Expenses of the sale will be paid from its proceeds. The auctioneer's certified account of the sales in detail, and the vouchers for the expenses of the sale, will be reported to the chief of the department to which the property belonged. The nett proceeds will be applied as the Secretary of War may direct.

928. No officer making returns of property shall drop from his return

any public property as worn out or unserviceable, until it has been condemned, after proper inspection, and ordered to be so dropped.

929. An officer issuing stores shall deliver or transmit to the receiving officer an exact list of them in duplicate invoices, and the receiving officer shall return him duplicate receipts.

930. When an officer to whom stores are forwarded has reason to suppose them miscarried, he shall promptly inform the issuing and forwarding officer, and the bureau of the department to which the property appertains.

931. When stores received do not correspond in amount or quality with the invoice, they will be examined by a board of survey, and their report communicated to the proper bureau, to the issuing and forwarding officer, and to the officer authorized to pay the transportation account. Damages recovered from the carrier or other party liable, will be refunded to the proper department.

932. On the death of any officer in charge of public property or money, the commanding officer shall appoint a board of survey to take an inventory of the same, which he shall forward to the proper bureau of the War Department, and he shall designate an officer to take charge of the said property or money till orders in the case are received from the proper authority.

933. When an officer in charge of public property is removed from the care of it, the commanding officer shall designate an officer to receive it, or take charge of it himself, till a successor be regularly appointed. When no officer can remain to receive it, the commanding officer will take suitable means to secure it, and report the facts to the proper authority.

934. Every officer having public moneys to account for, and failing to render his account thereof quarter-yearly, with the vouchers necessary to its correct and prompt settlement, within three months after the expiration of the quarter if resident in the Confederate States, and within six months, if resident in a foreign country, will be promptly dismissed by the President, unless he shall explain the default to the satisfaction of the President.

935. Every officer intrusted with public money or property shall render all prescribed returns and accounts to the bureau of the department in which he is serving, where all such returns and accounts shall pass through a rigid administrative scrutiny before the money accounts are transmitted to the proper officers of the Treasury Department for settlement.

936. The head of the bureau shall cause his decision on each account to be endorsed on it. He shall bring to the notice of the Secretary of War all accounts and matters of account that require or merit it. When an account is suspended or disallowed, the bureau shall notify it to the officer, that he may have an early opportunity to submit explanations or take an appeal to the Secretary of War.

937. When an account is suspended or disallowed in the proper office of the Treasury Department, or explanation or evidence required from the officer, it shall be promptly notified to him by the head of the military bureau. And all vouchers, evidence or explanation returned by him to the Treasury Department shall pass through that bureau.

938. Chiefs of the disbursing departments shall, under the direction

of the Secretary of War, designate, as far as practicable, the places where the principal contract and purchases shall be made and supplies procured for distribution.

939. All purchases and contracts for supplies or services for the army, except personal services, when the public exigences do not require the immediate delivery of the article or performance of the service, shall be made by advertising a sufficient time previously for proposals respecting the same.

940. The officer advertising for proposals shall, when the intended contract or purchase is considerable, transmit forthwith a copy of the advertisement and report of the case to the proper bureau of the War Department.

941. Contracts will be made with the lowest responsible bidder; and purchases from the lowest bidder who produces the proper article. But when such lowest bids are unreasonable, they will be rejected, and bids again invited by public notice; and all bids and advertisements shall be sent to the bureau.

942. When sealed bids are required, the time of opening them shall be specified, and bidders have privilege to be present at the opening.

943. When immediate delivery or performance is required by the public exigency, the article or service required may be procured by open purchase or contract at the places, and in the mode in which such articles are usually bought and sold, or such services engaged, between individuals.

944. Contracts shall be made in quadruplicate; one to be kept by the officer, one by the contractor, and two to be sent to the military bureau, one of which for the officer of the Second Comptroller of the Treasury.

945. The contractor shall give bond, with good and sufficient security, for the true and faithful performance of his contract, and each surety shall state his place of residence.

946. An express condition shall be inserted in contracts that no member of Congress shall be admitted to any share or part therein, or any benefit to arise therefrom.

947. No contract shall be made except under a law authorising it, or an appropriation adequate to its fulfilment except contracts by the Secretary of War for the subsistence or clothing of the army, or the Quartermaster's Department.

948. It is the duty of every commanding officer to enforce a rigid economy in the public expenses.

949. The commander of a geographical district or department shall require abstracts to be rendered to him, at least once in each quarter, by every officer under his orders who is charged with the care of public property or the disbursement of public money, showing all property received, issued and expended by the officer rendering the account, and the property remaining on hand, and all moneys received, paid or contracted to be paid by him, and the balances remaining in his hands; and where such officer is serving under any intermediate commander, as of the post, regiment, &c., the abstracts shall be revised by such commander; and both the accounting officer and the commanding officer shall accompany the abstracts with full explanations of every circumstance that may be necessary to a complete understanding, by the commander of the department, of all the items on the abstracts.

These abstracts, where the accounting officer is serving in more than one staff appointment, will be made separately for each.

950. The commander of the department shall promptly correct all irregularities and extravagances which he may discover. He shall also forward, as soon as practicable, the money abstracts to the bureau of the War Department to which the accounts appertain, with such remarks as may be necessary to explain his opinions and action thereon.

951. All estimates for supplies of property or money for the public service within a department shall be forwarded through the commander of the department, and carefully revised by him. And all such estimates shall go through the immediate commander, if such there be, of the officer rendering the estimate, as of the post or regiment, who shall be required by the department commander to revise the estimates for the service of his own command.

952. The administrative control exercised by department commanders shall, when troops are in the field, devolve on the commanders of divisions, or, when the command is less than a division, on the commander of the whole.

953. No land shall be purchased for the Confederate States except under a law authorizing such purchase.

954. No public money shall be expended for the purchase of any land, nor for erecting armories, arsenals, forts, fortifications or other public buildings, until the written opinion of the Attorney General shall be had in favor of the validity of the title to the land or site, nor, if the land be within any State of the Confederate States until a cession of the jurisdiction by the Legislature of the State.

955. No permanent buildings for the army, as barracks, quarters, hospitals, store-houses, offices, or stables, or piers, or wharves, shall be erected but by order of the Secretary of War, and according to the plan directed by him, and in consequence of appropriations made by law. And no alteration shall be made in any such public building without authority from the War Department.

956. Complete title papers, with full and exact maps, plans, and drawings of the public lands purchased, appropriated, or designed for permanent military fortifications, will be collected, recorded and filed in the Bureau of the Corps of Engineers; of the public lands appropriated or designated for armories, arsenals, and ordnance depots, will be collected, recorded, and filed in the Ordnance Bureau; of all other land belonging to the Confederate States, and under the charge of the War Department for barracks, posts, cantonments, or other military uses, will be collected, recorded and filed in the office of the Quartermaster General of the army.

957. A copy of the survey of the land at each post, fort, arsenal, and depot, furnished from the proper bureau, will be carefully preserved in the office of the commanding officer.

ARTICLE XLI.

QUARTERMASTER'S DEPARTMENT.

958. This department provides the quarters and transportation of the army; storage and transportation for all army supplies; army clothing; camp and garrison equipage; cavalry and artillery horses; fuel; forage; straw, and stationery.

959. The incidental expenses of the army paid through the Quartermaster's Department, include per diem to extra-duty men; postage on public service; the expenses of courts martial; of the pursuit and apprehension of deserters; of the burials of officers and soldiers; of hired escorts; of expresses, interpreters, spies, and guides; of veterinary surgeons and medicines for horses, and of supplying posts with water; and generally the proper and authorized expenses for the movements and operations of an army not expressly assigned to any other department.

BARRACKS AND QUARTERS.

960. Under this head are included the permanent buildings for the use of the army, as barracks, quarters, hospital, store-houses, offices, stables.

961. When barracks and quarters are to be occupied, they will be allotted by the quartermaster at the station, under the control of the commanding officer.

962. The number of rooms and amount of fuel for officers and men are as follows:

	Rooms.			Cords of wood per month.*	
	As quarters.	As kitchen.	As office.	From May 1, to Sept. 30.	From Oct. 1, to April 30.
A Brigadier-General or Colonel,	4	1	..	1	4
A Lieutenant-Colonel or Major,	3	1	..	1	$3\frac{1}{2}$
A Captain,	2	1	..	$\frac{3}{4}$	3
Lieutenant,	1	1	..	$\frac{1}{2}$	2
The General commanding the army,	..	..	3	..	3
The commanding officer of a division or department, an assistant or deputy Quartermaster-General,	..	..	2	..	2
The commanding officer of a regiment or post, Quartermaster, Assistant Quartermaster, or Commissary of Subsistence,	..	..	1	.	1
An Acting Assistant Quartermaster when approved by the Quartermaster-General,	..	..	..	..	..
Wagon and forage master, Sergeant-Major, Ordnance Sergeant, or Quartermaster Sergeant,	1	..	..	$\frac{1}{2}$	1
Each non-commissioned officer, musician, private, and washerwoman,	..	..	..	1-12	1-6
Each necessary fire for the sick in hospital, to be regulated by the surgeon and commanding officer, *not exceeding*,	..	..	..	$\frac{1}{2}$	2
Each guard fire, to be regulated by the commanding officer, *not exceeding*,	..	..	..	..	3
A commissary or quartermaster's storehouse, when necessary, *not exceeding*,	..	..	..	..	1
A regiment or post mess,	1	..	..	...	1
To every six non-commissioned officers, musicians, privates, and washerwomen, 256 square feet of room,					

*Or coal, at the rate of 1,500 pounds anthracite, or 30 bushels bituminous to the cord.

TABLE OF DAILY ALLOWANCE OF FUEL.

	1-12 cord per month			1-6 cord per month			½ cord p'r month			¾ cord p'r month.	
Days.	Cubic Feet.	Inches.	Days.	Cubic Feet.	Inches.	Days.	Cubic Feet.	Inches.	Days.	Cubic Feet.	Inches.
1		4	1		8	1	2	1	1	3	2
2		8	2	1	5	2	4	3	2	6	4
3	1	0	3	2	1	3	6	4	3	9	7
4	1	5	4	2	10	4	8	6	4	12	9
5	1	9	5	3	6	5	10	8	5	16	0
6	2	1	6	4	3	6	12	9	6	19	2
7	2	5	7	4	11	7	14	11	7	22	4
8	2	10	8	5	7	8	17	0	8	25	7
9	3	2	9	6	3	9	19	2	9	28	9
10	3	6	10	7	0	10	21	4	10	32	0
11	3	10	11	7	8	11	23	5	11	35	2
12	4	3	12	8	5	12	25	7	12	38	4
13	4	7	13	9	2	13	27	8	13	41	7
14	4	11	14	9	11	14	29	10	14	44	9
15	5	4	15	10	8	15	32	0	15	48	0
16	5	8	16	11	4	16	34	1	16	51	2
17	6	0	17	12	1	17	36	3	17	54	4
18	6	4	18	12	9	18	38	4	18	57	7
19	6	9	19	13	6	19	40	6	19	60	9
20	7	1	20	14	2	20	42	8	20	64	0
21	7	5	21	14	11	21	44	9	21	67	2
22	7	9	22	15	7	22	46	11	22	70	4
23	8	2	23	16	4	23	49	0	23	73	7
24	8	6	24	17	0	24	51	2	24	76	9
25	8	10	25	17	9	25	53	3	25	80	0
26	9	2	26	18	5	26	55	5	26	83	2
27	9	7	27	19	2	27	57	7	27	86	4
28	9	11	28	19	10	28	59	8	28	89	7
29	10	3	29	20	7	29	61	10	29	92	9
30	10	8	30	21	4	30	64	0	30	96	0

	1 cord per month.				2 cords per month.				3 cords per month.				3½ cords per month.				4 cords per month.		
Days.	Cords	Cubic Feet.	Inches.	Days.	Cords	Cubic Feet.	Inches.	Days.	Cords	Cubic Feet.	Inches.	Days.	Cords	Cubic Feet.	Inches.	Days.	Cords	Cubic Feet.	Inches.
1		4	3	1		8	6	1		12	9	1		14	11	1		17	
2		8	6	2		17	0	2		25	7	2		29	10	2		34	1
3		12	9	3		25	7	3		38	4	3		44	9	3		51	2
4		17	0	4		34	1	4		51	2	4		59	8	4		68	3
5		21	4	5		42	8	5		64	0	5		74	8	5		85	4
6		25	7	6		51	2	6		76	9	6		89	7	6		102	4
7		29	10	7		59	8	7		89	7	7		104	6	7		119	5
8		34	1	8		68	3	8		102	4	8		119	5	8	1	8	6
9		38	4	9		76	9	9		115	2	9	1	6	4	9	1	25	7
10		42	8	10		85	4	10	1			10	1	21	4	10	1	42	8
11		46	11	11		93	10	11	1	12	9	11	1	36	3	11	1	59	8
12		51	2	12		102	4	12	1	25	7	12	1	51	2	12	1	76	9
13		55	5	13		110	11	13	1	38	4	13	1	66	1	13	1	93	10
14		59	8	14		119	5	14	1	51	2	14	1	81	0	14	1	110	11
15		64	0	15	1	0	0	15	1	64	0	15	1	96	0	15	2	0	0
16		68	3	16	1	8	6	16	1	76	9	16	1	110	11	16	2	17	0
17		72	6	17	1	17	0	17	1	89	7	17	1	125	10	17	2	34	1
18		76	9	18	1	25	7	18	1	102	4	18	2	12	9	18	2	51	2
19		81	0	19	1	34	1	19	1	115	2	19	2	27	8	19	2	68	3
20		85	4	20	1	42	8	20	2			20	2	42	8	20	2	85	4
21		89	7	21	1	51	2	21	2	12	9	21	2	57	7	21	2	102	4
22		93	10	22	1	59	8	22	2	25	7	22	2	72	6	22	2	119	5
23		98	1	23	1	68	3	23	2	38	4	23	2	87	5	23	3	8	6
24		102	4	24	1	76	9	24	2	51	2	24	2	102	4	24	3	25	7
25		106	8	25	1	85	4	25	2	64	0	25	2	117	4	25	3	42	8
26		110	11	26	1	93	10	26	2	76	9	26	3	4	3	26	3	59	8
27		115	2	27	1	102	4	27	2	89	7	27	3	19	2	27	3	76	9
28		119	5	28	1	110	11	28	2	102	4	28	3	34	1	28	3	93	10
29		123	8	29	1	119	5	29	2	115	2	29	3	49	0	29	3	110	11
30	1			30	2			30	3			30	3	64	0	30	4		

963. Merchantable hard wood is the standard; the cord is 128 cubic feet.

964. No officer shall occupy more than his proper quarters, except by order of the commanding officer, when there is an excess of quarters at the station; which order the quartermaster shall forward to the Quartermaster General, to be laid before the Secretary of War. But the amount of quarters shall be reduced *pro rata* by the commanding officer when the number of officers and troops make it necessary; and when the public buildings are not sufficient to quarter the troops, the commanding officer shall report to the commander of the department for authority to hire quarters, or other necessary orders in the case. The department commander shall report the case and his orders therein to the Quartermaster-General.

965. A mess-room, and fuel for it, are allowed only when a majority of the officers of a post or regiment unite in a mess; never to less than three officers, nor to any who live in hotels or boarding houses. Fuel for a mess-room shall not be used elsewhere, or for any other purpose.

966. Fuel issued to officers or troops is public property for their use; what they do not actually consume, shall be returned to the Quartermaster and taken up on his quarterly return.

967. Fuel shall be issued only in the month when due.

968. In allotting quarters, officers shall have choice according to rank, but the commanding officer may direct the officers to be stationed convenient to their troops.

969. An officer may select quarters occupied by a junior; but, having made his choice, he must abide by it, and shall not again at the post displace a junior, unless himself displaced by a senior.

970. The set of rooms to each quarters will be assigned by the Quartermaster, under the control of the commanding officer; attics not counted as rooms.

971. Officers cannot choose rooms in different sets of quarters.

972. When public quarters cannot be furnished to officers at stations without troops, or to enlisted men at general or department headquarters, quarters will be commuted at a rate fixed by the Secretary of War, and fuel at the market price delivered. When fuel and quarters are commuted to an officer by reason of his employment on a civil work, the commutation shall be charged to the appropriation for the work. No commutation of rooms or fuel is allowed for offices or messes.

973. An officer is not deprived of his quarters and fuel, or commutation, at his station, by temporary absence on duty.

974. Officers and troops in the field are not entitled to commutation for quarters or fuel.

975. An officer arriving at a station shall make requisition on the Quartermaster for his quarters and fuel, accompanied by a copy of the order putting him on duty at the station. If in command of troops, his requisition shall be for the whole, and designate the number of officers of each grade, of non-commissioned officers, soldiers, and washerwomen.

976. Bunks, benches, and tables provided for soldiers' barracks and hospitals, are not to be removed from them, except by the Quartermaster of the station, or order of the commanding officers, and shall not be removed from the station except by order of the Quartermaster General.

977. The furniture for each office will be two common desks or tables,

six common chairs, one pair common andirons, and shovel and tongs.

978. Furniture will be provided for officers' quarters when special appropriations for that purpose are made. Sales to officers of materials for furniture may be made at cost, at posts where they cannot be otherwise obtained.

979. When buildings are to be occupied or allotted, an inspection of them shall be made by the commanding officer and Quartermaster. Statements, in triplicate, of their condition, and of the fixtures and furniture in each room, shall be made by the Quartermaster, and revised by the commanding officer. One of these shall be retained by the commanding officer, one by the Quartermaster, and the third forwarded to the Quartermaster-General.

980. Like inspection of all buildings in the use of troops will be made at the monthly inspection of the troops, and of all buildings which have been in the use of officers or troops, whenever vacated by them. Damages will be promptly repaired if the Quartermaster has the means. Commanding Officers will take notice, as a military offence, of any neglect by any officer or soldier to take proper care of the rooms or furniture in his use or occupancy; but such officer or soldier may be allowed to pay the cost of the repairs when the commanding officer deems that sufficient in the case. Commanding officers are required to report to the Quartermaster-General their proceedings in all cases of neglect under this regulation.

981. An annual inspection of the public buildings at the several stations shall be made at the end of June by the commanding officer and Quartermaster, and then the Quartermaster shall make the following reports: 1st, of the condition and capacity of the buildings, and of the additions, alterations and repairs that have been made during the past year; 2d, of the additions, alterations and repairs that are needed, with plans and estimates in detail.

These reports the commanding officer shall examine and forward, with his views, to the Quartermaster-General.

982. Necessary repairs of public buildings, not provided for in the appropriations, can only be made by the labor of the troops.

983. When private buildings, occupied as barracks or quarters, or lands occupied for encampments, are vacated, the commanding officer and Quartermaster shall make an inspection of them, and a report to the Quartermaster-General of their condition, and of any injury to them by the use of the Confederate States.

984. Military posts evacuated by the troops, and lands reserved for military use, will be put in charge of the Quartermaster's Department, unless otherwise specially ordered.

ARMY TRASPORTATION.

985. When troops are moved, or officers travel with escorts or stores, the means of transport provided shall be for the whole command. Proper orders in the case, and an exact return of the command, including company women, will be furnished to the Quartermaster who is to provide the transportation.

986. The baggage to be transported is limited to camp and garrison equipage, and officers' baggage. Officers' baggage shall not exceed (mess chest and all personal effects included) as follows:

	In the field.	Changing stations.
General officers, - - - - -	125 pounds.	1000 pounds.
Field officers, - - - - -	100 "	800 "
Captains, - - - - - -	80 "	700 "
Subalterns, - - - - -	80 "	600 "

These amounts shall be reduced *pro rata* by the commanding officer when necessary, and may be increased by the Quartermaster-General on transports by water, when proper, in special cases.

987. The regimental and company desk prescribed in army regulations will be transported; also for staff officers, the books, papers, and instruments necessary to their duties; and for medical officers, their medical chest. In doubtful cases under this regulation, and whenever baggage exceeds the regulated allowance, the conductor of the train, or officer in charge of the transportation, will report to the commanding officer, who will order an inspection, and all excesses to be rejected.

988. Estimates of the medical director, approved by the commanding officer, for the necessary transportation to be provided for the hospital service, will be furnished to the Quartermaster.

989. The sick will be transported on the application of the medical officers.

990. Certified invoices of all public stores to be transported will be furnished to the Quartermaster by the officer having charge of them. In doubtful cases, the orders of the commanding officer will be required.

991. Where officers' horses are to be transported, it must be authorized in the orders for the movement.

992. The baggage trains, ambulances, and all the means of transport continue in charge of the proper officers of the Quartermaster's Department, under the control of the commanding officers.

993. In all cases of transportation, whether of troops or stores, an exact return of the amount and kind of transportation employed will be made by the Quartermaster to the Quartermaster-General, accompanied by the orders for the movement, a return of the troops, and an invoice of the stores.

994. Wagons and their equipments for the transport service of the army will be procured, when practicable, from the Ordnance Department, and fabricated in the government establishments.

995. When army supplies are turned over to a Quartermaster for transportation, each package shall be directed and its contents marked on it; and duplicate invoices and receipts in bulk will be exchanged between the issuing and forwarding officer.

996. On transports, cabin passage will be provided for officers, and reasonable and proper accommodation for the troops, and, when possible, a separate apartment for the sick.

997. An officer who travels not less than ten miles without troops, escort, or military stores, and under special orders in the case from a superior, or a summons to attend a military court, shall receive ten cents mileage, or, if he prefer it, the actual cost of his transportation and of the transportation of his allowance of baggage for the whole journey, provided he has traveled in the customary reasonable manner.

Mileage will not be allowed where the travel is by government conveyances, which will be furnished in case of necessity.

998. If the journey be to cash treasury drafts, the necessary and actual cost of transportation only will be allowed, and the account must describe the draft and state its amount, and set out the items of expense, and be supported by a certificate that the journey was necessary to procure specie for the draft at par.

999. If an officer shall travel on urgent public duty without orders, he shall report the case to the superior who had authority to order the journey; and his approval, if then given, shall allow the actual cost of transportation. Mileage is computed by the shortest mail route, and the distance by the General Postoffice book. When the distance cannot be so ascertained, it shall be reckoned subject to the decision of the Quartermaster-General.

1000. Orders to an officer on leave of absence to rejoin the station or troops he left, will not carry transportation.

1001. Citizens receiving military appointments, join their stations without expense to the public.

1002. But assistant Surgeons approved by an examining board and commissioned, receive transportation in the execution of their first order to duty, and graduates of the Military Academy receive transportation from the Academy to their stations.

1003. When officers are permitted to exchange stations, the public will not be put to the expense of transportation, which would have been saved if such exchange had not been permitted.

1004. A paymaster's clerk will receive the actual expenses of his transportation while traveling under orders in the discharge of his duty, upon his affidavit to the account of expenses, and the certificate of the paymaster that the journey was on duty.

1005. Travel of officers on business of civil works will be charged to the appropriation for the work.

1006. No officer shall have orders to attend personally at the seat of government, to the settlement of his accounts, except by order of the Secretary of War on the report of the bureau, or of the Treasury, showing a necessity therefor.

FORAGE.

1007. The forage ration is fourteen pounds of hay and twelve pounds of oats, corn, or barley.

1008. In time of war, officers of the army shall be entitled to draw forage for horses according to grade, as follows: A Brigadier-General, four; the Adjutant and Inspector-General, Quartermaster-General, Commissary-General, and the Colonels of Engineers, Artillery and Cavalry, three each: all Lieutenant-Colonels, and Majors, and Captains of the general staff, Engineer Corps, Light Artillery and Cavalry, three each; Lieutenants serving in the Corps of Engineers, Lieutenants of Light Artillery and of Cavalry, two each. In time of peace, general and field officers, three. Officers below the rank of field officers in the general staff, Corps of Engineers, Light Artillery and Cavalry, two. Aids-de camp and Adjutant's forage for the same number of horses as allowed to officers of the same grade in the mounted service, in time of war and peace: provided, in all cases, that the horses are actually kept in service and mustered. No enlisted man in the service of the Confederate States shall be employed as a servant by any officer of the army.

1009. No officer shall sell forage issued to him. Forage issued to public horses or cattle is public property; what they do not actually consume, to be properly accounted for.

STRAW.

1010. In barracks, twelve pounds of straw per month for bedding will be allowed to each man and company woman.

1011. The allowance and change of straw for the sick is regulated by the Surgeon.

1012. One hundred pounds per month is allowed for bedding to each horse in public service.

1013. At posts near prairie land owned by the Confederate States, hay will be used instead of straw, and provided by the troops.

Straw not actually used as bedding shall be accounted for as other public property.

STATIONERY.

1014. Issues of stationery are made quarterly, in amount as follows:

	Quires writing paper.	Quires envelope paper.	Number quills.	Ounces wafers.	Ounces sealing wax.	Papers ink powders.	Pieces office tape.
Commander of an army, department, or division, (what may be necessary for himself and staff for their public duty.)							
Commander of a brigade, for himself and staff,	12	1	50	1	8	2	2
Officer commanding a regiment or post of not less than five companies for himself and staff,	10	1	40	1	6	2	1
Officer commanding a post of more than two and less than five companies,	8	½	30	½	5	1	1
Commanding officer of a post of two companies,	6	½	25	½	4	1	1
Commanding officer of a post of one company or less, and commanding officer of a company,	5	½	20	½	3	1	1
A Lieutenant-Colonel or Major not in command of a regiment or post,	3	¼	12	¼	2	1	1
Officers of the Inspector-General's Pay and Quartermaster's Department (the prescribed blank books and printed forms, and the stationery required for their public duty.)							
All officers, not enumerated above, when on duty and not supplied by their respective departments,	1½	⅓	6	¼	1	½	½

Steel pens, with one holder, to 12 pens, may be issued in place of quills, and envelopes in place of envelope paper, at the rate of 100 to the quire.

1015. When an officer is relieved in command, he shall transfer the office stationery to his successor.

1016. To each office table is allowed one inkstand, one stamp, one paper folder, one sand-box, one wafer-box, and as many lead pencils as may be required, not exceeding four per annum.

1017. Necessary stationery for military courts and boards will be furnished on the requisition of the recorder, approved by the presiding officer.

1018. The commander of an army, department or division, may direct orders to be printed, when the requisite dispatch and the number to be distributed make it necessary. The necessity will be set out in the order the printing, or certified on the account.

1019. Regimental, company, and post-books, and printed blanks for the officers of Quartermaster and Pay Departments, will be procured by timely requisition on the Quartermaster General.

1020. Printed matter procured by the Quartermaster General for use beyond the seat of Government, may be procured elsewhere, at a cost not to exceed the rates prescribed by Congress for the public printing, increased by the cost of transportation.

EXPENSES OF COURTS-MARTIAL.

1021. An officer who attends a general court-martial or court of inquiry, convened by authority competent to order a general court-martial, will be paid, if the court is not held at the station where he is at the time serving, one dollar a day while attending the court and travelling to and from it if entitled to forage, and one dollar and twenty-five cents a day if not entitled to forage.

1022. The Judge Advocate or Recorder will be paid, in addition to the above, a per diem of one dollar and twenty-five cents for every day he is necessarily employed in the duty of the court. When it is necessary to employ a clerk to aid the Judge Advocate, the court may order it; soldier to be procured when practicable.

1023. A citizen witness shall be paid his actual transportation or stage fare, and three dollars a day while attending the court and travelling to and from it, counting the travel at fifty miles a day.

1024. The certificate of the Judge Advocate shall be evidence of the time of attendance on the court, and of the time he was necessarily employed in the duty of the court. Of the time occupied in travelling, each officer will make his own certificate.

EXTRA-DUTY MEN.

1025. Duplicate rolls of the extra duty men, to be paid by the Quartermaster's Department, will be made monthly, and certified by the Quartermaster, or other officer having charge of the work, and countersigned by the commanding officer. One of these will be transmitted direct to the Quartermaster General, and the other filed in support of the pay-roll.

PUBLIC POSTAGE.

1026. Postage and despatches by telegraph, on public business, paid by an officer, will be refunded to him on his certificate to the account, and to the necessity of the communication by telegraph. The amount for postage, and for telegraph despatches, will be stated separately.

HORSES FOR MOUNTED OFFICERS.

1027. In the field, or on the frontier, the commanding officer may authorize a mounted officer, who cannot otherwise provide himself with two horses, to take them from the public at the cost price, when it can be ascertained, and when not, at a fair valuation, to be fixed by a board of survey, provided he shall not take the horse of any trooper. A horse so taken shall not be exchanged or returned. Horses of mounted officers shall be shod by the public farrier or blacksmith.

CLOTHING, CAMP AND GARRISON EQUIPAGE.

1028. Supplies of clothing and camp and garrison equipage will be sent by the Quartermaster General from the general depot to the officers of his department stationed with the troops.

1029. The contents of each package, and the size of clothing in it, will be marked on it.

1030. The receiving Quartermaster will give duplicate receipts for the clothing as invoiced to him, if the packages as received and marked agree with the invoice, and appear rightly marked, and in good order; if otherwise, an inspection will be made by a board of survey, whose report in case of damage or deficiency will be transmitted, one copy to the Quartermaster General and one to the officer forwarding the supplies. In case of damage, the board will assess the damage to each article.

1031. ALLOWANCE OF CAMP AND GARRISON EQUIPAGE.

	Tents in the field.	Spades.	Axes.	Pickaxes.	Hatchets.	Camp kettles.	Mess pans.
A General,	3		1		1		
Field or staff officer above the rank of Captain,	2		1		1		
Other staff officers or Captains,	1		1		1		
Subalterns of a company, to every two,	1		1		1		
To every 15 foot and 13 mounted men,	1	2	2	2	2	2	5

1032. Bed-sacks are provided for troops in garrison, and iron pots may be furnished to them instead of camp kettles. On the march and in the field, the only mess furniture of the soldier will be one tin plate, one tin cup, one knife, fork and spoon, to each man, to be carried by himself on the march. Requisitions will be sent to the Quartermaster General for the authorized flags, colors, standards, guidons, drums, fifes, bugles and trumpets.

ALLOWANCE FOR CLOTHING.

1033. A soldier is allowed the uniform clothing stated in the following table, or articles thereof of equal value. When a balance is due him at the end of the year, it is added to his allowance for the next.

CLOTHING.	FOR THREE YEARS.			Total in the three years.
	1st.	2nd.	3d.	
Cap, complete,	2	1	1	4
Cover,	1	1	1	3
Coat,	2	1	1	4
Trowsers,	3	2	2	7
Flannel shirts,	3	3	3	9
" drawers,	3	2	2	7
Bootees,* pairs,	4	4	4	12
Stockings, pairs,	4	4	4	12
Leather stock,	1			1
Great coat,	1			1
Stable frock (for mounted men,)	1			1
Fatigue overall (for engineers and ordnance,)	1	1	1	3
Blanket,	1		1	2

1034. One sash is allowed to each company for the first sergeant. This and the metalic scales, letters, number, castles, shells, and flames, and the camp and garrison equipage, will not be returned as issued, but borne on the return while fit for service. They will be charged to the person in whose use they are, when lost or destroyed by his fault.

1035. Commanders of companies draw the clothing of their men, and the camp and garrison equipage for the officers and men of their company. The camp and garrison equipage of other officers is drawn on their own receipts.

1036. When clothing is needed for issue to the men, the company commander will procure it from the Quartermaster on requisition, approved by the commanding officer.

1037. Ordinarily the company commander will procure and issue clothing to his men twice a year; at other times, when necessary in special cases.

1038. Such articles of clothing as the soldier may need will be issued to him. When the issues equal in value his allowance for the year, further issues are extra issues, to be charged to him on the next muster-roll.

1039. The money value of the clothing, and of each article of it, will be ascertained annually, and announced in orders from the War Department.

* Mounted men may receive *one* pair of "boots and *two* pair of bootees," instead of *four* pairs of bootees.

1040. Officers receiving clothing, or camp and garrison equipage, will render quarterly returns to the Quartermaster General.

1041. Commanders of companies will take the receipts of their men for the clothing issued to them, on a receipt roll, witnessed by an officer, or in the absence of an officer, by a non commissioned officer; the witness to be witness to the fact of the issue and the acknowledgment and signature of the soldier. The several issues to a soldier to be entered separately on the roll, and all vacant spaces on the roll to be filled with a cipher. This roll is the voucher for the issue to the quarterly return of the company commander. Extra issues will be so noted on the roll.

1042. Each soldier's clothing account is kept by the company commander in a company book. This account sets out only the money value of the clothing which he received at each issue, for which his receipt is entered in the book, and witnessed as in the preceding paragraph.

1043. When a soldier is transferred or detached, the amount due to or by him on account of clothing will be stated on his descriptive list.

1044. When a soldier is discharged, the amount due to or by him for clothing will be stated on the duplicate certificates given for the settlement of his accounts.

1045. Deserters clothing will be turned into store. The invoice of it, and the Quartermaster's receipt for it, will state its condition and the name of the deserter.

1046. The inspection report on damaged clothing shall set out, with the amount of damage to each article, a list of such articles as are fit for issue, at a reduced price stated.

1047. Commanding officers may order necessary issues of clothing to prisoners and convicts, taking deserters or other damaged clothing when there is such in store.

1048. In all cases of deficiency, or damage of any article of clothing, or camp or garrison equipage, the officer accountable for the property is required by law "to show by one or more depositions setting forth the circumstances of the case, that the deficiency was by unavoidable accident or loss in actual service, without any fault on his part, and in case of damage, that due care and attention were exerted on his part, and that the damage did not result from neglect."

RETURNS IN THE QUARTERMASTER'S DEPARTMENT.

1049. All officers and agents having money and property of the Department to account for, are required to make the monthly and quarterly returns to the Quartermaster General prescribed in the following articles:

1050. Monthly returns, to be transmitted within five days after the month to which they relate, viz: A summary statement (Form 1); report of persons and things (Form 2); roll of extra-duty men (Form 3); report of stores for transportation, &c., (Form 4); return of animals, wagons, harness, &c., (Form 5); report of forage (Form 6); report of fuel and quarters commuted (Form 7); report of pay due (Form 8); an estimate of funds for one month (Form 9) will be sent with the monthly returns. The estimate for it will be for the current month, or such subsequent month as may give time to receive the remittance. Other special estimates will be transmitted when necessary.

1051. Quarterly returns, to be transmitted within twenty days after the quarter to which they relate, viz: An account current of money (Form 10,) with abstracts and vouchers, as shown in Forms Nos. 11 to 22; a return of property (Form 23,) with abstract and vouchers, as shown in Forms 24 to 45. A duplicate of the property return without abstracts or vouchers; and a quarterly statement of the allowances paid to officers (Form 46.)

1052. A distinct account current will be returned of money received and disbursed under the appropriation for "contingencies of the army." (See Forms Nos. 47, 48, and 22, for the forms of the account current, abstracts, and vouchers.) Necessary expenditures by the Quartermaster from the Medical Department are entered on abstract C. (See Forms 49 and 50.) The account will, ordinarily, be transferred from "army contingencies" to the appropriation for the Medical and Hospital Department in the Treasury.

1053. Forms 51 and 52 are the forms of the quarterly returns of clothing, camp and garrison equipage and the receipt roll of issues to soldiers.

1054. When persons and articles hired in the Quartermaster's Department are transferred, a descriptive list (Form 53) will be forwarded with them to the Quartermaster to whom they are sent.

1055. Officers serving in the Quartermaster's Department will report to the Quartermaster General useful information in regard to the routes and means of transportation and of supplies.

PAY BUREAU OF THE QUARTERMASTER'S DEPARTMENT.

1056. The troops will be paid in such manner that the arrears shall at no time exceed two months, unless the circumstances of the case render it unavoidable, which the Quartermaster charged with the payment shall promptly report to the Quartermaster-General.

1057. The Quartermaster General shall take care, by timely remittances, that the Quartermasters have the necessary funds to pay the troops, and shall notify the remittances to the Quartermasters and commanding officers of the respective pay districts.

1058. The payments, except to officers and discharged soldiers, shall be made on muster and pay rolls; those of companies and detachments, signed by the company or detachment commander; of the hospital, signed by the surgeon; and all muster and pay-rolls, signed by the mustering and inspecting officer.

1059. When a company is paraded for payment, the officer in command of it shall attend at the pay-table.

1060. When a receipt on a pay-roll or account is not signed by the hand of the party, the payment must be witnessed. The witness to be a commissioned officer when practicable.

1061. Officers are paid on certified accounts, as in Form 57; discharged soldiers, on accounts according to Form 59, and certificates, Form 58. An officer retiring from service must make affidavit to his pay account, and to the certificate annexed to it, and state his place of residence and the date when his resignation or removal takes effect.

Pay accounts of post chaplains are to be certified by the commanding officer of the post.

1062. When an officer is dismissed from the service, he shall not be entitled to pay beyond the day on which the order announcing his dismissal is received at the post where he may be stationed, unless a particular day beyond the time is mentioned in the order.

1063. No officer shall receive pay for two staff appointments for the same time.

1064. Officers are entitled to pay from the date of the acceptance of their appointments, and from the date of promotion.

1065. No account of a restored officer for time he was out of service can be paid, without order of the War Department.

1066. As far as practicable, officers are to draw their pay from the Quartermaster of the district where they may be on duty.

1067. No officer shall pass away or transfer his pay account not actually due at the time; and when an officer transfers his pay account he shall report the fact to the Quartermaster-General and to the Quartermaster expected to pay it.

1068. No person in the military service, while in arrear to the Confederate States, shall draw pay. When the Secretary of War shall find by report of the Comptroller of the Treasury, or otherwise, that an officer of the army is in arrears to the Confederate States, the Quartermaster-General shall be directed to stop his pay to the amount of such arrears, by giving notice thereof to the Quartermasters of the Army, and to the officer, who may pay over the amount to any Quartermaster. And no Quartermaster shall make to him any payment on account of *pay*, until he exhibits evidence of having refunded the amount of the arrears, or that his pay accrued and stopped is equal to it, or until the stoppage is removed by the Quartermaster General.

1069. No officer or soldier shall receive pay or allowances for any time during which he was absent without leave, unless a satisfactory excuse for such absence be rendered to his commanding officer, evidence of which, in case of an officer, shall be annexed to his pay account.

1070. Every deserter shall forfeit all pay and allowances due at the time of desertion. Stoppages and fines shall be paid from his future earnings, if he is apprehended and continued in service; otherwise, from his arrears of pay.

1071. No deserter shall receive pay before trial, or till restored to duty without trial by the authority competent to order the trial.

1072. In case of a soldier's death, desertion, or discharge without pay, or the forfeiture of his pay by sentence of court-martial, the account due the laundress will be noted on the muster-roll.

1073. When an improper payment has been made to any enlisted soldier, and disallowed in the settlement of the Quartermaster's accounts, the Quartermaster may report the fact to the commander of the company in which the soldier is mustered, who will note on the muster-rolls the amount to be stopped from the pay of the soldier, that it may be refunded to the Quartermaster in whose accounts the improper payment has been disallowed.

1074. Authorised stoppages to reimburse the Confederate States, as for loss or damage to arms, equipments, or other public property; for extra issues of clothing; for the expense of apprehending deserters, or to reimburse individuals (as the Quartermaster, laundress, &c.;) forfeitures for desertion, and fines by sentence of court-martial, will be entered on the roll and paid in the order stated.

1075. The Quartermaster will deduct from the pay of the soldier the amount of the authorized stoppages entered on the muster-roll descriptive list, or certificate of discharge.

1076. The travelling pay is due to a discharged officer or soldier unless forfeited by sentence of a court-martial, or as provided in paragraph 1078, or the discharge is by way of punishment for an offence.

1077. In reckoning the travelling allowance to discharged officers or soldiers, the distance is to be estimated by the shortest mail route; if there is no mail route, by the shortest practicable route.

1078. Every enlisted man discharged as a minor, or for other cause involving fraud on his part in the enlistment, or discharged by the civil authority, shall forfeit all pay and allowance due at the time of the discharge.

1079. Quartermasters or other officers to whom a discharged soldier may apply, shall transmit to the Quartermaster-General, with their remarks, any evidence the soldier may furnish relating to his not having received or having lost his certificate of pay due. The Quartermaster-General will transmit the evidence to the Comptroller for the settlement of the account.

1080. No Quartermaster or other officer shall be interested in the purchase of any soldier's certificate of pay due, or other claim against the Confederate States.

1081. The Quartermaster-General will report to the Adjutant-General any cause of neglect of company officers to furnish the proper certificates to soldiers entitled to discharge.

1082. Whenever the garrison is withdrawn from any post at which a chaplain is authorized to be employed, his pay and emoluments shall cease on the last day of the month next ensuing after the withdrawal of the troops. The Quartermaster-General will be duly informed from the Adjutant-General's office whenever the appointment and pay of the Post Chaplain will cease under this Regulation.

1083. Funds turned over to other Quartermasters, or refunded to the Treasurer, are to be entered in account current, but not in the abstracts of payments.

1084. Whenever money is refunded to the Treasurer, the name of the person refunding, and the purpose for which it is done, should be stated in order that the officers of that Department may give the proper credits.

1085. When an officer of the army receives a temporary appointment from the proper authority, to a grade in the militia then in actual service in the Confederate States, higher in rank than that held by him in the army, he shall be entitled to the pay and emoluments of the grade in which he serves. But in no case can an officer receive the compensation of two military commissions or appointments at the same time.

1086. Whenever the Quartermaster-General shall discover that an officer has drawn pay twice for the same time, he shall report it to the Adjutant-General.

1087. The Quartermaster General shall transmit to the Second Auditor, in the month of May, a statement exhibiting the total amount during the year up to the 31st December preceding, of stoppages against officers and soldiers on account of ordnance and ordnance stores, that the amount may be refunded to the proper appropriations. These stoppages will be regulated by the tables of cost published by the chief of the Ordnance Department, and shall have precedence of all other claims on the pay of officers and soldiers.

1088. The following returns are to be transmitted to the Quartermaster-General after each payment:

1. Estimate for succeeding months, (Form 54.)
2. Abstract of payments (Form 60), accompanied by the vouchers.
3. General account current, in duplicate (Form 61.)
4. Monthly statement of funds, disbursements, &c., (Form 63.)

1093. The accounts and vouchers for the expenditures to the regular army must be kept separate and distinct from those to volunteers and militia.

1094. Pay-roll of militia will be according to Form 62, the certificate at the foot to be signed by all the company officers present.

1095. No militia or volunteers shall be paid till regularly mustered into service, as provided in the general regulations.

1096. When volunteers are furnished with clothing, by tailors or other persons, the furnisher may secure his pay at the first payment of the company, upon presenting to the paying Quartermaster the receipt of the individual furnished, verified by the certificate of the captain as to its correctness—but this receipt will not be respected for an amount above the twenty-five dollars allowed for six months' service.

FORMS.

No. 1.

MONTHLY SUMMARY STATEMENT.

The Confederate States in account with ——, *at* ——, *in the month of* ——, 186 .

Dr.			Cr.		
To amount of purchases within the month, ...			By balance per last statement, .		
To amount of expenditures within the month, ...			By cash received from ——, .		
To amount of advances made to officers per abstract, ...			By cash received from the Treasurer of the Confederate States, being amount of warrant No. —, . . .		
Balance due the Confederate States, carried to next statement, . .					
	$			$	

I certify that the above is a true statement of all the moneys which has come into my hands, on account of the Quartermaster's Department, during the month of ——, 186 ; and that the disbursements have been faithfully made. The balance due the Confederate States is deposited in ——.

A. B., *Quartermaster.*

Note.—No vouchers accompany this statement; abstracts of advances or transfers only, when the number of them makes the abstract necessary.

No. 2.

Report of Persons and Articles employed and hired at

Running Numbers.	No. of each class.	Names of persons and articles.	Designati'n and occupation.	Service during the month. From.	To.	Day.	Rate of hire or compensation. Amount.	Day, month, or voyage.	Date of contract, agreement or entry into service,
1	1	House, 3 rooms,	Quarters,	1	31	31	$40 00	Month,	July 1, 1850,
2	2	House, 4 rooms,	Storehouse,	3	31	31	31 00	Month,	Dec. 3, 1849,
3	3	House, 2 rooms,	Gua'd-ho'e,	1	31	31	19 00	Month,	Dec. 3, 1840,
1	1	Ship Fanny,	Transport,	1	31	31	22000 00	Voyage,	May 3, 1850,
2	2	Schr. Heroine,	Transport,	1	31	31	700 00	Month,	Jun. 4, 1850.
1	1	Wagon & team,	. . . .	1	31	31	100 00	Month,	Jan. 1, 1850,
1	1	Chas. James,	Clerk,	1	31	31	75 00	Month,	Dec. 3, 1850,
2		Isaac Lowd,	Interpreter,	7	10	4	2 00	Day,	Jan. 7, 1851,
3		Peter Keene,	Express,	7	12	9	40 00	Month,	Jan. 7, 1851,
4		John Peters,	Blacksm'h,	22	31	7	2 00	Day,	Jan. 1, 1851,
5		Thos. Cross,	Laborer,	1	31	31	20 00	Month,	May 3, 1850,
		Confeder'e States Steam'r Fashion.							
1		Jas. Corwin,	Captain,	1	31	3	150 00	Month,	Dec. 1, 1850,
2		Geo. Pratt,	Engineer,	1	31	3	100 00	Month,	Dec. 1, 1850,
3		John Paul,	Mate,	1	31	3	50 00	Month,	Dec. 1, 1850,

Amount of rent and hire during the month, ...

I certify, on honor, that the above is a true report of all the persons and that the observations under the head of Remarks, and the statement of
Examined

C. D.,

Commanding.

No. 2.

——, *during the month of* ——, *by* ——.

By whom owned.	Amou't of rent or pay in the month.	Remarks showing by whom the buildings were occupied and for what purpose, and how the vessels and men were employed during the month. (Transfer and discharges will be noted under this head.)	Time and amount due and remaining unpaid.		
			From.	To.	Amo't.
			1860.	1861.	
A. Byrne,	$40 00	Major 3d Infantry,	Dec. 1	Jan. 31	$80 00
Jas. Black.	29 00	Subsistence Store and Office,	Dec. 5	Jan. 31	60 00
Jas. Black,	10 00	Companies I & K, 3d Infantry,			
G. Wilkins,		Transporting stores to Benicia,	Voy'e	not com	pleted.
			1861.	1861.	
T. Browne,	700 00	Transporting stores to Brazos,	Jan. 1	Jan. 31	700 00
Jas. Barry,	100 00	Hauling stores to San Antonio,	Jan. 1	Jan. 31	100 00
	75 00	Quartermaster's Office.			
	8 00	Employed by Com'ing Gen'l.			
	7 00	Express to Indianola.			
	14 00	Shoeing public horses.			
	20 00	Helping blacksmith.			
	150 00	Steamship sent to Brazos,	July 1	July 31	150 00
	100 00	Steamship sent to Brazos,	July 1	July 31	100 00
	50 00	Steamship sent to Brazos,	July 1	July 31	50 00
	1303 74	Total amount due and remaining unpaid,			1240 00

articles employed and hired by me during the month of ——, 186 , and amounts due and remaining unpaid are correct.

E. F.,

Asst. Qr. Mr.

No. 3.

Roll of Non-commissioned Officers and Privates employed on extra duty, as Mechanics and Laborers, at ——, during the month of ——, 186 , by ——.

No.	Names.	Rank or designation.	Company.	Regiment.	Byw hose order empl'yd.	Nature of service.	Term of service.			Rate of pay or compensation.			How employed.
							From.	To.	No. days.	per diem. Cents.	Dolls.	Cts.	Remarks.
											$		

I certify that the above is a correct roll of non-commissioned officers, musicians and privates, employed on extra duty, under my direction, during the month of ——, 186 ; and that the remarks opposite their names are accurate and just.

A. B.,
Quartermaster (or officer commanding.)

Examined. C. D., *Commanding.*

No. 4.

Report of Stores received for Transportation and Distribution at ——, by ——, in the month of ——, 186 .

Time received.	Marks.	No.	Contents.	From whom received.	By whom received.	Time sent.	To whom sent, and where.	With whom sent.	Intermediate destination.	Ultimate destination.	Remarks.
186 June 1	W. S., &c.	1 to 3	Clothing.	Capt. A. B., Asst. Quarter-master.	Sloop Sally. Capt. A. W.	186	Capt. C., Asst. Quartermaster.	Ship George, Capt. I. B.			Received in good order.

I certify that the above report is correct.

E. A. O., *Quartermaster.*

No. 5.

Monthly Return of Public Animals, Wagons, Harness, and other means of Transportation in the possession of ——, at ——, during the month of ——, 186 :

Date.		Horses.	Mules.	Oxen.	Wagons.	Ambulances.	Carts.	Wheel harness, single sets of.	Lead harness, single sets of.	Wagon saddles.	Ships.	Schooners.	Sloops.	Steamers.	Boats and barges.	Skiffs and batteaux.	Remarks.
	On hand,																18 horses purchased; average cost $——.
	Purchased during the month,																Wagons purchased at ——.
	Received from officers,																6 horses received from ——.
	Total to be accounted for,																
	Transferred,																Horses transferred to ——.
	Sold and worn out,																Wagons transferred to ——.
	Died and lost,																1 horse sold;—horses died on the road to ——.
	Total issued and expended,																
	Remaining on hand,																

I certify that the above return is correct.

A. B., *Quartermaster.*

NOTE.—No other articles than those above enumerated will be placed on this return.

No. 6.

Monthly Report of Forage which has been issued to Horses, Mules and Oxen in the public service at ——, by ——, during the month of ——, 186 .

Date.	To whom issued.	Public.			Private		Total.	Quantity Issued.				Average cost of								Remarks.
		Horses.	Mules.	Oxen.	Horses.	Mules.	Animals.	Corn.	Oats.	Hay.	Fodder.	Corn per bushel, (56 lbs.)		Oats per bushel (32 lbs.)		Hay per 100 pounds.		Fodder per 100 pounds.		
								Pounds.		Pounds.		$	c.	$	c.	$	c.	$	c.	
	Field and staff officers.	6			12		18	6,480		1,350		1	00		50		50	1	00	Hay purchased at ——, at ——, per 100 lbs. Corn purchased at ——, and hauled at ——, per bush. Fodder delivered at the post, at —— per 100 lbs.
	Qr. Master's Departm't.	60	300	80			440	158,400		33,000										
	Total,	219	300	80	26		625	225,000		38,000	1,640									

I certify on honor, that the above report is correct.

A. B., *Quartermaster.*

No. 7.

Report of Officers of the Army stationed at ——, whose Quarters and Fuel are commuted, for the month of ——, 186 , by,——.

Names.	Rank.	Corps.	Period.		Quarters.					Fuel.							Under what order.	Remarks.
					Room No.	Rate per month.		Amount.		Wood.			Price per cord.		Amount.			
			From.	To.		Dolls.	Cts.	Dolls.	Cts.	Cords.	Feet.	Ins.	Dolls.	Cts.	Dolls.	Cts.		
																		Paid.
			Amount of Quarters, $							Amount of Fuel, $								

I certify on honor, that the above report is correct.

A. B., *Quartermaster.*

No. 8.

Report of Persons Hired and Employed in the Quartermaster's Department at ——, who have deceased, departed, or have been discharged the service with the pay due, during the month of ——, by ——.

No.	Names.	Occupation.	Rate of pay or hire.			Time for, and amount remaining unpaid.				Remarks.
			Dolls.	Cts.	Per day or month.	From.	To.	Dolls.	Cts.	
11	Geo. Peters,	Blacksmith;	2	00	Day,	1 Aug. 1860.	30 Sept. 1860.	52	00	Discharged 30th Sept. 1860; certificates given.
27	John Smith,	Teamster;	25	00	Month,	1 Sept. 1860,	15 Sept. 1860,	12	50	Deserted 16th Sept. 1860:
29	Peter Davis,	Laborer;	20	00	Month,	1 Sept. 1860,	15 Sept. 1860.	10	00	Died 24th Sept. 1860:
								$ 74	50	

I certify, on honor, that the above is a true report of all persons hired and employed by me in the Quartermaster's Department, who have deceased, deserted, or been discharged the service with pay due, and that the statement of time for, and amount remaining unpaid, and the remarks are correct and just.

A. B., *Quartermaster.*

NOTE.—This report must contain all the information required, to enable the Department to pay to the legal representatives of the deceased persons, to examine into the case of deserters, and to examine and verify the correctness of payments made on certificates of discharge.

No. 9.

Estimate of Funds required for the service of the Quartermaster's Department at ——, by ——, in the month of ——, 186 .

		Dolls.	Cts.
1	For Fuel,		
2	Forage,		
3	Straw,		
4	Stationery,		
5	Materials for building. (State what, and for what.)		
6	Hire for mechanics. (State for what work.)		
7	Hire for laborers. (State for what service.)		
8	Hire of teamsters. (State on what service.)		
9	Pay of extra-duty men. (State for what work.)		
10	Pay of wagon and forage masters,		
11	Hire of clerks, guides, escorts, expenses of courts-martial, of burials, of apprehending deserters, and other incidental expenses,		
12	Hire or commutation of officers' quarters,		
13	Hire of quarters for troops, or ground for encampment or use of military stations,		
14	Hire of store houses, offices, &c. (For what use.)		
15	Mileage to officers,		
16	Army transportation, viz:		
	Of troops and their baggage,		
	Of Quartermaster's subsistence, ordnance, and hospital stores,		
17	Purchase of horses and mules. (Q. M. Dep.,)		
18	Purchase of wagons and harness, do.		
19	Purchase of horses for mounted troops, viz:		
	Horses for Company —— Cavalry.		
	Horses for Company —— Artillery, &c.,		
20	Outstanding Debts,*		
	Deduct actual or probable balance on hand,		

*To be accompanied by a list giving the name and amount due each individual, or firm, and on what account due,

No. 10.

The Confederate States in account current with ——, Quartermaster Confederate States, on account of the Quartermaster's Department at ——, in the quarter ending on the —— day of ——, 186 .

DR.					CR.		
186				186			
March 31,	To amount of purchases per abstract A,			January 1,	By balance on hand, per last account,		
March 31,	To amount of expenditures, per abstract B,			January 15,	By cash received from Treasurer of the Confederate States, being amount of warrant No. ——, ...		
March 31,	To amount of transfers to officers, per abstract B *b*, ...			March 31,	By cash received of sundry officers, per abstract B *b b*, ...		
March 31,	To balance due the Confederate States, carried to new account, ...			March 31,	By cash received from sales of public property, as per account herewith, ...		

I certify that the above is a true account of all the moneys that have come into my hands on account of the Quartermaster's Department, during the quarter ending on the —— day of —— 186 , and that the disbursements have been faithfully made.

A. B., *Quartermaster.*

NOTE.—Moneys for clothing, camp and garrison equipage, and contingencies of the army, are not accounted for in this account current. Abstracts B *b* and B *b b* are used only where the number of transfers make them necessary.

No. 11—(Abstract A.)

Abstract of Purchases paid for at ——. in the quarter ending on the ——, 186 , by ——.

CLASSES.					FUEL.				FORAGE.				STRAW.	STATIONERY.															
Date.	No. of voucher.	Fr'm whom purchased.	Amount.		Wood.			Coal	Corn	Oats	Hay		Pounds.																
			Dolls.	Cts.	Cords	Feet	In	Lbs.	Bu.	Bu.	Lbs.																		
Purchased prior to the quarter,																													
Purchased within the quarter,																													
Total paid within the quarter,																													

Note.—This abstract will be supported by vouchers, (Form 12) and must exhibit all the articles paid for in the quarter, whether purchased within or prior to the quarter, except purchases of clothing, camp and garrison equipage, and purchases for "army contingencies,".

No. 12.—(Voucher for Purchases to Abstract A.)

The Confederate States,

To ——— ———. Dr.

Date of purchase.			Dollars.	Cents.
June 3, 1860,	20 cords of wood at ——— per cord,			
" 10, "	20,251 pounds of straw at ——— per 100 lbs.,			
" 29, "	100 bushels of coal at ——— per bushel,			
		$		

I certify that the above account is correct and just; the articles are to be (or have been) accounted for on my property return for the ——— quarter ending on the ——— day of ———, 186 .

A. B., *Quartermaster.*

Received at ———, the ——— of ———, 186 , of C. D., Quartermaster C. S. Army, ——— dollars and ——— cents, in full of the above account.

E. F.

(Signed duplicates.)

Note.—The certificate made by the officer who purchased the property. The receipt taken by the officer who paid it.

No. 13.—(Abstract B.)

Abstract of Expenditures on the Quartermaster's Department, by ——, *at* ——, *in the quarter ending on the* —— *of* ——, 186 .

Date of payment.	No. of voucher.	To whom paid.	On what account.	Amount.	
				Dolls.	Cts.
			$		

I certify that the above abstract is correct.

A. B., *Quartermaster.*

Note.—This abstract contains all payments in the account current, except purchases (Abstract) and transfers of funds.

No. 14.—(Abstract B b.)

Abstract of Advances made to officers for Disbursements on account of the Quartermaster's Department, by ——, *in the quarter ending the* ——, 186 .

Date of the advance.	No. of the recp't or voucher.	To what officer.	By whose order, for what purpose.	Amount.	
				Dolls.	Cts.
			$		

No. 15.—(VOUCHER TO ABSTRACT B.)

We, the subscribers, do hereby acknowledge to have received of ———, *Assistant Quartermaster C. S. Army at* ———, *the sums opposite to our names respectively, being in full of our pay for the period herein expressed, having signed duplicates hereof.*

Date.	No.	Names.	Occupation.	Period of service.				Rate of pay.			Amount of pay.		Am't of stop'ges.		Amount rec'd.		Signer's names.	Witnesses.	Remarks.
				From.	To.	Months.	Days.	Dollars.	Cents.	Pr. month or day.	Dollars.	Cents.	Dollars.	Cents.	Dollars.	Cents.			

I certify on honor, that the above receipt roll is correct and just.

A. B., *Quartermaster.*

No. 16.—(Voucher to Abstract B.)

The Confederate States,

To ——— ———, Dr.

Date.		Dolls.	Cts.
From —— of —— to —— of ——	For mileage from ———— to ————, being ———— miles, at ———— per mile,		

I certify, on honor, that the above is correct and just; that I performed the journey, and under the order hereto annexed, and not returning from leave of absence to the station or troops I had left; that I have not been furnished with public transportation, nor received money in lieu thereof, for any part of the route.

Received, ——— 186 , of ———, ——————— dollars and ——— cents, in full of the above account.

(Signed duplicate.)

No. 17.—(Voucher to Abstract B.)

The Confederate States,

To ——— ———, Dr.

Date.		Dollars.	Cents.
	For expenses incurred for transportation of self and allowance for baggage and porterage, in traveling from ——— to ———, per annexed statement,		

I certify on honor, that the above account is correct and just; that I have performed the journey, and on urgent public duty, without order, for the purpose of ———, and necessarily incurred the expenses as stated; that I have travelled in the customary reasonable manner, and not returning from leave of absence to the station or troops I left; that I have not been furnished with public transportation, or money in lieu thereof, for any part of the route. The approval of the journey by the proper authority is hereto annexed.

Received at ——— the ——— of ——— 186 , of ———, Assistant Quartermaster C. S. Army, ——— dollars and ——— cents, in full of the above account. (Signed in duplicate.)

Dolls. $\overline{100}$

Certificate in case of journey under orders.

I certify, on honor, that this account is correct and just; that I performed the journey, and under the order hereto annexed, and necessarily incurred the expenses as stated; that I travelled in the customary reasonable manner; that I was not returning from leave of absence to the station or troops I had left; that I have not been furnished with public transportation, nor money in lieu thereof, for any part of the route.

No. 18.—(VOUCHER TO ABSTRACT B.)

The Confederate States,

To —— ——, DR.

Date.		Dollars.	Cents.
	For mileage from —— to ——, pursuant to annexed copy of Orders No. ——, convening (or annexed summons to attend) a court-martial at ——, distance being —— miles, at —— cents per mile, —— days' attendance on said court-martial, being from the —— of —— to the —— of —— 186 , inclusive, (per annexed certificate) at $——, —— days' traveling on the —— of ——, going to, and on the —— of ——, returning from the court at $——,		

I certify, on honor, that the above account is correct and just; that I have actually performed the journeys herein charged for on the days stated, in obedience to the authority hereunto annexed; that I have not been furnished with public transportation, nor received money in lieu thereof, for any part of the route charged for.

Received at —— the —— of —— 186 , of ——, Assistant Quartermaster C. S. Army, —— dollars and —— cents, in full of the above account.

(Signed in duplicate).

No. 19.—(VOUCHER TO ABSTRACT B.)

The Confederate States,

To —— ——, DR.

Date.		Dollars.	Cents.
	For the actual expense of his transportation, while traveling under orders in the discharge of his duty as clerk to Major ——, Paymaster Confederate States Army, from —— to ——, per annexed statement,		

I certify, on honor, that —— was, during the time above specified, employed as clerk in the Pay Department, Confederate States Army, and that the journey charged for in the above account was performed by him in the discharge of his official duties, under my orders.

—— ——, *Paymaster C. S. Army.*

—— COUNTY, *ss.*

On this —— day of —— one thousand eight hundred and sixty ——, personally appeared before me, the subscriber, a justice of the peace in and for the county aforesaid, ——, and made oath in due form of law, that the above account is correct and just, and exhibits the actual expenses of his transportation for and during the journey above specified.

(Subscribed in duplicate.)

—— ——, *Justice of the Peace.*

Received at ——, the —— of —— 186 , of ——, Assistant Quartermaster Confederate States Army, —— dollars and —— cents, in full of the above account.

(Signed in duplicate.)

Dollars $\frac{}{100}$

No. 20.—(VOUCHER TO ABSTRACT B.)

The Confederate States,

To —— ——, DR.

Date.		Dollars.	Cents.
	For cash paid for postage on letters and packages on public service, received and sent by him from the —— of —— 186 , to the —— of —— 186 , inclusive,		

I certify, on honor, that the foregoing account is correct and just; that the letters and packages on which postage has been paid, as therein stated, were all on public service; that I have actually paid the amount charged.

Received at ——, the —— of ——186 , of ——, Assistant Quartermaster C. S. Army, —— dollars and —— cents, in full of the above account.

(Signed in duplicate.)

No. 21.—VOUCHER TO ABSTRACT B.)

The Confederate States,

To —— ——, DR.

Date.		Dolls.	Cts.
	For commutation of quarters at ——, from the —— of —— 186 , to the —— of —— 186 , inclusive, ...		
	For —— rooms, at —— dollars each, per month, ...		
	For commutation of fuel for the same period:		
	—— cords —— feet —— inches, at —— dollars per cord, ...		

I certify, on honor, that there were no quarters owned or hired by the public at the above station which could be assigned to —— during the above period, and that the fuel is charged at the average market price for the month.

A. B., *Quartermaster.*

I certify, on honor, that the above account is correct and just; that I have been regularly stationed on duty at ——, by ——, during the period charged for; that I have not been furnished with quarters, rent, or fuel, by the public, nor received a commutation of money in lieu thereof.

C. D.

Received at ——, the —— of ——, 186 , of ——, Quartermaster C. S. Army, —— dollars and —— cents, in full of the above account. (Signed in duplicate.)

C. D.

NOTE.—The certificate must show by whose order the officer was stationed, and the first account to be accompanied by a copy of the order.

No. 22.—(VOUCHER.)

The Confederate States,

To ——— ———, Dr.

Date.		Dolls.	Cts.

I certify, on honor, that the above account is correct and just; that the services were rendered as stated, and that they were necessary for the public service.

A. B., *Quartermaster.*

Received of ——, 186 , of ——, —— dollars and —— cents, in full of the above account.
(Signed duplicates.)

E. F.

NOTE.—This form will be used for miscellaneous disbursements, and will be entered in abstract B or C, according to the nature of the expenditure.

No. 23.

QUARTERLY RETURN OF QUARTERMASTER'S STORES.

Received, issued, and remain on hand at ——, *in the quarter ending on the* —— *of* ——, 186 .

A. B., *Quartermaster.*

NOTE.

The property on this return (which does not include clothing, camp and garrison equipage) will be classed as follows:

1. Fuel.
2. Forage.
3. Straw.
4. Stationery.
5. Barrack, Hospital, and office Furniture.
6. Means of Transportation, including Harness, &c.
7. Building Materials.
8. Veterinary Tools and Horse Medicines.
9. Blacksmiths' Tools.
10. Carpenters' Tools.
11. Wheelwrights' Tools.
12. Masons' and Bricklayers' Tools.
13. Miscellaneous Tools for Fatigue and Garrison purposes.
14. Stores for Expenditure, such as Iron, Steel, Horse-shoes, Rope, &c., &c., to be classed alphabetically.

No. 23.—*Quarterly Return of Quartermaster's Stores received and issued*

——. Co

Classes,			1. Fuel.				
			Wood.			Coal.	
Date.	Abstracts, &c.		Cords.	Feet.	Inches.	Anthracite.	Bituminous.
			No.	No.	No.	Lbs.	Bu.
	Per last return,	On hand,					
	Abstract D,	Received by purchase,					
	" E,	" from officers,					
	" N,	Fabricated, taken up, &c.,					
Total to be accounted for,							
	Per Abstract F,	Fuel,					
	" G,	Forage,					
	" H,	Straw,					
	" I,	Stationery,					
	" K,	Special issues,					
	" L,	Expended, sold,					
	" M,	Transferred,					
Total issued and expended,							
Total remaining on hand,							
Condition 1,		In good order,					
" 2,		Unfit for service, but repairable,					
" 3,		Totally unfit for service,					

at ——, *in the quarter ending on the* —— *of* ——, 186 , *by*
tinued.

2. Forage.				3. Straw.	Stationery.						
Corn.	Oats.	Hay.	Fodder.	For Bedding.	Foolscap Paper.	Letter Paper.	Folio Post Paper.	Envelope Paper.	Envelopes.	2 qr. blk. books.	3 qr. blk. books.
Lbs.	Lbs.	Lbs.	Lbs.	Lbs.	Qrs.	Qrs.	Qrs.	Qrs.	No.	No.	No.

No. 23.—*Quarterly return of Quartermaster's Stores, received and issued*

Stationery.											
Abstracts, &c.	4 qr. blk. books.	Ink.	Ink-powder.	Wafers.	Sealing-wax.	Steel-pens.	Quills.	Lead-pencils.	Office tape.	Inkstands.	Wafer-stamps.
	No.	Bottles	Papers	Ozs.	Ozs.	No.	Gross.	No.	Pcs.	No.	No.
O H, .											
D, .											
E, .											
N. .											
F, .											
G, .											
H, .											
I, .											
K, .											
L, .											
M, .											

at ——, *in the quarter ending on the* —— *of* ——, 186 , *by* ——.
tinued.

4. Stationery.

Erasers.	Paper-folders.	Sand-boxes.	Wafer-boxes.													
No.	No.	No.	No.													

I certify, on honor, that the foregoing return exhibits a true and correct statement of all the property which has come into my hands on account of the Quartermaster's Department, during the quarter ending on the —— of ——, 186

A. B., *Quartermaster.*

No. 24.—(ABSTRACT D.)

Abstract of Articles purchased at ——, *in the quarter ending on the* ——, 186 , *by* ——.

CLASSES.					FUEL.				FORAGE.			STRAW.			STATIONERY.																
Date.	No. of voucher.	From whom purchased.	Amount.		Wood.			Coal																							
			Dols	Cts.	Cords.	Feet	Ins.	Bus.																							
Articles purchased and paid for																															
Articles purchased and not paid for,																															
Total purchas'd within the quarter,																															

I certify that the above abstract is correct.

A. B., *Quartermaster.*

NOTE.—This abstract appertains exclusively to the *Property Return*, and is designed to show all the supplies purchased by the Quartermaster, *whether paid for or not.* No voucher of the purchase paid for accompany this abstract. They are in the second division of Abstract A. Purchase not paid for are vouched as in Form No. 25.

The Confederate States,

To ——— ———, Dr.

Date of purchase.		Dollars.	Cents.
	For ——— cords of wood, at ——— per cord, For ——— pounds of hay, at ——— per 100 pounds,		

I certify, on honor, that the above account is correct and just; that I purchased the articles above enumerated of the said ——, at the prices therein charged, amounting to —— dollars and —— cents, and that I have not paid the account. (Here state the cause of non-payment.)

A. B., *Quartermaster.*

No. 26.—(Abstract E.)

Abstract of Articles received from officers at ——, *in the quarter ending on* —— *of* —— 186 , *by* ——.

Classes.			Fuel.				Forage,			Straw.			Stationery.																	
			Wood.			Coal.																								
Date.	No. of voucher.	From whom received	Cords.	Feet.	Inches.	Bushels.																								
		Total received,																												

I certify that the above abstract is correct.

A. B., *Quartermaster.*

No. 27.—(Voucher to Abstract E.)

List of Quartermaster's Stores, &c., delivered by —— to ——, at ——, on the —— day of ——, 186 .

Number or quantity.		Articles.	Cost when new.	Condition when delivered.	Remarks.
40	Forty,	Felling axes,	$ 1 00 each,	New,	
300	Three hundred pounds,	Bar iron, assorted,	6 per pound,	New,	
1,000	One thousand pounds,	Cut nails,	5 per pound,	New,	
656	Six hundred and fifty-six bushels,	Corn,	1 00 per bushel,	Good,	
30,500	Thirty thousand five hundred lbs.	Hay,	1 00 pr hundred,	Good,	
10	Ten,	Wheelbarrows,	4 00 each,	Half-worn,	
5	Five,	Wagons, (4-horse,)	150 00 each,	Half-worn,	
5	Five,	Wagons, "	150 00 each,	New,	

I certify that I have this day delivered to A. B., Quartermaster Confederate States Army, the articles specified in the foregoing list.

C. D., *Quartermaster.*

Note.—When no invoice is received, the receiving officer will substitute for this form of voucher a list of the stores received, certified by himself. When the person responsible for the property entered without invoice is known, it will be entered in his name.

No. 28.—(Abstract F.)

Abstract of Fuel issued at ———, *in the quarter ending on the* ——— *of* ———, 180 , *by* ———.

Date.	No. of voucher	To whom issued.	For what period.	Wood.			Coal.		Remarks.
				Cords.	Feet.	Inches	Bush's	Lbs.	
Total issued.									

I certify that the abstract is correct.

A. B, *Quartermaster.*

Note.—For vouchers, see Forms No. 29 and No. 30. All fuel issued is entered on this abstract. Fuel transferred to other officers, to be accounted for by them, is entered on abstract M.

No. 29.—(Voucher to Abstract F.)

Requisition for Fuel for —— Company —— Regiment of ——, commanded by ——, for the month of —— 186 .

Station.	Captains.	Subalterns.	Non-commissioned officers. musicians and privates.	Laundresses.	Total.	Monthly allowance to each, in cords.	TOTAL ALLOWANCE.					Remarks.
							Wood.			Coal.		
							Cords.	Feet.	Inches.	Bush.	Pounds	
Total.												

I certify, on honor, that the above requisition is correct and just; and that fuel has not been drawn for any part of the time above charged.

R. S., *Commanding Company.*

Received, —— 186 , of ——, Assistant Quartermaster C. S. Army, —— cords —— feet —— inches of wood and —— of coal, in full of the above requisition

(Signed duplicates.)

R. S., *Commanding Company.*

No. 30.—(Voucher to Abstract F.)

Requisition for fuel for ——, stationed at ——, for the month of —— 186 .

				Wood.			Coal.		Remarks.
				Cords.	Feet.	Inches.	Bushels	Pounds.	
For myself, ...									
Total, ...									

I certify, on honor, that the above requisition is correct and just, and that I have not drawn fuel for any part of the time above charged.

Received, —— 186 , of ——, Assistant Quartermaster Confederate States Army, —— cords —— feet —— inches of wood and —— of coal, in full of the above requisition.

No. 31.—(Abstract G.)

Abstract of Forage issued at ——, *in the quarter ending on the* —— *of* ——, 186 , *by* ——.

Date.	No. of voucher.	To whom issued.	For what period.		Number of horses.	Number of mules.	Number of Oxen.	Total.	Total allowance.						Remarks.
									Corn.		Oats.		Hay.	Fodder.	
			From.	To.					Bushels. (56 lbs.)	Pounds.	Bushels. (32 lbs.)	Pounds.	Pounds.	Pounds.	
															Public. Private.
		Total,													

I certify that the above abstract is correct.

A. B., *Quartermaster*.

Note.—For vouchers, see Forms Nos. 32, 33, 34. All forage issued will be entered on this abstract. Forage transferred to other officers to be accounted for by them, will be entered on Abstract M.

No. 32.—(Voucher to Abstract G.

Requisition for Forage for Public Horses, Mules and Oxen, in the service of ——, for —— days, commencing the —— of ——, 186 , at ——.

Date of requisition.	Number of horses.	Number of mules.	Number of oxen.	Total number of animals.	Number of days.	Number of rations.	Daily allowance to each animal.					Total allowance.					Remarks.
							Pounds of corn.	Pounds of barley.	Pounds of oats.	Pounds of hay.	Pounds of fodder.	Corn.	Barley.	Oats.	Hay.	Fodder.	
												Pounds of.	Pounds of.	Pounds of.	Pounds of.	Pounds of.	
Required,																	
On hand, to be deducted,																	
To be supplied.																	

I certify, on honor, that the above requisition is correct and just; that I have now in service the number of animals for which forage is required, and that forage has not been received for any part of the time specified.

Received at ——, on the —— day of ——, 186 , of ——, Quartermaster C. S. Army, —— pounds of corn, —— pounds of barley, —— pounds of oats, —— pounds of hay, —— pounds of fodder, in full of the above requisition.

(Signed in duplicate.)

No. 33.—(Voucher to Abstract G.)

Requisition for Forage for —— Private Horses in the service of ——, C. S. Army, at ——, for —— days, commencing the —— of ——, and ending the —— of ——, 186 .

Date.	Period.		Number of horses.	Daily allowance for each.			Total allowance.						Remarks.
				Corn.	Oats.	Hay.	Corn.		Oats.		Hay.	Fodder.	
	From.	To.		Pounds.	Pounds.	Pounds.	Bushels. (32 lbs.)	Pounds.	Bushels. (32 lbs.)	Pounds.	Pounds.	Pounds.	
Total,													

I certify, on honor, that the above requisition is correct and just; and that I have not drawn forage for any part of the time above charged.

Received at ——, the —— of ——, 186 , of ——, Assistant Quartermaster C. S. Army, ——/56 bushels corn, ——/32 bushels oats, —— pounds hay, —— pounds fodder, in full of the above requisition.

(Signed in duplicate.)

No. 34.—(VOUCHER TO ABSTRACT G.)

Statement of Forage issued to and consumed by the Public Animals under my direction at ———, *during the month of* ———, 186 .

Period.			Number of animals.				Total allowance.						Remarks.
							Corn.	Oats.	Barley	Hay.	Fod-der.		
From.	To.	No. of Days.	Horses.	Mules.	Oxen.	Total.	Pounds of.	Pounds of.	Pounds of.	Pounds of.	Pounds of.		
Total, ...													

I certify, on honor, that the above statement is correct; that the forage was issued to the Public Animals as stated, and that the issues were necessary.

A. B., *Quartermaster.*

Approved.

R. S., *Commanding.*

No. 35.—(Abstract II.)

Abstract of Straw issued at ——, *in the quarter ending on the* —— *of* ——, 186 , *by* ——.

Date.	No. of voucher.	To whom issued.	For what period.		Non-commissioned officers, musicians, and privates.	Laundress.	Hospital.	Total allowance.	Remarks.
			From.	To.				Pounds.	
		Total,....							

I certify that the above abstract is correct.

A. B., *Quartermaster.*

Note.—For voucher, see Form 36. Issues on this abstract. Transfers on abstract M.

No. 36.—(Voucher to Abstract H.)

Requisition for Straw for —— *Company* —— *Regiment of* ——, *commanded by* ——, *for the month of* ——, 186 .

Station.	Non-commissioned officers, musicians, and privates.	Laundress.	Total drawn for.	Monthly allowance to each.	Total allowance.	Remarks.
				Pounds.	Pounds.	
Total,........						

I certify, on honor, that the above return is correct and just; and that straw has not been drawn for any part of the time above charged.

G. H., *Commanding Company.*

Received at ——, the —— of ——, 18 , of ——, C. S. Army, —— pounds of straw, in full of the above requisition.

(Signed duplicates.)

G. H., *Commanding Company.*

No. 37.—(Abstract I.)

Abstract of Stationery issued at ——, *in the quarter ending on the* —— *of* —— 186 , *by* ——.

Date.	No. of voucher.	To whom issued.	For what period. From	For what period. To.	Writing paper, quires.	Cartridge paper, sheets.	Quills, number.	Wafers, ounces.	Sealing-wax, ounces.	Ink powder, papers.	Blank books, number.				Remarks.
Total issued,															

I certify, that the above abstract is correct.

A. B., *Quartermaster.*

Note.—For voucher, see Form No. 38. **The stationery used by the Quartermaster in the public service is entered on this abstract, and all issues by him. Transfers on abstract M.**

No. 38.—(VOUCHER TO ABSTRACT L.)

Requisition for Stationery for ——, *stationed at* ——, *for the* ——, *commencing on the* —— *of* ——, *and ending on the* —— *of* ——, 186 .

	Quires of letter paper.	Quires of foolscap paper.	Sheets of cartridge paper.	Number of quills.	Ounces of wafers.	Ounces of sealing wax.	Pieces of tape.	Papers of ink-powder.						

I certify that the above requisition is correct, and that I have not drawn stationery for any part of the time specified.

Received at ——, on the —— of ——, 186 , of ——, Assistant Quartermaster C. S. Army, —— quires of letter paper, —— quires of foolscap paper, —— quills, —— ounces of wafers, —— ounces of sealing-wax, —— pieces of tape, —— sheets of cartridge paper, —— papers of ink-powder.

(Signed duplicate.)

No. 39.—ABSTRACT K.—FOR ALL ISSUES EXCEPT FUEL, FORAGE, STRAW, AND STATIONERY.

Abstract of Articles issued on Special Requisitions at ——, *in the quarter ending on the* —— *of* ——, 18 , *by* ——.

Classes,																									
Date.	From whom received.																								
Total,																									

I certify that the above abstract is correct.

A. B., *Quartermaster.*

NOTE.—For voucher see Form No. 40. Transfer to abstract M.

No. 40.—(Voucher to Abstract K.)

SPECIAL REQUISITION.

For

I certify that the above requisition is correct, and that the articles specified are absolutely requisite for the public service, rendered so by the following circumstances: [here the officer will insert such reasons as he may think fit to give, tending to show the necessity for the supplies.]

Captain J. B., Assistant Quartermaster Confederate States Army, will issue the articles specified in the above requisition.

C. D , *Commanding*.

Received at ——, the —— of ——, 18 , of ——, Assistant Quartermaster Confederate States Army [here insert the articles], in full of the above requisition. (Signed, duplicates.)

Note.—The cost of articles issued on special requisitions, and orders of commanding officers, will be entered on the requisition and on the list or invoice furnished the receiving officer.

No. 41.—(ABSTRACT L.)

Abstract of Articles Expended, Lost, Destroyed in the public service, sold, &c., at ——, under the direction of ——, in the quarter ending on the —— of ——, 186 .

Classes,																	
Date.	No. of certificates.	By whom made.															
Total, ...																	

I certify that the above abstract is correct.

A. B , *Quartermaster.*

No. 42.—(Voucher to Abstract L.)

List of Quartermaster Stores expended in public service at ——, under the direction of ——, in the month of ——, 186 .

o. or quantity.	Articles.	Application.

I certify, on honor, that the several articles of Quartermaster's stores, above examined, have been necessarily expended in the public service at this station, as indicated by the marginal remarks annexed to them respectively.

(Signed duplicates.) A. B., *Quartermaster.*

Note.—This list should be made out monthly, to enable the Quartermaster to know the exact state of his supplies.

No. 43.—(Voucher to Abstract L.)

List of Articles Lost or Destroyed in the public service at ——, while in the possession and charge of ——, in the month of ——, 186 .

No. or quantity.	Articles.	Circumstance and Cause.

I certify that the several articles of Quartermaster's stores, above enumerated, have been unavoidably lost or destroyed while in the public service, as indicated by the remarks annexed to them respectively. A. B., *Quartermaster.*

Approved: C. D., *Commanding.*

No. 44.—(VOUCHER TO ABSTRACT L.)

Abstract Sales of Articles of public property sold at auction at ———, *under the direction of* ———, *on the* ——— *of* ———, 186

No. or quantity.	Articles.	Purchaser.	Amount.
			$

I certify that the above account sales is accurate and just.

A. B., *Auctioneer.*

I certify that the above enumerated articles were sold at public auction as above stated, pursuant to—[state the orders or authority.]

C. D., *Quartermaster.*

No. 45.—(ABSTRACT M.)

Abstract of Articles transferred to ——, *at* ——, *in the quarter ending on the* —— *of* ——, 186 , *by* ——.

Classes,																		
Date.	No. of voucher.	To whom transferred.																
Total, ...																		

I certify that the above abstract is correct.

A. B., *Quartermaster.*

NOTE.—This abstract contains all transfers of stores to other officers, to be accounted for by them; the vouchers will be their receipts. When these are not received in time, the Quartermaster will substitute his own certified list of the stores sent, and the bill of lading. The receipts he will afterwards transmit when he receives them.

No. 45.—(ABSTRACT N.)

Abstract of Articles received at ——— , *during the quarter ending the* ——— *day of* ———, 186 .

Classes,			Fuel.				Forage.			Straw.	Stationery.
Date.	No. of invoice, &c.	From whence received.	Wood.			Coal.	Corn.	Oats.	Hay.		
			Cords.	Feet.	Inches.		Bushels, (35 lbs.)	Bushels, (32 lbs.)	Pounds.		
		Found at the post, Manufactured, Parts of articles broken up, Heretofore issued, but not consumed, Captured from the enemy,									
Total,											

I certify that the above abstract is correct.

A. B., *Quartermaster.*

NOTE.—This abstract contains all Quartermaster's property found at the post. not borne on the previous return all that may come to the Quartermaster's possession without his knowing who may be accountable for it; articles manufactured in the quarter; material or parts of articles that have been condemned or broken up; fuel or forage issued but not consumed, &c., &c. Separate lists of each class, with the necessary explanation, will be filed with the abstract.

No. 46.

Quarterly Statement of Allowances paid to Officers of the Army in money, the quarter end.

Officer's names.	Rank and Corps. (Rank being that for which they were paid, or allowances furnished.)	For Fuel.		Quarters.			
				In money.		In kind.	
		Period.	Am't. $ c.	Period.	$ c.	Period.	No. Rooms.
		1861.		1861.		1861.	
W.S	Major Genl.	July, Aug. Sep.	96 00	July, Aug. Sep.	120 00	–	–
J. T	Brig. Genl.	July, .	30 00	July, Aug. Sep.	80 00	–	–
K. J.	Col. Ajt. Gl.	August, .	30 00	July, Aug. Sep.	90 00	–	–
T. M	Col. Q. M. D.	August, .	30 00	July, Aug. Sep.	80 00	–	–
T. L	Maj. Pay Dt.	July, Aug. Sep.	30 00	Aug. Sep.	80 00	July, .	3
L. B	Col. Engrs.	July, Aug. Sep.	39 00	–	80 00	–	–
B. L	Mj. T. Engrs.	–	–	–	–	–	–
B. B	Cols. Drags.	–	–	–	–	July, Aug.	4
J. C	Col. Art.	July, Aug. .	20 00	–	–	July, Aug.	4
F. E.	Maj. Infty.	July, Aug. .	12 00	–	–	July, Aug.	4

or furnished in kind, with the money value thereof, by ——, at ——, in ing ———, 186 .

Rent.	For transportation of baggage.	Per diem on court-martial.	For forage issued in kind.	Stationery.	Total amount.	Abstract and voucher.	Remarks.
$ c.	$ c.	$ c.	$ c.	$ c.	$ c.		
-	120 00	40 00	-	20 00	306 00	B 1, 7, 9—19	
-	90 00	-	-	15 70	215 00	B 2, 11, 14—14	
-	-	-	-	-	120 00	B 17	
-	-	-	-	-	110 00	B 21	
30 00	60 00	-	30 00	-	230 00	B 4, 20—G 13	
-	-	-	-	-	130 00	B 19	
-	100 00	-	-	-	110 00	B 26, 27	
30 00	30 00	40 00	37 50	-	139 50	B 27, [illegible]—G 14	
35 00	70 00	-	-	-	126 50	B 28, 32—H 2	
	-	-	-	-	12 50	F 4—H 6,	Public quarters.

I certify that the above is correct. A. B., *Quartermaster.*

NOTE.—When officers occupy quarters owned by the public, the number of rooms only will be reported.

No. 47.

The Confederate States in account current with ———, *for expenditures on account of 'Contingencies of the Army and of the other Departments, in the quarter ending on the* ——— *day of* ———, 186 .

Date.		Dolls.	Cts	Date.		Dolls.	Cts.
Sept. 30,	To amount of expenditures, per Abstract C, ...			July 1,	By balance on hand, as per last account,		
				July 8,	By cash received of ——, ...		
Sept. 30,	To balance due the Confederate States, carried to new account,			Aug. 4,	By cash received from the Treasurer of the Confederate States, being amount of Warrant No. ——, ...		
	$				$		

I certify, on honor, that the above exhibits a true account of all moneys which have come into my hands on account of contingencies of the army, during the quarter ending on the —— of ——, 186 , and that the disbursements have been faithfully made.

A. B., *Quartermaster.*

No. 48—(ABSTRACT C)

Abstract of Disbursements on account of Contingencies of the Army and of other Departments, by ——————, in the quarter ending on the —— of ——, 186 , at ——.

Date of payment.	No. of voucher.	To whom paid.	On what account.	AMOUNT.	
				Dolls.	Cts.

A. B., *Quartermaster.*

NOTE.—For vouchers, see Forms ——. All payments for apprehending deserters must also be entered in this Abstract.

No. 49.—(VOUCHER TO ABSTRACT C.)

Requisition on the Quartermaster's Department for extra supplies of Medicines and Hospital Stores.

I certify, on honor, that the medicines and hospital stores above required are necessary for the use of the sick at this post in consequence of [here insert whether from loss, damage, &c.,] and that the requisition is agreeable to the supply table.

A. B., *Assistant Surgeon.*

Approved: C. D., *Commanding Officer.*

Received at ——, on the —— of ——, 186 , the articles above enumerated.

(Signed duplicates.)

A. B., *Assistant Surgeon.*

No. 50—(Voucher to Abstract C.)

Bill of Medicine, &c., when purchased by an Officer of the Quartermaster's Department.

The Confederate States,

To —— ——, Dr.

Date of purchase.		Dolls.	Cents.
	For		

I certify, on honor, that the prices of the articles above charged, for the use of the sick at ——, agreeable to the foregoing requisition, are reasonable and just.

A. B., *Surgeon.*

Received of ——, 186 , of ——, —— dollars and —— cents, in full of the above account.

(Signed duplicates.)

E. F.

Note.—The above certificate may be signed by the surgeon making the requisition, or by any surgeon or assistant surgeon belonging to the army. The requisition on which the purchase may be made must be attached to the bill of purchase, which will be entered in Abstract C, and the articles are noticed in the property returns.

No. 51.—*Quarterly Return of Clothing, Camp and Garrison Equi-*

day of ——

WHEN RECEIVED.	No. of invoice.	OF WHOM RECEIVED.	Cavalry hats.	Caps and bands.	Cap letters, castle, shell and flame.	Cap covers.	Pompons. Color.	
		On hand per last return.						
Total to be accounted for,								
WHEN ISSUED.	No. of roll	TO WHOM ISSUED.						
Total issued,								
On hand to be accounted for,								

page, received and issued at ———, *in the quarter ending on the* ——— 186 , *by* ———,

CLOTHING.														
		COATS.									METALLIC SEALS.			
Eagle and rings.	Plumes for cavalry.	Sergeant-majors'.	Quartermaster Sergeants'.	Ordnance Sergeants'.	Chief musicians'.	First sergeants'.	Sergeants'.	Corporals'.	Musicians'.	Privates.	Non-commissioned officers.	Sergeants'.	Corporals and privates'.	Sashes.

No. 51.—*Quarterly Returns of Clothing, Camp and Garrison*

CLOTHING.														
UNIFORM JACKETS.														
Sergeant-majors'.	Quartermaster Sergeants'.	First Sergeants.	Sergeants'.	Corporals'.	Privates.	Trowsers.	Yards of binding.		Flannel shirts.	Drawers, pairs of.	Boots, cavalry, pairs of.	Boots, infantry, pairs of.	Stockings, pairs of.	Leather stocks.

Equipage, received and issued, &c.—Continued.

CLOTHING.								EQUIPAGE.						
								BED SACKS						
Great-coats.	Great-coat straps, number of.	Talmas.	Blankets.					Single.	Double.	Axes.	Axe-helves.	Spades.	Camp kettles.	Mess pans.

No. 51.—*Quarterly Return of Clothing, Camp and Gar*

EQUIPAGE.														
													DRUMS.	
Camp hatchets.	Hatchet handles.	Hatchet handles.	Garrison flags.	Garrison flag halliards.	Storm flag.	Recruiting flags.	Recruiting flag halliards.	Camp colors.	Guidons.	Trumpets.	Bugles, with extra mouth pieces.	Fifes.	Complete.	Heads, batter.

rison Equipage, received and issued, &c.—Continued.

EQUIPAGE.																									
DRUMS.																				BOOKS AND BLANKS.					
Heads, snare.	Slings.	Sticks, pairs.	Drum-stick carriages.	Cords.	Snares, sets.	Wall-tents.	Wall-tent flies.	Wall-tent poles and pins, sets.	Common tents.	Common tent poles and pins, sets.	Iron pots.	Pickaxes.	Pickaxe handles.							Cloth'g ac't book.	Descriptive book.	Order book.	Clothing returns.	Receipt rolls.	Final statements.

No. 52.

We, the undersigned, Non-Commissioned Officers, Artificers, Musicians, —— *the several articles of Clothing*

Date of the issue.	Name and designation of the soldier.	Caps.	Cap covers.	Pompons.	Eagles and rings.	UNIFORM COATS.					UNIFORM JACKETS.				
						N. C. S.	Sergeants'	Corporals'	Musicians'	Privates'	Sergeants'	Corporals'	Musicians'	Privates'	

NOTES.—Erasures and alterations of entries are prohibited.

Regular and extra issues will be distinguished on the receipt-roll.

Each signature, whether written by the soldier or acknowledged *by mark*, must be witnessed.

Vacant space will be filled by a cipher.

Mounted men may receive *one* pair of "boots" and *two* pairs of "bootees," instead of *four* pairs of bootees.

No. 52.

and Privates of ———, do hereby acknowledge to have received of set opposite our respective names.

Trowsers, pairs.	Flannel shirts.	Drawers, pairs.	Boots, cavalry, pairs.	Booteees, infantry, pairs.	Stockings, pairs.	Leather stocks.	Great coats.	Fatigue overalls.	Stable frocks.	Blankets.								Signatures.	Witness.

As the metallic shoulder scales, letters, numbers, castles, and shells and flames will last for many years, they will be borne on the returns as company property, in the same manner as are sashes, and other articles of camp and garrison equipage, and will be charged to the soldier only when lost or destroyed through neglect.

No. 53.

Descriptive List of Persons and Articles employed and hired in the Quartermaster's Department, and transferred by ——, *at* ——; *to* ——, *Quartermaster at* ——, *on the* —— *day of* ——, 186

Number of each class.	Articles and names of persons.	Designation and occupation.	Period for which pay is due.				Rate of hire on compensation.			Amount due.		Date of contract, agreement, or entry into service.	By whom owned and where.	Remarks.
			From.	To.	Month.	Days.	Dollars.	Cents.	Month, day or voyage.	Dollars.	Cents.			
Total amount due,														

I certify, on honor, that the above is a true list of persons and articles transferred by me to ——, at ——, on the —— day of ——, 186 ; and that the periods of service, rates of hire or compensation, and amounts due, are correctly stated.

Pay and Allowances of the Army.

GRADE.	Pay in the Old Army	Pay. Per month.	Forage. No. of Horses time of war.	Forage. No. of Horses time of peace.
Brigadier-General,		$301 00	4	3
Aid to Brigadier-General in addition to pay of Lieutenant,		35 00		
Colonel of Engineers, Artillery, Cavalry, and of the General Staff, except the Medical Department;		210 00	3	3
Lieutenant-Colonel of Cavalry,		185 00	3	3
Major of Cavalry,		162 00	3	3
Captain of Cavalry,		140 00	3	2
First Lieutenant of Cavalry,		100 00	2	2
Second Lieutenant of Cavalry,		90 00	2	2
Adjutant, in addition to pay of Lieutenant,		10 00		
ARTILLERY.				
Colonel,		210 00	3	3
Lieutenant-Colonel,		185 00	3	3
Major,		150 00	3	3
Captain,		130 00		
First Lieutenant,		90 00		
Second Lieutenant,		80 00		
Adjutant, in addition to pay of Lieutenant,		10 00		

Pay and Allowances of the Army.—Continued.

GRADE.	Pay. Per month.	Forage. No. of Horses time of war.	Forage. No. of Horses time of peace.
INFANTRY.			
Colonel,	195 00	3	3
Lieutenant-Colonel,	170 00	3	3
Major,	150 00	3	3
Captaim,	130 00		
First Lieutenant,	90 00		
Second Lieutenant,	80 00		
Adjutant, in addition to pay as Lieutenant,	10 00		
MEDICAL STAFF.			
Surgeon-General, $3,000 per annum.			
Surgeon of ten years' service,	200 00	3	3
Surgeon of less than ten years' service,	162 00	3	3
Assistant Surgeon of ten years' service,	150 00	2	2
Assistant Surgeon of five years' service,	130 00	2	2
Assistant Surgeon of less than five years' service,	110 00	2	2
ENLISTED MEN.			
Sergeant or Master workmen of Engineers, Master Armorer, Master Carriage Maker, and Master Blacksmith, each,	34 00		

Corporal or Overseer of Engineers, Armorer, Carriage Maker and Blacksmith of Ordnance, each,	20 00	
Private—First Class, or Artificer of Engineers and Ordnance,	17 00	
Private—Second Class, or Laborer and Musician of Engineers, and Laborer of Ordnance,	13 00	
Sergeant-Major of Cavalry and Infantry,	21 00	
Quartermaster Sergeant of Cavalry and Infantry,	21 00	
Principal Musicians,	21 00	
Chief Bugler,	21 00	
First Sergeant of Cavalry and Infantry,	20 00	
Sergeant of Cavalry and Infantry,	17 00	
Corporal of Cavalry, Artillery, Infantry, Artificers, Farriers and Blacksmiths,	13 00	
Musician of Cavalry,	13 00	
Musician of Artillery and Infantry,	12 00	
Private—Cavalry,	12 00	
Private—Artillery and Infantry,	11 00	
Ordnance Sergeant,	21 00	
Hospital Steward appointed by the Secretary of War, and Hospital Steward at posts of more than four companies,	21 00	
Hospital Steward,	20 00	
Hospital Matron,	6 00	
Chaplain,	50 00	

NOTE.—Brigadier-General commanding in chief a separate Army actually in the field, $100 per month additional.

Lieutenants serving with the company of Sappers and Miners, and officers of Artillery serving in Light Artillery or on Ordnance duty, receive Cavalry pay.

In addition to pay, of above stated (excepting Surgeon-General) $3 per month is allowed for every five years' service in the Army of the United States and Confederate States.

Subalterns of the line detailed by the War Department as Assistant Quartermasters, or as Assistant Commissaries of Subsistence, receive in addition to pay in the line, $20 per month, while engaged in the duties of those Departments; but although the officer may be serving in both, he can draw this allowance for one Department only.

Tables of the Daily, Pay of the Army.

DAYS.	$5 per month.	$6 per month.	$6⅔ per month.	$7 per month.	$7½ per month.	$8 per month.	$9 per month.	$10 per month.	$11 per month.	$12 per month.	$13 per month.	$16 per month.	$20 per month.	$23 per month.	$25 per month.	$26⅔ per month.	$30 per month.	$33⅓ per month.	$40 per month.	$50 per month.	$60 per month.	$75 per month.
I,	16	20	22	23	24	26	30	33	36	40	43	53	66	76	83	88	1 00	1 11	1 33	1 66	2 00	2 50
II,	33	40	44	46	48	53	60	66	73	80	86	1 06	1 33	1 53	1 69	1 77	2 00	2 22	2 66	3 33	4	5 00
III,	50	60	66	70	73	80	90	1 00	1 10	1 20	1 30	1 60	2 00	2 30	2 50	2 66	3 00	3 33	4 00	5 00	6	7 50
IV,	66	80	88	93	97	1 06	1 20	1 33	1 46	1 60	1 73	2 13	2 66	3 06	3 33	3 55	4 00	4 44	5 33	6 66	8	10 00
[illegible]	83	1 00	1 11	1 16	1 22	1 33	1 50	1 66	1 83	2 00	2 16	2 66	3 33	3 83	4 16	4 44	5 00	5 65	6 66	8 33	10	12 50
VI,	1 00	1 20	1 33	1 40	1 46	1 60	1 80	2 00	2 20	2 40	2 60	3 20	4 00	4 60	5 00	5 33	6 00	6 66	8 00	10 00	12	15 00
VII,	1 16	1 40	1 55	1 63	1 71	1 86	2 10	2 33	2 56	2 80	3 03	3 73	4 66	5 36	5 83	6 22	7 00	7 77	9 33	11 66	14	17 50
VIII,	1 33	1 60	1 77	1 86	1 75	2 13	2 40	2 66	2 93	3 20	3 46	4 26	5 33	6 13	6 66	7 10	8 00	8 88	10 66	13 33	16	20 00
IX,	1 50	1 80	1 99	2 10	2 19	2 40	2 70	3 00	3 30	3 60	3 90	4 80	6 00	6 90	7 50	7 99	9 00	9 99	12 00	15 00	18	22 50
X,	1 66	2 00	2 22	2 33	2 44	2 66	3 00	3 33	3 66	4 00	4 33	5 33	6 66	7 66	8 33	8 88	10 00	11 11	13 33	16 66	20	25 00
XI,	1 83	2 20	2 44	2 56	2 68	2 83	3 30	3 66	4 03	4 40	4 76	5 86	7 33	8 43	9 16	9 77	11 00	12 22	14 66	18 33	22	27 50
XII,	2 00	2 40	2 66	2 60	2 93	3 20	3 60	4 00	4 40	4 80	5 20	6 40	8 00	9 20	10 00	10 66	12 00	13 33	16 00	20 00	24	30 00
XIII,	2 16	2 60	2 98	3 03	3 17	3 46	3 90	4 33	4 76	5 20	5 63	6 93	8 66	9 96	10 83	11 55	13 00	14 44	17 33	21 66	26	32 50
XIV,	2 33	2 80	3 10	3 26	3 42	3 73	4 20	4 66	5 13	5 60	6 06	7 46	9 33	10 73	11 66	12 44	14 00	15 55	18 66	23 33	28	35 00
XV,	2 50	3 00	3 33	3 50	3 66	4 00	4 50	5 00	5 50	6 00	6 50	8 00	10 00	11 50	12 50	13 33	15 00	16 66	20 00	25 00	30	37 50
XVI,	2 66	3 20	3 55	3 73	3 90	4 26	4 80	5 33	5 86	6 40	6 93	8 53	10 66	12 26	13 33	14 21	16 00	17 77	21 33	26 66	32	40 00
XVII,	2 83	3 40	3 77	3 96	4 15	4 53	5 10	5 66	6 23	6 80	7 36	9 06	11 33	13 03	14 16	15 10	17 00	18 88	22 66	28 33	34	42 50
XVIII,	3 00	3 60	3 99	4 20	4 39	4 80	5 40	6 00	6 60	7 20	7 50	9 60	12 00	13 80	15 00	15 99	18 00	19 99	24 00	30 00	36	45 00
XIX,	3 16	3 80	4 21	4 43	4 64	5 06	5 70	6 33	6 96	7 60	8 23	10 13	12 66	14 56	15 83	16 88	19 00	21 11	25 33	31 66	38	47 50
XX,	3 33	4 00	4 44	4 66	4 88	5 33	6 00	6 66	7 33	8 00	8 66	10 66	13 33	15 33	16 66	17 77	20 00	22 22	26 66	33 33	40	50 00
XXI,	3 50	4 20	4 66	4 90	5 13	5 60	6 30	7 00	7 70	8 40	9 10	11 20	14 00	16 10	17 50	18 66	21 00	23 33	28 00	35 00	42	52 50
XXII,	3 66	4 40	4 81	5 13	5 37	5 86	6 60	7 33	8 06	8 80	9 53	11 73	14 66	16 86	18 23	19 55	22 00	24 44	29 33	36 66	44	55 00
XXIII,	3 83	4 60	5 10	5 26	5 61	6 13	6 90	7 66	8 43	9 20	9 96	12 26	15 33	17 63	19 16	20 43	23 00	25 55	30 66	38 33	46	57 50
XXIV,	4 00	4 80	5 22	5 60	5 86	6 40	7 20	8 00	8 80	9 60	10 40	12 80	16 00	18 40	20 00	21 32	24 00	26 66	32 00	40 00	48	60 00
XXV,	4 16	5 00	5 55	5 83	6 10	6 66	7 50	8 33	9 16	10 00	10 83	13 33	16 66	19 16	20 83	22 21	25 00	27 77	33 33	41 66	50	62 50
XXVI,	4 33	5 20	5 77	6 06	6 35	6 93	7 80	8 66	9 63	10 40	11 26	13 86	17 33	19 93	21 66	23 10	26 00	28 88	34 66	43 33	52	65 00
XXVII,	4 50	5 40	5 99	6 30	6 59	7 20	8 10	9 00	9 90	10 80	11 70	14 40	18 00	20 70	22 50	23 99	27 00	29 99	36 00	45 00	54	67 50
XXVIII,	4 66	5 60	6 21	6 53	6 84	7 46	8 40	9 33	10 26	11 20	12 13	14 93	18 66	21 46	23 33	24 88	28 00	31 11	37 33	46 66	56	70 00
XXIX,	4 83	5 80	6 43	6 76	7 08	7 73	8 70	9 66	10 63	11 60	12 56	15 46	19 33	22 23	24 16	25 77	29 00	32 22	38 66	48 33	58	72 50
XXX,	5 00	6 00	6 66	7 00	7 33	8 00	9 00	10 00	11 00	12 00	13 00	16 00	20 00	23 00		26 66	30 00	33 33	40 00	50 00	60	75 00

Form No. 54.

Estimate of Funds required for the Pay, Forage, and Clothing of the —— Regiment of ——, stationed at ——, for —— month, founded on the actual number of said troops.

Enumeration of Troops.	Period. From	Period. To	Pay. $.	Pay. Cents.	Forage. $.	Forage. Cents.	Amount. $.	Amount. Cents.
— Colonel, . @ $ per month,								
— Lieut. Colonel, . @ $ "								
— Majors, . @ $ "								
— Surgeon, . @ $ "								
— Ass't Surgeon, . @ $ "								
— Captains, . @ $ "								
— 1st Lieutenants, . @ $ "								
— 2d Lieutenants, . @ $ "								
— Sergeant-major, . @ $ "								
— Qr. Mr. Sergeant, @ $ "								
— 1st Sergeants, . @ $ "								
— Sergeants, . @ $ "								
— Corporals, . @ $ "								
— Musicians, . @ $ "								
— Farriers and Blacksmiths, . @ $ "								
— Privates, . @ $ "								
— Add six months clothing allowance, for —— men, .								
		Total amount, ...						
		Deduct balance on hand, ...						
		Amount required, ...					$	

Examined and approved.

Commanding

—— ——, *Ass't Quartermaster.*

—— *Regiment of* ——.

FORM No. 55.

Consolidated Estimate of Funds required for the Pay, Forage, and Clothing of the following troops for —— months, commencing the —— of ——, 186 , and ending the —— of ——, 186 .

Regiment or corps.	Generals.	Aid-de-Camps.	Colonels.	Lieutenant-Colonels.	Majors.	Surgeons.	Assistant-Surgeons.	Captains.	1st Lieutenants.	2d Lieutenants.	Chaplains.	Sergeant-Majors.	Quartermaster-Sergeants.	1st Sergeants.	Sergeants.	Corporals.	Musicians.	Farriers and Blacksmiths.	Privates.	PAY.		FORAGE.		CLOTHING.		AMOUNT.	
																				Dolls.	Cts.	Dolls.	Cts.	Dolls.	Cts.	Dolls.	Cts.
Field and staff,																											
—Regiment of—																											
—Regiment of—																											
—Regiment of—																											
Total amount required,																									$		

Station ——.
Date ——.
Approved: —— ——, *Commanding.*

—— ——, *Chief A. Q. Master.*

FORM No. 56.

Receipts to be rendered by Quartermasters for Remittances.

Received of ——, this —— day of ——, 186 , at ——, in the State of ——, on ——, dated the —— day of ——, 186 , the sum of —— dollars and —— cents, on account of the pay, &c., of the Army of the Confederate States, as follows:

Pay, ...	$
Forage, ...	
Clothing, ...	
Amount, ...	$

For which sum I am accountable.

(Signed duplicates.)

—— ——, *Paymaster.*

NOTE.—One receipt for the Quartermaster-General, one for the Second Auditor, and one for the Treasurer.

FORM No. 57—OFFICERS, PAY ACCOUNT.

The Confederate States, to ——— ———, DR.

On what account.	Commencem't and expirat'n.		Term of service charged.		Pay per month.		Amount.		Remarks.
	From.	To.	Months.	Days.	Dolls.	Cts.	Dolls.	Cts.	
PAY—									
For myself, ...									
For myself for — years' service,									
FORAGE—									
For horse, ...									

I hereby certify that the foregoing account is accurate and just; that I have not been absent without leave during any part of the time charged for; that I have not received pay, forage, or received money in lieu of any part thereof, for any part of the time therein charged; that the horses were actually kept in service and were mustered for the whole time charged; that for the whole of the time charged for my staff appointment, I actually and legally held the appointment and did duty in the department; that I have been a commissioned officer for the number of years stated in the charge for every additional five years' service; that I am not in arrears with the Confederate States on any account whatsoever; and that the last payment I received was from ———, and to the ——— day of ———, 18 .

I at the same time acknowledge that I have received of ——— ———, this ——— day of ———, 18 , the sum of ——— dollars, being the amount in full of said account.

Pay, ...
To ——— years' service, ...
Forage, ...

(*Signed dup.*)

Amount, ...

FORM No. 58

Certificate to be given a soldier at the time of his discharge.

I certify that the within named —— a —— of Captain —— company, (——,) of the —— regiment of ——, born in ——, in the State of ——, aged —— years, — feet — inches high, —— complexion, —— eyes, and by —— a —— was enlisted by —— at —— on the —— day of —— 186 , to serve —— years, and is now entitled to discharge by reason of ——.

The said —— was last paid by ——, to include the — day of —— 186 , and has pay due him from that time to the present date.

There is due to him —— dollars travelling expenses from ——, the place of discharge to ——, to the place of enrollment, transportation not being furnished in kind.

There is due him ——.

He is indebted to the Confederate States —— dollars, on account of ——.

Given in duplicate at ——, this — day of —— 186 .

—— ——,
Commanding Company.

NOTE.—When this certificate is transferred it must be on the back, witnessed by a commissioned officer, if practicable, or by some other reputable person well known to the Quartermaster.

FORM No 59.

Account to be made by Quartermaster.

For pay from —— of —— 186 , to —— of —— 186 ; being —— months and —— days, at —— dollars per month, ...		
For pay for travelling from —— to ——, being —— miles, at ——, ...		
Amount, ...		
Deduct for clothing overdrawn, ...		
Balance paid, ...		

Received of ——, C. S. Army, this —— day of —— 186 , —— dollars and — cents, in full of the above account.

(Signed duplicates.)

Witness: —— ——.

Form No. 60.

Abstract of payments made by ——, Quartermaster, for the —— months of ——

No. of voucher.	Date of payment.	To whom paid.	Rank or grade.	Corps.	Commencement and expiration.		Pay.		Forage.						Amount.		Remarks.
					From.	To.	Dols.	Cts.	Dols.	Cts.	Dols.	Cts.	Dols.	Cts.	Dols.	Cts.	

I do hereby certify that the foregoing Abstract contains an accurate statement of the payments made by me, as therein expressed.

—— ——, *Quartermaster*.

FORM No. 61.—ACCOUNT CURRENT.

DR. *The Confederate States in account with ——, Quartermaster Confederate States Army,* CR.

Date.		Pay.		Subsistence.		Forage.		Amount.		Date.		Pay.		Subsistence.		Forage,		Amount.	
		Dolls.	Cents.	Dolls.	Cents.	Dolls.	Cents.	Dolls.	Cents.			Dolls.	Cents.	Dolls.	Cents.	Dolls.	Cents.	Dolls.	Cents.
18	For am't expended, as per abstr't and vouchers herewith, in paying the troops since the — of— 18—, the date of the last account rendered, ...										By balance to be accounted for, as stated in last account, ...								
	For amount turned over to ——,									18	By cash received of —, as per my receipt dated the – day of – 18—.								
	Due the Confederate States, to be accounted for in the next acc'nt,									18	By amount received of —, for —,								
	Amount, ...										Amount, ... $								
											By balance brought down, ...								

I certify that the above is a true account of all public money received by me, not heretofore accounted for, and that the disbursements have been fully made.

Stated at ——, this —— day of —— 18 :
(Duplicate)

—— ——, *Quartermaster.*

FORM No. 62.

We, the subscribers, do hereby acknowledge to have received of ——— ———, Quartermaster, the sums annexed to our names respectively, being the full of our pay and allowances for the period herein expressed, having signed duplicates thereof.

No.	Name.	Period of service.				Pay per month.	Amount of pay.	Forage.	40 cts. per day, use of horses, arms, &c.	Travelling allowance.		Total amount.	Stoppages.	Balance paid.	Signature.	Witness.	Remarks.
		Commencem't.	Expiration.	Months.	Days.												

We certify, on honor, that we actually owned and kept in service the horses for which we have received payment, for the whole of the time charged. We also certify that the non commissioned officers and privates of the company to which we belong, who are made up for pay, &c., as having horses and arms, actually owned and had them in service for the time paid for, although, in some cases, they may not have been valued. We also certify that we witnessed the payment of the whole company.

——— ———, *Captain.*
——— ———, *1st Lieut.*
——— ———, *2d Lieut.*
——— ———, *Ensign.*

FORM No. 63.

Statement of moneys received and expended, and on hand, for the month ending ——.

Date.		Pay.	Forage.	Effe diers.	Overdrawn clothing.	Ordnance.	Equipments.	Quartermaster's stores.	Militia.	Amount.	Remarks.
	Amount on hand from last month,..										
	Received from the Treasurer,.......										
	Received from Quartermaster,.......										
	Received from ——,...............										
	Total received,................$										
	Expended in paying the troops,.....										
	Turned over to Quartermaster,......										
	Total expended,...............$										
	Balance to be accounted for,.......$										

Accountable for —————— iron safe.

——, *Quartermaster.*

ARTICLE XLII.

SUBSISTENCE DEPARTMENT.

SUPPLIES.

1097. Subsistence stores for the army, unless in particular and urgent cases the Secretary of War shall otherwise direct, shall be procured by contract, to be made by the Commissary-General on public notice, to be delivered on inspection in the bulk, and at such places as shall be stipulated; the inspector to give duplicate inspection certificates (see Form No. 15), and to be a legal inspector where there is such officer.

1098. Purchases, to supply such corps and posts as by reason of their position, the climate, or for other sufficient cause the Secretary of War may specially direct to be supplied in that way, will be made in open market, on public notice, from the lowest bidder who produces the proper article.

1099. And whenever a deficiency of subsistence stores make it necessary to buy them, the commissary, where they are needed, will make a requisition for that purpose on the proper purchasing commissary, or buy them himself, of good quality, corresponding with the contract.

1100. When subsistence is received under contract, the commissary will receipt for it on the inspection certificates (see Form No. 15). He will deliver one of these to the contractor, and forward the other to the Commissary-General, with a report on the quality of the provisions and the condition of the packages.

1101. Whenever subsistence stores are purchased, the advertisements and bids, and a copy of the bill of purchase, with a statement of the cause of purchase, will be forwarded by the purchasing officer to the Commissary-General. This rule does not apply to the ordinary purchase of hospital supplies. Pork, salt beef, and flour must be inspected before purchase by a legal inspector where there is such officer. Duplicate certificates of inspection (see Form No. 15) will be taken as subvouchers to the vouchers for the payment.

1102. Fresh beef, when it can be procured, shall be furnished as often as the commanding officer may order, at least twice a week, to be procured by the commissary, when practicable, by contract. (For form of contract and bond, see Forms 27 and 28.) When beef is taken on the hoof, it will be accounted for on the provision return by the number of cattle and their estimated weight. When the pasture is insufficient, hay, corn, and other forage will be procured for public cattle.

1103. Good and suficient store-room for the subsistence stores will be procured by the commissary from the Quartermaster. Care shall be taken to keep the store-rooms dry and ventilated. Packages shall be so stored as to allow circulation of air among and beneath them. The flour should occasionally be rolled into the air.

1104. Before submitting damaged commissary stores to boards of survey, the commissary shall separate and re-pack sound parts.

1105. Wastage on issues, or from evaporation or leakage, will be ascertained quarterly, or when it can be most conveniently; and the actual wastage thus found will be charged on the monthly return. Loss, from whatever cause, exceeding ordinary waste, must be accounted for by the certificate of an officer, or other satisfactory evidence. Ordinary waste on issues should not exceed, say 10 per cent. on pork, bacon, sugar, vinegar, and soap, and 5 per cent. on hard bread, beans, rice, coffee, and salt.

1106. No wastage is admitted on issues of fresh beef furnished the company detachment, or regiment, directly from the butcher. But in beef on the hoof, errors in estimated weight, and losses on cattle strayed or stolen, will be accounted for by the certificate of an officer, or other satisfactory evidence. When cattle are transferred, they should be appraised, and loss in weight reported as wastage by the officer delivering them. Fair wastage in transportation of stores is accounted for by the receiving officer.

THE RATION.

1107. The ration is three-fourths of a pound of pork or bacon, or one and a fourth pounds of fresh or salt beef; eighteen ounces of bread or flour, or twelve ounces of hard bread, or one and a fourth pounds of corn meal; and at the rate, to one hundred rations of eight quarts of peas or beans, or, in lieu thereof, ten pounds of rice; six pounds coffee; twelve pounds sugar; four quarts of vinegar; one and a half pounds of tallow, or one and a fourth pounds adamantine, or one pound sperm candles: four pounds of soap, and two quarts of salt.

1108. The annexed table shows the quantity of each part of the ration in any number of rations from one to ten thousand.

1109. On a campaign, or on marches, or on board of transports, the ration of hard bread is one pound.

ISSUES.

1110. Returns for issues to companies, will, when practicable, be consolidated for the post or regiment (see Form 14). At the end of the month, the issuing commissary will make duplicate abstracts of the issues, which the commanding officer will compare with the original returns, and certify (see Form 2). This abstract is a voucher of the issue for the monthly return.

1111. Issues to the hospital will be on returns by the medical officer, for such provisions only as are actually required for the sick and the attendants. The cost of such parts of the ration as are issued will be charged to the hospital at contract or cost prices, and the hospital will be credited by the whole number of complete rations due through the month at contract or cost prices (see Note 7); the balance, constituting the *Hospital Fund*, or any portion of it, may be expended by the commissary, on the requisition of the medical officer, in the purchase of any article for the subsistence or comfort of the sick, not authorized to be otherwise furnished (see Form 3). At large depots or general hospitals, this fund may be partly expended for the benefit of dependent posts or detachments, on requisitions approved by the medical director or senior Surgeon of the district.

1112. The articles purchased for the hospital, as well as those issued from the subsistence store-house, will be included in the Surgeon's certificates of issues to the hospital, and borne on the monthly return of provisions received and issued. Vouchers for purchases for the hospital must either be certified by the Surgeon, or accompanied by his requisition.

1113. Abstracts of the issues to the hospital will be made by the commissary certified by the Surgeon, and countersigned by the commanding officer (see Form 3). When there is a hospital fund, every article supplied by the subsistence department for the use of the hospital, will be charged against that fund.

1114. In order that the authorized women of companies may draw their rations while temporarily separated from their companies, the officer commanding the company must make a report to the commanding officer of the post where the women may be left, designating such as are to draw rations as attached to his company. Their rations are not commuted, and they can only draw them at a military post or station where there are supplies.

1115. When provisions can be spared from the military supplies, commanding officers have discretion to order issues to Indians visiting military posts on the frontiers, or in their respective nations, and to order sales of subsistence to Indian agents for issues to Indians. The returns for issues, where there is no Indian agent, will be signed by the commanding officer. The sales will be for cash, at cost, including all expenses; to be entered on the monthly return, and credited on the quarterly account current.

1116. Issues to *volunteers* and *militia*, to *sailors*, to *marines*, to *citizens* employed by any of the departments, or to *Indians*, will be entered on separate abstracts to the monthly return.

1117. An extra issue of fifteen pounds of tallow or ten of sperm candles, per month, may be made to the principal guard of each camp and garrison, on the order of the commanding officer. Extra issues of soap, candles and vinegar, are permitted to the hospital when the Surgeon does not avail himself of the commutation of the hospital rations, or when there is no hospital fund; salt in small quantities may be issued for public horses and cattle. When the officers of the Medical Department find anti-scorbutics necessary for the health of the troops, the commanding officer may order issues of fresh vegetables, pickled onions, sour krout or molasses, with an extra quantity of rice and vinegar. (Potatoes are usually issued at the rate of one pound per ration, and onions at the rate of three bushels in lieu of one of beans.) Occasional issues (extra) of molasses are made—two quarts to one hundred rations—and of dried apples, of from one to one and a half bushels to one hundred rations. Troops at sea are recommended to draw rice and an extra issue of molasses in lieu of beans. When anti-scorbutics are issued, the medical officer will certify the necessity, and the circumstances which cause it, upon the abstract of extra issues, (see Form 4).

1118. When men leave their company, the rations they have drawn, and left with it, will be deducted from the next return for the company; a like rule when men are discharged from the hospital will govern the hospital return.

RECRUITING SERVICE.

1119. When subsistence cannot be issued by the Commissariat to recruiting parties, it will be procured by the officer in charge, on written contracts for complete rations, or wholesome board and lodging (see Form 26).

1120. The contractor will send, monthly or quarterly, as he may choose, his account for rations issued, to the Commissary-General for payment vouched by the abstract of issues (Form 17) certified by the officer.

1121. When convenience and economy require that the contract shall be for board and lodging, the officer in charge shall estimate the cost of the ration, for which the contractor shall be paid as before directed, and shall pay the amount due to lodging from the recruiting fund.

1122. At temporary rendezvous, advertising may be dispensed with, and a contract made conditioned to be terminated at the pleasure of the officer of the Commissary-General.

1123. The recruiting officer will be required, when convenient, to receive and disburse the funds for the subsistence of his party, and to render his accounts quarterly to the Commissary-General.

1124. When a contract cannot be made, the recruiting officer may pay the necessary expenses of subsisting and boarding his party.

1125. The expenses of subsistence at branch rendezvous, and all expenses of advertising for proposals, will be paid by the contractor at the principal station, and included in his accounts.

1126. Issues of provisions will be made on the usual provision returns, and board will be furnished on a return showing the number of the party, the days, and dates.

SUBSISTENCE TO OFFICERS.

1127. An officer may draw subsistence stores, paying cash for them at contract or cost prices, without including cost of transportation, on his certificate that they are for his own use and the use of his family. These certified lists the commanding officer shall compare with the monthly abstracts of sales, which he shall countersign, (see Form 5.) The commissary will enter the sales on his monthly return, and credit the money in his quarterly account current.

BACK RATIONS.

1128. When the supplies warrant it, back rations may be drawn, if the full rations could not have been issued at the time; except when soldiers have been sufficiently subsisted in lieu of the ration. The return for back rations shall set out the facts, and the precise time when rations were not issued, or the troops otherwise sufficiently subsisted, which shall appear on the abstract of issues.

COMMUTATION OF RATIONS.

1129. When a soldier is detached on duty, and it is impracticable to carry his subsistence with him, it will be commuted at seventy-five cents a day, to be paid by the commissary when due, or in advance, on the order of the commanding officer. The officer detaching the soldier will certify, on the voucher, that it is impracticable for him to carry his rations, and the voucher will show on its face the nature and extent of the duty the soldier was ordered to perform. (See Form 18.)

1130. The expenses of a soldier placed temporarily in a private hospital, on the advice of the senior Surgeon of the post or detachment, sanctioned by the commanding officer, will be paid by the Subsistence Department, not to exceed seventy-five cents a day.

1131. The ration of a soldier stationed in a city, with no opportunity of messing, will be commuted at sixty cents. The rations of the non-commissioned regimental staff, when they have no opportunity of messing, and of soldiers on furlough, or stationed where rations cannot be issued in kind, may be commuted at the cost or value of the ration at the post. The rations of Ordnance Sergeants may be commuted at thirty cents.

1132. When a soldier on duty has necessarily paid for his own subsistence, he may be refunded the cost of the ration. When more than the cost of the ration is claimed, the account must be submitted to the Commissary-General.

EXTRA-DUTY MEN.

1133. The commanding officer will detail a suitable non-commissioned officer or soldier from extra-duty, under the orders of the Commissary, and to be exempt from ordinary company and garrison duty. All extra-duty men employed in the Commissariat will be paid the regulated allowance (see Article XXXIX.) by the Commissary, if not paid extra-pay in any other department.

1134. Barrels, boxes, hides, tallow, &c., will be sold, and the proceeds credited in the quarterly account current.

ACCOUNTS.

1135. The following are the accounts and returns to be rendered to the Commissary-General:

Monthly.

Return of provisions and forage received and issued in the month,	Form	1
Invoices of subsistence stores received,	"	22
Abstracts of issues to troops, &c. (See paragraph 1116,)	"	2
Abstract of issues to hospitals,	"	3
Abstract of extra issues,	"	4
Abstract of sales to officers,	"	5
Abstract of purchases, without vouchers,	"	8
Receipts for subsistence transferred,	"	24
Summary statement of money received and expended during the month,	"	6
Report of persons and articles employed and hired,	"	20

Quarterly.

Account current,	Form	7
Abstract of all purchases of provisions and forage during the quarter,	"	8
Abstract of all expenditures in the quarter, except for purchase of provisions, and forage for cattle, (paragraph 1102,)	"	9
Consolidated abstract of sales to officers during the quarter,	"	10
Distinct abstract of other sales:		
Quarterly return of all property in the department, except provisions, and forage for cattle,	"	12
Estimate of funds required for next quarter,	"	11

1136. The abstracts of issues will show the corps or detachment. When abstracts require more than one sheet, the sheets will be numbered in series, and not pasted together; the total at the foot of each carried to the head of the next, &c., &c.

1137. All lists of subsistence shall run in this order: meat, breadstuff, rice and beans, coffee, sugar, vinegar, candles, soap, salt, antiscorbutics, purchases for hospital, forage for cattle.

1138. No charge for printing blanks, as forms, will be allowed.

1139. A book will be kept by the commissary at each post, in which will be entered the monthly returns of provisions received and issued, (Form 1.) It will show from what the purchases have been made, and whether paid for. It is called the Commissary's book, and will not be removed from the post.

1140. When any officer in the Commissariat is relieved, he will close his property accounts; but money accounts will be kept open till the end of the quarter, unless he ceases to do duty in the department.

1141. Commissaries of subsistence in charge of principal depots, will render quarterly statements of the cost and quality of the ration, in all its parts, at their stations.

NOTES.

1. Stores longest on hand will be issued first.

2. Armorers, carriage-makers and blacksmiths, of the Ordnance Department, are entitled to one and a half rations per day; all other enlisted men, one ration. Laundresses, one ration. No hired person shall draw more than one ration.

3. One ration a day may be issued to any person employed with the army, when the terms of his engagement require it, or on paying the full cost of the ration when he cannot otherwise procure food.

4. Lamps and oil to light a fort or garrison are not allowed from the Subsistence Department.

5. In purchasing pork for the Southern posts, a preference will be given to that which is put up in small pieces, say from four to six pounds each, and not very fat.

6. As soldiers are expected to preserve, distribute, and cook their own subsistence, the hire of citizens for any of these duties is not allowed, except in extreme cases. The expenses of bakeries are paid from the post fund, to which the profits accrue by regulations, (see paragraph 183,) such as purchase of hops, yeast, furniture; as sieves, cloths, &c., and the hire of bakers. *Ovens* may be built or paid for by the Subsistence Department, but not bake houses.

7. Mode of ascertaining the hospital ration: 100 complete rations consist of, say—

				Cost.
32	rations of	fresh beef is 40 lbs. at 4 cents,		$1 60
68	"	pork is 51 lbs. at 6 cents,		3 06
100	"	flour is 112 lbs. at 2 cents,		2 25
100	"	beans is 8 quarts at 4 cents,	32	0 46
or	"			
100	"	rice is 10 lbs. at 6 cents,	60	
100	"	coffee is 6 lbs. at 9 cents,		0 54

100 rations of sugar is 12 lbs. at 8 cents,		0 96
100 "	vinegar is 4 quarts at 5 cents,	0 20
100 "	candles is $1\frac{1}{2}$ lbs. at 12 cents,	0 18
100 "	soap is 4 lbs. at 6 cents,	0 24
100 "	salt is 2 quarts at 3 cents,	0 06
	Cost of one hundred rations,	$9 55

or 9 cents 5 mills per ration.

8. A box, 24 by 16 inches square, and 22 inches deep, will contain one barrel, or 10,752 cubic inches.

9. A box, 16 by 16.8 inches square, and 8 inches deep, will contain one bushel, or 2150.4 cubic inches.

10. A box, 8 by 8.4 inches square and 8 inches deep, will contain one peck, or 537.6 cubic inches.

11. A box, 7 by 4 inches square, and 4.8 inches deep, will contain a half gallon or 131.4 cubic inches.

12. A box, 4 by 4 inches square, and 4.2 inches deep, will contain one quart or 67.2 inches.

13. One bushel of	corn	weighs	56	pounds.
" "	wheat	"	60	"
" "	rye	"	56	"
" "	buckwheat	"	52	"
" "	barley	"	48	"
" "	oats	"	40	"
" "	beans	"	60	"
" "	potatoes	"	60	"
" "	onions	"	57	"
" "	dried peaches	"	33	"
" "	dried apples	"	22	"
" "	salt	"	50	"
Ten gallons	pickled onions	"	83	"
" "	sour krout	"	81	"

1142. Lieutenants, acting as Assistant Commissaries of Subsistence, are allowed $20 per month for such services, to be paid by the Pay Department, on accounts certified to by the Commissary-General, to the effect that proper returns were rendered for the period charged for.

1143. A Regimental or Depot Commissary of Subsistence may purchase, at first cost price, of the Captains or commanding officers of companies, in the service of the Confederate States, such articles or parts of the ration as are not drawn, nor consumed. But this applies only to such articles as were actually issued and not consumed, or would actually have been issued, and does not apply to such parts of the ration as the Commissary does not habitually have on hand for issue.

1144. The accounts for such purchases will be made in duplicate, (see Form No. 19,) and the articles will be taken up by the Commissary on his monthly return, as if it were an original purchase. The money paid to the Captains constitutes a company fund.

1145. 1st. Duplicate originals of all contracts on account of subsistence will be sent to the Commissary-General's office *through* the principal Commissary of Subsistence of the Military Department in which the contract is made. The *place of residence* of each surety to the bond must be named therein with particularity. Where the form is prescribed it will be followed; in all cases contracts must be drawn up and executed to meet the requirements of the law. Every contract, whether for services or for the furnishing of supplies, which contemplates a partial performance, from time to time, continuing until the whole duty is performed, or the whole delivery of the enumerated articles is effected, must provide in express terms for its earlier termination, if the Commissary-General shall so direct.

1146. Estimates for funds must be rendered in duplicate.

1147. In order to establish an invariable rule for ascertaining the nett weight of beef cattle received on the hoof, the following mode is adopted, and for the future, in all cases will be observed:

1. When practicable, cattle presented for acceptance must be weighed upon the scales. From the live weight of a steer, thus ascertained, his nett weight shall be determined by deducting forty-five per centum, when his gross weight exceeds thirteen hundred (1300) pounds, and fifty per centum when it is less than that, and not under eight hundred (800) pounds.

2. When it is impracticable to weigh upon the scales, one or more average steers must be selected, killed and dressed in the usual manner. The average nett weight of these (neck and shanks excluded) will be accepted as the average nett weight of the herd. In all written instruments for the delivery of cattle on the hoof, the manner prescribed above, for ascertaining nett weight, must, in express terms, be inserted; in verbal agreements, it must be understood and accepted by the party delivering the cattle. Vouchers for the payments of cattle will state the manner pursued in determining their nett weight, except where payment has been made on the certificate of an officer, in which case the certificate will state the mode followed.

3. With a view to the prevention of losses now so frequently occurring, from over-estimating the weight of cattle received on the hoof, the serious attention of officers and agents serving in this department is specially called to the exercise of greater care in the discharge of this important duty.

1148. When fresh beef can be provided, it will be issued to the troops five times per week. When the circumstances are favorable, and it can be done with advantage to the Government, the Subsistence Department will keep beef cattle to supply the issues.

1149. The following issues and substitutions may be made: When, from excessive fatigue or exposure, the commanding officer may deem it necessary, he may direct the issue of whiskey to the enlisted men of his command, not to exceed a gill per man for each day. Tea may be issued in lieu of coffee, at the rate of one and a half pounds per one hundred rations. Two "issues" per week of "desiccated vegetables" may be made in lieu of "beans" or "rice." Potatoes and onions, when issued, will always be in lieu of rice or beans. Potatoes at the rate of a pound per ration; onions at the rate of three pecks per hundred rations.

FORM 1.

Return of Provisions received and issued at ——, during the month
Confederate

DATE. (1860.)	No. of voucher.	FROM WHOM RECEIVED.	PORK. Barrels.	PORK. Pounds.	PORK. Ounces.
		Balance on hand, as per last return, . . .			
Oct. 16	1	2d Lieut. J. R., 4th Infantry, A. A. C. S. . .			
" 30	2	H. C., agent Subsistence Department, . .			
" 31	3	Major T. W. L., C. S., C. S. A., . . .			
" 31		W. J. R., contractor for fresh beef, ...			
" 31		Purchased this month, as per abstract, . .			
" 31		Gained in issuing, ...			
Total to be accounted for, ...					
Oct. 31	1	To troops (regulars) as per abstract, . . .			
" 31	2	To volunteers do . . .			
" 31	3	To citizens in the Qr. Mr's Dept., as per abstract, .			
" 31	4	To sick in hospital, as per abstract, . . .			
" 31	5	To extra issues, do . . .			
" 31	6	To sales to officers, do . . .			
" 15	7	Capt. G. T. H., A. C. S., mil. service, . .			
" 13	8	H. P. C., Agent Subsistence Department, . .			
" 23	9	Capt. W. W., A. Qr. M. for transportation, . .			
" 31	10	Wastage, as per certificate, ...			
		Total issued, ...			
Balance on hand, ...					

FORM 1.

of ——, 18 , *by* ——, *Assistant Commissary of Subsistence, States Army.*

FRESH BEEF.		SALT BEEF.			BACON.		HAMS.		FLOUR.			HARD BREAD.	CORN MEAL.	BEANS.			RICE.		COFFEE.		SUGAR.		CANDLES.		KROUT.
Pounds.	Ounces.	Barrels.	Pounds.	Ounces.	Pounds.	Ounces.	Pounds.	Ounces.	Barrels.	Pounds.	Ounces.	Pounds.	Pounds.	Bushels.	Quarts.	Gills.	Pounds.	Ounces.	Pounds.	Ounces.	Pounds.	Ounces.	Pounds.	Ounces.	Barrels.

FORM 1—Continued.

VINEGAR.			SOAP.		SALT.			MOLASSES.		PICKLES.			DRIED APPLES.		CHICKENS.	HAY.	CORN.	Remarks.
Gallons.	Quarts.	Gills.	Pounds.	Ounces.	Bushels.	Quarts.	Gills.	Gallons.	Quarts.	Barrels.	Half Barrels.	Kegs.	Bushels.	Pounds.	Pairs of.	Pounds.	Bushels.	

A. J.,
Assistant Commissary.

FORM 2.

Abstract of Provisions issued from the , 18 , to the , 18 , to the Troops of the Confederate States stationed at the post of , by , Commissary of Subsistence.

Date.	No. of return.	No. of men.	No. of women.	No. of days drawn for.	Commencing.	Ending.	Rations of pork.		Rations of fresh beef.		Rations of bacon.		Rations of flour.		Rations of hard bread.		Rations of beans.		Rations of rice.		Rations of coffee.		Rations of sugar.		Rations of vinegar.		Rations of candles (sperm or tallow.)		Rations of soap.		Rations of salt.		Names of companies or regiments.
Total number of rations, ...																																	
							Barrels.	Pounds.	Pounds.	Ounces.	Pounds.	Ounces.	Barrels.	Pounds.	Pounds.	Ounces.	Bushels.	Quarts.	Pounds.	Ounces.	Pounds.	Ounces.	Pounds.	Ounces.	Gallons.	Quarts.	Pounds.	Ounces.	Pounds.	Ounces.	Bushels.	Quarts.	
Quantity in bulk, ...																																	

I hereby certify that I have carefully compared the above abstract with the original returns now in my possession, and find that they amount to rations of fresh beef, rations of pork, rations of bacon, rations of flour, rations of hard bread, rations of beans, rations of rice, rations of coffee, rations of sugar, rations of vinegar, rations of candles, (sperm or tallow,) rations of soap, rations of salt.

——— ———, *Commanding.*

FORM 3.

Abstract of Provisions issued from the ——— to the ——— day of
charge of ——— ———, Assistant Surgeon, C. S. Army, by

Number of return.	Number of Men.	Number of days drawn for.	Commencing.	Ending.	Total number of rations due hospital.	Rations of Pork.	Rations of fresh beef.	Rations of flour.	Rations of hard bread.	Rations of rice.	Rations of coffee.	Rations of sugar.	Rations of Vinegar.	Rations of Candles.
						RATIONS ACTUALLY REQUIRED FOR CONSUMPTION IN THE HOSPITAL.								
1	5	8	Oct, 18	Oct'r 25	40	40		30	10	40	40	40	50	40
2			" 18											
3	27	4	" 20	" 23	108	108		108		108	108	108	108	108
4	78	6	" 20	" 25	468	100	168	468		368	200	468	300	468
5	46	4	" 22	" 25	184		84	130		184	184	184		184
6	122	6	" 26	" 30	732	130	300	697			402	732		732
7														
8												84		
Total rations due hospital,					1531									
Total quantity issued.						378	552	1433	10	700	934	1616	448	1532

	Pork: Barrels.	Pork: Pounds.	Pork: Ounces.	Fresh beef: Pounds.	Flour: Barrels.	Flour: Pounds.	Flour: Ounces.	Hard bread: Pounds.	Rice: Pounds.	Coffee: Pounds.	Sugar: Pounds.	Sugar: Ounces.	Vinegar: Gallons.	Vinegar: Quarts.	Vinegar: Gills.	Candles: Pounds.	Candles: Ounces.
Quantity in bulk.	1	83	8	690	8	44	2	10	70	56	193	14	4	1	7	15	5

I certify, on honor, that I have carefully compared the above "abstract" with the
seventy eight rations of pork, five hundred and fifty two rations of fresh beef, fourteen
rations of rice, nine hundred and thirty-four rations of coffee, sixteen hundred and six-
and thirty-two rations of candles, fifteen hundred and thirty two rations of soap, eight
purchases, amounting to two dollars and seventy eight cents, were required by me for,
consumption in the hospital.

Compared with returns of men in hospital, and found correct.

——— ———, *Commanding.*

FORM 3.

———, 18 , *to men in Hospital at New Orleans, Louisiana, under the Lieutenant J. T. J., 3d Infantry, A. C. S.*

REMARKS.

Rations of soap.	Rations of salt.	Gallons of molasses.
40	40	
		2
108	108	
468	200	
184		
732	400	
		10
	100	
1532	848	12

Pounds.	Ounces.	Quarts.	Gills.	Gallons.
61	4	16	7	12

MONTHLY STATEMENT OF THE HOSPITAL FUND.

DR. To balance due hospital last month,						$0	00
1532 rations, being whole amount due this month, at 9½ cents per ration,						145	54
ISSUED.							
CR. By the following provisions at contract prices:							
283½ pounds of pork at 6 cents per pound,			17	01			
690 pounds of fresh beef at 4 cts. per pound,			27	60			
1612⅛ pounds of flour at 2 cts. per pound,			32	24¼			
10 pounds of hard bread at 3½ cts. per pound,				35			
70 pounds of rice at 6 cts. per pound,			4	20			
56 pounds of coffee at 9 cts. per pound,			5	04			
193⅞ pounds of sugar at 8 cts. per pound,			15	51			
17⅛ quarts of vinegar at 5 cents per quart,				85⅝			
15 5-16 pounds of candles at 12 cts. per pound,			1	83¾			
61⅛ pounds of soap at 6 cts. per pound,			3	67⅜			
16⅝ quarts of salt at 3 cts. per quart,				50⅝			
12 gallons of molasses at 28 cts. per gallon.			3	36			
			112	18¾			
PURCHASED.							
2 pairs of chickens at 87½ cts. per pair,	1	75					
4 quarts of milk at 7 cts. per quart,		28					
3 dozen oranges at 25 cts. per dozen,		75					
			2	78			
Total expended,						114	96¾
Balance due this month,						30	57¼

original returns now in my possession, and find that they amount to three hundred and
hundred and thirty-three rations of flour, ten rations of hard bread, seven hundred
teen rations of sugar, four hundred and forty-eight rations of vinegar, fifteen hundred
hundred and forty-eight rations of salt, and twelve gallons of molasses; and that the
and issued to, the sick, and that the rations drawn in kind were actually required for

(DUPLICATES.)

J. C. J. *Assistant Surgeon C. S. Army.*

FORM 4.

Abstract of extra issues to the troops at , during the month of , by . A. C. S.

Date.	Number of return.	Number of rations.	Number of pounds of candles.	Gallons of pickled onions.	Bushels of dried apples.	Remarks.
						Guard at ——. Sick of ——. Anti-scorbutics.

I certify that the anti-scorbutics were necessary to the health of the troops, rendered so by the following circumstances:

Surgeon.

I certify that I have carefully compared the above abstract with the original returns now in my possession, and find that they amount to rations of and pounds of candles, and

Commanding.

FORM 5.

Abstract of Provisions sold to officers at , during the month of , by , A. C. S.

ARTICLES AND QUANTITIES SOLD.	AMOUNT.	
	Dolls.	Cts.
—— pounds of pork, ...		
—— pounds of fresh beef, ...		
—— barrels of flour, ...		
—— bushels of beans, ...		
—— pounds of soap, ...		
—— pounds of candles, ...		
—— bushels of salt, ...		
—— gallons of vinegar, ...		
—— pounds of sugar, ...		
—— pounds of coffee, ...		
Total, ...		

I certify that the above is a correct statement of all sales of subsistence stores made to officers at this post during the month of , 186 .

A. C. S.

I certify that I have compared the above abstract with the officers' certified list of purchases for their own use and the use of their families, and find the abstract correct.

Commanding.

FORM 6.

Monthly Summary Statement of Funds received and disbursed at , in , 186 .

To amount disbursed this month,.....			By balance as per last account, ...		
			By cash received from the treasury of Confederate States this month, ...		
			By cash from agents, sales, &c.,...............		
To balance due the Confederate States,					

I certify that the above is a true statement of all moneys received and expended by me on account of subsistence during the month, and the balance is in

, *Assistant Commissary of Subsistence.*

FORM 7.

DR. *The Confederate States, on account of Army Subsistence, in the quarter ending the day of 186 , in account with Lieutenant , Regiment Assistant Commissary of Subsistence at* CR.

Date.		Dolls.	Cts.	Date.		Dolls.	Cts.
	To amount disbursed per abstract of purchases,........................	667	18		By balance as per last statement,.........	156	78
	To amount disbursed per abstract of contingencies,........................	300	70		By cash received from Treasury of Confederate States,........................	1200	00
	To amount turned over to Lieut. John Forbes as per receipt,................	550	00		By cash from sales to officers,............	550	10
	To balance due Confederate States,.....	449	00		By cash from other sales, &c.,.............	60	00
		1966	88			1966	88

I certify that the above account current exhibits an accurate and true statement of all money received and expended by me on account of the subsistence of the army, not heretofore accounted for; and that the balance of dollars and cents is due from , and is deposited in in funds.

, A. B., *Assistant Commissary of Subsistence.*

FORM 8.

Abstract of Purchases made on account of Subsistence of the Army, by , at , in the quarter ending .

Date.	Number.	From whom purchased.	Fresh Beef.	Pork.	Flour.	Beans.	Rice.	Coffee.	Sugar.	Vinegar.	Candles.	Soap.	Salt.	Chickens.	Hay.	Corn.	Amount.	
			Pounds.	Barrels.	Barrels.	Bushels.	Pounds.	Pounds.	Pounds.	Gallons.	Pounds.	Pounds.	Bushels.	Pairs of.	Pounds.	Bushels.	Dollars.	Cents.
		Total amount,																

I certify that the purchases were made agreeably to the above abstract, and that the sums were actually paid as charged; and, also, that I was wholly uninterested in the purchases, and that the articles were purchased at the lowest market price.

FORM 9.

Abstract of Disbursements, on account of contingencies, by Lieut. , Assistant Commissary of Subsistence, in the quarter ending the day of , 186 .

Date.	Number of voucher.	To whom paid.	On what account.	Remarks.	Amount.
			Commutation of rations.		
			Weights and measures.		
			Clerk, ...	By authority, October 16.	
			Stationery.		
			Per diem to extra-duty men.		

Lieut., Reg't,
Assistant Commissary of Subsistence.

FORM 10.

Consolidated Abstract of Provisions sold to officers at , in the quarter ending , by , A. C. S.

Month.	Fresh beef, pounds of.	Bacon, pounds of.	Pork, pounds of.	Salt beef, pounds of.	Flour, pounds of.	Coffee, pounds of.	Sugar, pounds of.	Hard bread, pounds of.	Rice, pounds of.	Candles, pounds of.	Soap, pounds of.	Salt, quarts of.	Vinegar, gallons of.		TOTAL AMOUNT.		Remarks.	
																	Pounds of fresh beef, at Pounds of bacon, at. . . Pounds of pork, at. . . . Pounds of salt beef, at Pounds of flour, at. . . . Pounds of coffee, at. . Pounds of sugar, at. . . . Pounds of hard bread, at Pounds of rice, at. . . . . Pounds of candles, at. . Pounds of soap, at. . . .	
Total,																		
Price,																		

I certify that the above is correct.

Estimate of funds required for purchasing Fresh Beef, and for contingences for the troops stationed at , for the quarter ending , 18 .

Troops.	Strength.	Number of weeks.	Number of rations per week.	Number of pounds per week.	Total number of pounds required.	Price pr. pound.	Total amount.		Stationery.	Hospital.	Total amount required.		Remarks.
						Cts.	Dols	Cts.	Dols	Dols	Dols	Cts.	
Company of ——, ...													
Hospital contingences, ...													
Amount, ...													
Deduct the probable amount that will remain on hand, quarter ending													
Total amount required to meet the expenditures in the quarter ending													

—— ——, *Commissary.*

FORM 12.

Return of Commissary Property received, issued, and remaining on hand, at , during the quarter ending the day of , 186 , by , A. C. S.

From whom received.	Date.	No. of voucher.	Stationery.	Office Furniture.	Scales, Weights, &c.	Tools.
On hand per last return,........ Received from Lieut. Hall,.....						
Total to be accounted for,.......						
Turned over to Capt. Johns,....						
Total issued and expended,....						
Remaining on hand,...........						

I certify that the above return is correct, and that the articles specified were actually and necessarily expended in the public service.

FORM 13.

Provision Return for Captain , Company , Regiment , for days, commencing , and ending

Post or station.	Number of men.	Number of women.	Total.	Number of days.	Number of rations.	Rations of.												Remarks.
						Fresh be f.	Pork.	Flour.	Beans.	Rice.	Coffee.	Sugar.	Vinegar.	Candles.	Soap.	Salt.		

——— ———, *Commanding Company.*

The A. C. S. will issue agreeably to the above return.

——— ———, *Commanding Post.*

FORM 14.

Consolidated Provision Return for Regiment of , for days, commencing , and ending .

Post or Station.	Number of men.	Number of women.	Total.	Number of days.	Number of rations.	Rations of. Fresh beef.	Pork.	Flour.	Beans.	Rice.	Coffee.	Sugar.	Vinegar.	Candles.	Soap.	Salt.	Remarks.
																	See the remark

——— ———, *Commanding Regiment.*

The A. C. S. will issue on the above return.

——— ———, *Commanding Officer.*

10

COUNTY OF ——— ———,
State of ——— ———,

Personally appeared before me, ——— ———, inspector for said county, and made oath that, at the request of the parties concerned, he inspected the quality of provisions below enumerated, delivered as supplies for the troops at Fort ———, on the contract of ———, for the year ———, and found them to be of the quantity and quality undermentioned:

——— barrels of corn-fed pork, excluding the parts directed in the contract, and in quality as therein designated.
——— barrels of superfine flour.
——— bushels of good sound beans.
——— gallons of good cider or wine vinegar.
——— pounds of good hard soap.
——— pounds of tallow candles with cotton wicks.
——— bushels of clean dry salt.

S. T., *Inspector.*

Sworn and subscribed before me this ——— day of ———.

A. B., *Justice of the Peace.*

Received, Fort ———, 10th August, 1861, the provisions above enumerated.

C. D., *Lieut., and A. C. S.*

FORM 1d.

Dr. *The Confederate States,*

To —— ——, Special Contractor.

For rations issued to recruits under the command of ——, at ——, from —— to ——, as per accompanying abstract:

Complete rations, at —— cents, ...	$
—— lbs. extra soap, at —— cents, ...	
—— lbs. extra candles, at —— cents.	
Due contractor, ...	$

Received from the Confederate States, (or Lieutenant B., recruiting officer,) —— dollars and —— cents, in full of the above account.

Abstract of Rations issued to recruits stationed at , under command of , from to , by special contract.

Date.	No. of return.	No. of men	No of women.	Commencing.	Ending.	No. of days drawn for.	No. of complete rations,	Remarks.
Total number of complete rations,								

I certify that I have carefully compared the above abstract with the original returns now in my possession, and they amount to complete rations.

———— ————, *Recruiting Officer.*

FORM 88.

The Confederate States

To Sergeant James McMullen, DR.

Date.			
1861. June 30.	For commutation of rations while on detached service, returning to his branch rendezvous, en route from , to , from the 8th to the 12th June, 1861—five days, at 75 cents per day, ...	$ 3	75

I certify, that the above account is correct; that the commutation was made by my order, and was necessary for the public service, it being impracticable to take rations in kind.

—— ——, *Recruiting Officer.*

Received, at , 30th June, 1861, from , three dollars and seventy-five cents, in full of the above.

JAMES H. McMULLEN.

FORM 19.

The Confederate States

To A. B. DR.

Date.			Dolls.	Cts.
(The place and time of purchase.)	For 100 barrels flour @	$6 00	600	00
	" 500 pounds bacon @	10	50	00
			$650	00

I certify that the above account is correct and just, and that the articles were (or will be) accounted for on my returns for the month of , 1861, and that the purchases were made by the order of (state by whom).

Signed C. D. (rank), *Commissary of Subsistence.*

(DUPLICATES.)

Received at , on the of , 1861, of , Commissary of Subsistence C. S. A., dollars cents, in full of the above account.

(Signed) "A. B."

NOTE.—When the officer making the purchases does not pay the account, he will add that statement to the certificate and state the cause of non-payment.

FORM 20.

Report of Persons and Articles employed and hired at , du

Running Numbers.	No. of each class.	Names of persons and articles hired.	Designati'n and occupation.	Service during the month.			Rate of hire or compensation.			Date of contract, agreement or entry into service,
				From.	To.	Days.	Amount.		Day or month.	
							Dols	Cts.		
1	1	House, 3 rooms,	Quarters,	1	31	31	40	00	Month,	July 1, 1861,
2	2	House, 4 rooms,	Storehouse,	3	31	29	31	00	Month,	Dec. 3, 1860,
3	3	House, 2 rooms,	Guard,	1	31	31	10	00	Month,	Dec. 3, 1860,
1	1	Chas. James,	Clerk,	1	31	31	83	33	Month,	May 3, 1861,
2	1	John Johns,	Storekeeper	7	10	4	50	00	Month,	Jun. 4, 1861,
3	1	Slave Tom,	Messenger,	7	12	6	20	00	Month,	Jan. 1, 1861,
4	1	Peter Jones,	Laborer,	22	31	7	30	00	Month,	Dec. 3, 1860,
5	1	M. Murphy,	Laborer,	1	31	31	30	00	Month,	Jan. 7, 1861,

Amount of rent and hire during the month,

I certify, on honor, that the above is a true report of all the persons and that the observations under the head of Remarks, and the statement of

Examined: (DUPLICATES.)

C. D., *Commanding*

NOTE.—Houses must not be hired except in cases where they cannot be monthly.)

FORM 20.

ring the month of , 186 , by Capt. A. B., A. C. S., C. S. A.

By whom owned.	Amount of pay or rent in the month. Dols	Cts.	Remarks, showing by whom the buildings were occupied, and for what purpose; and how the men were employed during the month. (Transfers and discharges noticed under this head.)	Time and amount due and remaining unpaid. From 1860	To 1861.	Amount. Dols.	Cts.
A. Brewer,	40	00	Major 3d Infantry,	Dec. 1,	Jan 31,	80	00
B. Gott,	29	00	Subsistence store and office,	Dec. 3,	Jan 31,	60	00
C. Robinson,	10	00	Guard for sub. stores.				
	83	33	Office of A. C. S., C. S. A.				
	6	66	By order Commiss'y Gen'l.				
N O Anderson	4	00	" " "				
	7	00	" " "				
	30	00	" " "				
	209	99	Total amount due and unpaid,			140	00

and articles employed and hired by me during the month of , 186
amounts due and remaining unpaid are correct.

A. B., *Capt. and A. C. S.*

furnished by the Quartermaster's Department. (This report to be rendered

FORM 21.

We, the undersigned, do hereby acknowledge to have received of Capt. A. B. the sums set opposite our names respectively, it being in full for services for the time stated.

Date.	Names.	Occupation.	Time.	Rate of Hire.		Amount.		Signatures.	Witness.
				Dolls.	Cts.	Dolls.	Cts.		
Aug. 31.	N. O. Anderson,	Clerk,	1 mo.	83	33	83	33	N. O. Anderson.	
	John James,	Store-keeper,	1 mo.	50	00	50	00	John James.	
	Tom (slave),	Messenger,	1 mo.	20	00	20	00	A.S. Brewer (owner).	N. O. Anderson, [Clerk.
	Jim (slave),	Laborer,	15 days.	1	00	15	00	John Smith (owner).	

I certify that the above Roll is correct and just, and that the services were actually rendered as stated, and were necessary for the public service.

(DUPLICATES.)

NOTE.—This is a voucher of abstract of Disbursements (Form 9).

FORM 22.

Invoice of Subsistence Stores (Provisions) delivered by , to , at , on the day of , 186 .

Number and quantity.	Articles.	Cost.	Condition when transferred.	Remarks.
500 barrels.	Pork,	$20 per barrel,	Good,	Well coopered.
200 "	Flour,	$6 " "	"	Superfine, (well coopered).
390 lb. 10 oz.	Bacon,	12 cts. per lb.	"	Loose, or in boxes or casks.

I certify that I have this day transferred to , Commissary of Subsistence C. S. Army, the articles specified in the foregoing list.

(Signed) A. B., (rank,)
Commissary of Subsistence.

(DUPLICATES.)

NOTE.—Duplicates to be given. When no invoices are received, the receiving officer will substitute for this form of voucher a list of the stores received, certified to by himself. When the person sending the articles without invoice is known, it will be entered in his name.

FORM 23.

Invoice of Commissary Property, (Stationery, Measures, Scales, &c., &c.,) delivered by , *to* , *at* , *on this* *day of* , 186 .

Number and quantity.	Articles.	Cost.	Condition when transferred.	Remarks.
6 reams,	Letter paper,	$2 per ream,	New.	
2 "	Cap "	$1.50 per ream,	"	
5 setts,	Dry measures,	$3 per sett,	Half worn.	
5 "	Liquid measures,	$2 " "	Worn out.	
12 (twelve)	Faucetts,	12 cents each,	New.	
4 (four),	Molasses gates,	25 " "	"	
6 (six),	Butcher knives,	37 " "	"	

I certify that I have this day transferred to , Commissary of Subsistence C. S. Army, the articles specified in the foregoing list.

(Signed) A. B., (rank,)
Commissary of Subsistence.

(DUPLICATES.)

NOTE.—Same as an invoice of stores.

FORM 24.

Received at , *the* *day of* , 186 , *of* , *Commissary of Subsistence, the following articles of Subsistence Stores, (Provisions.)*

Number or quantity.	Articles.	Condition.	Remarks.
100 barrels,	Pork,	In good order.	
300 "	Flour,	" "	
1,000 pounds,	Bacon,	" "	

(Signed) A. B., (rank,)
Commissary of Subsistence.

(DUPLICATE.)

NOTE.—To be given in duplicate.

FORM 25.

Descriptive List of Persons and Articles employed and hired in the Commissary's Department, and transferred by , *at* , *to* , *Assistant Commissary C. S. A., at* , *on the* *day of* , 186 .

No. of each class.	Articles and names of persons.	Designation and occupation.	Period for which pay is due.				Rate of hire or compensation.			Amount due.		Date of contract, agreement, or entry into service.	By whom owned and where.	Remarks.
			From.	To.	Month.	Days.	Dollars.	Cents.	Month or day.	Dollars.	Cents.			
Total amount due,………………														

I certify that the above is a true list of persons and articles transferred by me to , at , on the day of , 186 , and that the periods of service, rates of hire or compensation, and amounts due are correctly stated.

NOTE.—To be given in duplicate, by the officer transferring the charge of a depot or station

FORM 26.

ARTICLES OF AGREEMENT made and entered into this day of , Anno Domini one thousand eight hundred and sixty- , between , an officer in the Confederate Army, on the one part, and , of the county of , and State of , of the other part.

This agreement witnesseth, That the said , for and on behalf of the Confederate States of America, and the said heirs, executors and administrators, have covenanted and agreed, and by these presents do mutually covenant and agree, to and with each other, as follows, viz:

First. That the said heirs, executors and administrators shall supply, or cause to be supplied and issued, at , all the rations, to consist of the articles hereinafter specified, that shall be required for the use of the Confederate States recruits stationed at the place aforesaid, commencing on the day of , one thousand eight hundred and sixty- , and ending on the day of , eighteen hundred and , or such earlier day as the Commissary General may direct, at the price of cents mills for each complete ration.

Second. That the ration to be furnished by virtue of this contract shall consist of the following articles, viz: One and a quarter pounds of fresh beef, or three-quarters of a pound of salted pork, eighteen ounces of bread or flour, and at the rate of eight quarts of beans or ten pounds of rice, six pounds of coffee, twelve pounds of sugar, four quarts of vinegar, one and a half pounds of tallow, or one pound of sperm candles, four pounds of soap, and two quarts of salt to every hundred rations, or the contractor shall furnish the men with good and wholesome board and lodgings, at the option of the recruiting officer; and the recruiting party shall have the privilege of hanging out a flag from the place of rendezvous.

Third. That fresh beef shall be issued at least twice in each week, if required by the commanding officer.

Fourth. It is clearly understood that the provisions stipulated to be furnished and delivered under this contract shall be of the first quality.

Fifth. Should any difficulty arise respecting the quality of the provisions stipulated to be delivered under this contract, then the commanding officer is to appoint a disinterested person, to meet one of the same description to be appointed by the contractor. These two, thus appointed, will have power to decide on the equality of the provisions; but should they disagree, then a third person is to be chosen by the two already appointed, the whole to act under oath, and the opinion of the majority to be final in the case.

Witness,

FORM 27.

ARTICLES OF AGREEMENT made this day of , eighteen hundred and sixty- , between , Assistant Commissary of Subsistence in the service of the Confederate States of America, of the one part, and , of , in the State of , of the other part.

This agreement witnesseth, That the said , for and on behalf of the Confederate States of America, and the said , for himself, his heirs, executors and administrators, have mutually agreed, and by these presents do mutually covenant and agree, to and with each other, in the manner following, viz :

First. That the said shall deliver at ; *fresh beef*, of a good and wholesome quality, in quarters, with an equal proportion of each, (necks and shanks to be excluded,) in such quantities as may be from time to time required for the troops, not exceeding thrice in each week, on such days as shall be designated by the Assistant Commissary of Subsistence.

This contract to be in force for months, or such less time as the Commissary General may direct, commencing on the day of , eighteen hundred and sixty-

Second. The said shall receive cents and mills per pound for every pound of *fresh beef* delivered and accepted under this contract.

Third. Payment shall be made monthly for the amount of *fresh beef* furnished under this contract; but in the event of the Assistant Commissary of Subsistence being without funds, then payment to be made as soon after as funds may be received for that purpose.

Fourth. That whenever and as often as the *beef* specified to be issued by this contract shall, in the opinion of the commanding officer, be unfit for issue, or of a quality inferior to that required by the contract, a survey shall be held thereon by two officers, to be designated by the commanding officer; and in case of disagreement, a third person shall be chosen by those two officers; the three thus appointed and chosen shall have power to reject such parts or the whole of the *fresh beef* as to them appear unfit for issue, or of a quality inferior to that contracted for.

Fifth. That in case of failure or deficiency in the quality or quantity of the *fresh beef* stipulated to be delivered, then the Assistant Commissary of Subsistence shall have power to supply the deficiency by purchase; and the said will be charged with the difference of cost.

In witness whereof, the undersigned have hereunto placed their hands and seals, the day and date above written.

Witness,

FORM 28.

BY THESE PRESENTS: That we, and , are held
l to the Confederate States of America in the sum of
ioney of the Confederate States; for which payment well
iade, we bind ourselves, and each of us, our and each of
ors and administrators, for and in the whole, jointly and
by these presents.
ır seals, dated the day of , in the year of our
ındred and sixty-
his obligation is such, That if the above bounden
and administrators, or any of them, shall and do in all
truly observe, perform, fulfill, accomplish and keep, all
covenants, conditions and ageements whatsoever, which,
e said , heirs, executors or administrators, are or
ierved, performed, fulfilled, accomplished and kept, comned in certain articles of agreement or contract, bearing
thousand eight hundred and sixty- , between
, concerning the supply and delivery of *fresh beef* to the
or rations to recruits at , according to the true intent
the said articles of agreement or contract, then the above
void: otherwise to remain in full force and virtue.

TABLE SHOWING THE WEIGHT AND BULK OF RATIONS.

Number of rations.	Tare in pounds.	Nett weight in pounds.	Gross weight in pounds.	Bulk in barrels.	Kind of ration.
1000	655.9301	2391.25	3047.1801	11.8224	Pork, flour, beans, and small rations.
1	.6559	2.3912	3.0471	.01182	Do do do
1000	402.9968	2016.25	2419.2468	16.2656	Bread, (12 oz.) bacon and do
1	.4029	2.0162	2.4192	.01626	Do do do
1000	460.2257	2266.25	2726.4757	19.2827	Bread, (16 oz.) do do
1	.4662	2.2662	2.7264	.019[illegible]	Do do do
One thousand rations of Pork,	468.75	750.	1218.75	3.75	
Bacon,	153.1861	750.	903.1861	4.9019	
Flour,	109.0561	1125.	1234.0561	5.7397	
Pilot bread,	171.6867	750.	921.6867	9.031	¾ lb. to one ration.
do	228.9156	1000.	1228.9156	12.048	1 lb. " "
Beans,	22.3187	155.	177.3187	0.7142	
Rice,	14.5	100.	114.5	0.4629	
Coffee,	10.901	60.	70.901	0.3488	
Sugar,	15.625	120.	135.625	0.5	
Vinegar,	15.	92.5	107.5	0.333	
Candles,	2.5	15.	17.5	0.0925	Tallow candles.
Soap,	6.8965	40.	46.8962	0.1877	
Salt,	4.8828	33.75	38.6328	0.1562	

By A. B. E.

RATION TABLE

Of Desiccated Potatoes, and Desiccated and Mixed Vegetables, from 1 *to* 100,000.

Desiccated Potatoes.				Desiccated and Mixed Vegetables.			
No.	lbs.	oz	1/100	No.	lbs.	oz	1/100
1		1	41	1			88
2		2	82	2		1	76
3		4	23	3		2	64
4		5	64	4		3	52
5		7	05	5		4	40
6		8	46	6		5	28
7		9	87	7		6	16
8		11	28	8		7	04
9		12	69	9		7	92
10		14	10	10		8	80
20	1	12	20	20	1	1	60
30	2	10	30	30	1	10	40
40	3	8	40	40	2	3	21
50	4	6	50	50	2	14	00
60	5	4	60	60	3	4	80
70	6	2	70	70	3	13	60
80	7	0	80	80	4	6	40
90	7	14	90	90	4	15	20
100	8	13	00	100	5	8	00
1,000	88	2	00	1,000	55	00	00
10,000	881	4	00	10,000	550	00	00
100,000	8,812	8	00	100,000	5,500	00	00

Table Showing the Quantity in Bulk or

Number of Rations.	Pork. Barrels.	Pork. Pounds.	Pork. Ounces.	Beef. Pounds.	Beef. Ounces.	Flour. Barrels.	Flour. Pounds.	Flour. Ounces.	Beans. Bushels.	Beans. Quarts.	Beans. Gills.	Rice. Pounds.	Rice. Ounces.
1			12	1	4		1	2			0.64		1.6
2		1	8	2	8		2	4			1.28		3.2
3		2	4	3	12		3	6			1.92		4.8
4		3		5			4	8			2.56		6.4
5		3	12	6	4		5	10			3.20		8.0
6		4	8	7	8		6	12			3.84		9.6
7		5	4	8	12		7	14			4.48		11.2
8		6		10			9				5.12		12.8
9		6	12	11	4		10	2			5.76		14.4
10		7	8	12	8		11	4			6.40	1	
20		15		25			22	8		1	4.80	2	
30		22	8	37	8		33	12		2	3.20	3	
40		30		50			45			3	1.60	4	
50		37	8	62	8		56	4		4		5	
60		45		75			67	8		4	6.40	6	
70		52	8	87	8		78	12		5	4.80	7	
80		60		100			90			6	3.20	8	
90		67	8	112	8		101	4		7	1.60	9	
100		75		125			112	8		8		10	
1,000	3	150		1,250		5	145		2	16		100	
10,000	37	100		12,500		57	78		25			1,000	
100,000	375			125,000		573	192		250			10,000	

any Number of Rations, from 1 *to* 100,000.

Coffee.		Sugar.		Vinegar.			Candles.		Soap.		Salt.		
Pounds.	Ounces.	Pounds.	Ounces.	Gallons.	Quarts.	Gills.	Pounds.	Ounces.	Pounds.	Ounces.	Bushels.	Quarts.	Gills.
	0.96		1.92			0.32		0.24		0.64			0·16
	1.92		3.84			0.64		0.48		1.28			0.32
	2.88		5.76			0.96		0.72		1.92			0.48
	3.84		7.68			1.28		0.96		2.56			0.64
	4.80		9.60			1.60		1.20		3.20			0.80
	5.76		11.52			1.92		1.44		3.84			0.96
	6.72		13.44			2.24		1.68		4.48			1.12
	7.68		15.36			2.56		1.92		5.12			1.28
	8.64	1	1.28			2.88		2.16		5.76			1.44
	9.60	1	3.20			3.20		2.40		6.40			1.60
1	3.20	2	6.40			6.40		4.80		12.80			3.20
1	12.80	3	9.60		1	1.60		7.20	1	3.20			4.80
2	6.40	4	12.80		1	4.80		9.60	1	9.60			6.40
3		6			2			12.00	2			1	
3	9.60	7	3.20		2	3.20		14.40	2	6.40		1	1.60
4	3.20	8	6.40		2	6.40	1	0.80	2	12.80		1	3.20
4	12.80	9	9.60		3	1.60	1	3.20	3	3.20		1	4.80
5	6.40	10	12.8		3	4.80	1	5.60	3	9.60		1	6.40
6		12		1			1	8 00	4			2	
60		120		10			15		40			20	
600		1,200		100			150		400		6	8	
6,000		12,000		1,000			1,500		4,000		62	16	

ARTICLE XLIII.

MEDICAL DEPARTMENT.

1150. The Surgeon General is charged with the administrative details of the medical department, the government of hospitals, the regulation of the duties of surgeons and assistant surgeons, and the appointment of acting medical officers, when needed, for local or detached service. He will issue orders and instructions relating to the professional duties of medical officers; and all communications from them, which require his action, will be made directly to him.

1151. The Medical Director of an army corps will have the general control of the medical officers.

1152. The Medical Director will inspect the hospitals under his control, and see that the rules and regulations with regard to them and the duties of the surgeons and assistant surgeons are enforced.

1153. He will examine the case books, prescription and diet books, and ascertain the nature of diseases which may have prevailed, and their probable causes; recommend the best method of prevention, and also make such suggestions relative to the situation, construction and economy of the hospitals, and to the police of the camps, as may appear necessary for the benefit and comfort of the sick, and the good of the service.

1154. From the monthly reports of the medical officers of the command (Form 1), he will make to the Surgeon General a consolidated monthly report of the sick and wounded.

1155. He will make to the Surgeon General a monthly return (Form 2) of the medical officers of the command.

1156. The Medical Purveyor will, under the direction of the Surgeon General, purchase all medical and hospital supplies required for the medical department of the army.

1157. Medical Purveyors will make to the Surgeon General, at the end of each fiscal quarter, returns in duplicate (Form 3,) of medical supplies received, issued, and remaining on hand, stating to whom, or from whom, and when and where issued or received. Other medical officers in charge of medical supplies will make similar returns semi-annually, on the 30th of June and the 31st of December; and all medical officers will make them when relieved from the duty to which their returns relate. The returns will show the condition of the stores, and particularly of the instruments, bedding, and furniture. Medical purveyors will furnish abstracts of receipts and issues, with their returns, (Form 4).

1158. Medical disbursing officers will, at the end of each fiscal quarter, render to the Surgeon General, in duplicate, a quarterly account current of moneys received and expended, with the proper vouchers for the payments, and certificates that the services have been rendered and the supplies purchased and received for the medical service, and transmit to him an estimate of the funds required for the next quarter.

1159. The medical supplies for the army are prescribed in the Standard Supply Tables for Hospitals and Field Service.

1160. Medical and hospital supplies will be obtained by making requisitions, in duplicate (Form 5), on the Surgeon General, forwarding them through the Medical Director of the command. If an army be in the field, and there be a Medical Purveyor in charge of supplies, requisitions will be made on him, after receiving the approval of the Medical Dictator. The quantities on hand, of the articles wanted, must be stated in all requisitions.

1161. When it is necessary to purchase medical supplies, those which are indispensable may be procured by the quartermaster, if recourse cannot be had to a medical disbursing officer, on a special requisition (Form 6), and account (Form 7).

1162. In every case of *special* requisition, a duplicate of the requisition shall, at the same time, be transmitted to the Surgeon General for his information.

1163. An officer transferring medical supplies, will furnish a certified invoice to the officer who is to receive them, and transmit a duplicate of it to the Surgeon General. The receiving officer will transmit duplicate receipts (specifying articles and quantities) to the Surgeon General, with a report of the quality and condition of the supplies, and report the same to the issuing officer. A medical officer who turns over medical supplies to a quartermaster for storage or transportation, will forward to the Surgeon General, with the invoice, the quartermaster's receipts for the packages.

1164. Medical officers will take up and account for all medical supplies of the army that come into their possession, and report, when they know it, to whose account they are to be credited.

1165. Medical supplies are not to be detained or diverted from their destination, except in cases of absolute necessity, by commanding generals, who will promptly report the circumstances to the Adjutant General, that orders may be given for supplying the deficiency; and the medical officer receiving them will immediately report the fact to the Surgeon General: and, also, when practicable, notify the officer for whom they were intended.

1166. In all official lists of medical supplies, the articles will be entered in the order of the Supply Tables.

1167. The senior medical officer of each post, regiment, or detachment, will, with the approbation of the commanding officer, select a suitable site for the erection of a hospital, or of hospital tents.

1168. The senior medical officer of a hospital will distribute the patients, according to convenience, and the nature of their complaints, into wards or divisions, under the particular charge of the several assistant surgeons, and will visit them himself each day as frequently as the state of the sick may require, accompanied by the assistant, steward, and nurse.

1169. His prescriptions of medicine and diet are to be written down at once in the proper book, with the name of the patient and the number of his bed; the assistants will fill up the diet table for the day, and direct the administration of the prescribed medicines. He will detail an assistant surgeon to remain at the hospital day and night, when the state of the sick requires it.

1170. In distributing the duties of his assistants, he will ordinarily require the aid of one in the care and preparation of the hospital reports, registers, and records, the rolls, and descriptive lists; and of another, in the charge of the dispensary, instruments, medicines, hospital expenditures, and the preparation of the requisitions and annual returns.

1171. He will enforce the proper hospital regulations to promote health and prevent contagion, by ventilated and not crowded rooms, scrupulous cleanliness, frequent changes of bedding and linen, occasional refilling of the bed sacks and pillow ticks with fresh straw, regularity in meals, attention to cooking, &c.

1172. He will cause to be printed, or written in a legible hand, and hung up in a conspicuous place in each ward, such rules and regulations as he may deem necessary for the guidance of the attendants, and the order, cleanliness, and convenience of the patients.

1173. He will require the steward to take due care of the hospital stores and supplies; to enter in a book, daily, (Form 8), the issues to the wardmasters, cooks, and nurses; to prepare the provision returns, and receive and distribute the rations.

1174. He will require the wardmaster to take charge of the effects of the patients; to register them in a book, (Form 9;) to have them numbered and labeled with the patient's name, rank, and company; to receive from the steward the furniture, bedding, cooking utensils, &c., for use, and keep a record of them, (Form 10), and how distributed to the wards and kitchens, and once a week to take an inventory of the articles in use, and report to him any loss or damage to them, and to return to the steward such as are not required for use.

1175. Assistant Surgeons will obey the orders of their senior surgeon, see that subordinate officers do their duty, and aid in enforcing the regulations of the hospital.

1176. The cooks and nurses are under the orders of the steward. He is responsible for the cleanliness of the wards and kitchens, patients and attendants, and all articles in use. He will ascertain who are present at sunrise and sunset, and tattoo, and report absentees.

1177. At surgeon's call the sick then in the companies will be conducted to the hospital by the first sergeants, who will each hand to the Surgeon, in his company book, a list of all the sick of the company, on which the surgeon shall state who are to remain or go into the hospital; who are to return to quarters as sick or convalescent; what duties the convalescents in quarters are capable of; what cases are feigned; and any other information in regard to the sick of the company, he may have to communicate to the company commander.

1178. Soldiers in hospital, patients or attendants, except stewards, shall be mustered on the rolls of their company, if it be present at the post.

1179. When a soldier in hospital is detached from his company so as not to be mustered with it for pay, his company commander shall certify and send to the hospital his descriptive list, and account of pay and clothing, containing all necessary information relating to his accounts with the Confederate States, on which the surgeon shall enter all payments, stoppages, and issues of clothing to him in hospital. When he leaves the hospital, the medical officer shall certify and remit his descriptive list, showing the state of his accounts. If he is discharged from the service in hospital, the surgeon shall make out his final statements for pay and clothing. If he dies in hospital, the surgeon shall take charge of his effects, and make the reports required in the general regulations concerning soldiers who die absent from their companies.

1180. Patients in hospital are, if possible, to leave their arms and accoutrements with their companies, and in no case to take ammunition into the hospital.

1181. When a patient is transferred from one hospital to another, the medical officer shall send with him an account of his case, and the treatment.

1182. The regulations for the service of hospitals apply, as far as practicable, to the medical service in the field.

1183. In the field, the senior medical officer will inspect camps, and urge the enforcement of stringent rules of police.

1184. The senior medical officer of each hospital, post, regiment, or detachment, will keep the following records, and deliver them to his successor: A register of patients, (Form 11;) a prescription and diet book, (Form 12;) a case book; copies of his requisitions, returns of property, and reports of sick and wounded; and an order and letter book, in which will be transcribed all orders and letters relating to his duties.

1185. He will make the muster and pay rolls of the hospital steward and laundress, and of all soldiers in hospital, sick or on duty, detached from their companies, on the forms furnished from the Adjutant and Inspector-General's office, and according to the directions expressed on them.

1186. The extra pay allowed to soldiers acting as cooks and nurses in hospitals, will be paid by the Quartermaster Department, the extra service being noted on the hospital muster rolls.

1187. The senior medical officer will select the cooks, nurses, and laundresses, with the approval of the commanding officer. Cooks and nurses, taken from the privates, will be exempt from other duty, but shall attend the parades for muster and weekly inspection of their companies at the post, unless specially excused by the commanding officer. They will not be removed except for misdemeanor, and at the request of the medical officer, unless in cases of urgent necessity, and then only by the order of the commanding officer.

1188. Cooks and nurses, other than enlisted men or volunteers, are subject to military control. They will be paid on the hospital muster rolls, by the Quartermaster Department, at the rates at which they have been engaged, which, in no case, will exceed $18.50 per month, being the pay proper of an enlisted man, together with extra pay allowed in paragraph 1186. They should not be employed for a less period than a calendar month.

1189. Ordinarily, hospital attendants are allowed as follows: To a general hospital, one steward, one nurse as wardmaster, one nurse to ten patients, one laundress to twenty, and one cook to thirty; to a hospital where the command exceeds five companies, one steward and wardmaster, one cook, two laundresses, and four nurses; to a post or garrison of one company, one steward and wardmaster, one nurse, one cook, and one laundress; and for every two companies more, one nurse; at arsenals, where the number of enlisted men is not less than fourteen, one laundress is allowed. The allowance of hospital attendants on the field will be, for commands of one company and not exceeding five, one steward, one cook, and for each company, one nurse; for regiments, or commands of over five companies, one steward, two cooks, and for each company, one nurse.

1190. Medical officers, where on duty, will attend the officers and enlisted men, and the laundress authorized by law; and at stations where other medical attendance cannot be procured, and on marches, the hired men of the army. Medicines will be dispensed to the families of officers and soldiers, and to all persons entitled to medical attendance; hospital stores to enlisted men.

1191. Medical officers, in giving certificates of disability, (Form 13,) are to take particular care in all cases that have not been under their charge; and especially in epilepsy, convulsions, chronic rheumatism, derangement of the urinary organs opthalmia, ulcers, or any obscure disease, liable to be feigned or purposely produced; and in no case shall such certificate be given until after sufficient time and examination to detect any attempt at deception.

1192. In passing a recruit, the medical officer is to examine him stripped; to see that he has free use of his limbs; that his chest is ample; that his hearing, vision, and speech are perfect; that he has no tumors, or ulcerated or extensively cicatrized legs; no rupture, or chronic cutaneous affection; that he has not received any contusion, or wound of the head, that may impair his faculties; that he is not a drunkard; is not subject to convulsions, and has no infectious disorder, nor any other that may unfit him for military service.

1193. Medical officers attending recruiting rendezvous will keep a record (Form 14) of all the recruits examined by them. Books for this purpose will be procured by application to the Surgeon General, to whom they will be returned when filled.

1194. As soon as a recruit joins any regiment or station, he shall be examined by the medical officer, and vaccinated when it is required.

1195. The senior medical officer of each hospital, post, regiment, or detachment, will make monthly to the Medical Director, and quarterly to the Surgeon General, a report of sick and wounded, and of deaths, and of discharges for disability, (Form 1;) and transmit to the Surgeon General a copy of the *Monthly Statement of the Hospital Fund*, (Form 19.)

1196. After surgeon's call, he will make a morning report of the sick to the commanding officer, (Form 15.)

1197. Every medical officer will report to the Surgeon General and to the Medical Director, the date when he arrives at a station, or when he leaves it, and his orders in the case, and at the end of each month, whenever not at his station, whether on service or on leave of absence; and when on leave of absence, his post-office address for the next month.

1198. They will promptly acknowledge the receipt of all orders relating to their movements; and in all official communications, when at stations the positions of which are not well known, they will state the nearest post-office.

1199. When it is necessary to employ a private physician as medical officer, the Medical Director, or if circumstances preclude reference to him, the commanding officer, may execute a written contract, (notifying the Medical-Director,) conditioned as in Form 16, at a stated compensation, not to exceed $50 a month when the number of officers and men, with authorized laundresses, is 100 or more; $40 when it is from 50 to 100, and $30 when it is under 50.

1200. But when he is required to abandon his own business, and give his whole time to the public service, the contract may be not to exceed $80 a month; and not to exceed $100, besides transportation in kind, to be furnished by the Quartermaster's Department, where he is required to accompany troops on marches or transports. But a private physician will not be employed to accompany troops on marches or transports, except by orders from the War Department, or, in particular and urgent cases, by the order of the officer directing the movement.

1201. And when a private physician is required to furnish medicines, he will be paid in addition from 25 to 50 per cent., to be determined by the Surgeon General, on the amount allowed by contract.

1202. In all cases, a duplicate of the contract, with a particular statement of the circumstances which make it necessary, appended, will be transmitted forthwith to the Surgeon General for approval; and the commanding officer for the time being will at once discontinue it, whenever the necessity for it ceases, or the Surgeon General may so direct.

1203. The physician's account of pay due must be sent to the Surgeon General for payment, vouched by the certificate of the commanding officer, that it is correct and agreeable to contract, and that the services have been duly rendered. But on the frontier or in the field, when it cannot conveniently be submitted to the Surgeon General, the contract having already received his approval, the account may be paid on the order of the commanding officer, not to exceed the regulated amount, by a Quartermaster or a medical disbursing officer.

1204. Private physicians, employed by contract, will conform to the regulations, and accordingly will keep all the records, and make the reports, requisitions, and returns required from medical officers.

1205. When medical attendance is required by officers or enlisted men on service, and the attendance of a medical officer cannot be had, the officer, or if there be no officer, then the enlisted man, may employ a private physician, and a just account therefor will be paid by the Medical Bureau.

1206. The account will set out the name of the patient, the date of and charge for each visit, and for medicines. The physician will make a certificate to the account in case of an officer, or affidavit in case of an enlisted man, that the account is correct, and the charges are the customary charges of the place.

1207. The officer will make his certificate, or the enlisted man his affidavit, to the correctness of the account, that he was on service at the place, and stating the circumstances preventing him from receiving the services of a medical officer.

1208. When the charge is against an officer, he will pay the account if practicable, and transmit it to the Medical Bureau for reimbursement. In all other cases, the account will be transmitted to the Medical Bureau for settlement.

1209. If the charge is against a deceased officer or enlisted man, the physician will make the affidavit, before required, to the account, and that he has been paid no part of it.

1210. No charges for consultation fees will be paid by the Medical Bureau; nor will any account for medical attendance or medicines be paid, if the officer or enlisted man be not on service.

1211. A board of not less than three medical officers will be appointed from time to time, by the Secretary of War, to examine applicants for appointment of assistant surgeons in the regular army, and assistant surgeons for promotion. And no one shall be so appointed or promoted until so examined and found qualified.

1212. The board will scrutinize rigidly the moral habits, professional acquirements, and physical qualifications of the candidates, and report favorably, either for appointment or promotion, in no case admitting of a reasonable doubt.

1213. The Secretary of War will designate the applicants to be examined for appointment of assistant surgeon. They must be between 21 and 25 years of age. The board will report their respective merits in the several branches of the examination, and their relative merit from the whole; agreeably whereto, if vacancies happen within two years thereafter, they will receive appointments and take rank in the medical corps.

1214. When an assistant surgeon has served five years, he is subject to be examined for promotion. If he decline the examination, or be found not qualified by moral habits or professional acquirements, he ceases to be a medical officer of the army.

1215. An applicant for appointment failing at one examination, may be allowed a second after two years; but never a third.

1216. The Secretary of War will appoint, on the recommendation of the Surgeon General, from the enlisted men of the army, or cause to be enlisted, as many competent hospital stewards as the service may require.

1217. The senior medical officer of a command requiring a steward, may recommend a competent non-commissioned officer or soldier to be appointed, which recommendation the commanding officer shall forward to the Adjutant and Inspector-General of the Army, with his remarks thereon, and with the remarks of the company commander.

1218. When no competent enlisted man can be procured, the medical officer will report the fact to the Surgeon General. Applications and testimonials of competency, from persons seeking to be enlisted for hospital stewards, may be addressed to the Surgeon General.

1219. The commanding officer may re-enlist a hospital steward at the expiration of his term of service, on the recommendation of the medical officer.

1220. No soldier, or citizen, will be recommended for appointment who is not *known* to be temperate, honest, and in every way reliable, as well as sufficiently intelligent, and skilled in pharmacy, for the proper discharge of the responsible duties likely to be devolved upon him. Until this is *known*, he will be appointed an acting steward by the medical officer, with the approval of the commanding officer, and will be entitled to the pay and allowances of hospital steward.

1221. Hospital stewards, appointed by the Secretary of War, whenever stationed in places whence no post return is made to the Adjutant General's office, or when on furlough, will, at the end of every month, report themselves, by letter, to the Adjutant General and Surgeon General, as well as to the Medical Director of the military department in which they may be serving; to each of whom they will also report each new assignment to duty, or change of station, ordered in their case, noting carefully the number, date, and source of the order directing the same. They will likewise report monthly, when on furlough, to the medical officer in charge of the hospital to which they are attached.

1222. The jurisdiction and authority of courts martial are the same with reference to hospital stewards as in the cases of other enlisted men. When, however, a hospital steward is sentenced by an inferior court to be reduced to the ranks, such sentence, though it may be approved by the reviewing officer, will not be carried into effect until the case has been referred to the Secretary of War for final action. In these cases of reduction, the application of the man for discharge from service, though not recognized as of right, will generally be regarded with favor, if his offence has not been of too serious a nature, and especially when he has not been recently promoted from the ranks.

1223. As the hospital stewards, appointed by the Secretary of War, are permanently attached to the Medical Department, their accounts of pay, clothing, &c., must be kept by the medical officers under whose immediate direction they are serving, who are also responsible for certified statements of such accounts, and correct descriptive lists of such stewards, to accompany them in case of transfer; as, also, that their final statements and certificates of discharge are accurately made out, when they are at length discharged from service.

Standard Supply Table for General and Post Hospitals.

[In General Hospitals, detached from troops, the supplies for every 100 sick will correspond with the allowance to commands of 500 men.]

ARTICLES.		Quantities for one year for commands of				
		From 100 to 200	From 200 to 300	From 300 to 400	500 men	1000 men
MEDICINES.						
Acaciæ, - - -	lb.	2	4	6	8	16
Acidi acetici, - - -	lb.	½	1	2	2½	5
" arseniosi, - -	oz.	½	1	2	2½	5
" benzoici, - -	oz.	1	2	3	4	8
" citrici, - - -	lb.	1	2	3	4	8
" muriatici, - -	lb.	½	1	2	2½	5
" nitrici, - - -	lb.	1	2	3	4	8
" sulphurici, - -	lb.	1	2	3	4	8
" " aromatici, -	lb.	1	2	3	4	8
" tannici, - - -	oz.	2	4	6	8	16
" tartarici, - - -	lb.	2	4	6	8	16
Aetheris sulphurici loti, -	lb.	2	4	6	8	16
Alcoholis, - - -	bott.	24	48	72	96	192
Aluminis, - - -	lb.	1	2	3	4	8
Ammoniaci, - - -	lb.	½	1	2	2½	5
Ammoniæ carbonatis, - -	oz.	8	16	24	32	64
" muriatis, - -	lb.	½	1	2	2½	5
Anthemidis, - - -	lb.	1	2	3	4	8
Antimonii et potassæ tartratis, -	oz.	3	6	9	12	24
Argenti nitratis, (crystals,) -	oz.	1	2	3	4	8
" " (fused,) -	oz.	1	2	3	4	8
Arnicæ, - - -	lb.	1	2	3	4	8
Assafœtidæ, - - -	oz.	4	8	12	16	32
Bismuthi subnitratis, - -	oz.	4	8	12	16	32
Camphoræ, - - -	lb.	2	4	6	8	16
Cardamomi, - - -	oz.	8	16	24	32	64
Catechu, - - -	lb.	½	1	2	2½	5
Ceræ albæ* - - -	lb.	2	4	6	8	16
Cerati resinæ, - - -	lb.	2	4	6	8	16
" simplicis, - -	lb.	8	16	24	32	64
" zinci carbonatis, -	lb.	2	4	6	8	16
Chloroformi, - - -	lb.	1	2	3	4	8
Collodii, - - -	oz.	2	4	6	8	16
Copaibæ, - - -	lb.	5	10	15	20	40
Creasoti, - - -	oz.	2	4	6	8	16
Cretæ preparatæ, - -	lb.	1	2	3	4	8
Cupri sulphatis, - -	oz.	2	4	6	8	16

* To be issued to posts where simple cerate cannot be sent without becoming rancid.

Supply Table for Hospitals—Continued.

ARTICLES.		Quantities for one year for commands of: From 100 to 200	From 200 to 300	From 300 to 400	500 men	1000 men
Emplastri adhæsivi,	yds.	5	10	15	20	40
" cantharadis,	lb.	3	6	9	12	24
" ferri,	lb.	1	2	3	4	8
" hydrargyri,	lb	½	1	2	2½	5
" ithyocollæ,	yds.	3	6	9	12	24
Extracti belladonnæ,	oz.	2	4	6	8	16
" buchu fluidi,	lb.	1	2	3	4	8
" colocynthidis, comp.	oz.	8	16	24	32	64
" colombæ fluidi,	lb.	1	2	3	4	8
" conii,	oz.	1	2	3	4	8
" cubebæ fluidi,	lb.	1	2	3	4	8
" gentianæ fluidi,	lb.	1	2	3	4	8
" glycyrrhizæ,	lb.	6	12	18	24	48
" hyoscyami,	oz.	2	4	6	8	16
" ipecacuanhæ fluidi,	lb.	½	1	2	2½	5
" piperis fluidi,	oz.	1	2	3	4	8
" pruni virg. fluidi,	lb.	1	2	3	4	8
" rhei fluidi,	lb.	1	2	3	4	8
" sarsaparillæ fluidi,	lb.	2	4	6	8	16
" senegæ fluidi,	lb.	½	1	2	2½	5
" sennæ fluidi,	lb.	1	2	3	4	8
" taraxaci fluidi,	lb.	1	2	3	4	8
" valerianæ fluidi,	oz.	8	16	24	32	64
" zingiberis fluidi,	lb.	½	1	2	2½	5
Ferri iodidi,	oz.	2	4	6	8	16
" et quiniæ citratis,	oz.	4	8	12	16	32
" sulphatis,	oz.	2	4	6	8	16
Gambogiæ,	oz.	½	1	2	2½	5
Glycerine,	oz.	2	4	6	8	16
Guaiaci resinæ,	lb.	½	1	2	2½	5
Hydrargyri chloridi corr:	oz.	½	1	2	2½	5
" " mitis,	lb.	1	2	3	4	8
" cum creta,	lb.	½	1	2	2½	5
" iodidi,	oz.	1	2	3	4	8
" oxidi rubri,	oz.	1	2	3	4	8
Iodinii,	oz.	2	4	6	8	16
Lini,	lb.	4	8	12	16	32
Liquoris ammoniæ,	lb.	4	8	12	16	32
" ferri iodidi,	lb.	1	2	3	4	8
" potass: arsenitis,	oz.	2	4	6	8	16
" sodæ chlorinatæ,	bott.	3	6	9	12	24
" zinci chloridi,	bott.	3	6	9	12	24
Magnesiæ,	lb	½	1	2	2½	5

Supply Table for Hospitals—Continued.

ARTICLES.		Quantities for one year for commands of				
		From 100 to 200	From 200 to 300	From 300 to 400	500 men	1000 men
Magnesiæ sulphatis,	lb.	25	50	75	100	200
Massæ pil: hydrargi,	oz.	8	16	24	32	64
Mellis despumati,	lb.	2	4	6	8	16
Morphiæ sulphatis,	dr.	2	4	6	8	16
Myrrhæ,	lb.	½	1	2	2½	5
Olei anisi,	oz.	1	2	3	4	8
" cajuputi,	oz.	1	2	3	4	8
" caryophilli,	oz.	1	2	3	4	8
" cinnamomi,	oz.	1	2	3	4	8
" menthæ piperitæ,	oz.	2	4	6	8	16
" morrhuæ,	bott.	8	16	24	32	64
" olivæ,	bott.	8	16	24	32	64
" origani,	dr.	4	8	12	16	32
" ricini,	qt. bott.	12	24	36	48	96
" terebinthinæ,	qt. bott.	4	8	12	16	32
" tiglii,	dr.	2	4	6	8	16
Opii,	lb.	½	1	2	2½	5
Piscis abietis,	lb.	1	2	3	4	8
Plumbi acetatis,	lb.	1	2	3	4	8
Potassæ acetatis,	lb.	1	2	3	4	8
" bicarbonatis,	lb.	1	2	3	4	8
" bitartratis,	lb.	2	4	6	8	16
" chloratis,	lb.	1	2	3	4	8
" nitratis,	lb.	1	2	3	4	8
" sulphatis,	lb.	½	1	2	2½	5
Potassii cyanureti,	dr.	1	2	3	4	8
" iodidi,	oz.	8	16	24	32	64
Pruni virginianæ,	lb.	½	1	2	2½	5
Pulveris acaciæ,	lb.	2	4	6	8	16
" aloes,	oz.	4	8	12	16	32
" cantharidis,	oz.	2	4	6	8	16
" capsici,	lb	1	2	3	4	8
" cinchonæ.	lb.	1	2	3	4	8
" ferri,	oz.	2	4	6	8	16
" " per sulphatis,	oz.	1	2	3	4	8
" glycyrrhizæ,	oz.	4	8	12	16	32
" ipecacuanhæ,	lb.	½	1	2	2½	5
" " et opii,	lb.	½	1	2	2½	5
" jalapæ,	oz.	4	8	12	16	32
" lini,	lb.	8	16	24	32	64
" opii,	lb.	½	1	2	2½	5
" rhei,	lb.	¼	½	¾	1	2
" sabinæ,	oz.	1	2	3	4	8

Supply Table for Hospitals—Continued.

ARTICLES.		Quantities for one year for commands of				
		From 100 to 200	From 200 to 300	From 300 to 400	500 men	1000 men
Pulveris sinapis nigræ,	lb.	6	12	18	24	48
" ulmi,	lb.	2	4	6	8	16
Quassiæ,	lb.	1	1	2	2½	5
Quiniæ sulphatis,	oz.	10–20	20–40	30–60	40–80	80–160
Rhei,	oz.	4	8	12	16	32
Sacchari,	lb.	20	40	60	80	160
Saponis,	lb.	4	8	12	16	32
Scillæ,	oz.	4	8	12	16	32
Serpentariæ,	lb.	½	1	2	2½	5
Sodæ bicarbonatis,	lb.	2	4	6	8	16
" boratis,	lb.	½	1	2	2½	5
" et potass: tartratis,	lb.	3	6	9	12	24
Speigeliæ,	lb.	½	1	2	2½	5
Spiritûs ammon: aromatici,	oz.	2	4	6	8	16
" ætheris compositi,	lb.	½	1	2	2½	5
" " nitrici,	lb.	2	4	6	8	16
" lavandulæ comp:	lb.	½	1	2	2½	5
" vini gallaci	bott.	12	24	36	48	96
Strychniæ	dr.	1	2	3	4	8
Sulphuris loti,	lb.	1	2	3	4	8
Syrupi scillæ,	lb.	3	6	9	12	24
Tincturæ aconiti radicis,	lb.	1	2	3	4	8
" digitalis,	oz.	4	8	12	16	32
" ergotæ (Dublin),	oz.	4	8	12	16	32
" ferri chloridi,	lb.	½	1	2	2½	5
" veratri veridis,	oz.	4	8	12	16	32
Unguenti hydrargyri,	lb.	1	2	3	4	8
" " nitratis,	lb.	½	1	2	2½	5
Veratriæ,	dr.	1	2	3	4	8
Vini colchici seminis,	lb.	½	1	2	2½	5
Zinci acetatis,	oz.	1	2	3	4	8
" chlorid,	oz.	¼	1	1	2	3
" sulphatis,	oz.	1	2	3	4	8
INSTRUMENTS.						
Amputating,	sets.	1	1	1	1	2
Ball forceps,	no.	1	1	1	1	2
Bougies, gumelastic, (1 to 12)	no.	6	6	6	6	6
" metallic, (assorted,)	no.	6	6	6	6	6
Buck's sponge-holder for the throat,	no.	1	1	1	1	1
Cathetors, gumelastic, (2 to 10,)	no.	6	6	6	6	6
" silver, (3, 6, 9,)	no.	3	3	3	3	3

Supply Table for Hospitals—Continued.

ARTICLES.		Quantities for one year for commauds of From 100 to 200	From 200 to 300	From 300 to 400	500 men	1000 men
Gathetors, cases,	no.	1	1	1	1	1
Cupping glasses, or tins,	no.	12	12	18	18	24
Dissecting,	sets.	1	1	1	1	1
Lancets, spring,*	no.	1	1	1	1	2
" thumb,†	no.	2	2	3	4	6
Needles, surgeons', with cases,	no.	6	6	6	6	12
Obstetrical,	sets.	1	1	1	1	1
Pocket,	sets.	1	1	1	1	1
Prabungs,	no.	6	6	6	6	6
Pulleys,	sets.	1	1	1	1	1
Scarificators,	no.	2	2	2	3	4
Splints, (assorted,)	sets.	1	1	1	1	1
Stethescopes,	no.	1	1	1	1	1
Stomach-pump and case,	no.	1	1	1	1	1
Syringe, enema,‡	no.	3	3	3	3	6
" penis, glass,	no.	2	4	6	8	16
" " metallic,	no.	6	12	18	24	36
" vagina,‖	no.	3	3	3	3	6
Teeth extracting,	sets.	1	1	1	1	2
Tongue depressor, (hinge,)	no.	1	1	1	1	2
Tourniquets, field,	no.	4	4	6	6	10
" spiral,	no.	1	1	2	2	4
Trepanning,	sets,	1	1	1	1	1
Trocars, (1 smalll,)	no.	1	1	1	1	2
Trusses, hernia,	no.	3	6	9	12	24
BOOKS.						
Anatomy,	cop.	1	1	1	1	1
Chemistry,	cop.	1	1	1	1	1
Dispensatory,	cop.	1	1	1	1	1
Medical Dictionary,	cop.	1	1	1	1	1
" Formulary,	cop.	1	1	1	1	1
" Jurisprudence and Toxicology,	cop.	1	1	1	1	1
" Practice,	cop.	1	1	1	1	1
Obstetrics,	cop.	1	1	1	1	1
Regulations for Med. Dept.	cop.	1	1	1	2	2
Surgery,	cop.	1	1	1	1	1
Blank,	cop.	2	2	2	3	4

* Four extra fleams to each lancet. † With cases. ‡ 1 Davidson's; 1, 4, 1, 8 oz. ‖ 1 hard India Rubber; 2 glass.

ARTICLES.		Quantities for one year for commands of From 100 to 200	From 200 to 300	From 300 to 400	500 men	1000 men.
Case,	no.	1	1	1	1	1
Order and Letter,	no.	1	1	1	1	1
Prescription,	no.	1	1	1	1	1
Register,	no.	1	1	1	1	1
Requisitions, Returns, Reports of sick,	no.	1	1	1	1	1
HOSPITAL STORES.						
Arrow root,	lb.	5	10	15	20	40
Barley,	lb.	20	40	60	80	160
Cinnamon,	lb.	½	1	2	2½	5
Cloves,	oz.	4	8	12	16	32
Cocoa,	lb.	10	20	30	40	80
Farina,	lb.	5	10	15	20	40
Ginger, ground, (Jamaica,)	lb.	½	1	2	2½	5
Nutmegs,	oz.	4	8	12	16	32
Tea,	lb.	20	40	60	80	160
Whiskey, bottles of,	doz.	2	4	6	8	16
Wine, bottles of,	doz.	2	4	6	8	16
BEDDING.						
Bed sacks,	no.	10	20	30	40	80
Bedsteads, iron,	no.	6–10	12–20	18–30	24–40	48–86
Blankets, woollen,	no.	10–20	20–40	30–60	40–80	80–160
Coverlets,	no.	10	20	30	40	80
Gutta percha cloth,	yds.	4	6	8	10	16
Mattresses,	no.	2	4	6	8	16
Mosquito bars,	no.	6–10	12–20	18–30	24–40	48–80
Pillow cases,	no.	25	50	75	100	200
" ticks,	no.	10	20	30	40	80
Sheets,	no.	40	80	120	200	400
FURNITURE, DRESSING, &C.						
Bandages, suspensory,*	no.	4	8	12	16	32
Binder's boards,†	no.	4	6	8	12	16
Corks, assorted,	doz.	12	24	36	48	96
Cork screws,	no.	1	1	2	2	3

* Assorted. † 18 inches by 4.

Supply Table for Hospitals—Continued.

ARTICLES.		Quantities for one year for commands of: From 100 to 200	From 200 to 300	From 300 to 400	500 men	1000 men
Cotton batting,	lb.	1	2	3	4	8
" wadding,	lb.	1	2	3	4	8
Flannel, red,	yds.	5	10	15	20	40
Funnels, glass,	no.	1	1	2	2	4
" tin,	no.	1	1	2	2	2
Hatchets,	no.	1	1	2	2	2
Hones, (in wood,)*	no.	1	1	1	1	1
Ink powder,	papers.	2	2	3	3	4
Inkstands,	no.	1	1	2	2	2
Linen,	yds.	5	10	15	20	40
Lint,	lb.	4	6	8	10	20
Measures, graduated,	no.	3	3	4	6	6
" tin,	sets.	1	1	1	1	1
Medicine cups and glasses,†	no.	3	6	9	12	24
Mills, coffee,	no.	2	2	2	3	4
Mortars and pestles, glass,	no.	1	1	2	2	2
" " " iron,	no.	1	1	1	1	1
" " " wedgewood,	no.	1	2	2	3	3
Muslin,	yds.	25	50	75	100	200
Needles, sewing,	no.	25	25	25	25	50
Oiled silk, or gutta percha tissue, or India rubber tissue,	yds.	4	6	6	8	12
Pans, bed,	no.	2	2	3	4	5
Paper envelopes,‡	no.	100	125	150	200	250
Paper, filtering,	quires.	½	1	2	2	3
" wrapping	quires.	10	12	15	15	20
" writing,‖	quires.	12	20	20	20	20
Pencils, hair,	no.	12	18	24	30	50
" lead,	no.	6	8	10	12	18
Pens, steel,	doz.	2	3	3	4	6
Pill boxes,	papers.	3	6	9	12	24
" machine,	no.	1	1	1	1	1
Pins, assorted,	papers.	2	4	6	8	16
Quills,	no.	25	25	50	50	50
Rain guages,	no.	1	1	1	1	1
Razors,	no.	1	1	1	1	2
" strops,	no.	1	1	1	1	2
Scales and weights, apothecary's,	sets.	1	1	2	2	2
" " " shop,	sets.	1	1	1	1	1

*4 inches by 1. †2 cups to 1 glass. ‡Assorted, 3 sizes—"Official business" printed on each. ‖ Foolscap, letter and note—white; blue ruled.

Supply Table for Hospitals—Continued.

ARTICLES.		Quantities for one year for commands of				
		From 100 to 200	From 200 to 300	From 300 to 400	500 men	1000 men
Scissors,	no.	2	2	2	3	4
Sheep skins, dressed,	no.	4	6	8	10	12
Silk, surgeons',	oz.	¼	¼	½	½	1
" green,	yds.	½	1	2	2½	5
Spatulas,	no.	3	3	4	6	12
Sponge,	lb.	½	½	¾	¾	1
Tape,*	pieces.	4	8	12	16	32
Thermometers and hydrometers,	no.	2	2	2	2	2
Thermometers,	no.	1	1	1	1	1
Thread, linen,	oz.	4	4	6	6	8
Tiles,	no.	2	3	3	3	4
Tow,	lb.	1	2	2	3	5
Towels,	no.	20	30	50	75	150
Twine,	lb.	1	1	1½	1½	3
Urinals,	no.	2	3	5	6	10
Vials, assorted,	doz.	6	12	18	24	48
Wafers, (½ oz. boxes,)	no.	1	1	2	2	3
Wax, sealing,	sticks.	3	3	4	4	6

* One quarter, woollen; three quarters, cotton.

If the following articles of Hospital Furniture cannot be obtained with the hospital fund, they may be procured from a quartermaster or medical disbursing officer, by special requisition:

ARTICLES.

Basins, wash.
Bowls.
Boxes, for pepper and salt.
Brushes.
Buckets.
Candlesticks.
Clothes Lines.
Cups.
Dippers and Ladles.
Graters.
Gridirons.
Kettles, tea.
Knives and Forks.
Lanterns.
Locks and keys.
Mugs.
Pans, frying.
" sauce.
Pitchers.
Plates.
Pots, chamber and chair.
Pots, coffee and tea.
" iron.
Sadirons.
Shovels, fire.
Skillet, with cover.
Snuffers.
Spoons.
Tongs and pokers.
Tumblers.
Woodsaws.

Standard Supply Table for Field Service.

Articles.		Quantities. Reg't 3 mos	Bat. 3 mos	Comp 3 mos
MEDICINES.				
Acidi nitrici,	lb.	$\frac{1}{4}$	$\frac{1}{8}$	$\frac{1}{8}$
" sulph. aromatici,	lb.	1	$\frac{1}{2}$	$\frac{1}{4}$
" tannici,	oz.	2	1	1
Alcoholis,	bott.	6	4	2
Aluminis,	lb.	1	$\frac{1}{2}$	$\frac{1}{4}$
Ammoniæ carbonatis,	oz.	16	8	4
Antimonii et potass, tartratis,	oz.	2	1	1
Argenti nitratis (fused),	oz.	4	2	1
Camphoræ,	lb.	4	2	1
Cerati resinæ,	lb.	2	1	$\frac{1}{2}$
" simplicis,	lb.	8	4	2
Chloroformi,	lb.	2	1	1
Copaibæ,	lb.	2	1	$\frac{1}{2}$
Creasoti,	oz.	2	1	1
Cupri sulphatis,	oz.	4	2	1
Emplastri adhæsivi,	yds.	15	8	4
" cantharidis,	lb.	4	2	1
" ichthyocollæ,	yds.	2	1	1
Extracti colocynthidis comp.	oz.	16	8	4
" glycyrrhizæ,	lb.	2	1	$\frac{1}{2}$
Hydrargyri chloridi corrosivi,	oz.	$\frac{1}{2}$	$\frac{1}{2}$	$\frac{1}{2}$
" " mitis,	lb.	2	1	$\frac{1}{2}$
Iodinii,	oz.	4	2	1
Liquoris ammoniæ,	lb.	4	2	1
" potass, arsenitis,	oz.	4	2	1
Magnesiæ sulphatis,	lb.	25	15	10
Massæ pil: hydrargyri,	oz.	16	8	4
Morphiæ sulphatis,	dr.	4	2	1
Olei menthæ piperitæ,	oz.	2	1	1
" olivæ,	bott.	8	4	2
" ricini,	qt. bott.	12	6	3
" terebinthinæ,	qt. bott.	8	4	2
" tiglii,	dr.	2	1	1
Pilul: cathartic: comp.: (U. S.),	doz.	8	4	2
" opii, (U. S.),	doz.	8	4	2
Plumbi acetatis,	lb.	2	1	$\frac{1}{2}$
Potassæ bitartratis,	lb.	2	1	$\frac{1}{2}$
" chloratis,	lb.	2	1	$\frac{1}{2}$
" nitratis,	lb.	1	$\frac{1}{2}$	$\frac{1}{4}$
Potassii iodidi,	oz.	8	4	2
Pulveris acaciæ,	lb.	4	2	1
" capsici,	lb.	$\frac{1}{2}$	$\frac{1}{4}$	$\frac{1}{4}$

Supply Table for Field Service—Continued.

Articles.		Quanities.	
	Reg't 3 mos	Bat. 3 mos	Comp 3 mos
Pulveris ferri per sulphatis, ... oz.	4	2	1
" ipecacuanhæ, ... lb.	1	½	¼
" " et opii, ... lb.	½	¼	¼
" lini, ... lb.	16	8	4
" opii, ... lb.	2	1	½
" rhei, ... lb.	½	¼	¼
" sinapis nigræ, ... lb.	12	6	3
Quiniæ sulphatis, ... oz.	24	12	6
Sacchari, ... lb.	10	5	2
Saponis, ... lb.	8	4	2
Sodæ bicarbonatis, ... lb.	1	½	¼
Spiritûs ammoniæ aromatici, ... oz.	4	2	2
" ætheris nitrici, ... lb.	2	1	½
" vini gallici, ... bott.	12	6	4
Syrupi sciliæ, ... lb.	3	2	1
Tincturæ cinchonæ comp., ... lb.	4	2	1
" columbæ, ... lb.	4	2	1
" ferri chloridi, ... lb.	1	½	¼
" gentianæ comp., ... lb.	4	2	1
" opii, ... oz.	16	8	6
Unguenti hydrargyri, ... lb.	1	½	¼
" " nitratis, ... lb.	½	¼	¼
Vini colchici seminis, ... lb.	1	½	½
Zinci acetatis, ... oz.	2	1	1
" sulphatis, ... oz.	2	1	1
INSTRUMENTS.			
Amputating, ... sets.	2	1	1
Ball forceps, ... no.	2	1	1
Bougies, gumelastic, (1 to 12), ... no.	6	6	6
" metallic, (assorted), ... no.	6	6	6
Catheters, gumelastic, (2 to 10), ... no.	6	6	6
" silver, (3, 6, 9), ... no.	3	3	3
" cases, ... no.	1	1	1
Cupping glass or tins,* .... no.	12	8	6
Lancets, spring, ... no.	1	1	1
" thumbs, (with cases), ... no.	4	2	2
Needles, surgeons', (with cases,) ..... no.	12	6	6

* Half glass, half tin.

Supply Table for Field Service—Continued.

Articles.	Quantities. Reg't 3 mos	Bat. 3 mos	Comp 3 mos
Pocket, ... sets.	2	1	1
Probangs, ... no.	6	4	2
Scarificators, ... no.	2	1	1
Splints, (assorted), ... sets.	1	1	1
Syringes, enema, (assorted),*........ no.	4	2	1
" penis, glass, ... no.	8	4	2
" " India rubber, ... no.	8	4	2
Teeth extracting, ... sets.	1	1	1
Tongue depressor, (hinge), ... no.	1	1	1
Tourniquets, field, ... no.	12	6	3
" spiral, ... no.	2	1	1
Trepanning, ... sets.	1	1	1
Trocars, (1 small), ... no.	2	1	1
Trusses, hernia, ... no.	6	3	2
BOOKS.			
Anatomy, (surgical), ... cop.	1	1	1
Medical Practice, ... cop.	1	1	1
Regulations for medical department,. cop.	1	1	1
Surgery, (operative), ... cop.	1	1	1
Thompson's Conspectus, ... cop.	1	1	1
Blank, ... no.	5	5	5
HOSPITAL STORES.			
Arrow-root, ... lb.	10	5	3
Candles, (sperm),† .... lb.	2	1	1
Farina, ... lb.	10	5	3
Ginger, (fluid extract,) .... lb.	1	½	¼
Nutmegs, ... oz.	8	4	2
Tea, ... lb.	30	15	7
Whiskey, bottles of, ... doz.	3	2	1
BEDDING.			
Bed sacks, ... no.	20	10	5
Blankets, (woollen,) .... no.	30	15	8

* 1 Davidson's; 1 hard rubber, 6 oz.
† To be reserved for use in surgical operations in the night

Supply Table for Field Service—Continued.

ARTICLES.		Quantities.		
		Reg't 3 mos	Bat. 3 mos	Comp 3 mos
Gutta percha cloth,	yds.	20	10	5
Mosquito bars,	do.	20	10	5
Pillow ticks,	no.	20	10	5
FURNITURE AND DRESSINGS.				
Bandages (1), roller, assorted,	doz.	14	7	4
" suspensory, assorted,	no.	12	6	4
Binders' boards (18 inches by 4),	no.	18	9	5
Corks, assorted,	doz.	12	6	3
Corkscrews,	no.	2	1	1
Cotton batting,	lb.	2	1	½
" wadding,	lb.	2	1	½
Flannel (red),	yds.	5	3	2
Hatchets,	no.	2	1	1
Hones (4 inches by 1, in wood),	no.	1	1	1
Ink, 2-ounce bottles,	no.	12	6	3
Knapsacks, hospital (2),	no.	2	1	1
Lanterns,	no.	4	2	1
Lint,	lb.	8	4	2
Litters and stretchers, hand,	no.	10	5	2
" horse (3),	no.			

(1) 1 dozen, 1 inch wide, 1 yard long.
2 " 2 " 3 "
2 " 2½ " 3 "
1 " 3 " 4 "
½ " 3½ " 5 "
½ " 4 " 6 "

(2) According to pattern of same dimensions with ordinary knapsacks, and of light material; to be divided into four compartments or drawers, and to be covered with canvas. It is to be carried on a march or in battle, by a hospital orderly, who is habitually to follow the medical officer. The purpose of this knapsack is to carry such instruments, dressings, and medicines, as may be needed in an emergency on the march or in the field.

(3) Horses litters required for service on ground not admitting the use of two wheeled carriages, to be composed of a canvas bed similar to the present stretcher, and of two poles, each sixteen feet long, made in sections, with head and foot pieces constructed to act as stretchers to keep the poles apart.

Supply Table for Field Service.—Continued.

ARTICLES.		Quantities.		
		Reg't 3 mos	Bat. 3 mos	Comp. 3 mos.
Measures, graduated, assorted (4),	no.	4	2	2
Medicine chests,	no.	1	1	1
" cups and glasses (5),	no.	6	3	2
" panniers,	no.			
Mess chests (see note),	no.	1	1	1
Mills, coffee,	no.	2	1	1
Mortars and pestles, wedgewood (small),	no.	2	1	1
Muslin,	yds.	20	10	5
Needles, sewing (assorted, in a case),	no.	25	25	25
Oiled silk or gutta percha tissue, or India rubber tissue,	yds.	8	4	2
Pans, bed (6),	no.	2	1	1
Paper envelopes, assorted (7),	no.	100	50	25
Paper, wrapping,	quires	6	3	1
" writing (8),	quires	12	6	3
Pencils, hair,	no.	24	12	6
" lead (of Faber's make, No. 2),	no.	12	6	3
Pens, steel,	doz.	4	2	1
Pill boxes (wood),	papers	2	1	1
" (tin),	no.	6	6	6
Pins, assorted (large and medium),	papers	4	2	2
Razors,	no.	1	1	1
" strops,	no.	1	1	1
Scales and weights, apothecary's,	sets.	1	1	1
Scissors,	no.	4	2	2
Sheep skins, dressed,	no.	4	2	1
Silk, surgeons'	oz.	½	¼	¼
" green,	yds.	1	½	½
Spatulas,	no.	6	3	2
Sponge (washed),	lb.	1	½	¼
Store chest,	no.	1	1	1

(4) 6 oz., 2 oz. minim.
(5) 2 cups to 1 glass.
(6) Of hard India rubber or other material. Shovel.
(7) 50 letter, 25 note, 25 large. "Official Business" prin[illegible]
(8) 2 foolscap, 6 letter, 4 note, white; blue ruled.

Supply Table for Field Service.—Continued.

ARTICLES.		Quantities. Reg't. 3 mos	Bat. 3 mos	Comp 3 mos
Tape,	pieces,	4	2	1
Thread linen,	oz.	2	1	1
Tiles,	no.	2	1	1
Towels,	no.	40	20	10
Twine,	lb.	½	¼	¼
Vials, assorted (1 oz. and 2 oz.),	doz.	4	2	1
Wafers, (½ oz. boxes),	no.	1	1	1
Wax, sealing,	sticks.	2	1	1

NOTE TO PRECEDING TABLE.

FURNITURE OF MESS CHEST.

6 Basins, tin.
2 Boxes, pepper and salt.
6 Cups, tin.
4 Canisters (for tea, coffee, sugar and butter.)
2 Dippers and ladles.
1 Grater.
1 Gridiron.
1 Kettle, tea, iron.
12 Knives and forks.
6 Mugs (Britannia, half-pint).
1 Pan, frying.
1 Pan, sauce.
8 Plates (6) and dishes (2) tin.
1 Pot, iron.
2 Pots, coffee and tea, tin.
12 Spoons, iron [table (6) and tea (6)].
1 Skillet, with cover.
1 Tray, tin.
6 Tumblers, tin.

The Standard Supply Tables contain all the articles to be purchased by medical purveyors, except on the orders of the Surgeon General; but any less quantity may be required or any article omitted at the discretion of the medical officer.

FORM 1.

Report of the Sick and Wounded at , for the ending 18 .

CLASSES OF DISEASES.	TAKEN SICK OR RECEIVED INTO HOSPITAL DURING THE QUARTER.										
	Month,	First.		Second,		Third.		Total by each disease.		Total by each class.	
	Specific diseases.	Cases.	Deaths	Cases.	Deaths	Cases.	Deaths	Cases.	Deaths	Cases.	Deaths
Fevers	Febris Congestiva,										
	Febris Continua Communis,										
	Febris Intermittens Quotidiana,										
	Febris Intermittens Tertiana,										
	Febris Intermittens Quartana,										
	Febris Remittens,										
	Febris Typhoides,										
	Febris Typhus,										
	Febris Typhus Icterodes,										
	All other diseases of this class,										
Eruptive Fever	Erysipelas,										
	Rubeola,										
	Scarlatina,										
	Variola,										
	Varioloides,										
	All other diseases of this class,										

Diseases of the organs connected with the digestive system.	Cholera Asiatica,								
	Cholera Morbus,								
	Colica,								
	Constipatio,								
	Diarrhœa Acuta,								
	Diarrhœa Chronica,								
	Dysenteria Acuta,								
	Dysenteria Chronica,								
	Dyspepsia,								
	Enteritis								
	Gastritis,								
	Hæmatemesis,								
	Hepatitis Acuta,								
	Hepatitis Chronica,								
	Icterus,								
	Parotitis,								
	Peritonitis,								
	Splenitis,								
	Tonsillitis,								
	All other diseases of this class,								
Diseases of the respiratory system.	Asthma,								
	Bronchitis Acuta,								
	Bronchitis Chronica,								
	Catarrhus Epidemicus,								
	Catarrhus,								
	Hæmoptysis,								
	Laryngitis,								
	Phthisis Pulmonalis,								
	Carry forward,								

Form 1—Continued.

CLASSES OF DISEASES.	TAKEN SICK OR RECEIVED INTO HOSPITAL DURING THE QUARTER.										
	Month,	First.		Second.		Third.		Total by each disease.		Total by each class.	
	Specific Diseases.	Cases.	Deaths	Cases.	Deaths	Cases.	Deaths	Cases.	Deaths	Cases.	Deaths
	Brought forward,										
	Pleuritis,										
	Pneumonia,										
	All other diseases of this class,										
Diseases of the circulatory system.	Anæmia,										
	Aneurisma,										
	Angina Pectoris,										
	Carditis,										
	Endocarditis,										
	Pericarditis,										
	Phlebitis,										
	Varicocele,										
	Varix,										
	All other diseases of this class,										
	Apoplexia,										
	Cephalalgia,										
	Cerebritis,										
	Chorea,										
	Delirium Tremens,										
	Epilepsia,										
	Ictus Solis,										

Diseases of the brain and nervous system.	Irritatio Spinalis,										
	Mania,										
	Melancholia,										
	Meningitis,										
	Neuralgia,										
	Paralysis,										
	Tetanus,										
	All other diseases of this class,										
Diseases of the urinary and genital organs, and venereal affections.	Bubo Syphiliticum,										
	Calculus,										
	Cystitis,										
	Diabetes,										
	Enuresis,										
	Gonorrhœa,										
	Ischuria et Dysuria,										
	Nephritis,										
	Orchitis,										
	Sarcocele,										
	Strictura Urethræ,										
	Syphilis Primitiva,										
	Syphilis Consecutiva,										
	Ulcus Penis Non Syphiliticum,										
	All other diseases of this class,										
Diseases of the serous exhalent vessels.	Anasarca,										
	Ascites,										
	Hydrarthrus,										
	Hydrocele,										
	Carry forward,										

FORM 1—Continued.

CLASSES OF DISEASES.	TAKEN SICK OR RECEIVED INTO HOSPITAL DURING THE QUARTER. Month,	Frist.		Second.		Third.		Total by each disease.		Total by each class.	
	Specific Diseases.	Cases.	Deaths	Cases.	Deaths	Cases.	Deaths	Cases.	Deaths	Cases.	Deaths
	Brought forward,										
	Hydrothorax,										
	All other diseases of this class,										
Diseases of the fibrous and muscular structures.	Lumbago,										
	Podagra,										
	Rhuematismus Acutus,										
	Rhuematismus Chronicus,										
	All other diseases of this class,										
Abscesses and ulcers.	Abscessus,										
	Anthrax,										
	Fistula,										
	Paronychia,										
	Phlegmon,										
	Ulcus,										
	All other diseases of this class,										
	Ambustio,										
	Concussio Cerebri,										
	Compressio Cerebri,										
	Contusio,										
	Fractura,										
	Gelatio,										

Wounds and injuries.	Hernia,										
	Luxatio,										
	Morsus Serpentis,										
	Punitio,										
	Sub-luxatio,										
	Vulnus Incisum,										
	Vulnus Contusum vel Laceratum,										
	Vulnus Punctum,										
	Vulnus Sclopeticum,										
	All other diseases of this class,										
Diseases of the eye.	Amaurosis,										
	Cataracta,										
	Hemeralopia,										
	Iritis,										
	Nyctalopia,										
	Ophthalmia,										
	Retinitis,										
	All other diseases of this class.										
Diseases of the ear.	Otalgia,										
	Otitis,										
	Otorrhœa,										
	Surditas,										
	All other diseases of this class,										
	Anchylosis,										
	Atrophia,										
	Bubo simplex,										
	Carry forward,										

FORM 1—Continued.

CLASSES OF DISEASES.	TAKEN SICK OR RECEIVED INTO HOSPITAL DURING THE QUARTER.										
	Month,	First.		Second.		Third.		Total by each disease.		Total by each class.	
	Specific diseases.	Cases.	Deaths	Cases.	Deaths	Cases.	Deaths	Cases.	Deaths	Cases.	Deaths
	Brought forward,										
All other diseases.	Cachexia,										
	Debilitas,										
	Ebrietas,										
	Epistaxis,										
	Exostosis,										
	Hæmorrhois,										
	Hæmatocele,										
	Morbi Cutis,										
	Necrosis,										
	Nostalgia,										
	Odontalgia,										
	Prolapsus Ani,										
	Pyæmia,										
	Scirrhus,										
	Scorbutus,										
	Scrofula,										
	Suicidium,										
	Toxicum,										
	Tumores,										
	Vermes,										
	Morbi Varii,										
	Total,										

Form 1—Continued.

GENERAL SUMMARY.

Remaining at last Report			Taken sick during the quarter.	Aggregate.	Sent to general hospital.	Returned to duty.	On furlough.	Discharged.	Deserted.	Died.	Remaining.			MEAN STRENGTH.				Number treated.	Deaths.	Ratio per 1000 of mean strength.	
Sick.	Convalescent.	Total.									Sick.	Convalescent.	Total.	Months.	Offi'rs.	Enlisted men.	Total			Cases.	Deaths.
														Total,							
														Ratio per qr.							

Directions.—In regard to this report, the utmost punctuality and exactness will be required, and its nomenclature will be strictly observed. It will be accompanied with a general Sanitary Report, to be written on alternate pages of foolscap paper, with a margin of one inch on the left side of each page, and to be folded in four equal folds; in which the medical officer will furnish information respecting all those agencies which may have influenced the sickness and mortality of the troops—such as the medical topography of the station; the climate; prevalent diseases in the vicinity; the duty and employment of the troops; the nature of their barrack and hospital accommodations; diet; water; clothing; and general habits of the men as to cleanliness, temperance, &c. Cases of unusual interest will be reported in detail. Diseases of women and children, if given, must be reported separately. No duplicate of this report is required. It will be rendered to the Surgeon General March 31, June 30, September 30, and December 31.

In consolidated and other monthly reports of sick and wounded, the general arrangement and the nomenclature of this form will be followed.

FORM 1—Continued.

Discharges on Surgeon's Certificate, and Death.

Name.		Rank.	Regim't.	Company.	Disease.	Date of disch'ge from service.	Date of death.
Surname.	Christian name.						

REMARKS.

NOTES.—Discharges on Surgeon's certificate, and deaths occurring among those of the command *not* on sick report, will be also reported, but separated from the others by a double line drawn across the page. The remarks will, in each case, specify the manner in which the disease originated, when it is known.

In every case of the death of an officer, whether on duty or not, a special report is to be made to the Surgeon General.

FORM 1—Continued.

ENDORSEMENT.

Report of Sick and Wounded for the

Quarter ending 186 .

Station:

SURGEON.

Command.

REGIMENTS.	COMPANIES.

FORM 2.

Return of the Medical Officers of the Regular Army, Volunteer Corps, and Militia, including Physicians employed under contract, serving in the Department of ——, for the month of ——, 186 .

No.	Names.	Rank.	Post or Station	With what troops serving.	Remarks.

NOTE.—The names will be arranged in the following order: 1st, Medical Officers of the Regular Army; 2d, those of Volunteer Corps and Militia; 3d, Private Physicians. In the column of "Remarks" will be noted all changes in the position of medical officers and private physicians, whether on duty or on leave of absence; giving the number, date, and source of the order directing or authorizing such change, the time of the departure of the officers from their posts, and the date of their return to duty. If to a new post, its position must be indicated by reference to some known point, as —— miles north from —— river, town, or post-office. The remarks opposite the names of Private Physicians will state, in addition to the above, the name and rank of the party making the contract, the date thereof, the monthly compensation, and the date of their discharge from service.

The Medical Directors will require from the Medical Officers and Private Physicians in their respective Departments, monthly reports, to enable them to make out and transmit this Return to the Surgeon General.

FORM 3.

RETURN OF MEDICAL AND HOSPITAL PROPERTY.

Articles, and Characters, and Quantities.	On hand at last return.	Rec'd since last return.	Total.	Expended with the sick.	Issued.	Lost or destroyed by unavoidable accident.	Worn out, or unfit for use.	Total expended, &c.	On hand.	Remarks.

I certify, on honor, that the above return is correct, to the best of my knowledge, and that the medicines and stores have been expended with the sick belonging to the army alone.

——— ———, *Surgeon.*

NOTE.—Returns will always be transmitted in duplicate, and by different mails.

Articles purchased with the Hospital Fund will not be accounted for on this Return.

FORM 4.

Abstract of Medical and Hospital Property received and issued at ———, in the quarter ending on the ——— day of ——— 186 , by ——— ———, Medical Purveyor.

Articles, and Characters or Quantities.	Received						Issued								
	Vou. No. 1.	Vou. No. 2.	Vou. No. 3.	Vou. No. 4.	Vou. No. 5.	Total.	Vou. No. 1.	Vou. No. 2.	Vou. No. 3.	Vou. No. 4.	Vou. No. 5.	Vou. No. 6.	Vou. No. 7.	Vou. No. 8.	Total.

I certify that the above abstract is correct.

———, *Medical Purveyor.*

NOTE.—Invoices and receipts must accompany this Abstract.

FORM 5.

REQUISITION FOR MEDICAL AND HOSPITAL SUPPLIES.

Station: ——. Period: ——.

From —— to ——.

Regiment ——, Colonel ——, Surgeon ——.

Command; Officers, ——; Enlisted men, ——; All others entitled to Medicines, ——; Total, ——.

Articles, and Characters or Quantities.	On hand.	Wanted.	Articles, and Characters or Quantities.	On hand.	Wanted.
Acaciæ, ... lb.					
Acidi acetici, ... lb.					
" arseniosi, ... oz.					

Dates: ——, *Surgeon.*

NOTE.—Requisitions will exhibit the quantity of each article "on hand." They will be transmitted in duplicate, and by different mails.

FORM 6.

SPECIAL REQUISITION FOR SUPPLIES OF MEDICINES, &c.

Requisition for Medicines (Hospital Stores, &c.,) required at ——, *for* ——.

Acidi tannici, oz. 2.
Pulveris opii, lb. 1.
&c., &c.
&c., &c.

I certify that the medicines above required are necessary for the sick at ——, in consequence of [here state whether from loss, damage, &c., &c.] and that the requisition is agreeable to the Supply Table.

—— ——, *Surgeon.*

Approved:

—— ——,
Commanding Officer.

FORM 7.

Account for Medicines, &c., Purchased by a Surgeon or an Officer of the Quartermaster's Department.

The Confederate States,

To A. B., Dr.

Acidi tannici, oz. 2, at 30 cents,	$ 60
Pulveris opii, lb. 1, at $9,	9 00
&c., &c., &c.	

I certify that the articles above charged, for the use of the sick at ———, are agreeable to the foregoing requisitions, and that the charges are reasonable and just.

——— ———, *Surgeon.*

Received, ———, 186 , of ———, ——— dollars and ——— cents, in full of the above account.

——— ———, A. B.

NOTE.—The above certificate may be signed by the Surgeon making the requisition, or by any Sutgeon, or Assistant Surgeon, belonging to the army.

FORM 8.

Account of Hospital Stores, Furniture, &c., Issued.

Date.	Rice.	Sugar.	Tea.	Wine.	Bra'dy	Coffee.	&c.	&c.	&c.			Remarks.
	Lbs.	Lbs.	Oz.	Qts.		Lbs.	&c.	&c.	&c.			

Form 9.

Account of Clothing, Arms, Equipments, &c., of Patients in Hospital.

Date.	Number.	Names.	Rank.	Regiment or corps.	Company.	Coats.	Jackets.	Overalls.	&c.	Muskets.	Knapsack.	&c.	&c.	&c.				When delivered.	Remarks.
																			The remarks will note to whom the articles were delivered; what money, &c., were left by those who die; and to whom they were given.

FORM 10.

Account of Furniture, Cooking Utensils, Bedding, &c., in use.

No. of ward or kitchen.	Bunks.	Bed sacks.	Sheets.	Blankets.	Kettles.	Spoons.	Knives.	Forks.	&c.	&c.										Lost.	Worn out.	Destroyed by order.	Returned to steward.	Remarks.
																								The remarks will state how articles have been lost, and by whom destroyed, or the persons suspected, &c.

FORM 11.

REGISTER.

Number.	Names.	Rank.	Regiment or corps.	Company.	Complaint.	Admitted.	Returned to duty.	Deserted.	Discharged from service.	Sent to general hospital.	On furlough.	Died.	Remarks.

NOTE.—Both christian and surname will be registered.

FORM 12.

Prescription Book, Diet Book, and Diet Table.

NAMES.	Sunday.	Monday.	Tuesday.	Wednesday.	Thursday.	Friday.	Saturday.

The spaces in the Prescription Book are to be filled up with the prescriptions at length, the times of administering the medicines, and the quantities to be given at each time. The diet of the patients will be divided into full, half, and low, to be designated in the Diet Book by the letters F. H. and L.; and in order that the steward may have precise instructions for delivering the hospital stores, &c., the surgeon will, from time to time, insert in the Diet Book written directions of the quantity of each article in his store-room which he may think necessary to each degree of diet. To each ten patients, for example, on low diet, a certain quantity of tea, sugar, &c. To each ten on half diet, a certain quantity of rice, milk, &c. These proportions will soon become familiar to the steward, who has only to refer to the letters in the Diet Book, to ascertain the whole quantity of any article to be delivered for the day, as well as the quantity for each ward. When any liquor is directed, or any other article not contained in these general instructions of the Surgeon, the precise quantity directed for each patient will be noted in the Diet Book. The Diet Tables are to be filled up daily from the Diet Book, and hung up in each ward of a general hospital.

FORM 13.

ARMY OF THE CONFEDERATE STATES.

Certificate of Disability for Discharge.

A. B., of Captain company, (—,) of the regiment of Confederate States , was enlisted by , of the regiment of , at , on the day of , to serve years. He was born in , in the State of , is years of age, feet inches high, complexion, eyes, hair, and by occupation, when enlisted, a . During the last two months said soldier has been unfit for duty days.

(The company commander will here add a statement of all the *facts* known to him concerning the disease or wound, or cause of disability of the soldier; the time, place, manner, and all the circumstances under which the injury occurred, or disease originated or appeared; the duty, or service, or situation of the soldier at the time the injury was received or disease contracted, or supposed to be contracted; and whatever facts may aid a judgment as to the cause, immediate or remote, of the disability, and the circumstances attending it.)

Station:
Date:

C. D., *Commanding Company.*

(When the *facts* are not known to the company commander, the certificate of any officer, or affidavit of other person having such knowledge, will be appended.)

I certify that I have carefully examined the said of Captain company, and find him incapable of performing the duties of a soldier because of (here describe particularly the disability, wound, or disease; the extent to which it deprives him of the use of any limb or faculty, or affects his health, strength, activity, constitution, or capacity to labor or earn his subsistence). The Surgeon will add, from his knowledge of the facts and circumstances, and from the evidence in the case, his professional opinion of the cause or origin of the disability.

E. F., *Surgeon.*

Discharged this day of , 186 , at

Commanding the Post.

NOTES—1. When a *probable* case for *pension*, *special care* must be taken to state the *degree* of disability.

2. The *place* where the *soldier* desires to be *addressed* may be here added. *Town*, —— *County*, —— *State* ——.

(Duplicates.)

[Blanks for this form are issued from the Adjutant General's office.]

Record of Recruits Examined by , at

Date.	Name.	Where Born.		Age.	Profession.	By whom enlisted.	Remarks.
		Town or county.	State or kingdom.				
							The remarks will state the cause of rejecting any who are examined, &c., &c.

——— ———, *Surgeon.*

FORM 15.

Morning Report of the Surgeon of a Regiment, Post, or Garrison.

Date.	Company.	Remaining at last report.		Taken sick.	Total.		Returned to duty.	Discharged.	Sent to general hospital.	Died.	Remaining.		Remarks.
		In hospital.	In quarters.		In hospital.	In quarters.					In hospital.	In quarters.	

FORM 16.

Contract with a Private Physician.

This contract, entered into this day of , 186 , at , State of , between , of the C. S. Army, and Dr. , of , in the State of , witnesseth, that for the consideration hereafter mentioned, the said Dr. promises and agrees to perform the duties of a medical officer, agreeably to the Army Regulations, at , (*and to furnish the necessary medicines.*) And the said promises and agrees, on behalf of the Confederate States, to pay, or cause to be paid, to the said Dr. the sum of dollars for each and every month he shall continue to perform the services above stated, which shall be his full compensation, and in lieu of all allowances and emoluments whatsoever, (*except that for medicines furnished, which shall be at the rate of per cent. on his monthly pay, to be determined by the Surgeon General.*) This contract to continue till determined by the said doctor, or the commanding officer for the time being, or the Surgeon General.

[SEAL.]

Signed, sealed, and delivered, in presence of —

[SEAL.]

"I certify that the number of persons entitled to medical attendance, agreeably to regulations, at , is ; that no competent physician can be obtained at a lower rate; and that the services of a private physician are necessary, for the following reasons: [Here make the particular statement required in paragraph 1202; reporting, also, whether a medical officer of the army was near, and if so, that his services could not be rendered; and when the contract allowed $80 per month, whether it was necessary for the physician to abandon his own business, and give his whole time to the public service.]

——— ———, *Medical Director,*
or Commanding Officer."

FORM 17.

Form of a Medical Certificate.

——— ———, of the regiment of , having applied for a certificate on which to ground an application for leave of absence, I do hereby certify that I have carefully examined this officer, and find that . [Here the nature of the disease, wound, or disability, is to be fully stated, and the period during which the officer has suffered under its effects.] And that, in consequence thereof, he is, in my opinion, unfit for duty. I further declare my belief that he will not be able to resume his duties in a less period than . [Here state candidly and explicitly the opinion as to the period which will probably elapse before the officer will be able to resume his duties. When there is no reason to expect a recovery, or when the prospect of recovery is distant and uncertain, it must be stated.]

Dated , this day of .

Signature of the Medical Officer, ——— ———.

FORM 18.

Provision Return for the Hospital at , for days, commencing , and ending

POST OR STATION.	Number of men.	Number of women	Total.	Number of days.	Number of rations.	RATIONS OF Fresh beef.	Pork.	Flour.	Beans	Rice.	Coffee.	Sugar.	Vinegar.	Candles.	Soap.	Salt.	Remarks.
Camp of Instruction, Richmond, Virginia.																	1 steward. 2 cooks. 3 laundresses. 5 nurses. 49 sick. — 60 total.
Rations due, ...	57	3	60	7	420	210	210	420	50	370	420	420	420	420	420	420	
Rations drawn, ...						110	50	400	40	280	420	420	300	420	420	300	
Rations commuted,						100	160	20	10	90	00	00	120	00	00	120	

The A. C. S. will issue agreeably to the above return.

Surgeon C. S. A.

———— ————, *Commanding Post.*

Form 19.

A Monthly Statement of the Hospital Fund at , for the month of , 186 .

Dr.	To balance due hospital last month, ...			$0 00
	1532 rations, being whole amount due this month, at 9½ cents per ration, ...			145 54
	ISSUED.			
Cr.	By the following provisions, at contract prices:			
283½	lbs. of pork, at 6 cents per pound, ...		$17 01	
690	lbs. of fresh beef, at 4 cents per pound, ...		27 60	
1612 2-16	lbs. of flour, at 2 cents per pound, ...		32 24¼	
10	lbs. of hard bread, at 3½ cents per pound, ...		35	
70	lbs. of rice, at 6 cents per pound, ...		4 20	
56	lbs. of coffee, at 9 cents per pound, ...		5 04	
193 14-16	lbs. of sugar, at 8 cents per pound, ...		15 51	
17⅛	qrts. of vinegar, at 5 cents per quart, ...		85⅝	
15 5-16	lbs. of candles, at 12 cents per pound, ...		1 83¾	
61¼	lbs. of soap, at 6 cents per pound, ...		3 67½	
16⅞	qrts. of salt, at 3 cents per quart, ...		50⅝	
12	galls. of molasses, at 28 cents per gallon, ...		3 36	
			112 18¾	
	PURCHASED.			
	2 pairs of chickens, at 87½ cents per pair, ...	$1 75		
	4 qrts. of milk, at 7 cents per quart, ...	28		
	3 dozen oranges, at 25 cents per dozen, ...	75	2 78	
	Total expended, ...			114 96¾
	Balance due this month, ...			30 57¼

——— ———, *Surgeon.*

[Date.]

ADDENDA.

---

1. Officers of the Medical Department, by virtue of their commissions, command enlisted men.

---

2. The Medical Director and the Medical Purveyor of a Military Department are each allowed one room as an office, and fuel from the 1st of October to the 30th of April, at the rate of one cord of wood per month for each office.

---

3. Ambulances are not to be used for any other than the specific purpose for which they are designed, viz: the transportation of the sick and wounded.

---

4. Hospital laundresses will be paid eight dollars per month, by the Quartermaster's Department, on the hospital muster rolls, and will be allowed one ration per diem.

---

5. A regiment, in the field, is allowed two four-wheeled, and the same number of two-wheeled ambulances; and one wagon for the transportation of hospital supplies.

---

6. Hospital tents, having on one end a lapel, so as to admit of two or more tents being joined and thrown into one with a continuous covering or roof, will be made of these dimensions:

Length, 14 feet; width, 15 feet; height (centre) 11 feet, with a wall 4½ feet, and a "fly" of appropriate size. The ridge pole will be made in two sections, measuring 14 feet when joined.

This tent will accommodate from eight to ten patients comfortably.

The following allowance of tents for the sick, their attendants, and hospital supplies, will be issued on requisitions on the Quartermaster's Department:

COMMANDS.	Hospital Tents.	Sibley Tents.	Common Tents.
For one company, ...	—	1	1
For three companies, ...	1	1	1
For five "	2	1	1
For seven "	2	1	1
For ten "	3	1	1

7. The following Blanks will be issued from the Surgeon General's office.

Monthly Reports of Sick and Wounded.

Quarterly Reports of Sick and wounded.

Consolidated Monthly Reports of Sick and Wounded, for Medical Directors.)

Returns of Medical Officers, (for Medical Directors.)

Returns of Medical and Hospital Property.

Abstracts of Medical and Hospital Property, (for Medical Purveyors.)

Requisitions for Medical and Hospital Supplies.

Medical Purveyors will be allowed to print only their blank Invoices and Receipts. Other medical officers will not have any blanks printed, except by special authority from the Surgeon-General.

Certificates of Disability for Discharge from the service, and Hospital Muster Rolls, are furnished from the Adjutant and Inspector-General's office.

---

8. Official *letters* addressed to the Surgeon General, by medical officers of the army, will be written on letter paper (quarto post) whenever practicable, and not on note or foolscap paper. The letter must be folded in three equal folds parallel with the writing, and endorsed across that fold which corresponds with the top of the sheet, thus:

(Name and rank of writer.)

(Post or station, and date of letter.)

(Analysis of the Contents.)

ARTICLE XLIV.

ORDNANCE DEPARTMENT.

1224. The senior officer of artillery on ordnance duty is, under the direction of the Secretary of War, charged with the superintendence and administration of the Ordnance Bureau. He shall be stationed at the seat of government, and may select an officer on ordnance duty as his assistant.

1225. The officers on ordnance duty shall, under the direction of the senior officer, have charge of all arsenals, (for special reasons the armory at Richmond is placed under the charge of a superintendent, authorized by law, to be appointed by the President,) the government manufactories of powder, ordnance depots and magazines, and all property appertaining to the Ordnance Bureau, not issued to the troops, for the safe-keeping and preservation of which they shall be held strictly responsible.

They shall furnish all arms, ordnance and ordnance stores required for the military service, on proper requisitions, and in conformity with the regulations of the Bureau.* .

Arsenals, being under the control of the Ordnance Bureau, will not be interfered with by any other branch of the service.

1226. No right of choice shall exist in the command of ordnance stations. Officers will be assigned to such commands, at the discretion of the chief of ordnance, in such manner as the public interest may require.

1227. Officers in command of ordnance stations will not be changed oftener than once in four years, except for special reasons, to be approved by the Secretary of War.

1228. The names of ordnance stations will be officially known and designated as follows, viz:

Names of Ordnance Stations.	Postoffice.
Fayetteville Arsenal and Armory,	Fayetteville, N. C.
Richmond Armory, Arsenal and Laboratory,	Richmond, Va.
Augusta Arsenal,	Augusta, Ga.
Baton Rouge Arsenal	Baton Rouge, La.
Charleston "	Charleston, S. C.
Mt. Vernon "	Mt. Vernon, Ala.
Apalachicola "	Chatahouchie, Fla.
Texas "	San Antonio, Texas.
Little Rock "	Little Rock, Ark.
Savannah Depot	Savannah, Ga.
Montgomery "	Montgomery, Ala.
Nashville "	Nashville, Tenn.
Government Powder Mills,	Augusta, Ga.

* For the present, the Ordnance Bureau will also furnish knapsacks, haversacks, and canteens.

1229. All orders received from the headquarters of the army, relating to the movement of the troops, or the discipline of the army, shall be circulated through and by the chief of ordnance to every ordnance station.

1230. The senior officer of artillery on ordnance duty, attached to an army in the field, shall have the charge and direction of the depots of ordnance and ordnance stores for the supply of such army. All orders relating thereto shall be regularly transmitted to him through the office of the Adjutant General acting with such army. He will communicate with the chief artillery officer, to ascertain the actual and probable wants of the army relative to his department, and be prepared to furnish supplies at the shortest notice. He will also correspond with the Chief of Ordnance, and with the officers at the nearest arsenals and laboratories, so as to anticipate, if possible, and provide for all the wants of the army connected with his department.

1231. The general denomination, "*Ordnance and Ordnance Stores*," comprehends all cannon, howitzers, mortars, cannon balls, shot and shells, for the land service; all gun carriages, mortar beds, caissons and traveling forges, with their equipments; and all other apparatus and machines required for the service and manœuvres of artillery, in garrisons, at sieges, or in the field; together with the materials for their construction, preservation, and repair. Also, all small arms, side-arms, and accoutrements, for the artillery, cavalry, infantry, and riflemen; all ammunition for ordnance and small arms, and all stores of expenditure for the service of the various arms; materials for the construction and repair of ordnance buildings; utensils and stores for laboratories, including standard weights, gauges and measures; and all other tools and utensils required for ordnance duty. The ordinary articles of camp equipage and pioneers' tools, such as axes, spades, shovels, mattocks, &c., are not embraced as ordnance supplies.

1232. Ordnance and ordnance stores shall be provided by open purchase, by fabrication or by contract, as may be most advantageous to the public service. They shall be provided by ordnance officers only, except when otherwise specially directed by the Chief of Ordnance, or in case of urgent necessity; and in such cases, a report and certificate showing the necessity, from the officer ordering the purchase, will be required for the admission of the account of purchase at the treasury.

INSPECTION OF NATIONAL ARMORIES, ARSENALS, POWDER WORKS, AND ORDNANCE DEPOTS.

1233. Inspections of national armories, of arsenals and ordnance depots, shall be made under the direction of the Chief of Ordnance, by such officers of the Ordnance Bureau as the Secretary of War may, from time to time, designate for that purpose.

1234. A thorough and complete inspection of the national armories, and arsenal of construction, shall be made annually, and all other ordnance stations at least once every two years. At these inspections it shall be the special duty of the inspecting officer to see that the laws, regulations, and orders of the Bureau are faithfully executed, and to give the necessary orders and instructions in writing, at the time of inspection, in correction of any neglect or departure therefrom. He will ascertain whether the persons employed in arsenal and armories are efficient in the performance of their duties: whether the number exceeds that required to execute, by constant employment, the business of the establishment; and in case of any excess beyond what may be necessary, he will report the number to the commanding officer for discharge, and immediately after report the same and the circumstances, with copies of all orders and instructions which he may have given during his inspections, to the Chief of Ordnance. It shall also be his duty specially to examine the annual reports, and to give such orders as, in his judgment, may tend to produce as much uniformity in the mode and amount of valuation of property as the circumstances at each place will admit.

1235. At the conclusion of each inspection of a national armory, arsenal or construction, or ordnance depot, the inspecting officer will report to the Chief of Ordnance the general and particular condition of each; and especially each and every departure from the established models and patterns in all articles fabricated; and also, how far the laws, regulations, and orders may have been violated, and in what respect they have not been carried into full operation. He shall keep books in which shall be recorded all reports which he is required to make, and all correspondence relating to his inspections.

SERVICE AT ARMORIES, ARSENALS AND ORDNANCE DEPOTS.

1236. The commanding officer of an armory shall have the management and direction of the business, and shall conduct the correspondence of the armory. He shall draw up and publish, under the direction of the Chief of Ordnance, all necessary regulations for its internal government; he shall provide the necessary tools and stores; he shall give directions to the store-keeper, acting as paymaster, in the disbursement of the public funds; he shall at all times have free access to the books of the store-keeper, and may require of him any information relative to the financial concerns of the establishment; he shall engage all workmen, determine their grades, appoint such number of foremen in each branch of the manufacture as he shall consider necessary, and he may displace or dismiss said workmen or foremen when he shall deem it expedient; he will be held responsible that the number of hired men employed at the armory, under his superintendence, shall not exceed the number necessary to execute, by constant employment, all the business of the armory. In the absence of the commanding officer, the charge of an armory shall devolve on the master armorer, unless the Chief of Ordnance shall otherwise direct.

1237. The commanding officer of an armory shall make annual reports of the inspection of all arms manufactured at the armory, in conformity with the directions in the form number 37; and the master armorer, under the direction of the commanding officer, shall keep a book in which shall be entered copies of all the inspection reports herein required. The originals of said reports shall be forwarded to the Chief of Ordnance on the completion of the inspections.

1238. The commanding officer of an armory shall authorize the issue of materials required for fabrication in the workshops in such quantities, and at such times, as may be considered necessary: provided the supply so issued (which shall in all cases be placed in charge of the master armorer) shall at no time exceed the quantity which may be required for use in the course of three months.

1239. At each national armory the master armorer shall keep accounts with the foremen for all tools and materials, rough and finished work delivered to, and received from, them respectively; he shall be careful to keep each particular branch of the manufacture in an equal state of advancement; he shall be the chief inspector of all materials and tools, and of all finished arms, to be delivered into the public storehouse; and he shall be responsible that the same shall have undergone the proofs required by the Ordnance Bureau, and shall be completed for service; he shall hold the foremen responsible for the faithful execution of the part of the work with which they may be respectively charged.

1240. The foremen at national armories shall keep accounts with the individual workmen employed in their respective branches, of tools and materials, and of work, rough and finished, delivered to, or received from, them respectively. They shall be inspectors and comptrollers, each in his proper department, of the work executed. Suitable marks are to be adopted to ensure the due inspection of all parts of the work, and the responsibility of the foremen.

1241. The foremen at each of the national armories shall make out and hand to the master armorer certified monthly rolls, specifying the names of the persons employed, the quantity of work performed by each during the month, and the amount due for the same, whether by the established regulations or particular stipulations. And the master armorer shall also certify to the correctness of said rolls, and hand them to the commanding officer, that he may cause the general monthly pay rolls to be made out. The pay-rolls shall exhibit the compensation due to each individual for the month, and will become the vouchers on which the payments will be made. The books and accounts of the master armorer and foremen shall be open to the inspection of the commanding officer and his clerks, and are to be carefully preserved, and ultimately deposited in the office of the commanding officer.

1242. The commanding officer of a national armory shall, under direction of the Chief of Ordnance, arrange all work connected with the fabrication of arms at the armory under classes or heads, not exceeding ten nor less than five, according to the different degrees of labor, skill or ability required in its execution; and each workman thereon employed shall be assigned to work under some one class; shall be denominated of that class, and shall receive a daily compensation corresponding thereto; such compensation shall be established on the following principles to-wit: First, of an estimated fair day's work for every variety of work under each class; second, of a just and reasonable per diem allowance, corresponding thereto, which shall be greater or less, according to the greater or less degree of labor, skill and ability required; third, of the amount of work done, so that each shall receive the per diem allowance if he perform the estimated fair day's work of his class; and if he perform more or less than such fair day's work, then his compensation shall be proportionately greater or less than such per diem allowance.

1243. Whenever at national armories, arsenals, or ordnance depots, any hired workman shall, through incompetency or design, spoil any piece of work, in the execution of which he may be engaged, it shall be the duty of the commanding officer to cause the amount of injury to be estimated, and give the necessary information to the paymaster to stop the same from the pay of such workman.

1244. At national armories or arsenals, where dwelling houses, belonging to the Confederate States, are occupied by workmen, a quarterly rent-roll, specifying the names of the occupants, the periods for which rents are charged, the price per quarter, and the amount due from each person, shall be prepared by the commanding officer, agreeably to form No. 14. The proper designation shall be added to the names of such persons as may be entitled to the use of dwellings rent free. If the officer who prepares the roll is not the disbursing officer, he shall furnish the latter with one copy and shall transmit another to the Chief of Ordnance. The disbursing officer shall retain the roll in his office, and shall credit the amount collected in his account current; and it is made his duty to collect the sums due from the several individuals charged, by retaining in his hands the proper amount when making the monthly payments; it is not required that the rents charged and collected shall be entered on the pay-rolls, the credit in the accounts current, with the proper rent-roll, being sufficient.

1245. Master armorers and clerks employed at the national armories shall be allowed quarters, rent free, where there are buildings belonging to the Confederate States sufficient for their accommodation.

1246. Fuel in kind shall be allowed to armory officers, occupying public quarters, at the following rates per annum, viz:

To a master armorer, . .	18 cords of wood.
To a clerk	12 " "

1247. Master armorers at the national armories, when traveling on duty under orders from the proper authority, shall be entitled to receive ten cents a mile for the distance traveled; all hired persons in the service of the Ordnance Bureau shall, under the same circumstances, be entitled to receive eight cents a mile.

1248. At the national armories, arsenals and ordnance depots where it may be considered necessary to enlarge the sites, to erect new buildings or machinery, to make additions or repairs to old buildings, to provide new wharves or enclosures, or to make any other permanent improvements, plans and estimates therefor shall be made by the commanding officer, and be transmitted in time to be received at the ordnance office in the month of August. Estimates for any of these purposes shall exhibit fully the objects contemplated, the reason or causes which render them necessary, the measures by which it is proposed to effect them, and their probable cost. The estimate, if approved by the Chief of Ordnance, shall be submitted to the Secretary of War, and, if sanctioned by him, shall be embodied in the general estimate submitted annually to Congress. Works of the description above mentioned shall in no case be undertaken or commenced but by special authority from the Chief of the Ordnance Bureau.

1249. Authority from the Chief of Ordnance, must, in all cases, be obtained before ornamental trees growing on the public grounds, at national armories, arsenals, or ordnance depots, can be removed or destroyed.

1250. Horses for the public service in the Ordnance Bureau, shall not be purchased without authority from the Chief of Ordnance. The horses must be strong, heavy-draught horses.

1251. Workmen or others employed by hire at national armories, arsenals, or ordnance depots, shall be engaged on daily wages and not on monthly wages or salaries. In places where it is found necessary to employ slaves on public works, and where the customs of the country do not permit of daily hire, slaves may be engaged on monthly wages. In such cases, parts of months will be set forth as in form No. 18.

1252. Workmen or others employed by hire in the Ordnance Bureau, shall be paid only for such days or parts of days as they may actually labor in the service of said Bureau, for which the certificate upon honor of the commanding officer shall be a necessary voucher. The working hours for hired men at the ordnance establishments shall be so arranged as to average ten hours a day throughout the year, working by daylight only. In cases where men labor more than the usual number of working days, the commanding officer will explain on the pay-roll the necessity therefor.

1253. No slave, the property of any officer or person in the service of the Confederate States, connected with the War Department, shall be employed in the Ordnance Bureau.

1254. Payments to hired persons in the Ordnance Bureau shall be made monthly, unless otherwise specially authorized.

1255. No receipt shall be taken in blank by a disbursing officer, nor unless the money be actually paid; and no due bills for money on public account shall be given; nor shall any officer or agent of the Ordnance Bureau be concerned, directly or indirectly, on private account, in any contract made for said Bureau, or in the purchase or sale of any articles which it may be his duty to purchase or sell on public account.

1256. When a change in the command of an armory, arsenal, or ordnance depot occurs, the officer relieved shall prepare and adjust all accounts, both for money and for stores; he shall state such accounts as may remain due at the time of his being relieved, and shall hand them, together with a certified abstract of the same, to the relieving officer, for settlement; no outstanding claims, other than those embraced in such accounts and abstract, shall be settled without instructions from the Ordnance Bureau.

1257. No money shall be disbursed at any national armory, arsenal, or ordnance depot, until the pay-roll or other account shall have been first examined, approved, and certified to be correct by the officer having charge of such armory, arsenal or depot; and the amount shall be stated in words and not in figures; and when the disbursements are not made by the commanding officer, such approval and certificate shall be a necessary voucher in the settlement of the accounts of the disbursing officer.

1258. It shall be the duty of the paymaster and store keeper at each of the national armories, to make all disbursements, to receive in charge, and receipt for, all materials procured, after they shall have been inspected by the master armorer; to re-issue the same on the order of the commanding officer, and to receive and receipt for all finished arms. He shall render accounts and returns according to the forms required by the Ordnance Bureau.

1259. A military store-keeper attached to a national armory, an arsenal, or an ordnance depot, shall have the charge of ordnance and ordnance stores at the armory, arsenal, or depot, excepting such ordnance tools, machines, or other stores, including public horses or oxen, as may be required for the current service of the post, which are placed in charge of the commanding officer thereof. (See Par. 1350.) The store-keeper shall be subject to the orders of such commanding officer in all matters which regard the inspection, preservation, and issue of the stores; and it shall be the duty of said commanding officer to furnish the store-keeper at all times with the necessary aid from the forces under his command, to assist in receiving, delivering, removing and arranging the ordnance and ordnance stores, and in repairing and preserving all public buildings in which they may be deposited.

1260. In case of an arsenal or ordnance depot being left without any other commissioned officer, the charge of the post shall devolve on the military store-keeper, who shall conform to such instructions as may be given him by the commanding officer on leaving the post.

1261. A military store-keeper of the Ordnance Bureau shall, when required by the Secretary of War, in addition to his other duties, disburse the funds for the ordnance service at the post where he may be stationed; and he shall in that case give a bond, with approved security, in such sum as the Secretary of War may direct, for the faithful performance of his duty.

1262. At arsenals of construction, and other ordnance depots, where there is no store-keeper, and at which the annual disbursements exceed five thousand dollars, the officer second in rank shall, if required by the Secretary of War, be the disbursing officer.

1263. Every disbursing officer of the Ordnance Bureau shall be held responsible for the safe-keeping of the funds placed in his hands, in the manner prescribed by the regulations of the War and Treasury Departments. A disbursing officer, on being relieved from duty at any post, shall pay over the unexpended balance in his hands to the person who may be designated by the Chief of Ordnance to receive it.

1264. The commanding officer of any armory, arsenal, or ordnance depot, having a military store-keeper, shall, at the time of the reception by the store-keeper of ordnance or ordnance stores, which may have been obtained by purchase or fabrication, furnish the store-keeper with an authenticated abstract for the fabrication, and an account for the purchase; and whenever the commanding officer shall receive ordnance or ordnance stores from the commanders of military posts, or other agents of the War Department, he shall in like manner hand over to the military store-keeper the invoices accompanying said property. (See Form No. 2.)

1265. All orders for the issue of ordnance and ordnance stores, in charge of any military store-keeper, shall be directed to the commanding officer of the armory, arsenal, or depot, to which such store-keeper is attached; and it shall be the duty of said commanding officer to see that such orders are faithfully and promptly executed. All issues of ordnance or ordnance stores in charge of the store-keeper at any arsenal, ordnance depot, or national armory, for the purposes of construction in the armory or ordnance shops, or for the current service of the arsenal, depot, or armory, shall be made only upon the written order of the commanding officer, or of some military or armory officer appointed by him for that purpose; and an abstract of such orders for current issues shall be made and presented by the storekeeper, at the end of each quarter, to the commanding officer, who shall authenticate the same. (See form No. 9.)

1266. Ordnance or ordnance stores shall not be issued for construction in the ordnance shops, or for the current service of any military post, except on the written authority of the commander, or that of some military officer, or other responsible person acting under his order; and such authority shall, in all cases, state the object of the issue, and be filed in the Ordnance or Adjutant's office of the post, in order that the quarterly abstract of materials expended or consumed at the post (see form No. 9) may be in conformity to the orders for issue.

1267. When an order for supplies is received at any armory, arsenal, or ordnance depot, the commanding officer shall cause the articles ordered to be carefully packed, and shall turn them over to the nearest quartermaster, with an invoice. (See form No. 2.) A duplicate of the invoice shall, at the same time, be transmitted to the officer to whom the stores are addressed, or for whose command they are designed. The dates when the order was received, and the articles turned over for transportation, will be stated in the next monthly statement of work done. (See form No. 29.)

1268. Requisitions for ordnance or ordnance stores, needed at any armory, arsenal, or ordnance depot, shall exhibit, in addition to the description and quantity of property asked for, the amount of similar articles on hand, with full explanations, showing the propriety of the issue. (See form No 24.) These requisitions shall be forwarded to the Chief of Ordnance, and, if approved by him, the requisite orders shall be given.

1269. In case of the authorized absence of a military storekeeper, and at arsenals or ordnance depots, where there is no storekeeper, the commanding officer will be held responsible for the safekeeping and preservation of all public property committed to his charge; but he may assign to a junior officer of the arsenal, or depot, the immediate charge of it, and also the duty of preparing the proper returns.

1270. To guard against the embezzlement of ordnance and ordnance stores, they shall be distinctly and permanently marked, so as to identify them as being the property of the Confederate States, previously to their being sent from the arsenals or ordnance depots.

1271. No hired or enlisted man engaged in the service of the Ordnance Bureau, at any national armory, arsenal, ordnance depot, or with any military command, shall be employed for the private benefit of officers or other persons, with or without compensation; and no public property appertaining to the Ordnance Bureau shall, under any pretence, be sold, exchanged, or used for the private benefit of any person or persons whatsoever. The public workshops, tools and materials, must be used solely for purposes of public benefit; and all private work in the public buildings, and all other application of public means to any other than public purposes, is expressly prohibited. It shall be the special duty of all officers or other agents of the Ordnance Bureau, and especially inspectors, to see that this regulation be strictly observed.

1272. The number of enlisted men authorized by law for the Ordnance Bureau, shall be assigned to the arsenals and depots by the Chief of Ordnance, who shall likewise determine the number of each specified grade of workmen to be employed at each arsenal or depot, all of whom shall be enlisted in the grade of laborer; from which grade promotions shall be made of such as may be found to merit it, at the discretion of the commanding officers of arsenals and depots, under the provisions contained in the next articles of these regulations.

1273. Enlisted men in the Ordnance Bureau will be mustered in either of the grades authorized by law, except that of master workman, at the discretion of the senior ordnance officer at the arsenal or depot at which they may be stationed; provided, that every enlisted man shall be efficient in the discharge of the duties required of him, according to his grade. Enlisted master workmen will be appointed, when required, by the Chief of Ordnance, upon recommendations of the senior officers of arsenals or depots. Ordnance men will be discharged by their commanders on expiration of enlistment; but for any other cause they can be discharged only by the War Department, or by sentence of a general court martial.

1274. Enlistments of ordnance men will be taken in duplicate, according to form No. 26, one to be forwarded to the Chief of Ordnance, and the other to be retained at the post or station where the man was enlisted.

1275. Enlisted soldiers who may be detailed from the line of the army for extra service, under the direction of an officer of the Ordnance Bureau, shall be allowed, while so employed, for every period greater than ten days continuously, a per diem of forty cents.

ORDNANCE SERGEANTS.

1276. The Secretary of War shall be authorized to select from the sergeants of the line of the army, who shall have faithfully served eight years in the service, four years of which in the grade of non-commissioned officer, as many ordnance sergeants as the service may require, not to exceed one for each military post, whose duty it shall be to receive and preserve the ordnance, arms, ammunition, and other military stores at the post, under the direction of the commanding officer of the same, and under such regulations as shall be prescribed by the Secretary of War, and who shall receive for their services twenty-one dollars per month.*

1277. The appointments and removals of ordnance sergeants stationed at military posts in pursuance of the above provisions of law, shall be reported by the Adjutant General to the Chief of Ordnance.

1278. An ordnance sergeant in charge of ordnance stores at a post where there is no commissioned officer, shall be held responsible for the safe keeping of the property, and he shall be governed by the regulations of the Ordnance Bureau, in making issues of the same and in preparing and furnishing the requisite returns. If the means at his disposal are not sufficient for the preservation of the property, he shall report the circumstance to the Chief of Ordnance, who shall take measures accordingly.

ORDNANCE STORES IN SERVICE.

1279. In time of war, arms, ordnance, and ordnance stores, for arm-

*The operation of this article is suspended until further orders.

ing, equipping, and supplying the troops in service, will be issued upon the order of any general or field officer commanding an army, garrison or detachment, whose order shall be transmitted to the Ordnance Burea by the officer or agent by whom the issue is made. The arming of permanent fortifications will be specially directed by the Secretary of War.

1280. Any officer commanding a district or geographical department, who, in time of peace, may require authority to call, at his discretion, for ordnance and ordnance stores from the arsenals and depots within the extent of his command, shall make application for that purpose to the Secretary of War through the Adjutant General's office.

1281. No arms nor ordnance stores shall be issued otherwise than as provided for in these regulations, except by special authority from the President of the Confederate States, or in cases of servile insurrection or foreign invasion. Whenever issues are made under this exception, the order therefor shall be immediately forwarded to the ordnance officer, accompanied by a statement of the reasons for the issue.

1282. Ordnance stores issued on urgent occasions, as provided in the next preceding article, shall, if not expended, be carefully stored at some convenient ordnance depot when the urgency ceases.

1283. One complete set of arms and accoutrements of each description may, if the state of the public supplies will permit, be issued to any officer of the army for his own use, and no other's, on his payment of the cost price thereof to the issuing officer.

1284. All ordnance stores issued for the personal use of officers, agreeably to Par. 1280, shall be accounted for on the quarterly return of property of the officer making the issue; and the voucher for such issue shall be the duplicate acknowledgment of the officer receiving the stores, stating the fact of having received the same and paid for them, the amount paid being likewise stated in the acknowledgment. (See form No. 21.) The disbursing officer of the arsenal, armory, or depot, from which the issue is made, will credit all moneys thus received in his next quarterly account current.

1285. Ordnance and ordnance stores in charge of any ordnance officer, or the command of any regiment, company, or detachment, or other agent of the Ordnance Bureau, shall in no case be issued or loaned to individuals, except as provided in Par. 1280, or authorized by law; nor shall they, under any circumstances, be used for private purposes by any officer or other agent of the army, or be diverted from their legitimate use, as indicated by the regulations and the laws appropriating moneys for the service of the Ordnance Bureau.

1286. Requisitions (according to form 24) for ordnance and ordnance stores for the use of regiments, companies, detachments, or military posts or stations, shall, in time of peace, be transmitted to the General or commander of the district or geographical department within which such regiment, company, detachment, or military post or station is situated, who will sanction, modify, or annul such requisition at his discretion. If sanctioned or modified, he shall transmit the same through the Adjutant General for the decision of the General-in-Chief.

1287. In cases of urgent necessity, the requisitions may be transmitted direct to the Adjutant General for the decision of the General-in-

Chief, duplicates thereof being immediately forwarded, as prescribed in the preceding article.

1288. The Chief of Ordnance shall examine all requisitions for ordnance supplies, and, under the direction of the Secretary of War, shall modify and regulate them in such manner as to curtail all extravagancies, to suit them to the exigencies of the service, to existing appropriations, and to just and proper views of economy; and in the performance of this part of his duty, he shall invariably communicate with the General-in-Chief of the army.

1289. It shall be the duty of the Chief of Ordnance, under the direction of the General-in-Chief, to see that a sufficient quantity of ordnance, ammunition and ordnance stores are deposited at every military post where troops are stationed.

1290. On the receipt of ordnance or ordnance stores by any officer of the Ordnance Bureau, or by any other officer or agent of the army, such officer or agent shall cause the same to be immediately examined and entered on the property return of the post, company, or detachment, and he shall transmit to the forwarding officer duplicate receipts for the same, (Form No. 7,) stating the number or quantity, and the condition of the articles received. If, on examination, it should appear that there are less than specified in the invoice; or have sustained material injury in the transportation, it shall be the duty of such officer or agent to report the amount of loss or damage to the Chief of Ordnance, and also to the proper officer of the Quartermaster's Department, to the end that, if such loss or damage has been caused by neglect of the agent of transportation, it may be deducted from the amount allowed him for that purpose.

1291. The receipt of ordnance stores at an arsenal or ordnance depot shall be noted on the monthly statement of work done. (Form No. 29.) The receipt of stores at any other military post, or by an officer in command of troops, shall be immediately reported to the Chief of Ordnance.

1292. When an officer or agent of the army, who shall have received an invoice of ordnance or ordnance stores to be forwarded to him, has reason to believe that they have been lost or miscarried, or are deposited in irresponsible hands, it shall be his duty to acquaint the forwarding officer of such failure. And it shall be the duty of both officers to make diligent inquiries along the route of transportation, of all persons into whose hands such ordnance or ordnance stores might probably have passed; the result of which shall be reported to the Chief of Ordnance. Should it be ascertained that the stores have been lost, then the officer to whom they were sent shall enclose a certificate (see Form No. 11) to the forwarding officer, who shall transmit the same, accompanied by one from himself, (see Form No. 12) to the Chief of Ordnance, to the end that he may be relieved from further responsibility on that account.

1293. The commander of any permanently embodied regiment, or (if separated by companies or detachments) the commander of each company or detachment, will be considered as having the immediate charge of, and will be held accountable for, all arms, ordnance and ordnance stores at the post, issued for the personal armament of the troops of his command. And the commander of each military post will be considered as having the immediate charge of, and will be held accountable for, all ordnance and ordnance stores at the post, which are not in the exclusive service of any regiment, company, or detachment, or not in charge of an officer or agent of the Ordnance Bureau.

1294. The commander of each company shall, as far as practicable, retain and keep in store such number of small arms and sets of accoutrements as may be sufficient, with those in use, to equip the full complement of men established by law for his command; and whenever any such arms and accoutrements become unserviceable for want of repairs, which cannot be made at the post, it shall be the duty of the commander of the regiment or post to send them to the nearest or most convenient arsenal with a requisition for immediate repair; but in no case shall such unserviceable small arms and accoutrements be exchanged for others when they can be made serviceable for repair, nor until they have been regularly condemned by an inspecting officer, or board of inspection organized by the commander of the department. It is made the duty of commanders of regiments to see that this regulation is strictly observed.

1295. Arms and accoutrements condemned as totally irreparable, under the provisions of the preceding article, shall be broken up, and the serviceable parts retained and accounted for by the commander of the company, to be used for repairs. The commander of each company shall also, on his requisition, made in the usual form, be furnished by the Ordnance Bureau with a due proportion of such spare parts as are necessary for repairs.

1296. Officers who may execute the duty of repairing arms and accoutrements, under the provisions of paragraph 1294, shall transmit to the Chief of Ordnance, in each case of repair, a statement of the cost thereof, in order that it may accompany to the treasury the quarterly return of the officer commanding the company to which the articles belonged, and that such officer may be held accountable for the damages, according to the regulations.

1297. Accoutrements and artillery equipments, only partly worn, which have become soiled or discolored by use in the field, and which are reported as yet sufficiently strong to endure much more service, shall be cleaned and furbished and restored to their original new appearance, as nearly as can be done, when they will be issued to the troops for service, on the usual requisitions.

1298. Whenever an enlisted soldier is transferred from one company to another, his arms and accoutrements shall be retained with the company to which he belonged, unless the urgency of the service shall otherwise require.

1299. In all cases in which ordnance or ordnance stores are lost or damaged by the negligence or misconduct of any officer, cadet, or enlisted man, the amount of said loss or damage shall be charged to the delinquent on the next muster roll, and the facts shall be recorded on the books of the company, detachment, military post, arsenal, or ordnance depot. On the next quarterly return of ordnance and ordnance stores, the name of the delinquent shall be noted, with the amount charged, the particular loss or damage for which the charge is made, and the date of the muster roll on which noted.

1300. When, in compliance with the preceding article, a charge for loss or damage of ordnance or ordnance stores is made against any individual, it shall be the duty of the commanding officer, provided it be requested by the individual charged, to assemble a *board of examination* (to be composed of commissioned officers, if practicable,) to investigate the facts, and report to him the cause of such loss or damage; and their report, with the remarks of the commanding officer thereon, shall accompany the next quarterly return to the Chief of Ordnance.

1301. All charges made in obedience to paragraphs 1299 and 1300, of these regulations, for loss or damage of ordnance or ordnance stores in the hands of the troops, shall have precedence of all other claims whatsoever on the pay of the troops; they shall be regulated by tables of cost, periodically published by the Chief of Ordnance. (See rates of prices of articles.)

1302. Whenever stoppages are noted on muster rolls, for loss or damage of ordnance or ordnance stores, it shall be the duty of the paymaster to withhold the amount charged, and that of the Paymaster General to transmit to the Second Auditor of the Treasury, in the month of May, annually, a statement exhibiting the total amount of such stoppages up to the 31st of December next preceding, to the end that such amount may be refunded to the appropriation to which it may legally belong.

1303. When any person shall fraudulently sell or otherwise dispose of any ordnance or ordnance stores, the property of the Confederate States, or convert the same to his own use, or deface their marks for the purpose of concealment, or wantonly waste or destroy such property, it shall be the duty of any military officer to whom the facts shall become known, either personally or on creditable report, to communicate the circumstances to the Chief of Ordnance, who shall adopt such measures in the case as the interest of the service may require.

1304. Surplus ordnance and ordnance stores in the hands of the troops shall be turned into store, in as good order as possible, at the most convenient ordnance depot, for which the officer or agent in charge of such depot shall give a receipt, stating their condition.

1305. Surplus ordnance and ordnance stores, at any military post, not an ordnance depot, which are considered by the commanding officer unnecessary for the service of the post, shall be transported to an arsenal or ordnance depot, provided the removal of such ordnance and ordnance stores shall be first sanctioned by an Inspector General, or by the commander of the department in which they are situated. Officers commanding posts will report all surplus stores to the commander of the department, or to the Inspector General, when present at the post on a tour of inspection, who shall designate the place to which they shall be removed.

1306. In case ordnance or ordnance stores are lost, or rendered unserviceable by unavoidable accident, the commanding officer shall assemble a *board of survey* to investigate the facts, and report to him the cause of such loss or damage. The board shall be composed of commissioned officers, when practicable, and their report shall be submitted to the commanding officer for his remarks or explanations, and shall be forwarded by the person responsible for the property with his next quarterly return of property to the ordnance office.

1307. Whenever any officer in charge of ordnance or ordnance stores shall leave his command or post, with a prospect of being absent for any period less than three months, it shall not be obligatory on him to take receipts for said ordnance or ordnance stores; but he may, at his own discretion, either close his accounts or place the ordnance or ordnance stores under charge of the officer next in command, who shall in that case, do all duty in regard to said ordnance or ordnance stores in the *name* of said absent officer, until his return to the command or post.

1308. At the decease of any disbursing officer of the Ordnance Bureau, or any officer or agent chargeable with ordnance or ordnance stores, and responsible for the returns required by paragraphs 1348 and 1350, a board of survey shall be assembled by the senior officer of the arsenal, depot, or post, to examine the state of the funds, ordnance or ordnance stores, for which said officer or agent was accountable. The board will make a report in duplicate, in the same order of classification as in Par. 1365, stating the kinds, quantity, and condition of said ordnance or ordnance stores, and the amount of funds on hand, which report will be immediately transmitted to the Chief of Ordnance; the duplicate will be handed to the successor of the deceased.

1309. The commander of each company in garrison shall constantly retain in store, and exhibit on his quarterly returns of property, the regulation arm chests hereinafter mentioned, in which all arms and accoutrements, not in the hands of the troops, shall be at all times securely packed for preservation, viz: to each company of infantry, and to each company of artillery armed as infantry, two m[illegible] arm-chests; and to each company of riflemen, two rifle arm-chests; to each company of cavalry, one pistol arm-chest; and if armed with carbines or rifles, then, in addition, one rifle or carbine arm-chest.

1310. The commanding officer of any regiment, garrison, company, or detachment, shall be responsible that all surplus chests or cases, other than packing boxes, in which arms or other ordnance stores have been conveyed to his command are carefully preserved. They will be receipted for and entered upon the property returns as other stores, and, in like manner, reported to the Ordnance Bureau.

1311. Every officer commanding a permanently embodied regiment, or a company, garrison or detachment, shall make a report every two months to the Ordnance Bureau, stating all damages to arms, equipments, and implements belonging to his command, noting those occasioned by negligence or abuse, and naming the party by whose negligence or abuse the said damages were occasioned; which reports shall be consolidated by the Chief of Ordnance, and transmitted with his remarks and orders thereon, every six months, to the superintendents of the national armories and inspecting officers of the Ordnance Bureau, in order to ascertain and correct any defects which may exist in the manufacture of arms.

UNSERVICEABLE ORDNANCE STORES.

1312. Whenever ordnance or ordnance stores are reported unserviceable, they shall be examined by an Inspector General, or some other officer specially designated by the Secretary of War for that purpose, who will note on the inventory such as he condemns and such as he considers repairable. (See form No. 13.) He shall recommend the stores condemned by him either to be broken up at the arsenal, depot, or military post, or to be sold, as may be deemed most advantageous to the public service; but should it appear to the inspector that the ordnance or ordnance stores condemned are of too little value to cover the expense of sale or breaking up, he shall recommend them to be dropped from the return as useless. Such arms and stores as the inspector may consider repairable he shall direct either to be repaired at the arsenal, depot, or military post, or to be transported to the nearest or most convenient arsenal or depot of construction or repairs. The list of condemned stores (see form No. 10) with the remarks and opinion of the inspector, shall be made in duplicate, and forwarded to the Chief of Ordnance for the further action of the President of the Confederate States. The inventory shall be left with the officer having charge of the ordnance and ordnance stores.

1313. All articles condemned and ordered for sale by the President of the Confederate States shall be disposed of at public auction, under the superintendence of such officers as may be designated for that purpose by the Chief of Ordnance, due public notice being given of the sale. An authorized auctioneer shall be employed, and the sale shall be conducted in conformity with the established usages of the place where made.

1314. An officer directing a sale of unserviceable ordnance stores will cause the articles to be offered in such lots as he may think will command the best prices; and he is authorized to bid in or suspend the sale of any articles when, in his opinion, they will command better prices at private sale. No article shall be sold at private sale until after it shall have been offered at auction, nor then at a price less than that offered at public sale.

1315. All sales shall be for cash. The auctioneer shall make certain bills of sale of the property and deliver them to the superintending officer, to whom the money shall be paid on delivery of the property. All expenses of the sale shall be paid from the proceeds. The auctioneer's certified account of sales in detail, and the vouchers for the expenses of the sale, shall be forwarded to the ordnance office unconnected with quarterly accounts, whence, after examination and record, they shall be transmitted to the proper auditor for settlement; the nett proceeds of the sale shall be disposed of in such manner as the Chief of Ordnance shall direct.

ISSUE OF ORDNANCE STORES TO MILITIA IN THE SERVICE OF THE CONFEDERATE STATES.

1316. Whenever any regiment, or company or detachment of militia shall be called into the service of the Confederate States, they are mustered and inspected by an inspector general, or some duly authorized officer of the regular troops, who shall ascertain the condition of the arms, accoutrements, ordnance and ordnance stores in their possession, and if it should be found necessary to supply them with arms and accoutrements, or ordnance and ordnance stores, belonging to the Confederate States, the commander thereof shall make requisition for the articles required, according to form No. 25, which if sanctioned by the inspecting officer, shall be submitted for approval or modification to the commander of the regular troops present or in the vicinity; and upon such requisition duly approved by such commander, any officer or agent of the Ordnance Bureau may issue the articles required taking duplicate receipts therefor, one of which shall be forwarded to the Chief of Ordnance, in order that the same may be charged on the books of the bureau to the officer who received them. And the commander of such regiment, battalion, company or detachment, shall be held responsible for the care and preservation of the articles thus received, and that the arms and accoutrements are issued to the men constituting his command, and that each individual is charged on the muster roll with the actual number of arms and accoutrements delivered to him; and the same shall be entered upon each successive muster roll until the men shall be discharged.

1317. When any militia are about to be discharged, they are mustered for payment by an inspector-general, or some other duly authorized officer of the regular troops, who shall, at the same time, critically inspect the arms and accoutrements in their possession, in order to ascertain if any loss or damage has accrued to them whilst in their possession, either by negligence or carelessness; and if any, shall charge the amount of said loss or damage, according to the rates established by the Ordnance Bureau, to each individual, opposite to his name on the muster roll, which amount the paymaster shall deduct from the pay due each individual at the time of his discharge. And it shall be the duty of the inspecting officer, or of an officer of the Ordnance Bureau, at the time of muster and inspection for discharge, to receive the arms and accoutrements, ordnance and ordnance stores, in the possession of the regiment, battalion, company or detachment, and to give duplicate receipts for the same to the commander thereof, in order that he may settle his accounts with the Ordnance Bureau.

1318. No payments shall be made to any militia called into the service of the Confederate States until they shall have been mustered, and shall have delivered up their arms and accoutrements, as set forth in the preceding article, unless they were absent by reason of sickness, or some other justifiable cause, at the time of the muster and inspection for discharge; and in such case they shall produce receipts to the paymaster that they have deposited their arms and accoutrements with some officer authorized to receive them, who shall state in the receipts the condition of the arms and accoutrements, and the amount of loss or damage, (if any has accrued whilst the same were in their possession,) according to the rates established by the Ordnance Bureau, which amount the paymaster shall deduct from the pay due them at the time of their discharge.

1319. In all cases when arms, accoutrements, ordnance, or ordnance stores, issued to any officer, non-commissioned officer, or soldier of the militia, called into the service of the Confederate States, shall have been lost by unavoidable circumstances, it shall be the duty of the inspecting officer, who shall muster and inspect the same for discharge, to require the affidavit of some officer or non-commissioned officer, testifying to the unavoidable circumstances of the loss, and such affidavit, if deemed satisfactory, shall be sufficient authority for the inspecting officer to relieve the individual who shall have been charged with the loss from all charges on account of such loss, which shall be entered with the affidavit on the proper muster roll.

INSPECTION OF ORDNANCE AND ORDNANCE STORES.

1320. Regulations, in detail, for the inspection and proof of all ordnance and ordnance stores shall be prepared by the Chief of Ordnance, with the approbation of the Secretary of War, and the mode of inspection and proof shall be the same for all articles of the same kind, whether fabricated at the ordnance establishments, or procured by contract or by open purchase.

I. *Inspection of Ordnance and Projectiles.*

1321. The inspection and proof of ordnance and projectiles shall be made under the direction of the Chief of Ordnance, by such officers of the Ordnance Bureau as he may, from time to time, designate for that purpose, who will be held strictly responsible that all ordnance and projectiles received by them for the Confederate States shall have been subjected to the inspection and proof required, and that they shall conform in all respects to the established models.

1322. The inspecting officer of ordnance and projectiles at the foundries shall give to the contractors triplicate certificates of inspection, according to form No. 32.

1323. Duplicate reports of inspection of ordnance and projectiles at the foundries (forms Nos. 33 and 34) shall be made immediately after each inspection; one copy to be forwarded to the Chief of Ordnance; and in the month of July a consolidated report (form No. 35) of all such inspections, made during the year ending 30th June, shall be forwarded by the inspecting officer to the Chief of Ordnance. The inspecting officer will keep books in which shall be recorded all reports which he is required to make, and all correspondence connected with this particular service. These books will be carefully preserved, and, in case of relief, turned over to his successor.

II. *Inspection of Small Arms and Accoutrements.*

1324. All small arms and accoutrements manufactured by contract, or purchased for the service of the Confederate States, shall, before being received, be inspected under the direction of the Chief of Ordnance, by officers of the Ordnance Bureau, designated for that purpose.

1325. It shall be the duty of the inspecting officer of the contract service, under the order of the Chief of Ordnance, to inspect all muskets, rifles, carbines, pistols, swords, sabres, or other small arms and accoutrements, that may be manufactured in the contract service for the Confederate States. He will be held strictly responsible that the said arms and accoutrements are in exact conformity with the models and patterns. To aid the inspecting officer in the performance of these duties, such number of assistants as may be required shall be detailed from the National armories, by the commanding officer, on the requisition of the inspecting officer.

1326. Each assistant inspector shall, previous to entering on the duty, take an oath before a competent magistrate for its faithful discharge; and it shall be the duty of the inspecting officer to see that no assistant be allowed to inspect the arms manufactured at the same private establishment oftener than twice in succession.

1327. The inspecting officer of contract arms shall in all cases, before receiving any such arms for the Confederate States, cause them to be taken to pieces in his presence, and the several parts to be closely examined by the assistants. When arms have been received by the inspecting officers for the use of the Confederate States at private armories, the principal inspector will cause them immediately to be boxed for transportation in his presence, and will secure each box by fixing his seals thereon.

1328. Inspections of small arms and accoutrements, made by contract, shall be made quarterly; and the inspecting officer shall make annual reports of inspections, (form No. 37,) and at each reception of articles furnished by contract, he shall give to the contractor triplicate certificates, according to form No. 36.

1329. The inspecting officer of contract arms and accoutrements shall keep books in which shall be copied such inspection reports as they are required to make, and all the correspondence connected with this particular service. The original reports shall be forwarded to the Chief of Ordnance as soon as the several inspections are completed. The books above mentioned shall be carefully preserved, and, in case of relief, turned over to the successors.

III. *Inspection of Gunpowder.*

1330. Gunpowder is ordinarily packed in barrels containing one hundred pounds each. The magazines in which it is kept shall be frequently aired in dry weather.

1331. Gunpowder in the magazines giving a proof-range, by the established eprouvette, less than one hundred and eighty yards, shall not be used in the *service charges*; but shall be separated from that of higher range, and legibly marked; to be used for firing salutes and for blank cartridge practice. That which gives a range less than one hundred and fifty yards shall be considered unserviceable.

1332. The inspecting officer shall cause each cask to be marked in the following manner, viz: on one end the place and year of fabrication and description of powder; on the other end the proof-range and date of proof, taking care to leave space for subsequent proofs.

1333. Reports of proof and inspection of powder received from contractors, and of that in the magazines, shall be made in duplicate according to form No 39; and the proving officer shall give to the contractor triplicate certificates of inspection according to form No. 38. One of the duplicate inspection reports of powder in the magazines, and of that received from contractors for the Confederate States, shall be forwarded to the Chief of Ordnance on the completion of the inspection; the other for powder in magazines, shall be recorded at the arsenal or depot; the duplicate for powder received for the Confederate States shall be retained by the proving officer.

1334. Standard powder for the reception proof of all kinds of fire-arms, whether manufactured at the national armories, foundaries, or by contract, shall be of such quality as to give a range of *not less* than *two-hundred and fifty yards* by the regulation eprouvette.

1335. All powder designed for the proof of fire-arms, shall be proved with the regulation eprouvette, immediately preceding the inspection, unless it shall have been so proved within one year, and there be no reason to suspect that it has become deteriorated.

CONTRACTS.

1336. No contract for the service of the Ordnance Bureau shall be made by any officer or agent thereof, except by special authority of the Chief of Ordnance, sanctioned by the Secretary of War: and all officers or agents making contracts, shall strictly observe the provisions of the laws on that subject. Contracts shall be made in triplicate, one of which shall be forwarded to the Chief of Ordnance, at the date of the contract, that it may be deposited in the office of the comptroller within ninety days thereafter.

1337. The rights vested in a contractor, for services to be performed, or supplies to be furnished for the Ordnance Bureau, shall in no case be transferred to any other person or persons; but such contractor shall be held to his legal responsibilities, and all payments shall be made to him only.

1338. Payments on account of any contract, to the amount of four-fifths of the value of the work done, or of services performed in part, may be made in case the contract embraces operations of long continuance. Such payments on account, under an unfulfilled contract not being admitted at the treasury, will not be charged in the quarterly accounts; but a statement of all such, specifying the amount of each, will be annexed to the duplicate account current, which is designed for the files of the ordnance office, in order that the true state of the funds on hand may be known.

ACCOUNTS.

1339. Every disbursing officer of the Ordnance Bureau shall transmit to the Chief of Ordnance, within twenty days after the expiration of each quarter, an account current of all moneys received, expended, and remaining on hand, with the necessary *vouchers* and *abstracts* made according to the forms hereinafter prescribed; which, after examination in the Ordnance office, will be transmitted to the treasury department for settlement.

1340. A duplicate of the *quarterly account current*, and of the *abstract* mentioned in the preceding paragraph, shall be transmitted at the same time to the Ordnance office, to be retained for use there. On a blank page of this duplicate account current there shall be endorsed a statement of receipts and expenditures under each appropriation, (form No. 22,) and the face of the abstract will show as far as practicable, the quantity and kind of articles purchased. (See form No. 19.) Individual accounts for services will show the dates and kind of service charged.

1341. Vouchers of articles purchased, for supplies furnished, for services rendered, or for other expenditures, will be made agreeably to one or the other of the forms No. 15, 16, 17 or 18, according to the nature of the case: *First:* Form No. 15 is the form of a voucher for supplies furnished, or for services rendered by an individual. *Second:* Form No. 16 is the form of an ordinary receipt-roll for services. *Third:* Form No. 17 is a pay-roll to be used at armories or arsenals, where work is done by the piece. *Fourth*: Form No. 18 is a pay roll for hired slaves. *Fifth:* In all the accounts of individuals against the Confederate States the matters and things charged for are to be clearly and accurately set forth. No substitution of names, dates, services, prices, or things of any kind shall be made; the transaction on which the charges are made in any account shall, in all cases, be truly represented on the face of the voucher. *Sixth:* In accounts for articles purchased, the date of each separate purchase, the name and the number or quantity of each article, the price of each, with the particular to which the price refers—as number, weight or measure, and the amount due for each, will be specified in the body of the account. If the public use of any article be not fully apparent from its name; or if, from any other cause, there be reason to apprehend that the charge may not be correctly comprehended by the accounting officers, the purpose for which it was procured, or other explanation, should be inserted opposite the article in the column of remarks. *Seventh*: If an account be for services rendered, the occupation or kind of service, the time employed, the dates within which the services were rendered, the wages and the amount, should be stated in the body of the account. If the service charged be of an unusual kind, or if it be charged at an unusual rate, or if, from any cause, the charge may be liable to misconception, the necessary explanation should be given under the head of remarks. The dates to be inserted in the left margin of the accounts should represent the time when the several sums charged were due to the creditors. *Eighth:* At armories and at arsenals, where the number of persons employed is considerable, the accounts for services rendered will be stated on monthly rolls, specifying the name and occupation of each, the number of days' service rendered by, the wages of, and the amount due to each, agreeably to forms No. 16 and 17. *Ninth:* In case the authority to direct and control expenditures reside in one officer, and the payments are made by another, the accounts must be sanctioned by the signature of the directing officer, in the manner indicated by forms No. 15, 16, 17 and 18, before payment is made; the date on which the sanction is given shall always be stated. *Tenth:* In the accounts for the transportation of stores or supplies, the articles carried, with the number or weight thereof, the places from and to which, and the distance conveyed, the period within which the service was performed, and the price, should be specified. If the charge be for transporting stores from the post to a distant place, an original bill of lading, and the receipt of the person to whom the articles were addressed, or other proper evidence of delivery, should be annexed to the voucher.

1342. VOUCHERS. *First:* An account for the transportation or travelling allowance of an armory officer, or other person, will state the distance travelled, the purpose of the journey, and at what time performed; and it must be sustained by the original order directing the service, or a certified copy of, or extract from it, with a certificate that the journey charged has been performed. *Second:* An account for postage of letters on public service must be accompanied by a certificate from the officer sending or receiving them, setting forth that the postage charged is due exclusively for letters on the public business committed to his charge. *Third:* If an account be founded upon a contract or agreement, reference should be made to the agreement in the body of the account, and the original agreement should be transmitted with the first account arising under it, if the same shall not have been previously transmitted; vouchers referring to a verbal agreement, without a specification of particulars, are inadmissible. *Fourth:* In case a charge is made by one person, for a payment made by him to another, for freight, wharfage, drayage, or other purpose, the particulars of the charge will be fully specified in the body of the account, and a receipt from the person to whom the payment is made must be annexed to the account as a sub-voucher. *Fifth:* The prices and amounts in all accounts and rolls will be stated in dollars and cents. *Sixth:* All accounts accruing during any quarter should, if practicable, be adjusted and paid during the current quarter, or within so short a period after its termination as to be embraced in the account for the appropriate quarter. *Seventh:* The receipt annexed to an account will express the sum paid by words written out in full and not by figures, and it will state the name of the person from whom, the place, where, and the date when, the money is received; the receipt will be signed, if practicable, by the person in whose name the account is stated, or if signed by another as agent, proper evidence that the agent was duly authorized by the principal to sign receipts must accompany the account. When the signature to a receipt does not legibly express the name of the writer, it should be witnessed. *Eighth:* If expenditures under different appropriations be contained in one voucher, the amount expended under each shall be separately stated; if this occur in an individual account, the items shall be appropriately designated in the body of it or in the column of remarks: if it happen in a pay-roll, the amount chargeable to such appropriation shall be stated at the bottom of the roll, and the several sums shall be separately stated in the appropriate columns of the abstract. *Ninth:* If the number of persons to be entered on the receipt-roll be so considerable as to require it, the roll will be made up into book form, similar to No. 17. *Tenth:* In all cases where the expenditures are made in pursuance of special orders or instructions from the Chief or Ordnance, a reference to such orders, specifying the date, will be made in the column of remarks on the voucher, in which the expenditure is charged. If the orders emanate from any other source than the Chief of Ordnance, then a certified copy will be appended to the voucher.

1343 ABSTRACTS. *First:* All expenditures, for one quarter, will be embodied in one abstract. Expenditures under different appropriations will be entered in separate columns (see form No. 19). *Second:* The vouchers for all expenditures in any quarter shall be numbered in one continued series, according to their dates. *Third:* If the abstract is so large as to require more than one sheet, it will be made on several sheets of the same kind stitched together in book form.

1344. *Accounts current* will be prepared according to form No. 20. They should always commence by entering—*First*, the balance from the last account; if that balance shall have been officially ascertained and stated to the disbursing officer, he will enter the official balance; if otherwise, he will enter the balance as stated by himself in his last account. *Second:* All money received since the last account was rendered will then be entered specifying, separately the several sums, the dates when, and from what source received. The expenditures will then be charged, entering the amount under each appropriation separately. *Third:* The account should then be balanced, certified and dated, agreeably to the prescribed form.

RETURNS AND REPORTS.

1345. The Chief of Ordnance shall transmit monthly, to the Adjutant General's office, a return, exhibiting the names, rank and stations of all officers and enlisted men attached to the corps of artillery in the service of the Ordnance Bureau.

1346. The officer having charge of each arsenal or ordnance depot shall transmit to the Chief of Ordnance, within five days after the termination of each month, and according to the forms hereinafter prescribed, the following monthly returns, viz: first, of the ordnance officers and enlisted men at the post (form No. 27); second, of the hired men employed (form No. 28); third, of the work done at the post (form No. 29). The commanding officer of each national armory shall transmit to the Chief of Ordnance, within the period above named, a monthly return of army officers and men employed, and of small arms and their appendages, manufactured at the armory (form No. 30). The commanding officer of each armory, arsenal, or depot, shall transmit, at the end of every month, a summary statement of money received and expended, (form No. 32,) which shall be made out by the disbursing officer.

1347. The commanding officer of each national armory, arsenal, or ordnance depot, shall transmit to the Chief of Ordnance, at the beginning of each quarter, an estimate of the funds required during the quarter. (Form No. 29.)

1348. Every person having the charge and custody of ordnance or ordnance stores, shall be held responsible for the same, and shall make and transmit to the Chief of Ordnance, within twenty days after the termination of the quarter, a quarterly return of the same, according to the forms referred to in paragraph 1353 of these regulations, which return, after having been duly examined, will be transmitted to the proper officer of the treasury.

1349. When an officer commands, at the same time, a military post and also a regiment or company, he shall make a return of ordnance and ordnance stores belonging to the post, separate and distinct from those belonging to the regiment or company.

1350. The commanding officer of an armory, arsenal, or ordnance depot, having a storekeeper, shall transmit to the Chief of Ordnance, in the month of July of each year, a return according to form No. 1, of all ordnance, tools, machines and other stores, including public horses and oxen, which may be in current service; and such commanding officer shall not be required to make the quarterly returns called for in the 1348th paragraph; but he shall, at the end of each month, turn over to the storekeeper all finished articles fabricated during the month, and other stores which may be required in the current service.

1351. Arms, ordnance, and ordnance stores, shall be arranged on the returns and inventories, according to the classification exemplified in paragraph 1365.

1352. Every person who is required by paragraph 1348, or 1350, to make a quarterly or annual return of ordnance or ordnance stores, shall make an exact inventory of the same in the month of June of each year, and shall certify, on the second quarter's return, that such inventory has been accurately made, and that said return has been compared with the inventory, and corrected accordingly, if necessary. This inventory shall be made according to form No. 13, and shall, if required, be exhibited to the Inspector-General, or to any other inspecting officer who may visit the post.

1353. All returns of property required by paragraphs 1348 and 1350 of these regulations shall be made according to the forms hereinafter prescribed, that is to say, quarterly and annual returns of property, (according to form No. 1;) invoices and vouchers in support thereof, viz: of articles received, (according to form No. 2;) abstract of articles fabricated, (form No. 3;) abstract of articles purchased, (form No. 4;) abstract of articles required, (form No. 5;) statement of materials obtained from condemned stores, (form No. 6;) receipts for stores issued to the army, (forms No. 7 and 21;) receipt for stores issued to the militia, (form No. 8;) abstract of articles expended or consumed for purposes of construction in the ordnance workshops, or for current service, (form No. 9;) list of condemned stores stricken from the return by order of the President of the Confederate States, (form No. 10;) certified invoice, (form No. 2;) of stores turned over to the Quartermaster's Department for transportation, for which a receipt shall not have been obtained in time to accompany the return; such receipt, when obtained, shall be marked to correspond with the invoice and the return to which it belongs, and shall be forwarded with the next quarterly return; *certificates of the loss* of ordnance stores in transportation, (forms Nos. 11 and 12;) original orders for issue in certain cases, (according to paragraphs 1280 and 1281.) All *abstracts* required above shall be furnished *in duplicate* to the ordnance office. If the vouchers for receipts or issues of property are too numerous to be stated separately on the face of the return, an abstract of them will be made in a form corresponding with that of the return. In all the vouchers and abstracts accompanying a property return, the articles should be arranged in the same order as in the body of the return.

1354. Each commanding officer, or other agent of the ordnance department, who is required by paragraphs 1248 and 1250 to make returns, shall constantly keep at his station recorded copies of said returns, to be turned over to his successor in the same manner as other property; and all the books and files of papers required by this and the next following article shall be submitted to the Inspector General and other inspecting officers on their tours of inspection, who shall state in their reports the order in which they are kept.

1355. Each officer, or other agent of the Ordnance Department, required by paragaphs 1339, 1340, 1346, 1347, and 1358 of these regulations, to make the monthly returns, accounts current, and abstracts of reports therein referred to, shall constantly keep at his station, to be turned over to his successor, the following books and files of papers, viz: *First: A monthly return book*, containing copies of all monthly returns and statements, except the company return, form 28. *Second: A company return book*, made by binding together the duplicate returns which are retained at the post. *Third: An account book*, containing copies of all quarterly accounts current, of all abstracts of money disbursed, of the statements endorsed on such accounts and abstracts, and of the estimates for funds. *Fourth: A letter book*, containing copies of all official letters written by such officer or agent. *Fifth: An annual inventory book*, made by binding together the duplicate inventories retained at the post. *Sixth: Files of letters received*, containing all original official letters received on ordnance service, regularly endorsed and bundled, according to the years in which they are written. *Seventh: Files of orders received,* containing all original orders, regulations and circular letters received, endorsed and bundled according to the years in which they are written. *Eighth:* At armories and arsenals of construction, such books will be kept as may be necessary to show the nature and extent of operations, and the details of the applications of funds.

1356. It shall be the duty of the Chief of Ordnance to report to the Second Auditor of the Treasury, in the month of June of each year, all persons who shall have failed to transmit returns within the periods prescribed by the 1248th and 1250th paragraphs of these regulations.

1357. Should an officer or other agent of the Ordnance Bureau, charged with ordnance and ordnance stores, fail to render the prescribed returns thereof, within a reasonable time after the termination of a quarter, a settlement shall be made out of his accounts at the treasury, and the *money value* of the supplies with which he stands charged shall be reported against him for collection. The delinquency will also furnish matter of military accusation, at the discretion of the proper authority.

1358. The commanding officer of each armory, arsenal, or ordnance depot, shall transmit to the Chief of Ordnance, in the month of August of each year, an annual inventory and report of operations for the year ending the 30th June, according to form No. 31. This inventory will be made in duplicate, one copy to be retained at the post.

1359. A general statement, in a condensed form, will be transmitted with the annual inventory and report, showing the principal operations at the post during the year ending June 30th. This statement will embrace experiments, (their objects and results;) the construction of buildings, machinery, or other important works; extensive repairs or alterations, and the general character of the operations at the armories and arsenals of construction and in the foundry and inspection service.

TRANSMITTING PAPERS TO THE ORDNANCE OFFICE.

1360. All papers transmitted to the Chief of Ordnance (except the annual inventories and the returns of stores, with their vouchers,) shall be folded in such manner that the packet shall not exceed three and a half inches in width and eight and a quarter inches in length, and shall be, as near as practicable, of those dimensions. They shall be endorsed according to the prescribed forms. The duplicate papers designed for the Chief of Ordnance will have the additional words, "*Ordnance Office,*" written on the back of each.

1361. All returns, statements, or other papers, which may be transmitted to the Chief of Ordnance, shall be accompanied by a letter of advice.

1362. The printed blank forms required by these regulations for the service of the Ordnance Bureau shall, when not otherwise directed, be furnished from the ordnance office to the several posts and stations, on requisitions to be made annually, in the month of *May,* by the commanders of such posts or stations, showing the number of each form required for one year's consumption.

The printed forms are as follows, viz: Nos 15, 16, 17, 18, 19, 20, 26, 27, 28, 30, 31, 33.

RATES OF PRICES OF SMALL ARMS AND ACCOUTREMENTS.

PARTS.	PERCUSSION LOCK.		
	Musket.	Rifle.	Pistol.
	D. C.	D. C.	D. C.
Barrel with sight, without breech,	4 90	5 28	2 40
Breech screw,	12	12	09
Bayonet or band stud,	01		
Tang screw,	06	06	05
Breech sight,		07	
Cone,	11	11	11
Lock plate,	60	60	48
Tumbler,	32	32	30
Tumbler screw,	04	04	04
Bridle,	19	19	17
Sear,	24	24	20
Sear spring,	12	12	10
Main spring,	32	32	30
Lock screws, each,	04	04	04
Hammer,	72	72	54
Side plate, (with band for pistol,)	09	12	48
Side screws, each,	05	05	01
Upper band,	46	54	
Middle band,	28		
Lower band,	18	22	
Upper band spring,	11	11	
Middle band spring,	10		
Lower band spring,	10	10	
Guard plate,	50	60	42
Guard plate screws, each,	04	04	02
Guard bow without swivels,	36	42	24
Guard bow nut, each,	02	02	02
Swivels and rivets, each,	12	12	
Trigger,	14	14	11
Trigger screw,	02	02	02
Butt plate,	36	63	35
Butt plate screw, each,	03	03	03
Ramrod,	60	60	30
Ramrod spring,	14	14	
Ramrod wires,	01	01	
Ramrod stop,	01	01	
Stock,	1 74	2 22	1 08
Bayonet,	1 63		
Bayonet clasp,	19		
Bayonet clasp screw,	02		
Box plate,		86	
Box catch,		06	
Box spring,		12	

PRICES OF SMALL ARMS—Continued.

PARTS.	PERCUSSION LOCK.		
	Musket.	Rifle.	Pistol.
	D. C.	D. C.	D. C.
Box spring screw, ...		02	
Box screw, each, ...		03	
Ramrod swivel and rivet, . . .			
Ramrod swivel and rivet screw, .			30
Sword bayonet blade, . . .		2 00	02
Sword bayonet hilt without clasp, .		2 00	
Sight base, ...	40		
Long branch (leaf) . . .	17		
Short, ...	24		
Sight screws, each, . . .	03		
Sight complete, ...	1 00		
Barrel complete, ...	5 16	5 48	
Lock complete, ...	2 70	2 70	
Guard complete, ...	1 27	1 49	
Bayonet complete, . . .	1 95		
Box plate complete, . . .		1 16	
Arm complete, ...	15 60	16 90	
Appendages for all arms:			
Screw driver and cone wrench.			
Wiper.			
Ball screw.			
Spring vice.			
Bullet mould, (rifle calibre.)			

SWORDS AND SABRES,

PARTS.		Cavalry sabre.	Horse Artillery Sabre.	Artillery Sword.	Musketoon Sword Bayonet.	Non-commissioned Officer's Sword	Musician's Sword.
		D. C.	D. C.	D. C.	D. C.	D. C.	D. C.
Hilt	Gripe,	40	34			48	40
	Head,	1 40	88	1 74	3 20	1 00	88
	Guard,	2 20	1 16			2 40	88
Blade,		5 60	3 96	4 26	4 26	4 40	3 84
Scabbard	Mouth-piece,	40	20				
	Body,	2 40	2 00	1 00	1 24	1 32	1 00
	Bands and rings,	1 20	1 20				
	Ferrule and stud,	30	26	50	80	70	50
	Tip,			50	50	70	60
Arm complete,		14 00	10 00	8 00	10 00	11 00	3 00

ACCOUTREMENTS—(Black Leather Belts.)

PARTS.	Infantry.	Artillery.	Cavalry.	Rifle.
	D. C.	D. C.	D. C.	D. C.
Cartridge box,	1 75			1 60
Cartridge box belt,	75			
Bayonet scabbard and frog,	75			
Waist belt—private's,	60			60
Cap pouch and pick,	65		65	65
Gun sling,	35		35	35
Sabre belt,		1 35	1 35	
Sword belt,		1 00		
Carbine or gun sling,			1 25	
Powder flask—tin,	30		30	30
Canteen,	25	25	25	25
Canteen strap,	20	20	25	25
Knapsacks,	3 25	3 25	3 25	3 25
Haversacks,	20	20	20	20

1365—*Classification of Ordnance and Ordnance Stores.*

PART FIRST.

Artillery, Small Arms, Ammunition, and other Ordnance Stores.

CLASS I.—CANNON.

18 pdr.	brass cannon,	Mexican, trophy,	weight,	pounds.
12 pdr.	"	French,	"	"
9 pdr.	"	Spanish,	"	"
8 pdr.	"	French,	"	"
6 pdr.	"	English, trophy,	"	"
4 pdr.	"	French,	"	"
3 pdr.	"	English, trophy,	"	"
12 pdr.	"	field, U. S. pattern, 1840,	"	"
6 pdr.	"	" "	"	"
6 pdr.	"	old pattern,	"	"
8 inch	brass howitzers,	English, trophy,	"	"
6 inch	"	French,	"	"
24 pdr.	"	field, U. S. pattern, 1840,	"	"
12 pdr.	"	" "	"	"
16 inch	brass stone mortars,	French,	"	"
12 inch	brass mortar,	French,	"	"
42 pdr.	iron cannon,	U .S. pattern, 1831,	"	"
42 pdr.	"	" 1819,	"	"
42 pdr.	"	" 1840,	"	"
32 pdr.	"	" 1840,	"	"
32 pdr.	"	rifled,	"	"
24 pdr.	"	U. S. pattern, 1819,	"	"
24 pdr.	"	" 1839,	"	"
24 pdr.	"	old pattern, round breech,	"	"
24 pdr.	iron cannon,	rifled,	"	"
18 pdr.	"	old pattern, round breech,	"	"
18 pdr.	"	model 1819,	"	"
18 pdr.	"	model 1839,	"	"
12 pdr.	"	garrison, model 1819,	"	"
13 pdr.	"	" 1839,	"	"
12 pdr.	"	field, model 1819,	"	"
12 pdr.	iron cannon,	field, inspected 1834,	"	"
6 pdr.	"	" "	"	"
3 inch	"	field, rifled,	"	"
100 pdr.	Columbiads,	smooth bore,	"	"
50 pdr.	"	"	"	"
10 inch	"	"	"	"
10 inch	"	rifled,	"	"
8 inch	"	smooth bore,	"	"
8 inch	"	rifled,	"	"
8 inch	iron howitzers,	sea coast, model 1840,	"	"
8 inch	"	" " 1839,	"	"
8 inch	"	siege, model 1839,	"	"
24 pdr.	"	field, inspected 1834,	"	"
24 pdr.	"	for flank defence,	"	"
24 pdr.	"	field, old pattern, light,	"	"
12 pdr.	"	field, inspected 1834,	"	"

10 inch iron mortars, sea coast, model 1839,	weight,	pounds.
10 inch " " " 1819,	"	"
8 inch " siege, model 1840.	"	"

Unserviceable.

9 pdr. brass cannon, field,	"	"
6 pdr. " "	"	"
8 inch brass howitzers, American, old,	"	"
24 pdr. " "	"	"
10 inch brass mortars,	"	"
24 pdr. iron cannon, cascable broken,	"	"
6 pdr. " old, various patterns,	"	"
6 pdr. " wrought iron,	"	"

NOTE.—The mean weight of each kind of ordnance, as well as the number of pieces, should be entered on the inventories.

CLASS II.—ARTILLERY CARRIAGES.

12 pdr. field gun carriages, complete, stock-rail, pattern 1835.
12 pdr. " " " " " 1840.
6 pdr. " " " " " "
24 pdr. howitzer, field carriages, " " " "
12 pdr. " " " " " "
24 pdr. siege gun carriages, " " " "
Mountain howitzer carriages, " " " "
Caissons for 12 pounder guns, complete, stock trail, pattern 1840.
" 6 pdr. guns, " " " "
" 24 pdr. howitzers, " " " "
" 12 pdr. " " " " "
Caissons for 3 inch rifle guns, " " " 1861.
Travelling forges.
Battery wagons.
Portable forges for mountain service.
Chests, with carriage-maker's tools, for mountain service.
Field battery wagons, with tools and stores complete, C.
Field travelling forges, with " " " A.
Mortar wagons, for siege service, complete.
8 inch Columbiad casemate gun carriages.
8 inch Columbiad casemate chassis.
32 pdr. casemate gun carriages.
32 pdr. casemate chassis.
32 pdr. casemate gun carriages, wood.
24 pdr. " " cast iron.
24 pdr. " chassis.
24 pdr. howitzer casemate carriages, for flank defence, complete.
8 inch sea-coast howitzer, barbette carriages and chassis.
32 pdr. barbette gun carriages.
32 pdr. " chassis.
24 pdr. " gun carriages.
24 pdr. " chassis.
10 inch see-coast mortar beds, iron.
10 inch " " wood.
10 inch " " iron.
8 inch " " iron.

Unserviceable.

6 pdr. field carriages, Gribeauval pattern, require repairs.
6 pdr. " Stocktrail. }
Caissons. } Maj. ———————'s battery.
Battery wagons. }
Travelling forges. }

NOTE.—The "field carriage, complete," includes the limber and ammunition chest, but no implements. The "casemate or barbette carriage, complete," includes the upper or gun carriage and the chassis, with all the wheels, but no implements; it is better, however, to enter the gun carriages and the chassis separately as above.

CLASS III.—ARTILLERY IMPLEMENTS AND EQUIPMENTS.

Axes, felling.
Bricoles.
Buckets, sponge, iron for field guns.
" " wood for garrison guns.
" tar, iron for field guns.
" water, for field forge.
" watering, leather.
Budge barrels.
Cannon locks, left side, for guns with lock pieces.
" " without "
Cannon spikes.
Chocks, for casemate carriages.
Drag ropes.
Fuze augers.
" extractors.
" gimlets.
" mallets.
" plug reamers.
" rasps.
" saws.
" setters, brass.
" " wood.
Gunner's callipers.
" gimlets for siege and garrison guns,
" " field guns.
" haversacks,
" levels.
" pincers.
" quadrants.
Handspikes, trail, for field carriages.
" manœuvring, for garrison carriages.
" shod, " "
" truck, iron, casemate "
" roller, " " "
Harness, viz:
Sets for two wheel horses, pattern 1840.
" leading " "
" wheel " with Grimsley's saddles, &c.
" leading " "
Draught for mountain howitzer carriage.

Pack saddles and bridles for mountain howitzer carriage.
Nose bags.
Whips.
Ladles and staves for 32 pdr. gun.
" 24 pdr. gun.
" 12 pdr. gun.
Lanterns, common.
" dark.
Lanyards for friction primers.
Lead apron and straps.
Linstocks.
Lock covers.
Men's harness.
Pass boxes.
Pendulum hausses for 12 pdr. field guns.
" 6 pdr. "
" 32 pdr. field howitzers.
" 24 pdr. "
" 12 pdr. "
Pick axes.
Plummets.
Pointing wires.
Portfire cases.
Portfire shears.
Portfire stocks.
Powder funnels, copper.
Powder measures.
Priming horns.
Priming wires for siege and garrison guns.
" for field "
Prolonges.
Rammers and staves, viz:
For 32 pdr. garrison guns.
For 24 pdr. "
Rammers and staves—*continued.*
For 12 pdr. garrison guns.
For 10 inch Columbiads.
For 8 inch sea-coast howitzers.
Shell hooks.
Shell plug screws.
Splints.
Shovels.
Sponges, wollen, 8 inch.
" " 32 pdr.
" " 24 pdr.
" " 12 pdr.
" " 6 pdr.
Sponge covers, 32 pdr.
" " 24 pdr.
" " 6 pdr.
Sponges and rammers, viz:
For 8 inch siege howitzers.
For 24 pdr. field "
For 12 pdr. field guns.
For 6 pdr "

Sponges and staves, viz:

For 42 pdr. guns.
For 32 pdr. guns.
For 12 pdr. guns, siege and garrison.
For 10 inch Columbiad, bore.
For " " chamber.
For 8 inch sea-coast howitzer.

Tangent scales for 12 pdr. field guns.
" 6 pdr. "
" 24 pdr. field howitzer.
" 12 pdr. "

Tarpaulins, large.
" small.

Thumb-stalls.

Tompions and collars 12 pdr. field guns.
" " 6 pdr, "

Tompions for 8 inch mortars.

Tow hooks.

Tube pouches.

Vent covers.

Vent pouches.

Worms and staves, viz:

For siege and garrison guns.
For 12 pdr. field guns.
For 6 pdr. "

NOTE.—A set of harness for two horses includes everything required for them except *whips* and *nose-bags*, which are reported separately.

CLASS IV.—ARTILLERY PROJECTILES, AND THEIR APPENDAGES, UNPREPARED FOR SERVICE.

12 pdr. shot for 12 pdr. gun,	fixed,	rounds
12 pdr spherical-case shot for 12 pdr. gun,	"	"
12 pdr. canisters for 12 pdr. gun,	"	"
6 pdr. shot,	"	"
6 pdr. spherical case shot,	"	"
6 pdr. canisters,	"	"
12 pdr. howitzer shells,	"	"
12 pdr. " spherical case shot,	"	"
12 pdr. " canisters,	"	"
32 pdr. howitzer spherical case shot, with metal fuzes,	"	"
12 pdr. spherical case for 12 pdr. field gun,		
12 pdr. shell " "	"	"

8 inch shells, strapped for Columbiad.
8 inch " " sea-coast howitzer.
12 pdr. howitzer shell, strapped.
12 pdr. howitzer spherical case shot strapped.
12 pdr. canister, for 12 pdr. field gun.
6 pdr. shot, strapped.
6 pdr. canisters.
12 pdr. grape shot, stands of.
42 pdr. cannon wads, junk.
32 pdr. " hay.
24 pdr. " grommet.

NOTE.—A "*round of fixed ammunition*" is here used to indicate the *projectile with its cartridge* prepared for use, although, in some cases, they are not actually connected together. A "*shot strapped*," or a "canister, "stand of grape," &c., indicates the projectiles prepared for making fixed ammunition, or for service.

CLASS VI.—SMALL ARMS.

Muskets complete, viz:
- National armory, bright, percussion new.
- National armory, brown, flint, 4th class, short.
- National armory, bright. altered to percussion.
- National armory, brown, " "
- Contract, brown, " "
- Contract, bright, " "
- Musketoons, artillery, percussion.
- " cavalry, "
- " sappers, "

Rifles, viz:
- Harper's Ferry percussion, new.
- Harper's Ferry percussion, repaired.
- Contract, full stocked, brown, flint.
- Hall's patent, new, without bayonets.
- Hall's patent, new, with bayonets.

Pistols, viz:
- Percussion, new model.
- Colt's patent.

Hall's carbines, new, percussion.
Wall pieces, rifle, 4 oz. calibre.
Cavalry sabres, pattern 1840.
Horse artillery sabres, privates, pattern 1840.
Non-commissioned officers' swords, pattern 1840.
Musicians' swords, pattern 1840.
Artillery swords, new pattern.
Cavalry sabres, English.
Sergeants' swords, Prussian.
Foot officers' swords, new pattern, 30½ inches.
Foot officers' swords, new pattern, 32 inches.
Field officers' swords.

Unserviceable.

Muskets, without bayonets.
Rifles, require repairs.
Carbines, Hall's patent, irreparable.

CLASS VII.—ACCOUTREMENTS, IMPLEMENTS AND EQUIPMENTS FOR SMALL ARMS.

Infantry cartridge boxes.
Cartridge box plates.
Cartridge box belts, black leather.
" " white leather.
Cartridge box belt plates.
Bayonet scabbards, 16 inches.
Bayonet scabbards, 18 inches, black frogs.
Gun slings.
Ball screws for percussion rifles.
Bullet moulds for percussion rifles, round balls.
Bullet moulds for percussion rifles, conical balls.
Spring vices.
Cartridge boxes for pistols.
Cartridge box plates for pistols.
Spring vices. "

Waist belts, black leather.
Waist belt plates, inf'ry, privates.
" " " sergeants.
Wipers for percussion muskets.
Ball screws " "
Screw drivers " "
Spring vices for muskets.
Cones for new muskets.
Cones for altered muskets.
Cap pouches.
Cone picks.
Rifle cartridge boxes.
Rifle cartridge box plates.
Rifle flasks.
Rifle ball pouches.
Rifle pouch and flask belts, white.
" " black.
Bayonet scabbard, Hall's rifles.
Bayonet scabbard belts, Hall's rifles.
Wipers for percussion rifles.
Screw drivers for percussion rifles.
Spare cones "
Screw drivers for pistols.
Bullet moulds " "
Ball screws " "
Spare cones " "
Screw drivers for Colt's pistols.
Spring vices "
Powder flasks "
Bullet moulds "
Artillery sword belts.
Cavalry sabre belts, white, old pattern.
Cavalry sabre-belt plates, old pattern.
Non-comm'd officers' sword belts, double frogs, black leather.
Non-commissioned officers' sword belt plates.
Horse artillery sabre belts, black.
Holsters.
Housings.
Musket flints.
Rifle flints.

CLASS VIII.—POWDER, AMMUNITION FOR SMALL ARMS, &C., AND MATERIALS.

Cannon powder, pounds.
Musket powder, "
Rifle powder, "
Mealed powder, "
Fulminate of mercury, "
Nitre, refined, "
Sulphur, crude, "
Sulphur, roll, "
Sulphur, flowers, "
Sulphur, pulverized, "
Pulverized charcoal, "
24 pdr. cartridges, 6 "
12 pdr. " 2½ "
6 pdr. " 1¼ "
42 pdr. cartridge bags, paper, with flannel bottoms.
32 pdr. cartridge bags, paper, with flannel bottoms.
24 pdr. cartridge bags, flannel.
12 pdr. " field, "
6 pdr. " " "
Musket buck and ball cartridges for percussion arms.
Musket buck and ball cartridges for flint-lock arms.
Rifle ball cartridges for percussion arms.
Pistol ball cartridges for percussion arms.
Expanding ball cartridges, calibre 58, percussion.
Pistol ball cartridges, flint.
Musket blank cartridges.
Rifle " "
Cartridges for Colt's pistols.
Musket balls, pressed, (for proving muskets,) pounds.
Musket balls, pressed, "
Rifle balls " "
Buckshot, "
Laboratory paper, viz:
No. 1, (musket cartridge,) pounds.
No. 2, (wrapping,) "
No. 3, (blank cartridge,) "
Wrap'g paper, (No. 2,) waxed, "
Wrapping paper, quires.
Priming tubes, filled.
Portfires.
Quick match, pounds.
Slow match, "
Percussion caps for small arms.
Percussion caps for Colt's pistols.
Percussion primers for Maynard's locks.
Percussion primers for cannon, Hidden's.
Friction tubes.
Rockets, war, congreve.
Rockets, Hale's 3¼ inch.
Rockets, " 2¼ inch.
Rockets, 1 inch, signal.
Fuzes, 10 inch, filled.

Fuzes, 8 inch, filled.
Fuzes, paper, for field ammunition.
Fuzes, wooden, "
Blue lights.
Fire balls.

CLASS IX.—PARTS, OR INCOMPLETE SETS OF ANY OF THE ARTICLES INSERTED IN THE PRECEDING CLASSES.

Parts of barbette carriage, viz:
Bevil washers for 32 pdr.
" 24 pdr.
Elevating screws.
Iron work for 24 pdr. carriages and chassis, complete sets.
Lunettes.
Naves.
Pintles.
Pintle plates, 32 pdr.
Pipes, 32 pdr.
Rollers, 32 pdr.
Rollers, 24 pdr.
Traverse wheels.

Parts of casemate carriages, viz:
Bed plates for elevating screws.
Elevating screws.
Handles for elevating screws.
Iron work for 32 pdr. carriages, complete sets.
Pintles, cast iron.
Traverse wheels, large.
" small.
Truck wheels.
Trunion plates, 32 pdr., pairs.

Parts of field cartridges, viz:
Air backs for forges.
Axle trees for 6 pdr. gun caringes.
" limbers.
Cap squares, 6 pdr.
Cap square chains.
Cold shut, S links, No. 3.
" No. 5.
Elevating screws and nuts.
Fellies.
Iron work for 6 pdr. carriages, complete sets.
Keys for ammunition chests.
Linch pins.
Lock chains.
Nails, No. 1 and 2, pounds.
Nave bands.
Nave boxes, cast iron.
Nuts, assorted.
Pintle hooks, keys and chains.
Poles, spare, ironed.
Pole props.
Pole yokes.
Rondelles, 6 pdr., large.
" " small.
Splinter bars.
Spokes.
Stocks, 6 pdr. carriage, ironed.
" caisson, "
" battery wagon, "
Tire bolts, nuts and washers.
Washers for axle trees, linch.
" " shoulder.
" for bolts, assorted.
Wheels, spare.

Parts of artillery implements.
42 pdr. rammer heads.
24 pdr. "
12 pdr. "
6 pdr. "
42 pdr. sponge heads.
24 pdr. "
12 pdr. "
6 pdr. "
8 inch Columbiad sponge head sand staves, for bore.
8 inch Columbiad sponge head and staves, for chamber.
24 pdr. sponge heads and staves.
6 pdr. sponge and rammer staves.
6 pdr. worm staves.
12 pdr. ladles.
Worms for siege and garrison guns.
Thimbles for prolonges.

Parts of artillery harness, viz:
Drivers' saddles, Grimsley's pat'n.
Valise " "
Bridles, Grimsley's pattern.
Bits, brass plated.
Halters.
Halter chains.
Collars.
Girths.
Traces, leading, leather.
Traces, wheel, "
Leg guards.
Breast straps.
Breech straps.
Hames, prs.

Parts of small arms, viz:
Stocks for percussion muskets.

Tumbler screws for percus'n musk's.
Bridle screws "
Sears for "
Sear screws "
Main springs "
Main spring screws "
Sear springs "
Sear spring screws "
Bayonet for Hall's rifles.

Parts of prepared ammuni'n, viz:
Sabots for 12 pdr. field gun.
Sabots for 12 pdr. howitzer.
Cylinders and caps for 6 pounder field ammunition.
Plates for 12 pdr. canisters.
Plates for 24 pdr. grape.
Rocket cases, 2½ inches, Hale's.
Rocket cases, paper, 1 in., signal.

CLASS X.—MISCELLANEOUS.

Garrison gins, old pattern.
" with ratchet windlass.
Casemate gins, "
Field and siege gins, "
Sling carts, large.
Sling carts, hand.
Casemate trucks.
Hand carts.
Store trucks.
Lifting jacks.
Falls for casemate gins.
Falls for garrison gins.
Falls for siege and gins.
Treble blocks, iron.
Double " "
Single " "
Gin hand-spikes.
Hand-spikes for mechanical manœuvres.
Long rollers for mechan. manœ's.
Short rollers "
Half rollers "
Blocks "
Half blocks "
Quarter blocks "
Gun chocks "

Wheel chocks for mechan. manœ's.
Roller chocks "
Skids "
Shifting planks "
Trunion chains.
Mortar eprovettes.
Beds for "
Balls for "
Rocket conductors, Hale's.
Star gauges with rings for inspecting cannon.
42 pdr. ring gauges for shot, large.
" small, old.
" " new.
13 in. ring gaug. for shells, large.
" small, old.
" " new.
42 pdr. grape shot gauges, large.
" small.
Can'r shot gauges for 12 pdr. gun.
" " for 12 pdr. how'r.
Shell callipers for thick. of sides.
" " " bottom.
42 pdr. cylinder gauges for shot.
32 pdr. " " " "

PART SECOND.

TOOLS AND MATERIALS.

Cloths, Ropes, Thread, &c.

Canvass,	yards.	Thread, shoe,	pounds.
Cotton cloth,	"	Thread, patent,	"
Duck, cotton,	"	Tow,	"
Linen, brown,	"	Twine, bundling,	"
Marlin,	pounds.	Worsted stuff,	yards.
Rope, hemp,	"	Yarn, cotton,	pounds.
Rope, manilla,	"	Yarn, packing,	"
Sash cord,	"	Yarn, woollen,	"

Forage.

Bran, bushels.
Hay, pounds.
Oats, bushels.
Straw, pounds.

Ironmongery.

Bolts, door, number.
Brass, sheet, pounds.
Buckles, iron, number.
" brass, "
Chains, iron, pounds.
Chalk, "
Copper, sheet, "
" bar, "
" cake, "
" scrap, "
Emory, - "
Files, assorted, number.
Glue, pounds.
Hinges, iron, butt, pairs.
" brass, " "
Horse shoes, " "
Iron, bar, pounds.
" sheet, "
" plate, "
" scrap, "
" castings, "
Lead, pig, "
" sheet, "
" scrap, "
Locks, assorted, number.
" magazine, "
Mica, sheet, pounds.
Nails, iron, cut, "
" wrought, "
" finishing, "
" horseshoe, "
" bellows, "
Nails, copper, "
Pullies, brass, number.
Rasps, "
Rivets and burrs, iron, pounds.
" " copper, "
Sandpaper, quires.
Screws, wood, assorted, number.
Spelter, solder, pounds.
Steel, cast, "
" blister, "
" shear, "
" scrap, "
Tacks, iron, paper.
" copper, pounds.
Tin, block, pounds.
" sheet, "
Tubing, wrought iron, feet.
Wire, iron, pounds.
" brass, "
" steel, "
Acid, nitric, "
Acid, muriatic, "
Alcohol, "
Antimony, sulphuret, "
Borax, "
Beeswax, "
Camphor, "
Chlorate, potash, "
Chloride lime, "
Flour, "
Gum arabic, "
Gum shellac, "
Nitrate barytes, "
Nitrate strontia, "
Quicksilver, "
Rosin, "
Sal ammoniac, "
Soap, "
Sponge, "
Tallow, "
Whiskey, gallons.

LUMBER.

Gun Carriage Timber and Building Materials.

For 12 pdr. stocktrail carriage:
Gun carriage stocks.
Axle bodies.
For 6 pdr. stocktrail carriage:
Gun carriage stocks.
Axle bodies.
Cheeks.
Axle bodies for limbers.
Poles for limbers,
Hounds "
Forks "
Splinter bars "
Front footboards "
Axle bodies for caissons.
Stocks "
Middle rails "

Side rails for caissons.
Cross bars "
Front footboards "
Hind footboards "
Stocks for forges.
Axle bodies "
Side rails "
Middle rails "
Cross bars "
Studs, plates and guides "
Ends for coal boxes.
Sides " "
Bottoms " "
Lids " "
Axle bodies for battery wagons,
Stocks " "
Lower side rails for " "
Upper side rails for " "
Ridge poles for " "
Ends for ammunition chests.
Sides " "
Frames for covers for ammunition chests.
Panels for ammunition chests.
Bottoms " "
Cover linings for ammunition chests.
Principal partitions for ammunition chests.
Naves for field carriages.
Spokes " "
Fellies " "
Trail handspikes for field carriages.
Legs for siege and garrison gins.
Pry poles for siege and garrison gins.
Windlasses for siege and garrison gins.
Upper braces for siege and garrison gins.
Middle braces for siege and garrison gins.
Lower braces for siege and garrison gins.
Building materials:
Brick, red, number.
" fire, number.
Fire clay, barrels.

Handspikes for gins.
For 32 pdr. casemate gun carriage:
Cheeks.
Front transome.
Rear "
Slides.
Axletrees.
For 32 pdr. casemate chassis:
Tongues.
Hurters and guides.
Rails.
Front transoms.
Rear "
For 32 pdr. barbette top car'ge:
Uprights.
Braces.
Front transoms.
Middle "
For 32 pdr. barbette chassis:
Tongues.
Rails.
Hurters.
Front transoms.
Middle "
Rear "
Props.
Spokes for barbette carriages.
Handspikes " "
Plank, poplar, for interior of ammunition chests, feet.
Plank, ash, for implements, feet.
" walnut, "
" cherry, "
" beech, "
" white pine, "
" yellow pine, "
Scantling, maple, for rammer heads, feet,
Scantling, poplar, for sponge heads, feet,
Scantling, ash, feet.

Lime, barrels.
Sand, loads.
Slates.

Note.—The number of pieces of timber for each part of a gun carriage, &c., should be reported separately, as above. Miscellaneous plank, scantling, &c., should be stated in board measure.

LEATHER AND MATERIALS FOR HARNESS WORK.

Leather, buff, sides.
" bridle, "
" kip, "

Leather, sole, pounds.
Sheep skins with wool, number.
" tanned. "

Leather thong, sides,
" collar. "
" harness, pounds.
" band, "
" skirting, "

Black wax, pounds.
Bristles, "
Hair, "
Raw hides, number.
Whip stocks, "

PAINTS, OILS, GLASS, &c.

Chrome, green, pounds.
Coal tar, gallons.
Copperas, pounds.
Glass, window, feet.
Lacker, for cannon, gallons.
Lampblack, pounds.
Lead, white, "
Litharge, "
Oil, linseed, gallons.
Oil, neatsfoot, "
Oil, sperm, "
Ochre, yellow, pounds.
Putty, "

Pumice stone, pounds.
Prussian blue, "
Paint, mixed, olive, "
" " black, "
Spirits of turpentine, gallons.
Tar, "
Umber, pounds.
Varnish, copal, gallons.
" Japan, "
Vermillion, pounds.
Whiting, "
Zinc paint, white, "

STATIONERY.

Books, office, blank.
Ink, black, gallons.
Ink, red, pints.
India, rubber, pieces.
Paper, letter, quires.
" cap, "
" envelope, "
" blotting, "
" drawing, sheets.

Pencils, lead, number.
Pens, steel, "
Pasteboard, pounds.
Quills, number.
Sealing wax, pounds.
Tape, pieces.
Wafers, pounds.
Ordnance Manuals.
Ordnance Regulations.

TOOLS.

Adzes, carpenter's.
" cooper's.
Alphabets, sets.
Andirons, pairs.
Anvils.
Augers, assorted.
Awls, saddler's.
Axes, broad.
" felling.
" hand,
Bellows, hand.
Benches, laboratory.
Bevils, assorted.
Bick irons.
Bits, auger.
Blocks for tackle.
Braces.
Brace-bits.
Brushes, dusting.

Forks, straining.
Formers, cast iron, assorted.
" laboratory, "
" for musket cartridges.
" for rifle "
Fullers, assorted.
Funnels, copper.
" glass.
Furnaces, tinner's.
Gauges, assorted.
" wire.
" cutting.
" for rockets.
" for portfires.
Gimlets, assorted.
Glue pots.
Gouges, carpenter's.
" turner's.
" stockers'.

Brushes, paint.
Brushes, white-wash.
Chasing tools.
Cherries.
Chisels, cold.
" firmer.
" framing.
" splitting.
" for turning wood.
Clamps, wood.
" iron.
Claw tools.
Compasses.
Counter-sinks.
Diamonds, glaziers'.
Drawing knives.
Dredging boxes.
Drifts, assorted.
Drills, "
Drill bows.
Figure stamps, sets.
Fire buckets.
Fire engines.
Flasks, moulders, wood.
" " iron.
Flatners.
Forks, hay.
Ladles, large.
" lead.
Lanterns.
Lathes, hand.
" engine.
Level and plumb.
Mallets.
Mandrills, assorted.
Marline spikes.
Measuring lines.
Milling tools,
Mortars and pestles, brass.
Nippers, cutting.
Oil stones.
Paint mills.
Pans, copper.
" paste.
" stone.
Pick axes.
Pincers, saddler's,
Plyers.
Punches, saddler's.
" cutting rifle patches.
" for stencils.
Rakes.
Reamers, assorted.
Rules, carpenter's.
Saws, compass.
Grindstones.
Hacksaw frames.
Hammers, bench.
" copper.
" creasing.
" hand.
" planishing.
" trimming.
Hand barrows.
Hardies.
Hatchets, assorted.
Heading tools.
Hoes.
Holdfasts, bench.
Horses, draught.
Horses, saddler's, wood.
Instruments, drawing, cases of.
Jugs.
Kettles, lead.
" copper.
" varnish.
Knives, pallet.
" putty.
" round, saddler's.
" shoe.
Ladders.
" step.
Shears, tinner's.
Shears, small.
Shovels.
Shoeing tools, sets of.
Sickles.
Sieves, composition.
" parchment.
" assorted.
Sledges.
Soldering irons.
Spades.
Spatulas.
Spirit levels.
Spoke shaves.
Spy glasses.
Squares, trying.
Stakes, bench.
Straight edges.
Swedges.
Sand screens.
Taps, screws.
Ticklers.
Tongs, tinner's grooving.
" smith's.
Tools for cutting wood screws.
" turning iron.
Tools for making paper fuzes.
" bending sheet iron.

Saws, cross-cut.
" circular.
" hand.
" tenon.
" web.
" whip.
Saw sets.
Scales and beams, large.
" " small.
Scales, counter.
" graduated.
Scissors.
Scoops, copper.
Screw plates and taps.
Screw-drivers.
Scythes.
Scythe snaths.
Sets, nail.
Tools for making metal fuzes,
Trammels.
Trestles.
Tube moulds.
Tube wires.
Vices, bevil.
" bench.
" breeching.
" hand.
Water buckets.
Watering pots.
Wheels, buffing.
Wheel barrows.
Wheel cutters.
Wrenches, screw.
" tap.
" assorted.

MISCELLANEOUS ARTICLES.

Arm chests.
Bands.
Baskets.
Boxes, packing.
Brooms.
Canisters, tin.
Carboys.
Corks.
Coal, bituminous, bushels or tons.
Coal, anthracite, pounds.
Coal, charred, bushels.
Demijohns.
Lightning rod points.
Oil cans, large.
Pumps.
Ploughs.
Safes, iron.
Salt, bushels.
Wood, oak, cords.
" pine, "

FORMS.

FORM No. 1.—(See paragraphs 1350, 1353.)

RETURN

Of Ordnance and Ordnance Stores received, issued, and remaining on hand, at Arsenal, commanded by Major A. B., during the quarter ending , 18 .

N. B.—All Articles should be entered on Property Return in the order of classification prescribed in paragraph 1365.

PART FIRST.

ARTILLERY, SMALL ARMS, AMMUNITION, AND OTHER ORDNANCE STORES.

FORM 1.

Date. 18 .		Number of voucher.	SECOND QUARTER, 18 .
April	1		On hand from last quarter, ...
"	15	1	Received from C. D., military store-keeper, ...
May	10	2	" " E. F., contractor at ——, ...
"	22	3	" " Capt. G. A., —— regiment of artillery,
June	30	4	Fabricated at the post, during the quarter, per abstract,
"	30	5	Purchased during the quarter, per abstract, ...
"	30	6	Repaired during the quarter, ...
			Total to be accounted for, ...
May	15	7	Condemned and dropped from the return, by order of the President of the Confederate States, ...
June	30	8	Issued to sundry persons, per abstract, ...
"	30	9	Expended at the post, per abstract, ...
"	30	10	Issued for current service, per abstract, ...
"	30	6	Repaired during the quarter, ...
			Total issued and expended, ...
			Remaining on hand, to be accounted for next quarter,

FORM 1—Continued.

CLASS I.—ORD-

Brass Guns.						Brass Howitzers.		Brass Mortars.		Iron Guns.					Iron Howitzers.	
English trophies.		Mexican.	U. S.			U. S.		French.								
6 pdr., weight 674 lbs.	3 pdr., weight 215 lbs.	18 pdr. trophies, weight 4,384 lbs.	6 pdr., old pattern, 800 lbs.	12 pdr., pattern 1840, 1,770 lbs.	6 pdr., pattern 1840, 885 lbs.	24 pdr., 1312 lbs.	12 pdr., 783 lbs.	16 inch stone, 1,050 lbs.	10 inch, 785 lbs.	10 inch columbiad, S. B.	10 inch columbiad, rifled.	8 inch columbiad, S. B.	8 inch columbiad, rifled.	12 pdr., garrison, model of 1839.	10 inch sea-coast, model 1840.	8 inch sea-coast, model 1840.

Form 1—Continued.

NANCE.						Class II.—Artillery Carriages.										
Unserviceable.						Field Artillery.				Barbette.		Casemate.				
Brass Guns.			Iron Guns.													
24 pdr.	6 pdr., old pattern, weight 660 lbs.	3 pdr., old pattern, 318 lbs.	24 pdr., old pattern, 5,376 lbs.	18 pdr., old pattern, 4,238 lbs.	6 pdr., old pattern, 844 lbs.	12 pdr. stock-trail gun carriages, pattern 1840.	6 pdr. caissons, pattern 1840.	Travelling forges, pattern 1840.	Battery wagons, pattern 1840.	24 pdr. gun-carriages.	24 pdr. chassis.	8 inch columbiad gun-carriages.	8 inch columbiad chassis.	32 pdr. gun carriages.	32 pdr. chassis.	24 pdr. howitzer, for flank defence, complete.

FORM 1—Continued.

Class III.—Artillery Equipments and Implements.																
Cannon Locks.		Handspikes.						Sponges.						Worms and Staves.		
Percussion, left side, for guns with lock pieces.	Do. without lock pieces.	Trail, for field carriages.	Manœuvring.	Shod.	Linstocks.	Port-fire cases.	Shell hooks.	32 pdr.	24 pdr	10 inch columbiad bore.	Tarpaulins, large.	Tarpaulins, small.	Tube pouches.	For siege and garrison guns.	For 12 pdr. field guns.	For 6 pdr. field guns.

Class IV.—Cannon Balls.								Class V.—Fixed Ammunition, &c.										
Shot.			Shells.		Spherical Case.			Shot, Fixed.		Spherical case, fixed.			Strapped Shot.					
42 pdr.	32 pdr.	24 pdr.	10 inch for mortars.	8 inch for columbiads.	24 pdr.	12 pdr.	6 pdr.	12 pdr. shot for 12 pdr. gun, rounds.	12 pdr. canister do. do.	For 12 pdr. gun, do do.	For 12 pdr. howitzer.	For 6 pdr. gun.	12 pdr. shot for 12 pdr. field gun.	6 pdr. shot.	12 pdr. canister for 12 pdr. howitzer.	12 pdr. grape.		

FORM 1—Continued.

Class VI—Small Arms.									Class VII—Accoutrements.							
Muskets.		Rifles.		Pistols.		Swords and Sabres.			For Muskets.			For Rifles.			Cavalry.	
National Armory, percussion, bright.	National Armory, altered to percussion, brown.	Hall's patent flint.	Percussion, new.	Percussion, new model.	Colt's.	Cavalry Sabres, pattern 1840.	Horse artillery sabres, pattern 1850.	Non-commissioned officers', swords.	Infantry cartridge boxes.	Infantry cartridge box plates.	Cartridge box belts.	Wipers.	Ball screws.	Bullet moulds.	Holsters.	Cavalry cartridge boxes.

Form 1—Continued.

Class VIII—Powder, &c.								Class IX—Parts of				
Powder, lbs.			Cartridges.			Lead Balls, lbs.						
Cannon.	Rifle.	Fulminate of mercury.	Musket buck and ball.	Pistol ball.	Rifle blank.	Musket pressed.	Buck shot.	Elevating screws for barbette carriages.	Flange rollers for barbette carriages.	Pintles for casemate chassis.	Sets of iron work 24 pdr. barbette carriages, complete.	Traverse wheels for barbette chassis.

ARTILLERY CARRIAGES.				CLASS X—MISCELLANEOUS.					
Spare parts for field carriages.									
Fellies.	Nave bands.	Pole yokes.	Spokes.	Sling carts, large.	Garrison gins.	Hand carts.	Casemate trucks.	Falls for garrison gins.	Double blocks, iron.

PART SECOND.

TOOLS AND MATERIALS.

FORM 1—Continued.

CLOTH, ROPE, THREAD, &c.									FORAGE.			IRON-	
Cotton cloth, yards.	Marline, pounds.	Rope, hemp, do.	Thread, patent do.	Twine, bundling, do.	Worsted stuff, yards.	Yarn, cotton, pounds.			Hay.	Oats.		Buckles, No.	Horse shoes.

FORM 1—Continued.

MONGERY, &c.					LABORATORY STORES.					
Iron.		Nails.								
Bar, pounds.	Sheet, do.	Copper, do.	Iron, cut, do.		Alcohol, gallons.	Beeswax, pounds.	Gum Arabic, do.	Quicksilver, do.	Rosin, do.	

FORM 1—Continued.

Gun Carriage Timber.											Paints and		
For Field Carriage.				For 24 pdr. Barbette Carriages.									
12 pdr. Gun Carriages.		Caissons.		Gun Carriages.			Chassis.						
Stocks.	Axle bodies.	Stocks.	Middle rails.	Uprights.	Braces.	Axle bodies.	Rails.	Tongues.	Front transoms.	Middle transoms.	Lead, white, pounds.	Ochre, yellow, do.	Oil, linseed, gallons.

FORM 1,—Continued.

OILS.		STATIONERY.				TOOLS.				MISCELLANEOUS.			
Oil, sperm, gallons.	Paint, olive, pounds.	Paper, letter, quires.	Paper, drawing, sheets.	Ink, black, quarts.	Ordnance Regulations.	Axes, hand.	Hammers, saddlers'.	Planes, bench.	Rules, carpenters'.	Carboys.	Coal, bituminous, tons.	Lime, barrels.	Sand, loads.

I certify that the foregoing return exhibtis a correct statement of the public property in my charge during the —— quarter, 18 .

A. B., *Captain Commanding.*

C. S. Arsenal, (Armory or Post.)
—— ——, 18 .

NOTE.—For the quarter ending 30th June, add a certificate that an accurate inventory of property has been made, and the return corrected accordingly. Abstracts of the receipts and issues will be made when their number makes it more convenient.

FORM 2.—(See paragraphs 1264, 1267, 1353.)

Invoice of Ordnance and Ordnance Stores turned over by A. B., Captain or Military Store-keeper, to Lieutenant C. D., Assistant Quartermaster, for transportation to Arsenal, in obedience to order for supplies, No. .

No. of boxes or packages.	Marks.	Total contents.	Weight or Measurement.
From 1 to 7,	Capt. A. B., commanding arsenal, near A., Georgia,	140 muskets, complete, N. A. new, brown,	2,100 pounds.
From 8 to 10,	Lieutenant A. B. commanding arsenal near C., South Carolina.	300 cartridge boxes, infantry; 300 cartridge box belts? 300 gun slings,	1,000 "

I certify that the above is a correct invoice of ordnance and ordnance stores, turned over by me this of , 18 , to Lieutenant C. D., Assistant Quartermaster, for transportation to Arsenal.

A. B., *Captain Commanding, or Military Store-keeper.*

(Signed duplicates,)

FORM 3.—(See paragraph 1353.)

Abstract of Articles fabricated at Arsenal during the quarter of , 18 .

Appropriation.	6 pounder field carriages.	32 pounder casemate carriages.	24 pounder casemate carriages.	10 inch sea-coast mortar beds.	6 pounder strapped shot.	Rifle flasks,	Cavalry sabre belts.	Holsters, pairs.	Musket ball cartridges.	Port-fires.	Quick-match, pounds.	Cones.	Cone seats.	Hammers.
Ordnance service in all its branches,	8	2	1	4	200	210	100	60	10,000	250	35			
Purchase, manufacture and alteration of small arms,												500	500	1,000
Total,	8	2	1	4	200	210	100	60	10,000	250	35	500	500	1,000

I certify that the above is correct.

A. B., *Captain Commanding.*

NOTE.—This abstract is designed to include such articles only as are completed, and are in a suitable condition to be issued for service. (To be made in triplicate.)

Endorsement to be as follows: [See paragraph 1360.]

"No. ——.

"Articles fabricated at —— Arsenal,

—— quarter, 18 ."

FORM 4.—(See paragraph 1353.)

Abstract of Articles purchased at *Arsenal during the* *quarter of* 18 .

Appropriation.	Hemp, rope, lbs.	Hay, lbs.	Bar iron, lbs.	Screws (assorted), No.	Gum arabic, lbs.	White pine boards, feet.	Harness leather, lbs.	White lead, lbs.	Linseed oil, galls.	Letter paper, qrs.	Axes, No.	Anthracite coal, lbs.	Cast steel, lbs.	Olive oil, bbls.
Ordnance service in all its branches,	550	1,570		864	5	1,520	100	1,150	140	20	10	4,489		
Purchase, manufacture and alteration of small arms,			2,750										1200	2
	550	1,550	1,750	864	5	1,520	100	1,150	140	20	10	4,480	1200	2

I certify that the above abstract is correct. (See Vouchers, Nos. 2, 5, 7, 8, 12, of the cash accounts for this quarter.)
(To be made in triplicate.)

A. B., *Captain Commanding.*

Endorsement to be as follows: (See paragraph 1360.)

"No.——.

"Abstract of articles purchased at —— Arsenal,
—— quarter, 18 ."

FORM 5.—(See paragraph 1353.)

Statement of Articles repaired at , during the quarter of , 18 .

Articles.	Number transferred from unserviceable to serviceable, or made up from unserviceable articles into serviceable articles.	
	From.	To.
6 pounder field carriages,	2 unserviceable,	2 serviceable.
24 " barbette chassis,	5 "	5 "
12 " sponges and rammers,	7 "	6 "
Bayonets,	170 } 170 } "	170 muskets complete.

I certify that the above statement is correct.

Signed, A. B., *Captain Commanding.*

[Triplicates.]

Endorsement to be as follows: (See paragraph 1360.)

" No. ——.
" Article repaired at —— Arsenal,
—— quarter, —— 18 .

FORM 6.—(See paragraph 1353.)

Statement of the serviceable materials obtained from the breaking up of condemned Ordnance or Ordnance Stores, by order of the Secretary of War, of , 18 .

See FORM No. 10.

400	pounds wrought iron.
200	" cast iron.
50	" brass.
30	" copper.
50	" old rope for junk.
20	" leather.

Signed,

A. B., *Captain Commanding.*

(In duplicate.)

Endorsement to be as follows:

"No. ——.

"Materials obtained from condemned stores,

—— quarter, —— 18 ."

FORM 7.—(See paragraphs 1290, 1353.)

Received this day of , 18 , of Captain , commanding , the following Ordnance and Ordnance Stores, viz :—

4	32 pounder iron cannon.
3	24 " casemate carriages, complete.
3	24 " barbette carriages, complete.
500	Muskets, new, brown.

C. D., *Major Commanding.*

(In duplicate.)

Endorsement to be as follows:

" No. ——.

" Receipt for issues to the Army,

—— quarter, —— 18 ."

FORM 8.—(See paragraph 1353.)

I hereby acknowledge to have received of the Confederate States, by the hands of , of the Confederate States Army, the following stores and accoutrements, viz:

100 common rifles, equal in value to	123	1-13	muskets.
100 sets accoutrements (black leather) for rifles, equal in value to	21	11-13	"
350 pistols, equal in value to	215	5-13	"
50 artillery swords, " "	16	4-13	"
175 cavalry sabres, " "	80	10-13	"
175 " " belts, " "	15	4-13	"
1000 muskets, " "	1000		"
500 sets accoutrements for muskets, (black leather,) equal in value to	115	10-13	"
4 6 pdr. iron cannon, 4 6 pdr. field carriages with equipments complete, } equal in value to	110	3-13	"
Total,	1698	9-13	"

The whole being equivalent to sixteen hundred and ninety-eight and nine thirteenths muskets, which are received on account of the quota of arms due to the of , under the act of , 18 . for arming the whole body of the militia, and for which I have signed triplicate receipts.

Given at , this day of , 18 .

Signed, A. B., *Governor, or*
Agent of the State of .

(To be given in triplicate.)

Endorsement to be as follows:

No. ——.

Receipt for issues to the Militia.

Form 9.—(See paragraphs 1265, 1266, 1253.)

Abstract of Materials, &c., expended or consumed at Arsenal, during the quarter of , 18 .

EXPENDED OR CONSUMED.	Powder, cannon, lbs.	Powder, rifle, lbs.	Musket balls, pressed, lbs.	Bundling twine, lbs.	Hay, lbs.	Bar iron, lbs.	Cast steel, lbs.	Gumarabic, lbs.	Uprights for 32 pdr. barbette carriages.	White pine boards, feet.	Pressed bricks, No.	Calf skins, No.	White lead, lbs.	Letter paper. qrs.
In experimental firing, &c., ordnance,	39	50						4						
In making musket and rifle cartridges, "		100	500	2										
In repair and preservation of the post, "										100				
n preservation of stores, "										260				
n repair of tools and machinery, "							38					2		
In office duties, "														20
On account of public horses, "					3500									
In repair and preservation of buildings, arsenals,											100		50	
In making sea-coast carriages, fortifications,						270			20				230	
In making field and siege guns, ordnance stores,						350							20	
In fixing ammunition, " "			1000											
Total expended,	39	150	1500	2	3500	620	38	4	20	360	100	2	300	20

I certify that the above abstract is correct, and that the stores therein referred to have been issued for the above purposes by my orders, agreeably to the articles of the regulations.

(To be signed in triplicate by the commanding officer of the Arsenal or Post.)

(To be furnished in duplicate.) Endorsement as follows: (See paragraph 1360.)

" No. ——.

" Abstract of articles expended or consumed at ——, —— quarter, ——, 18 ."

FORM 10.—(See paragraphs 1312, 1353.)

List of Ordnance and Ordnance Stores condemned at , by Inspector , at an inspection made on the of 18 .

ARTICLES CONDEMNED.	IN WHAT MANNER DISPOSED OF.				
	Broken up.	Sold.	Dropped.	Total.	Remarks.
12 pounder brass guns, French,				2	
6 pounder field carriages,	2	1		3	
Sets of harness for two-wheel horses,			2	2	
Muskets,		170		170	
Infantry cartridge boxes,	54	26	5	85	

I certify that the above enumerated articles have been regularly inspected by me, in conformity to the regulations, and are hereby recommended to be disposed of as above.

(Duplicates.) R. L. B., *Inspector.*

Approved: J. D., *President Confederate States.*

NOTE.—The stores embraced in the above are to be retained on the property return until the purposes of the condemnation, as approved by the President, shall have been finally executed.

Endorsement to be as follows:

"No. ——.
"Condemned stores, ——— Arsenal,
——— quarter, ———, 18 ."

FORM 11.—(See paragraphs 1292, 1353.)

I certify that, in obedience to article   of the Regulations, I have made diligent inquiries for the ordnance and ordnance stores, (referred to in Captain A. B.'s invoice accompanying my third quarter's return of 18 ,) which ordnance stores have not reached my post after a lapse of   days; and that the loss or miscarriage of said stores, as far as can be ascertained, must be attributed to the following circumstances, viz:

(Signed duplicates.)   C. D., *Captain Commanding, or Receiving Officer.*

Endorsement to be as follows:

"Certificate of Lost Stores."

FORM 12.—(See paragraphs 1292, 1353.)

I certify that, in obedience to article   of the Regulations, I have made diligent inquiries for the ordnance and ordnance stores, (referred to in my certified invoice of stores forwarded to Capt. C. D., at   on the   ,) which stores, as appears after a lapse of   days, have not arrived at his post; and that the loss or miscarriage of said stores, as far as I have been able to ascertain, must be attributed to the following circumstances:

(Signed,)   A. B., *Captain, Forwarding Officer.*

NOTE.—The certificate of Captain C. D., in regard to the same stores, is hereunto annexed.

Endorsement to be as follows:

"Certificate of Lost Stores."

FORM 13.—(See paragraphs 1312, 1353.)

Inventory of Ordnance and Ordnance Stores on hand at , commanded by , inspected al , 18 .

Number or quantity.	Articles.	Location.	Commanding Officer's remarks.	Inspector's recommendations.
6	12 pdr. brass cannon, 1770 lbs.	Arsenal yard.	Serviceable, model of 1840.	
2	4 " " " 350 "	" "	" French.	
1	3 " " " 216 "	" "	" English trophy, captured at Yorktown.	
8	18 pdr. iron cannon, 3800 "	" "	Heavy, old pattern.	To be sold.
6	18 " " " 3200 "	" "	Light, " "	
2	12 " brass cannon, 1800 "	" "	Unserviceable, French, worn out.	To be exchanged for new guns.
1	6 " " " 670 "	" "	Unserviceable Yankee trophy, captured at Manassas.	
8	6 " field carriages, stocktrail.	Gun house.	New, serviceable.	
2	6 " " "	" "	Unserviceable, irrepairable.	To be broken up.
15 gallons	Linseed oil.	Store-house cellar.		
			To be signed by the commanding officer.	To be signed by the Inspector-General or other authorized inspector.

NOTE.—The stores will be entered upon the inventory in the order of the classification, (paragraph 1365,) which order should be observed as nearly as practicable in the arrangement of the articles in store.

The commanding officer will describe, in the columns of remarks, the kind, quality and condition of the several articles, more in detail than is practicable to do in the quarterly returns. He will also express his opinion, in the columns of remarks, with regard to all such stores as may come within the provisions of the 1312th and 1353d paragraphs of these Regulations.

Endorsement to be as follows:

"No. ——.

"Inventory for inspection," or "for the correction of second quarter's return of property."

FORM 14.—(See paragraph 1244.)

RENT ROLL.

Statement of Dwelling Houses belonging to the Confederate States at armory, (or arsenal,) and of the rents due thereon, on , 18. .

Houses. No.	Houses. Of what kind.	By whom occupied.	Time occupied. Months.	Rent per quarter. D. C.	Amount. D. C.
1	Brick, two story.	A. B., com'g officer's clerk.			
2	Wood, "	C. D., master armorer.			
3	" "	E. F., storekeeper.			
4	" one story.	G. H.	3	3 25	3 25
5	Brick, "	J. K.	2	3 00	2 67
6	" "	L. M.	3	3 50	3 50
7	" two story.	N. O.	1½	3 00	1 50
		P. Q.	3	3 00	3 00
		R. S.	1½	3 00	1 50
8	" one story.	T. U., paymaster's clerk.			
9	Stone, "	V. W.,	3	2 75	2 75
	" "	X. Z.	2	2 70	1 83
10	" "	Unoccupied.			

I certify that the foregoing roll exhibits a correct account of the dwelling houses at this armory, and of their occupation, and of the amount of rent now due on each.

A. B., *Commanding Officer.*

—— Armory,
——, 18 .

Endorsement to be as follows:

"No. ——.
Rent Roll.
—— Armory, —— quarter.

FORM 15.—(See paragraphs 1341, 1342.) (To be printed.)

The Confederate States,

To DR.

18 .					
		Ordnance Service.			*Remarks.*
September	10,	For 2000 feet oak timber, $40 per M., . . .		$80 00	Gun carriages.
		Purchase, Manufacture and Alteration of Small Arms.			
November	8,	For 100 bushels charcoal, at 5 cents per bushel, .	$5 00		Smith's shop.
"	15,	" 75 cords oak wood, $3 50 per cord, . .	262 00		Fuel for workshops.
"	17,	" 5560 feet of pine boards, at 10 50 per M., .	58 38		For arm chests.
"	"	" 2 days' services as laborer, at 75 cents per day,	1 50	327 38	Packing arms.
				$407 38	

Approved, for four hundred and seven dollars and thirty-eight cents.
, 18 . (Signed duplicates.) A. M., *Commanding Officer*.

Received from , paymaster, dollars cents, in full of the above account.
Arsenal or Armory, }
, 18 . }

Endorsement to be as follows (See paragraph 1360):

"No. , A. B.
November , 18. .

Ordnance Service, ...	$80 00
Purchase, Manf. and Alt'n Small Arms,	327 38
	$407 38

FORM 16.—(See paragraph 1341.) (To be printed.)

We, the subscribers, hereby acknowledge to have received of the sums set opposite to our names, respectively, being in full for our services at Arsenal, during the month of , 18 , having signed duplicate receipts.

No.	Address.	Occupation.	No. of days employed.	Pay per day.		Amount.		Signatures.	Witnesses.
				Dols	Cts.	Dols	Cts.		
1	A. B.	Master armorer,	26	2	50	65	00		
2	C. D.	Blacksmith,	24	1	50	36	00		
3	E. F.	Carpenter, &c.	20	1	20	24	00		
						125	00		

I certify, on honor, that the foregoing Pay Roll is correct, and that the men labored during the time charged for; it is accordingly approved for one hundred and twenty-five dollars cents, to be charged as follows:

Date.

Ordnance service in all its branches, ...	$90 00
Purchase, manufacture and alteration of small arms, .	35 00
	$125 00

Signed by Commanding Officer.

Endorsement to be as follows (see paragraph 1360):

No. , hired men, for October , 18 .

Ordnance service in all its branches, ...	$90 00
Manufacture, purchase and alteration of small arms,	35 00
	$125 00

FORM 17.—(See paragraphs 1341, 1342.) (To be printed.)

Pay-Roll of Clerks, Armorers, and others employed at the C. S. Armory, , during the month of , 18 .

We, the subscribers, acknowledge to have received from , paymaster, the sums set opposite our respective names in the last column of figures, in full for our services during the month of , 18 .

No.	Names.	Occupation or Employment.	Time or number.	Wages or prices.	Amount.	Ordnance service. Arms and appendages. Musk't	Ordnance service. Arms and appendages. Rifle.	Ordnance service. Special work.	Amounts.	Signed in Duplicate. Signatures.	Signed in Duplicate. Witnesses.
1	A. B.	Clerk, commanding officer's office,	1 month.	$55 00	$55 00			$55 00	$55 00	A. B.	
2	C. D.	Foreman, armorer,	25 days.	2 00	50 00	$50 00			50 00	C. D.	
3	E. F.	Machinist,	20 "	1 50	30 00				30 00	E. F.	
4	G. H.	{ Forging barrels,	248	20	49 60		$44 80		44 80	G. H.	
		{ Dr. for bursted barrels,	16	30	4 80						
									$179 80		

I certify, on honor, that the foregoing pay-roll is correct; that the work has been done as stated, and that the men employed by the day have labored during the time charged for; it is accordingly approved for dollars cents, to be charged as follows:

Ordnance service, $

Purchase, manufacture and alteration of small arms,

$

B. H., (*B. H., Commanding Officer.*)

Endorsement to be as follows; (See paragraph 1360.)

"No. ——.

Hired men for ——, 18 .

Ordnance service, ... $

Purchase, manufac. and alteration of small arms,

$

NOTE.—The printed form will contain the requisite heads for disbursements under various appropriations. The amount on each page of the roll will be footed up separately, and these several amounts will be recapitulated on the last page.

FORM 18.—(See paragraphs 1251, 1341.) (To be printed.)

We, the subscribers, hereby acknowledge to have received of the sums set opposite our names respectively, being in full for the services of our slaves at Arsenal, during the month of , 18 , having signed duplicate receipts.

From whom hired.	Name and occupation.	Time employed.	Wages per month.	Amount for each slave.	Amount received.		Signatures.
A. B.	A., laborer,	1 month.	$12 00	$12 00			
	C., "	22—26 "	15 00	12 69			
	D., blacksmith,	20—26 "	18 50	14 23			
	E., laborer,	19—26 "	14 00	10 23			
					$49	15	A. B.
C. D.	F., "	1 "	16 00	16 00			
	G., "	25—26 "	14 50	13 94			
	H., "	1 "	14 50	14 50	43	44	
					$92	59	

NOTE.—In cases where it may be difficult to obtain the proper signatures on the roll, because of the distant residence of the owners of the slaves, separate receipts may be taken and appended to the roll.

I certify, on honor, that the above pay-roll is correct, and that the slaves labored during the time charged for; it is accordingly approved for dollars, cents, to be charged to the following appropriations:

Ordnance service in all its branches,	$71 40
Purchase, manufacture, and alteration of small arms,	21 19
	$92 59

Endorsement to be as follows: (See par. 1360.)

"No. ——.

Slave Roll for ——, 18 .

Ordnance service in all its branches,	$71 40
Purchase, manufac. and alteration of small arms,	21 19
	$92 59

[Date.]

(Signed duplicates.)

A. B., *Commanding Officer.*

FORM 19.—(See paragraphs 1340, 1343.) (To be printed.)

Abstract of Disbursements at Arsenal, by , in the quarter ending , 18 .

Date of payment.	No. of vouchers.	To whom paid.	*Nature of the Disbursement.* If the voucher is for services, add from to , 18 , or for the month of , 18 . If for articles, and there is sufficient room on the one line, state the quantity of each; or if not room for this, then say, "iron, nails and paint brushes," or whatever the voucher may be for.	Ordnance service in all its branches.		Purchase, manufacture and alteration of small arms.		Total.	
				Dolls.	Cts.	Dolls.	Cts.	Dolls.	Cts.
18 .									
May 5,	1	A. B.	500 lbs. bar iron; 20 lbs. cast steel,	20	00	15	00	35	00
10,	2	C. D.	100 lbs. harness leather; 4 calf skins,	26	00			26	00
June 30,	3	E. F.	50 bushels oats; 1,000 lbs. hay,	500	00			500	00
30,	4	Hired men,	Services for the month of June,	300	00	700	00	1,000	00
				846	00	715	00	1,561	00

(To be signed in duplicate by the disbursing officer.)

Endorsement to be as follows: (See paragraph 1360.)

"Abstract of disbursements,
—— quarter, ——, 18 .

Ordnance service in all its branches,	$846 00
Purchase, manufacture, and alteration of small arms,	715 00
	$1,561 00

FORM 20.—(See paragraph 1344.) (To be printed.)

DR. *The Confederate States in account current with Captain A. B.* CR.

Dates.	To Expenditures.	Amount.	Dates.	By Cash received.	Amount.
18 .			18 .		
Dec. 31,	For ordnance service, per abstract, ...	$	Oct. 1,	Balance due from last account, per official statement, ...	$
	Purchase, manufac'e and alterat'n of small arms,		" 20,	Amount of treasury warrant, No. ——, issued on requisition, No. ——, ...	
	Balance to new account,		Nov. 15,	Amount received of Major ——, for a sword,	
			Dec. 31,	Amount of rent roll for 4th quarter, ...	
				Dollars, ...	
			Dec. 31,	Balance due the Confederate States carried to new account, ...	

I certify, on honor, that the foregoing account is just and true, as stated; that the expenditures have been faithfully made, and for the objects expressed in the voucher, and for no other; and that they are correctly classed in the abstract; and, also, that the credits given in this account include all public money received by me, and not heretofore accounted for. (To be signed in duplicate by the disbursing officer.)

Arsenal,
, 18 .

Endorsement to be as follows: (See paragraph 1360.)

"Account Current.
Capt. A. B.
—— Arsenal,
—— quarter, 18 ."

FORM 21.—(See paragraph 1284.)

Received, Arsenal, 18 , of Major ,

One field officer's sword,
One pair percussion pistols,

For which I have paid to the said Major the cost prize, dollars.

W. A. N.,
Major Artillery.

(To be made in duplicate.)

Endorsement to be as follows:

No. ——.
Receipt for Stores,
Issued to Major W. A. N.,
For his own use.

FORM 22.—(See paragraphs 1340, 1346.)

Statements of Receipts and Expenditures under each appropriation, for the month of , (or for the quarter,) 18 .

	Ordnance service in all its branches.	Purchase, manufacture, and alterat'n of small arms.	Amount.
Due to the Confederate States from last account, or last month,	69 72	87 21	156 83
Received in quarter, or month,	1,500 00	1,500 00	3,000 00
Total to be accounted for,	1,369 62	1,587 21	3,156 83
Due from the C. S. from last account, or last month,		1,200 00	1,200 00
Expended in quarter, or month,	900 00	550 00	1,450 00
	90 00	1,750 00	2,650 00
Balance due , 18 , To the C. S.,	669 62		669 62
From the C. S.,		162 79	162 79
	Due to the Confederate States.		$506 33

FORM 23.—(See paragraph 1347.)

Estimate of Funds required at Arsenal, during the fourth quarter of 18 .

Ordnance service in all its branches.		
Police and preservation of post,	$430 68	
Placing arms in racks,	500 00	
Tools and machinery,	300 00	
Fuel for steam engine,	350 00	
Public horses,	150 00	
Office duties,	200 00	
Making sling carts,	1,027 48	
Making lifting jacks,	300 00	
Purchase of lumber for packing boxes, &c.,	150 00	
	$3,408 16	
Due C. S. from last quarter,	408 16	
		$3,000 00

Required in sums as follows:

Month.	Ordnance service in all its branches.	Amount.
October,	$1,200 00	$1,200 00
November,	800 00	800 00
December,	1,000 00	1,000 00
Total,	$3,000 00	$3,000 00

(To be signed by the commanding officer.)

FORM 24.—(See paragraphs 1268, 1286.)

Requisition for Ordnance and Ordnance Stores for Arsenal or Post, (date.)

Post or Place.	6 pdr. gun carriages.	Infantry cartridge boxes.	Cannon, powder, pounds.	Slow match, pounds.	Shot gauges, sets.	&c. &c.				REMARKS
On hand, (date.) Required , 18 .	2 3	100 106	200 1000	5 50	0 1					
To be supplied,	1	6	800	45	1					

[Here follow the explanations demanding the issue.]

(Signed) A. B., *Commanding.*

Endorsement to be as follows:

"**Requisition for Ordnance Stores for [post or place].**"

(Date.)

FORM 25.—(See paragraph 1316.)

Requisition for Ordnance and Ordnance Stores, for the use of Militia in the service of the Confederate States.

	6 pdr. brass cannon.	6 pdr. carriages.	Muskets, complete.	Non-com. officers' swords.	Cartridge boxes.	Cartridge box belts.	Bayonet scabbards.	Waist belt plates.	Gun slings.	6 pdr. shot fixed.	Musket ball cartridges.	REMARKS.
	2	2	49	9	49	49	49	51	49	120	2500	Company of infantry of fifty-eight non-commissioned officers and privates. Same form for Artillery, Riflemen, and Cavalry.
Total,	2	2	49	9	49	49	49	51	49	120	2500	

I certify that there are non-commissioned officers, musicians and privates under my command, called into the service of the Confederate States, and that the above requisition is made in conformity thereto.

(Signed) A. B., *Captain of the 5th Regiment of Militia of the State of Tennessee.*

Nashville, June 1, 18

The above requisition has been examined in conformity to the article of the Ordnance Regulations and is approved.

(Signed) C. D., *Major in Confederate States Army.*

Nashville, June 5, 18

Endorsement to be as follows

Requisition for Ordnance and Ordnance Stores, ——, 18

FORM 26.—(See paragraph 1274.) [To be printed.]

State of:

I, , born in , aged years, and by occupation a , do hereby acknowledge to have voluntarily enlisted this day of , 18 , as a of ordnance, in the army of the Confederate States of America, for the period of five years, unless sooner discharged by proper authority; do also agree to accept such bounty, pay, rations, and clothing as is or may be established by law. And I, , do solemnly swear that I will bear true and faithful allegiance to the Confederate States of America, and that I will serve them honestly and faithfully against all their enemies and opposers whomsoever; and that I will observe and obey the orders of the President of the Confederate States, and the orders of the officers appointed over me, according to the rules and articles of war, and the regulations which govern enlisted men of Ordnance.

Sworn and subscribed to at , } this day of , 18 . } J. G., *Recruit.*

S. M., *Magistrate.*

I certify, on honor, that I have carefully examined the above-named recruit, and that, in my opinion, he is free from all bodily defects and mental infirmity which would, in any way, disqualify him from performing the duties of a of ordnance. A. B., *Examining Surgeon.*

I certify, on honor, that I have minutely inspected the recruit, , previously to his enlistment, who was entirely sober when enlisted; and that, to the best of my judgment and belief, he is of lawful age, and a competent mechanic, (carriage-maker, or otherwise, as the case may be.) This recruit has eyes, hair, complexion, is feet inches high.

(Duplicates.) C. D., *Recruiting (or Enlisting) Officer.*

Endorsement to be as follows:

"No. ——
Jonas Gould.
K —— Arsenal,
February ——, 18—."

ARTICLE XLV.

CORPS OF ENGINEERS.

1366. The duties of these corps usually relate to the construction of permanent and field fortifications; works for the attack and defence of places; for the passage of rivers; for the movements and operations of armies in the field; and such reconnoisances and surveys as may be required for these objects, or for any other duty which may be assigned to them. By special direction of the President of the Confederate States, officers of engineers may be employed on any other duty whatsoever. (See 63d Article of War.)

1367. No permanent fortification, or other important work assigned to either corps, shall be undertaken, until the plans have been submitted to a board composed of such officers of the corps as the Secretary of War may designate. The report of the board, with complete drawings and specifications of the work, and detailed estimates of the cost, shall be made to the bureau of the corps in the War Department, and be submitted to the Secretary of War, without whose sanction no plan shall be adopted. A dissenting member of the board may present his own project, memoir, plans, and estimates.

1368. The chief engineer, with the approbation of the Secretary of War, will regulate and determine the number, quality, form, and dimensions, &c., of the necessary vehicles, pontons, tools, implements, arms, and other supplies for the use and service of the engineer company of sappers, miners, and pontoniers, to be procured, as far as practicable, by fabrication in the government establishments of the Engineer and Ordnance Departments.

1369. In any work carried on under the direction of the chief of either corps, his authority must be obtained for the erection of any temporary buildings required in the progress of the work, or the purchase of any vessel or boat, or for furnishing medicines or medical attendance to hired men, and to determine the number and wages of clerks, foremen, and overseers.

1370. An engineer superintending a work or operation shall disburse the money for the same; and when informed of the funds applicable to the work, he will furnish to the bureau or office through which he receives his instructions, a detailed report of the manner in which he proposes to apply the funds.

1371. Public works in charge of either corps shall be inspected once a year, and when completed, by such officers of the corps as the Secretary of War shall designate. A report of each inspection shall be made to the Secretary of War through the bureau of the corps.

1372. On the completion of any fortification or other work, the officer in charge will transmit to the appropriate bureau all the books, papers, and drawing relating to it. Of fortifications, the following drawings are required: a plan of the finished work and the environs within the scope of investment, on a scale 12 inches to a mile; a plan of the main work and outworks, on a scale of 1 inch to 50 feet, with sections, profiles, and elevations, on a scale of 1 inch to 25 feet; and a plan of the masonry, on a scale of 1 inch to 50 feet, with profiles and elevations, on a scale of 1 inch to 25 feet; and such other drawings as may be necessary to show important details of the work.

1373. An officer charged with a survey will procure the books and instruments for the execution of the duty by requisition on the appropriate bureau, and upon his return from field operations will report to it the condition of the instruments in his charge; on the completion of the survey he will transmit to the bureau a full report thereof, with the field notes, and all necessary drawings.

1374. The following reports and returns for a work or operation under the direction of the chief of either corps are to be sent to the appropriate bureau of the corps by the officer in charge:

1375. Monthly returns, within five days after the month to which they relate, viz.: report of operations, Form 1; return of officers and hired men, Form 2; money statement, Form 3;

1376. An estimate of funds for one month, in time to receive the remittance for the service of the month;

1377. Quarterly returns, within twenty days after the quarter to which they relate, viz.: a money account current, Form 4; with abstract of disbursements, Form 5, and vouchers, Forms 6, 7, 8; and a return of property, Form 9, with abstracts of receipts and issues, Forms 10, 11, 12, 13, and 14.

1378. A quarterly return of instruments, books, &c., Form 15, by every officer accountable for them;

1379. A report, in time to reach the bureau by the 20th of October, of the operations on the work or survey during the year ending 30th of June, with the necessary drawings, and showing the condition of the work, the extent and cost of the principal operations (as brick-work, stone-work, earth-work, surveys), accompanied by a summary statement of the expenditures during the year, with an estimate of the funds required for the next year, and an estimate of the amount required to complete the work.

1380. When disbursements are made by the same individual on account of different works, a separate set of accounts for each must be kept and rendered, as above required, as well as separate estimates, returns, and reports; the quarterly accounts being accompanied by a general statement, Form 3, of receipts and expenditures during the quarter on all the works.

1381. The following books and files for each work will be kept by the officer in charge: a letter book, for copies of his official letters; file of letters received; file of orders received; a journal, containing a daily record of the occupations of the persons employed on the work; a book of materials, in which must be entered, under the appropriate head, every kind of material received, specifying date of delivery and payment, from whom received, the kind, quality, price, and cost—in this book the various articles will be entered under the same heads as in the quarterly return of property; a ledger, in which an account will be opened with every person of whom materials or supplies are purchased for the work, including every person not on the rolls; an account-book, containing entries, according to Form 5, of all expenditures and copies of the quarterly accounts current, and estimates of funds; a roll-book, showing the name, occupation, rate of pay, of each hired person, and time made by him daily in each month; a book of miscellanies, containing accounts of experiments and miscellaneous information relating to the work.

1382. Printed forms allowed will be furnished from the bureaus, unless otherwise directed, on requisition in May for a year's supply.

FORM 1.

Report of Operations at Fort for the month of September, 18 .

Masons have been employed in setting coping, N. and W. fronts; roofing casemated traverse, S. W. exterior front; building breast-height and traverse walls, covert way, S. E. front; pointing interior counterscarps, S. E. and S. W. fronts.

Laborers, embanking breakwater, S. W. front; embanking parapet of high covert way; excavating for and laying foundations of breast-height walls, covert way, S. E. front; sodding S. E. glacis coupé; quarrying stone for masons at S. E. quarry; aiding masons and carpenters; receiving materials.

Teamsters, levelling S. E. glacis; transporting stone for and embanking breakwater, S. W. front; aiding masons and carpenters; receiving materials.

Carpenters, on quarters, E. front; making and repairing tools and machinery.

Wheelrights and Smiths, making and repairing tools and machinery.

Plumbers, covering arches, W. front; leading breast-height walls, covert way, S. E. front.

State any important result during the month, as the condition of a front, bastion, battery, &c.; progress of a survey.

Probable operations of the month of October.

Masons, as in September: to commence laying the foundations of S. E. exterior front, and to lay the traverse circles in the exterior battery of N. front.

Laborers, as in September: to finish breakwater, S. W. front, and commence the embankment of parapet of W. front.

Teamsters, as in September.

Carpenters, making and repairing tools and machinery.

Wheelwrights and Smiths, do do. do.

Plumbers, covering arches: to finish the W. front, and commence the S. W. front.

——— ———,
Maj. Engineers.

FORT , ,
October 10, 18 .

Endorsement to be as follows:

FORT

Report of Operations for the month of September, 18 .

FORM 2.

Return of Officers and Hired Men at Fort , for the month of September, 18 .

OFFICERS.

Present.	Absent.
Major A. B. relieved Lieutenant E. F., in charge September 15, by special order No. 14, of August 2. Post-office address for October, Fort .	Lieutenant E. F. at G. Island on service by order of Major A. B. Post-office address for October, Fort . Lieutenant O. P. left September 10, on leave of absence by order ——. Post-office address for October, Indianola, Texas.

HIRED MEN.

No.	Trade or occupation.	Time or piece work.	Wages.	Amount.
30	Masons,	700 days,	$ 2 25	$1575 00
10	Do.	200 days,	1 75	350 00
20	Do. at piece work,	700 sup. ft. of granite,	at 15 cts.	105 00
10	Carpenters,		2 00	
	Do.		1 50	
	Laborers,		1 00	
	Do.		90	
1	Clerk,	1 month,	60 00	
2	Foreman,	1 do.	80 00	
1	Overseer,	1 do.	40 00	
	Amount,			

C. D., *Major Engineers.*

Endorsement:

Officers and Hired Men.

Fort .

September, 18 .

FORM 3.

Statement of Money received and expended, under each appropriation, in the month of September, 18

	Fort	Fort B.	Contingencies of fortifications.	Total.
Due C. S. from last month,	$ 70 00	$ 80 00		$ 150 00
Received in the month,	450 00	8000 00	$300 00	8750 00
Total to be accounted for,	520 00	8080 00	300 00	8900 00
Due from C. S. last month,			400 00	400 00
Expended in the month,	400 00	7000 00		7400 00
Total accounted for,	400 00	7000 00	400 00	7800 00
Due 1st Oct. to the C. S.,	120 00	1080 00		1200 00
Do. from the C. S.,			100 00	100 00
			Due C. S.	1100 00

C. D., *Major Engineers.*

FORM 4.

Dr. *The Confederate States in account current with Major C. D.*, *Corps of Engineers, at Fort* : Cr.

18					18				
Sept.	30	To amount paid for purchases and expenditures during the 3d quarter of 18 , as per accompanying vouchers and abstracts,			July	1	Due the Confederate States, as per account current rendered for the 2d quarter of 18 :		
		Balance,			"	4	By the following Treasury drafts on War Warrant No. 5868, viz: No. 8169, on Collector of 8170, on Collector of 8171, on Treasurer of C. S.		
					Aug.	3	By the following articles sold from Fort , viz: 4950 lbs. scrap iron, at 1½ cent per lb. 26 wheelbarrows, $5 each, sold A. B., as per accompanying certificate of sale.		
					Sept.	30	By this amount disallowed at the Treasury Department, being the item in Voucher No. 16 of the accounts for Fort , for the 2d quarter of 1838, viz:		
							$		
					Oct.	1	Due the Confederate States,		

I certify that the foregoing is a true account of all money received by me for Fort not heretofore accounted for, and that the disbursements have been faithfully made.

E. E.

Fort October 4, 18 .

C. D., *Major Engineers.*

Endorsement to be as follows:

Fort .
Account Current of
Major C. D., C. S. Engineers, for the 3d quarter, 18 .

FORM 5.

Abstract of Disbursements on account of Fort during the quarter ending on the 30th of September, 18 .

No. of voucher.	Nature of purchase or expenditure.	To whom paid or of whom purchased.	Amount. Dolls.	Cts.
1	Lime,	Henry King,	200	00
2	Stone,	Joseph King,	500	00
3	Bricks,	Stephenson & Co.,	300	00
4	Sundries,	Smith & Co.,	60	00
5	Cement,	Samuel Jones,	100	00
6	Services,	Hired men,	826	52
7	Granite, lime, and bricks,	Aaron Brown,	3737	50
		Dollars.	5724	02

E. E.

C. D., *Major Engineers.*

Fort

October 4, 18 .

Endorsement, to be as follows:

Fort .
Abstract of Disbursements by

Major C. D., C. S. Engineers, during the 3d quarter, 18 .

FORM 6.

The Confederate States, for Fort ,

To AARON BROWN, DR.

Date.	Designation.	Application.	Cost. Dolls.	Cts.
18 . July 4.	For 600 cubic yards dressed granite at per yard.	Scarp wall.		
	For 30 tons broken granite, at per ton.	Backing of scarp.		
	For cutting 700 feet of granite, at per foot.	Scarp:		
August 1	For 20 M hard bricks, at per M	Casemate arches.		
	For 100 barrels lime, 3 bushels each, at per barrel.	Foundation of scarp and piers,		
		Dollars,	3737	50

I certify that the above account is correct and just; the articles to be (or have been) accounted for in my property return for —— quarter of —.

(Signed) C. D., *Major Engineers.*

Received at Fort , this 24th day of September, 18—, from Major C. D., Corps of Engineers, the sum of three thousand seven hundred and thirty-seven dollars and fifty cents, in full payment of the above account.

(Signed in duplicate.) AARON BROWN.

$3737 50

Endorsement to be as follows:

Fort
Voucher No. 8.
Aaron Brown.
September 24th, 18—.
Granite, Lime, Bricks, $3737 50.

FORM 7.

We, the subscribers, hereby acknowledge to have received of ——— the sums set opposite our names respectively, being in full for our services at Fort A——— during the month of ———. 18—, having signed duplicate receipts.

No.	Name.	Occupation.	Time employed.	Rate of Pay.	Amount. Dolls.	Amount. Cts.	Signatures.	Witn's
1	A. B.	Clerk.	1 month.	$80 00	80	00	A. B.	
2	C. D.	Overseer.	1 do.	40 00	40	00	C. D.	
3	E. F.	Master Mason.	24 days.	2 00	60	00	E. F.	
4	G. H.	Mason.	20 do.	1 75	35	00	G. H.	A. B.
5	I. K.	Laborer.	24 do.	1 00	24	00	I. x K.	
					239	00		

I certify that the foregoing pay-roll is correct and just,

J. M., *Captain Engineers*.

Endorsement:

Fort A———.
No. ———.
Pay-roll for ——, 18—
$239 00

FORM 8.

We, the subscribers, acknowledge to have received of Captain ——— the sums set opposite our names respectively, being in full for the services of our slaves at Fort A——— during the month of ——, 18. having signed duplicate receipts.

From whom hired.	Name and occupation.	Time employed.	Rate of wages.	Amount for each slave.	Amount received. Dolls.	Amount received. Cts.	Signatures.
A. B.	A., mason.	1 month.	$40 00	$40 00			
Do.	C., bl'ksmith.	25 days.	2 00	50 00			
Do.	D., laborer.	1 month.	20 00	30 00			
					$110	00	A. B.
E. F.	G., laborer.	12 days.	$25 a mo	12 00			
Do.	H., do.	1 month.	20 00	20 00			
					32	00	E. F.
					142	00	

I certify that the above pay-roll is correct and just.

J. M., *Captain Engineers.*

Endorsement:

Fort A———,
No. —.
Slave-roll for ———, 18—.
$142 00

FORM 9.

Return of Engineer Property at Fort ——, for the quarter ending 30th June, 18 .

Date.	Vouchers or Abstracts.	Second Quarter, 18 .	Building Materials. Stone. Granite, cubic yards.	Building Materials. Stone. Marble, tons.	Building Materials. Bricks, M.	Building Materials. Lime, casks.	Building Materials. Cement, casks.	Lumber. Scantling, M.	Lumber. Boards, white pine, M.	Boats, No.	Horses, No.	Carts.	Harness, sets.	Tools.	Tools.	Tools.	For'ge. Corn, lbs.	For'ge. Hay, lbs.	Provisions. Pork.	Provisions. Flour.	Provisions. Potatoes.	Miscellaneous.
18		On hand.																				
	Abstract A.	Purchases paid for.																				
	Abstract B.	Purchases not paid for.																				
	Abstract C.	Fabricated.																				
	Abstract D.	Rec'd from other posts.																				
Total to be accounted for,																						
	Abstract E.	Materials used,																				
	Abstract F.	Forage issued,																				
	Abstract G.	Provisions issued,																				
Total issued and expended.																						
Remaining on hand 30th June,																						

I certify that the foregoing return is a true statement of the public property in my charge at Fort A——, ending the —— quarter 186 .

J. M., *Captain Engineers.*

Form 10.

Abstract of Purchases received and paid for at Fort A——, in the —— quarter of 186

No. of vouchers.	To whom paid.	STONE. Granite cubic yards.	STONE. Coping, superficial, feet.	Bricks, M.	Hay, lbs.	Flour, barrels.	IRONMONGERY. Screws, No.	IRONMONGERY. Nails, pounds.	IRONMONGERY. Hinges, No.	IRONMONGERY. Locks, No.	IRONMONGERY. Bar iron, lbs.	IRONMONGERY. Steel, pounds.
1	A. B., ...	800		10,000								
2	C. D., ...		700									
3	E. F., ...				4000							
4	M. N., ...					20	500	1000	50	20	2000	100
5	O. P., ...											
	Total, ...	800	700	10,000	4000	20	500	1000	50	20	2000	100

I certify that the above abstract is correct.

J. M., *Major Engineers.*

FORM 11.

Abstract of Purchases received, and not paid for, at Fort A——, —— quarter, 18

	Of whom purchased.	Bricks, M.	Bar iron, lbs.	Oats, bushels.	Hay, lbs.				
	R. .	50,000							
	S. .		4000						
	T. .			100	2000				
	X. .								
	Y. .								
Amount, .		50,000	4000	100	2000				

I certify that the above abstract is correct.

J. M., *Captain Engineers.*

FORM 12.

Abstract of Materials expended at Fort A——, —— quarter, 18

For what purpose.	Stone, cub. yds.	Bricks, M.	Lime, barrels.	White pine boards, feet.	Yellow pine scantling.		
Scarp wall bastion 1.	2000						
Casemate do		50,000	50				
Stable.				1500	300		
Amount, .	2000	50,000	50	1500	300		

I certify that the above abstract is correct; that the issues and expenditures were made, and were necessary.

J. M., *Captain Engineers.*

FORM 13.

Abstract of Forage issued at Fort ——— during the quarter ending on the 30th September, 18

Description of forage.	Issued during the quarter.	No. of rations.	Distribution of the issues.							Remarks.
			Horses.	Days.	Mules.	Days.	Oxen.	Days.	Rations.	
Hay, pounds.	13,664	976	6	92					552	
			2	65					130	Half rations — horses at grass.
			4	40					80	
					3	10			30	
							2	92	184—976	
Oats, bushels.	233¼	862	6	92					552	
			2	65					130	
			2		3	60			180—862	
Corn, bush.	210	440	4	40					160	
					3	32			96	
							2	92	184—440	

I certify that the above abstract is correct; that the issues were made, and were necessary. C. D., *Major Engineers.*

Endorsement to be as follows:

Fort ———.

Forage Return for the 3d quarter of ———.

Form 14.

Abstract of Provisions issued at Fort during the quarter ending on the 30th September, 18 .

Description of provisions.		Issued in the quarter.	No. of Rations.	No. of men to whom issued.	Remarks.
Pork,	pounds.	1500	2000	40 men employed 92 days, 3680 rations. 8 " 40 " 320 " — 4000 rations.	
Beef—fresh,	do.	2500	2000		
Beef—salt,	do.				
Flour,	do.				
Meal,	do.				
Bread,	do.	4500	4000		
Beans,	quarts.	320	4000		
Vinegar,	do.	160	4000		
&c.,					

I certify that the above abstract is correct; that the issues were made, and were necessary. C. D., *Major of Engineers.*

Endorsement to be as follows:

Fort .

Provision Return for the 3d quarter of 18 .

Form 15.

Return of Instruments, Books, Maps, Charts, and Plans, belonging to the Corps of Engineers, for the quarter

Post or Place.	Instru												
Fort ;	Sextants.	Box sextants.	Artificial horizons.	Theodolites.	Spirit levels.	Level staffs.	Surveyor's compasses.	Pocket compasses.	Boat compasses.	Azimuth compasses.	Reconnoitering or spy-glass.	Boxes drawing instruments.
On hand per last return,												
Received during the quarter,												
To be accounted for,												
Disposed of since last return,												
On hand the 30th Sept., 18												

Books, Maps, Charts,

	Vauban's Fortifications.	Bousmard's Fortification.	Army Regulations.	Eng. Dep. Regulations.	Map of	Map of harbor.	General plan of	Sheets of detailed drawings of Fort				
On hand per last return,												
Received during the quarter,												
To be accounted for,												
Disposed of since last return,												
On hand the 30th Sept., 18												

Endorsement to be as follows:

Return of Instruments, &c.,
in charge of
Major C. D., C. S. Engineers, in 3d quarter, 18

FORM 15.

Confederate States, received and accounted for by Major C. D., of the ending on the 30th of September, 18 .

MENTS.																	REMARKS.
Cases drawing instruments.	Beam compasses.	Proportional compasses.	Triangular compasses.	Dividers.	Protractors.	Boxes of colors.	Brass scales.	Ivory scales.	Surveying chains.	Measuring tapes.	Barometers.	Thermometers.	Tin paper-cases.				Exhibiting the purchase, repair, disposition, &c., of the articles.

AND PLANS.

I certify that the foregoing return is correct.

C. D., *Major Engineers.*

, *October* 1, 18 .

ARTICLE XLVI.

RECRUITING SERVICE.

1383. The recruiting service will be conducted by the Adjutant and Inspector General, under the direction of the Secretary of War.

1384. Field officers will be detailed to superintend the recruiting districts, and lieutenants to take charge of the recruiting parties. The recruiting service will form a special roster. The Adjutant and Inspector General will detail the field officers, and announce in orders the number of lieutenants to be detailed from each regiment by its Colonel. When the detail is not according to the roster, the special reason of the case shall be reported and laid before the Secretary of War.

1385. A recruiting party will consist generally of one lieutenant, one non-commissioned officer, two privates, and a drummer and fifer. The parties will be sent from the principal depots, and none but suitable men selected.

1386. Officers on the general recruiting service are not to be ordered on any other duty, except from the Adjutant General's Office.

DUTIES OF SUPERINTENDENTS.

1387. As soon as a recruiting station is designated, the superintendent sends estimates for funds to the Adjutant General, and requisitions on the proper departments (through the Adjutant and Inspector General) for clothing, camp equipage, arms, and accoutrements.

1388. Subsequent supplies for the stations in his district are procured by the superintendent on consolidated estimates; these are made quarterly for funds, and every six or twelve months for clothing, equipage, arms, and accoutrements. Estimates for funds will be in the following form:

Estimate of Recruiting Funds required for the —— during the quarter ending ——, 18 .

1389. Funds and supplies of clothing, camp and garrison equipage, arms and accoutrements, when ordered, will be sent direct to each station.

1390. The superintendents will transmit to the Adjutant Inspector General consolidated monthly returns of the recruiting parties under their superintendence, according to directions on the printed blanks, accompanied by one copy of the enlistment of each recruit, enlisted within the month. Also a quarterly return of deceased soldiers to the Adjutant Inspector General and Second Auditor.

1391. When recruits should be sent to regiments, a superintendent will report to the Adjutant and Inspector General for instructions in reference thereto.

1392. When recruits are sent from a depot or rendezvous to a regiment or post, *a muster and descriptive roll*, and an *account of clothing* of the detachment, will be given to the officer assigned to the command of it; and a duplicate of the muster and descriptive roll will be forwarded to the Adjutant and Inspector General by the superintendent, who will note on it the names of all the officers on duty with the detachment, and the day of its departure from the depot or rendezvous.

1393. The superintendent will report all commissioned or non-commissioned officers who may be incapable or negligent in the discharge of their functions. Where a recruiting party fails to get recruits from any cause other than the *fault* of the officer, the superintendent will recommend another station for the party.

1394. When a rendezvous is closed, the superintendent will give the necessary instructions for the safe-keeping or disposal of the public property, so as not to involve any expense for storage.

1395. Tours of inspection by superintendents will be made only on instructions from the Adjutant and Inspector General's Office. Officers on the recruiting service will not be sent from place to place without orders from the same source.

DUTIES OF RECRUITING OFFICERS.

1396. Success in obtaining recruits depends much on the activity and *personal attention* of recruiting officers, and they will not entrust to enlisted men the duties for which themselves only are responsible. They will in no case absent themselves from their stations without authority from the superintendent.

1397. Recruiting officers will not allow any man to be deceived or inveigled into the service by false representations, but will in person explain the nature of the service, the length of the term, the pay, clothing, rations, and other allowances to which a soldier is entitled by law, to every man before he signs the enlistment. If minors present themselves, they are to be treated with great candor; the names and residences of their parents or guardians, if they have any, must be ascertained, and they will be informed of the minor's wish to enlist, that they may make their objections or give their consent.

1398. With the sanction of superintendents, recruiting officers may insert in not exceeding two newspapers, brief notices directing attention to the rendezvous for further information.

1399. Any free white male person above the age of eighteen and under thirty-five years, being at least five feet four and a half inches high, effective, able-bodied, sober, free from disease, of good character and habits, and able to speak and understand *well* the English language, may be enlisted. This regulation, so far as respects the *height* and *age* of the recruit, shall not extend to musicians, or to soldiers who may "re-enlist," or have served honestly and faithfully a previous enlistment in the army.

1400. No person under the age of twenty-one years is to be enlisted without the written consent of his parent, guardian, or master. The recruiting officer must be very particular in ascertaining the true age of the recruit, and will not accept him when there is a doubt of his being of age.

1401. After the nature of the service and terms of enlistment have been fairly explained to the recruit, the officer, before the enlistments are filled up, will read to him, and offer for his signature, the annexed declaration, to be appended to each copy of his enlistment:

I, ———, desiring to enlist in the Army of the Confederate States for the period of five years, do declare that I am ——— years and——— months of age; that I have neither wife nor child; that I have never been discharged from the Confederate States service on account of disability, or by a sentence of a court martial, or by order before the expiration of a term of enlistment; and I know of no impediment to my serving honestly and faithfully as a soldier for five years.

Witness: ———.

———.

1402. If the recruit be a minor, his parent, guardian, or master must sign a consent to his enlisting, which will be added to the preceding declaration, in the following form:

I, ———, do certify that I am the (*father only surviving parent, legal master, or guardian*) of ———; that the said ——— is ——— years of age; and I do hereby freely give my consent to his enlisting as a soldier in the Army of the Confederate States for the period of five years.

Witness: ———.

——— ———.

1403. The forms of declaration, and of consent in case of a minor, having been signed and witnessed, the recruit will then be duly inspected by the recruiting officer, and surgeon, if one be present, and if accepted, the 20th and 87th Articles of War will be read to him; after which he will be allowed time to consider the subject until his mind appears to be fully made up before the oath is administered to him.

1404. As soon as practicable, and at least within six days after his enlistment, the following oath will be administered to the recruit:

"I, A— B—, do solemnly swear or affirm, (as the case may be,) that I will bear true allegiance to the Confederate States of America, and that I will serve them honestly and faithfully against all their enemies or opposers whatsoever, and observe and obey the orders of the President of the Confederate States, and the orders of the officers appointed over me, according to the rules and articles for the government of the armies of the Confederate States." (See 10th Art. War.)

1405. Under the Article of War above cited, a justice of the peace, the chief magistrate of any town or city corporate, (not being an officer of the Army,) a notary public, or when recourse cannot be had to such civil magistrates, a judge advocate, or any commissioned officer of the army, may administer the above oath.

1406. It is the duty of the recruiting officer to be present at the inspection of the recruit by the medical officer. In passing a recruit the medical officer is to inspect him stripped; to see that he has free use of all his limbs; that his chest is ample; that his hearing, vision, and speech are perfect; that he has no tumors, or ulcerated, or extensively cicatrized legs; no rupture or chronic cutaneous affection; that he has not received any contusion, or wound of the head, that may impair his faculties; that he is not a drunkard; is not subject to convulsions; and has no infectious disorder, nor any other that may unfit him for military service.

1407. Recruiting officers will not employ private physicians, without authority from the Adjutant and Inspector General's office, for the special purpose of inspecting the recruits prior to their enlisting.

1408. If it be necessary, as in the case of sickness, to employ a physician, the recruiting officer may engage his services by contract, on reasonable terms, by the visit, or by the month. If by the month, the inspection of the recruits must be stated in the contract as part of his duty. The physician will be paid from the recruiting funds.

1409. Enlistments must, in all cases, be taken in triplicate. The recruiting officer will send one copy to the Adjutant General with his quarterly accounts, (paragraph 1280, No. 1,) a second to the superintendent with his monthly return, (paragraph 1280, No. 6,) and a third to the depot at the same time the recruits are sent there. In cases of soldiers re-enlisted in a regiment, or of regimental recruits, the third copy of the enlistment will be sent at its date to regimental headquarters for file.

1410. When ordnance sergeants re-enlist, the recruiting officer will immediately send the second copy of the enlistment direct to the Adjutant General, and the third copy to the station of the ordnance sergeant for file.

1411. A non-commissioned officer, musician, or private soldier, who may re-enlist into his company or regiment within two months before, or one month after the expiration of his term of service, shall receive a bounty of three months' extra pay—that is to say, the pay be was receiving as pay of his grade, and as additional pay for length of service and for certificate of merit. This bounty shall be paid by the recruiting officer at the time of enlistment, and noted on the descriptive list, and timely notice of probable re-enlistments in a company must be given beforehand to the proper authority, that the necessary funds may be provided. Ordnance sergeants and hospital stewards are non commissioned officers entitled to the bounty in the case provided.

1412. Enlistments must, in no case, be antedated so as to entitle a soldier to bounty who applies after the period allowed for "*re-enlisting*" has expired.

1413. A premium of two dollars will be paid to any citizen, non-commissioned officer, or soldier, for each accepted *recruit* that he may bring to the rendezvous; but not for soldiers who receive bounty for "re-enlisting."

1414. The recruiting officer will see that the men under his command are neat in their personal appearance, and will require the permanent party to wear their military dress in a becoming manner, especially when permitted to go abroad.

1415. Only such articles of clothing as are indispensable for immediate use, will be issued to recruits at the rendezvous. Their equipment will not be made complete till after they have passed the inspection subsequent to their arrival at the depot.

1416. The instruction of the recruits will commence at the rendezvous from the moment of enlistment. The general superintendent will see that all recruiting officers give particular attention to this subject.

1417. Recruits will be sent from rendezvzous to depots every ten days, or oftener, if practicable, provided the number disposable exceeds three. The detachments of recruits will be sent from rendezvous to depots under charge of a non-commissioned officer.

1418. Commutation for fuel and quarters, when allowed, is paid from the recruiting funds on the usual vouchers receipted by the officer himself.

1419. Every officer commanding a recruiting party will procure the necessary transportation, forage, fuel, straw, and stationery, taking the requisite vouchers; but no non-commissioned officer or soldier is to be allowed to become a contractor for the supplying of any article which may be required.

1420. The transportation of recruits to depots, and from one recruiting station to another, will be paid from the recruiting funds; transportation of officers and enlisted men on the recruiting service will be paid in the same manner, except when first proceeding to join that service, or returning to their regiments after having been relieved.

1421. No expenses of transportation of officers will be admitted that do not arise from orders emanating from the Adjutant and Inspector General's Office, except they be required to visit branch or auxiliary rendezvous under their charge, when they will be allowed the stage, steamboat, or railroad fare, porterage included.

1422. Whenever an officer is relieved or withdrawn from the recruiting service, he will pay over the balance of any unexpended recruiting funds in his possession to the officer appointed to succeed him, or to the paymaster, if no officer be so designated; and if there be no paymaster or other proper officer convenient to receive such balance, the amount will be deposited to the credit of the Treasurer of the Confederate States, with the most convenient Assistant Treasurer, or other depositary of public money. In either case the officer will forward to the Adjutant and Inspector General the evidence of the disposition he may make of the funds, and report the fact to the superintendent, or to his colonel, if on regimental recruiting service.

RENDEZVOUS, QUARTERING AND SUBSISTING RECRUITS.

1423. Written contracts will be made by recruiting officers for the rent of a rendezvous upon the most reasonable terms possible. The rent will be paid from the recruiting fund. The terms of the contract will be immediately reported to the Adjutant and Inspector General.

1424. When subsistence cannot be issued by the commissariat to recruiting parties, it will be procured by the officer in charge. Written contracts will be made for the subsistence of the recruits, (*see form* A,) due public notice being first given inviting proposals for furnishing complete rations, (or board—see paragraph 1425.) The original advertisement, bids, contracts, and bond, will be forwarded to the Commissary General of Subsistence, and copies be kept for the use of the recruiting station.

1425. When convenience and economy require that the contract shall be for *board and lodging*, the officer in charge shall estimate the cost of the ration for which the contractor shall be paid from the subsistence funds, as before directed; and shall pay the amount due to *lodging* from the recruiting funds.

1426. Issues will be made, or board furnished, (as the case may be,) on regular *provision returns*, specifying the number of men, and days and dates. A ration in kind may be allowed to one laundress at each principal rendezvous. The contractor will forward his accounts either monthly or quarterly to the Commissary General of Subsistence, (*see form* B.) This account will be supported by an *abstract* of issues, duly certified by the recruiting officer, (*see form* C.)

1427. At temporary rendezvous, advertising may be dispensed with, and a contract made conditioned to be terminated at the pleasure of the officer or the Commissary General.

1428. The recruiting officer will be required, when convenient, to receive from the Commissary General and disburse the funds for the subsistence of his party, and to render his accounts quarterly to the Commissary General.

1429. When a contract cannot be made, the recruiting officer may pay the necessary expenses of subsisting and boarding his party; rendering distinct accounts for amounts paid from the subsistence and recruiting funds, as in paragraph 1425.

1430. The expenses of subsistence at branch rendezvous, and all expenses of advertising for proposals, will be paid by the contractor at the principal station and included in his accounts.

BLANKS.

1431. Officers on recruiting service will make timely requisitions for printed blanks, direct, as follows:

To the Adjutant General.—For enlistments; re-enlistments; forms for medical inspection of recruits; muster-rolls; muster and descriptive rolls; monthly returns; tri-monthly reports; recruiting accounts current; accounts of clothing issued; posters or handbills.

To the Quartermaster General.—For estimates of clothing, camp and garrison equipage; clothing receipt rolls; quarterly returns of clothing, camp and garrison equipage.

1432. No blanks of the above kinds will be used, except the printed forms furnished. Blanks of other kinds, when required, must be ruled.

1433. Blanks for the regimental recruiting service are furnished to the company commanders.

FURNITURE AND STATIONERY.

1434. The articles of furniture and police utensils which may be absolutely necessary at a recruiting station may be procured by the officer in charge of the rendezvous, on the special authority of the superintendent.

1435. Necessary stationery will be purchased monthly or quarterly, not to exceed, per quarter at each station, six quires of paper, twenty-four quills, or twenty-four steel pens and two holders, half an ounce of wafers, one paper of inkpowder, one bottle of red ink, four ounces of sealing wax, one quire of cartridge paper, or one hundred envelopes, one fourth quire of blotting paper, and one piece of tape. If necessary, an additional supply of one-fourth of these rates will be allowed to the recruiting officer having charge of one or more auxiliary rendezvous distant from his permanent station. At the principal depots the allowance must be fixed by the wants of the public service.

1436. To each office table is allowed one inkstand, one wafer stamp, one wafer box, one paper folder, one ruler, and as many lead pencils, as may be required, not exceeding four per annum.

1437. Such blank books as may be necessary are allowed to the general superintendent and at permanent recruiting depots; also, one descriptive book for the register of recruits at each permanent station. Blank books will be purchased by recruiting officers, under instructions from the superintendent.

1438. When a recruiting officer is relieved, the blanks, the books, and unexpended stationery, with all the other public property at the station, will be transferred to his successor, who will receipt for the same.

ACCOUNTS, RETURNS, ETC.

1439. The following are the accounts, returns, &c., to be rendered by officers on recruiting service:

To the Adjutant General.

1. *Recruit accounts current,* quarterly, with abstract, (form D,) vouchers, (form E.) and one set of enlistments. An account will be rendered by every officer who may receive funds, whether he makes expenditures or not during the quarter.

2. *A quarterly return* of stationery, books, fuel, straw, and such other property as may have been purchased with the recruiting funds.

3. *A monthly summary statement* of money received, expended, and remaining on hand, (form F,) to be transmitted on the last day of each month.

4. *A muster roll* of all enlisted men at the rendezvous, including the names of all who may have joined, died, deserted, been transferred or discharged, during the period embraced in the muster roll.

5. *Tri-monthly reports* of the state of the recruiting service, according to the prescribed form.

To the Superintendent.

6. *A monthly return* of recruits and of the recruiting party, accompanied with one copy of the enlistment of every recruit enlisted within the month.

7. Duplicate *muster rolls for pay* of the permanent recruiting party, which may be sent direct to the nearest paymaster, when authorized by the superintendent. A triplicate of this roll will be retained at the station.

8. *Muster and descriptive rolls* and an account *of clothing* of every detachment of recruits ordered to the principal depot. If the recruits be ordered to proceed from the rendezvous *direct*, to join any regiment or post, these rolls and accounts of clothing will be delivered to the officer in command of the detachment, a duplicate of each muster and descriptive roll only being then made and sent to the superintendent.

9. Copy of the quarterly abstract of contingent expenses, to be forwarded within three days after the expiration of each quarter.

10. *Quarterly estimates* for funds.

11. *Estimates* for clothing, and camp and garrison equipage, and for arms and accoutrements, for six or twelve months, or for such times as may be directed by the superintendent.

12. Copy of the return No. 13.

To the Quartermaster General.

13. *A quarterly return* of clothing and camp and garrison equipage, and of all quartermaster's property in his possession, not including such as is purchased with the recruiting funds.

To the Ordnance Department.

14. *A quarterly return* of arms, accoutrements, ammunition, and of all ordnance stores.

RULES FOR MAKING ACCOUNTS AND PAPERS.

1440. The following rules must be observed in making out and forwarding accounts and papers:

1. Letters addressed to the Adjutant General "*on recruiting service*," will be so endorsed on the envelopes, under the words "official business."

2. Each voucher must be separately entered on the abstract of contingent expenses, (form F,) and only the gross amount of the abstract must be entered on the account current.

3. No expenditure must be charged without a proper voucher to support it. (See form E.)

4. The receipt to the voucher must be signed, when practicable, by a principal. When this is not practicable, the recruiting officer will add to his own certificate a statement that the agent is duly authorized to sign the receipt.

5. When an individual makes "his mark" instead of signing his name to the receipt, it must be witnessed by a third person.

6. Expenditures must be confined to items stated in the Regulations. In an unforeseen emergency, requiring a deviation from this rule, a full explanation must be appended to the voucher for the expenditure; and if this be not satisfactory, the account will be charged in the Treasury against the recruiting officer.

7. In all vouchers, the different items, with dates, and cost of each, must be given. To vouchers for tranportation of officers, a copy of the order under which the journey was performed, must be appended.

8. In vouchers for medical attendance and medicines, the name of each patient, date of, and charge for each visit, and for medicines furnished, must be given, and the certificate of the physician added, that the rates charged are the usual rates of the place.

9. On all vouchers for premiums for bringing recruits, and fees for oaths of enlistment, the names of the recruits for whom the expenditure is made must be given in alphabetical order, according to the num-

bering of the enlistments. The vouchers may be made in form of consolidated receipt rolls, authenticated by the officer's certificate that they are correct.

10. The fee usually allowed for administering the oath of enlistment being twenty-five cents for each recruit, when a greater amount is paid, the officer must certify on the voucher that it is the rate allowed by law of the State or Territory.

11. To each voucher for notices inserted in newspapers a copy of the notice will be appended.

12. Quarterly accounts current must exhibit the numbers of Treasury drafts and dates of their receipt; and when funds are transferred, the names of officers from whom they are received, or to whom they are turned over, with the dates of transfer.

13. Fractions of cents are not to be taken up on accounts current.

14. Enlistments must be filled up in a fair and legible hand. The *real* name of the recruit must be ascertained, correctly spelled, and written in the same way wherever it occurs; the *Christian* name must not be abbreviated. Numbers in the body of the enlistment must be written and not expressed by figures. Each enlistment must be endorsed as follows:

No. —.
A—— B——,
enlisted at
—— ——
January —, 18—,
By Lt. C—— D——,
— Regiment of ——

The number *in each month* to correspond with the names alphabetically arranged.

15. Whenever a soldier re-enters the service, the officer who enlisted him will endorse on the enlistment, next below his own name and regiment, "second (or third) enlistment," as the case may be, together with the name of the regiment and the letter of the company in which the soldier last served, and date of discharge from former enlistment. This information the recruiting officer must obtain, if possible, from the soldier's discharge, which he should in all cases be required to exhibit. (See 22d Art. of War.)

16. Re-enlistments must be forwarded with recruiting accounts, although the bounty due on them may not be paid. When the bounty is subsequently paid, the soldier's receipt is to be taken on a voucher showing date and place of re enlistment, company and regiment, and by whom re-enlisted.

17. The filling up of, and endorsement on, the enlistment, will be in the handwriting of the recruiting officer, or done under his immediate inspection.

18. To facilitate the final settlement of accounts of discharged soldiers, the name of the *State*, as well as the town, where each recruit is enlisted, will be recorded on all muster, pay, and descriptive rolls.

DEPOTS FOR COLLECTING AND INSTRUCTING RECRUITS.

1441. The depots for recruits are established by orders from the Adjutant and Inspector-General's office.

1442. To each *depot* there will be assigned a suitable number of officers to command and instruct the recruits; and when necessary, such number of enlisted men as may be designated at the Adjutant and Inspector General's office, will be selected for the permanent party, to do garrison duty and for drill masters.

1443. The number of recruits at depots to be assigned to each arm and regiment is directed from the Adjutant and Inspector General's office.

1444. The recruits are to be *dressed in uniform* according to their respective arms, and will be regularly mustered and inspected. They are to be well drilled in the infantry tactics, through the school of the soldier to that of the battalion, and in the exercise of field and garrison pieces. Duty is to be done according to the strict rules of service.

1445. The general superintendent will cause such of the recruits as are found to possess a natural talent for music, to be instructed (besides the drill of the soldier) on the fife, bugle and drum, and other military instruments; and boys of twelve years of age and upward may, under his direction, be enlisted for this purpose. But as recruits under eighteen years of age and under size must be discharged, if they are not capable of learning music, care should be taken to enlist those only who have a natural talent for music, and, if practicable, they should be taken on trial for some time before being enlisted.

1446. Regiments will be furnished with field music on the requisitions of their commanders, made, from time to time, direct on the general superintendent; and when requested by regimental commanders, the superintendents will endeavor to have suitable men selected from the recruits, or enlisted for the regimental bands.

1447. To give encouragement to the recruits, and hold out inducements to good conduct, the commanding officer of the depot may promote such of them to be *lance corporals and lance sergeants* as exhibit the requisite qualifications, not exceeding the proper proportion to the number of recruits at the depot. These appointments will be announced in orders in the usual way, and will be continued in force until they join their regiments, unless sooner revoked. No allowance of pay or emoluments is to be assigned to these appointments; they are only to be considered as recommendations to the captains of companies and colonels of regiments for the places in which the recruits may have acted; but such non-commissioned officers are to be treated with all the respect and to have all the authority which may belong to the stations of sergeant and corporal.

1448. *Permanent* parties at depots, and *recruiting parties*, will be mustered, inspected, and paid in the same manner as other soldiers. Recruits will be mustered for pay only at depots, and when paid there one half of their monthly pay will be retained until they join their regiments.

1449. When recruits are received at a garrisoned post, the commanding officer will place them under the charge of a commissioned officer.

1450. Recruits are not to be put to any labor or work which would interfere with their instruction, nor are they to be employed otherwise than as soldiers, in the regular duties of garrison and camp.

1451. Every enlisted man discharged as a minor, or for other cause involving fraud on his part in the enlistment, or discharged by the civil authority, shall forfeit all pay and allowances due at the time of the discharge.

1452. The Rules and Articles of War are to be read to the recruits every month, after the inspection; and so much thereof as relates to the duties of non-commissioned officers and soldiers will be read to them every week.

INSPECTION OF RECRUITS AT DEPOTS AND POSTS.

1453. The superintendent or commanding officer will cause a minute and critical inspection to be made of every recruit received at a depot two days after his arrival; and should any recruit be found unfit for service, or to have been enlisted contrary to law or regulations, he shall assemble a *Board of Inspectors*, to examine into the case. A board may also be assembled in a special case, when a concealed defect may become manifest in a recruit, at any time during his detention at the depot.

1454. Every detachment ordered from a depot to any regiment or post shall, immediately preceding its departure, be critically inspected by the superintendent or commanding officer and surgeon; and, when necessary, a Board of Inspectors will be convened.

1455. Recruits received at a military post or station shall be carefully inspected by the commanding officer and surgeon, on the third day after their arrival; and if, on such inspection, any recruit, in their opinion, be unsound or otherwise defective in such degree as to disqualify him for the duties of a soldier, then a Board of Inspectors will be assembled to examine into and report on the case. (See paragraphs 1438, 1439, 1440.)

1456. *Boards* for the inspection of recruits will be composed of the three senior regimental officers present on duty, with the troops, including the commanding officer, and the senior medical officer of the army present.

REJECTED RECRUITS.

1457. In all cases of *rejection*, the reasons therefor will be stated at large in a special *report*, to be made by the board; which, together with the surgeon's certificate of disability for service, will be forwarded by the superintendent or commandant of the post direct to the Adjutant and Inspector General. In all such cases, the commanding officer will cause the articles of clothing which may have been issued to the recruit, with the price of each article, to be endorsed on the certificate of disability. If the recommendation of the board for the discharge of the recruit be approved, the authority therefor will be endorsed on the certificate, which will be sent back to be filled up and signed by the commanding officer, who will return the same to the Adjutant and Inspector General's office.

1458. The board will state in the report whether the disability, or other cause of rejection, existed before his enlistment, and whether, with *proper care and examination*, it might not have been discovered.

RECRUITS SENT TO REGIMENTS.

1459. An officer entrusted with the command of recruits ordered to regiments will, on arriving at the place of destination, forward the following papers:

1. To the *Adjutant and Inspector General* and the *Superintendent*, each, a descriptive roll and an account of clothing of such men as may have deserted, died, or been left on the route from any cause whatever, with date and place; also, a special report of the date of his arrival at the post, the strength and condition of the detachment when turned over to the commanding officer, and all circumstances worthy of remark which may have occurred on the march.

2. To the *Commanding Officer* of the regiment or post, the muster and descriptive roll furnished him at the time of setting out, properly signed and completed by recording the names of the recruits *present*, and by noting in the column for remarks, opposite the appropriate spaces, the time and place of death, desertion, apprehension, or other casualty that may have occurred on the route.

1460.* Should an officer be relieved in charge of a detachment *en route*, before it reaches its destination, the date and place, and name of the officer by whom it is relieved, must be recorded on the detachment roll. Without the evidence of such record, no charge for extra pay for clothing accountability of a detachment equal to a company will be allowed.

1461. The "original muster and descriptive roll" of every detachment, with remarks showing the final disposition of each recruit, and the regiment and letter of the company to which he may be assigned, will be signed and forwarded to the Adjutant and Inspector General by the commanding officer who makes the assignment. If the recruits embraced in one roll happen to be assigned to different posts, the original roll is to continue with the last detachment to its destination, each commander completing it so far as concerns the recruits left at his post. When this is not practicable, extracts from the original roll are to be made by the authority which distributes the recruits, to accompany the several detachments and to be forwarded to the Adjutant and Inspector General as in case of the original roll.

REGIMENTAL RECRUITING SERVICE.

1462. The regimental recruiting will be conducted in the manner prescribed for the general service.

1463. Every commander of a regiment is the superintendent of the recruiting service for his regiment, and will endeavor to keep it up to its establishment, for which purpose he will obtain the necessary funds, clothing, &c., by requisition to the Adjutant General.

1464. At every station occupied by his regiment, or any part of it, the colonel will designate a suitable officer to attend to the recruiting duties; which selection will not relieve such officer from his company or other ordinary duties. The officer thus designated will be kept constantly furnished with funds, and, when necessary, with clothing and camp equipage. (See paragraph 1441.)

1465. The regimental recruiting officer will, with the approbation of the commanding officer of the station, enlist all suitable men. He will be governed, in rendering his accounts and returns, by the rules prescribed for the general service; and when leaving a post, will turn over the funds in his hands to the senior company officer of his regiment present, unless some other be appointed to receive them.

Form A.

Articles of agreement made and entered into this day of , Anno Domini one thousand eight hundred and , between , an officer in the Confederate States Army, on the one part, and , of the county of , and State of , of the other part.

This agreement witnesseth, That the said , for and on behalf of the Confederate States of America, and the said , heirs, executors, and administrators, have covenanted and agreed, and by these presents do mutually covenant and agree, to and with each other, as follows, viz:

First. That the said , heirs, executors, and administrators, shall supply, or cause to be supplied and issued, at ; all the rations, to consist of the articles hereinafter specified, that shall be required for the use of the Confederate States recruits stationed at the place aforesaid, commencing on the day of , one thousand eight hundred and , and ending on the day of , one thousand eight hundred and , or such earlier day as the Commissary General may direct, at the price of cents mills for each complete ration.

Second. That the ration to be furnished by virtue of this contract shall consist of the following articles, viz; One and a quarter pound of fresh beef or three-quarters of a pound of salted pork, eighteen ounces of bread or flour, and at the rate of eight quarts of beans or ten pounds of rice, six pounds of coffee, twelve pounds of sugar, four quarts of vinegar, one and a half pound of tallow or one pound of sperm candles, four pounds of soap, and two quarts of salt, to every hundred rations, or the contractor shall furnish the men with good and wholesome board and lodgings, at the option of the recruiting officer; and the recruiting party shall have the privilege of hanging out a flag from the place of rendezvous.

Third. That fresh beef shall be issued at least twice in each week, if required by the commanding officer.

Fourth. It is clearly understood that the provisions stipulated to be furnished and delivered under this contract shall be of the first quality.

Fifth. Should any difficulty arise respecting the quality of the provisions stipulated to be delivered under this contract, then the commanding officer is to appoint a disinterested person to meet one of the same description to be appointed by the contractor. These two thus appointed will have power to decide on the quality of the provisions; but should they disagree, then a third person is to be chosen by the two already appointed, the whole to act under oath, and the opinion of the majority to be final in the case.

Witness:

FORM B.

DR. *The Confederate States,*

To ———, *Special Contractor.*

For rations issued to recruits under the command of ———, at ———, from ——— to ———, as per accompanying abstract:

—— complete rations, at —— cents, ...	$
—— lbs. extra soap, at —— cents, ...	
—— lbs. extra candles, at —— cents.	
Due contractor, ...	$

Received from the Confederate States —— dollars and —— cents, in full of the above account.

——————

Special Contractor:

FORM C.

Abstract of rations issued to recruits stationed at ——, under command of ——, from —— to ——, by ——, Special contractor.

Date.	No. of return.	No. of men.	No. of women.	Commencing.	Ending.	No. of days drawn for.	No. of complete rations.	Remarks.
Total number of complete rations.								

I certify, on honor, that I have carefully compared the above abstract with the original returns now in my possession, and they amount to —— complete rations.

FORM D.

Abstract of disbursements on account of contingencies of the recruiting service, by ———, in the quarter ending ———, 18 , at ———.

No. of voucher.	Date of payment.	To whom paid.	On what account.	Amount.	
				Dolls.	Cts.
			$		

Recruiting Officer.

FORM E.

The Confederate States,

To DR.

Date.		Dolls.	Cts.
	For		

I certify that the above account is correct.

Recruiting Officer.

Received —— this —— day of ——, 18—, of —— —— ——, recruiting officer, —— dollars and —— cents, in full of the above account.

$

(Duplicate.)

FORM F.

MONTHLY SUMMARY STATEMENT.

The Confederate States in account with ——— ———, *at* ——— ———, *in the month of* ———, 18—.

DR.			CR.		
To amount of expenditures within the month			By balance per last statement		
To amount of advance made to			By cash received from ——— ———		
			By cash received from Treasurer of the Confederate States, being amount of warrant No. —		
Balance due the Confederate States carried to next statement,					
$			$		

I certify that the above is a true statement of all the moneys which have come into my hands, on account of the recruiting service, during the month of ———, 18 , and that the disbursements have been faithfully made. The balance due the Confederate States is deposited in ——— ———.

——— ———,
Recruiting Officer.

NOTE.—No vouchers accompany this statement.

ARTICLE XLVII.

UNIFORM AND DRESS OF THE ARMY.

COAT.

For Commissioned Officers.

1466. All Officers shall wear a frock-coat of gray cloth, known as cadet gray; the skirt to extend half way between the hip and the knee; double breasted for all grades.

1467. For a *Brigadier General*—Two rows of buttons on the breast, eight in each row, placed in pairs; the distance between the rows four inches at top and three inches at bottom; stand up collar, to rise no higher than to permit the chin to turn freely over it; to hook in front at the bottom, and slope thence up and backward, at an angle of thirty degrees, on each side; cuffs two and a half inches deep on the under side, there to be buttoned with three small buttons, and sloped upwards to a point at a distance of four inches from the end of the sleeve; pockets in the folds of the skirt, with one button at the hip and one at the end of each pocket, making four buttons on the back and skirt of the tunic, the hip buttons to range with the lowest breast buttons.

1468. For a *Colonel*—the same as for a Brigadier General, except that there will be only seven buttons in each row on the breast, placed at equal distances.

1469. For a *Lieutenant-Colonel, Major, Captain* and *Lieutenant*—the same as for a Colonel.

For Enlisted Men.

1470. The uniform coat for all enlisted men shall be a double-breasted frock coat of gray cloth, known as cadet gray, with the skirt extending half way between the hip and the knee; two rows of buttons on the breast, seven in each row; the distance between the rows four inches at top and three inches at bottom; stand-up collar, to rise no higher than to permit the chin to turn freely over it; to hook in front at the bottom, and slope thence backwards at an angle of thirty degrees on each side; cuffs two and a half inches deep at the under seam, to button with two small buttons, and to be slightly pointed on the upper part of the arm; pockets in the folds of the skirts. The collars and cuffs to be of the color prescribed for facings for the respective arms of service, and the edges of the coat to be trimmed throughout with the same colored cloth. Narrow lining in the skirts of the coat of gray material.

Facings.

1471. The facing for General Officers, and for Officers of the Adjutant General's Department, the Quartermaster General's Department, the Commissary General's Department, and the Engineers—buff. The coat for all officers to be edged throughout with the facings designated.

1472. For the Medical Department—black.

1473. For the Artillery—red.
1474. For the Cavalry—yellow.
1475. For the Infantry—light blue.

1476. For fatigue purposes, a light gray blouse, double breasted, with two rows of small buttons, seven in each row; small, turn-over collar, may be issued to the troops.

1477. On all occasions of duty, except fatigue, and when out of quarters, the coat will be buttoned and hooked at the collar. Officers on bureau duty may wear the coat open.

Buttons.

1478. For General Officers and Officers of the General Staff—bright gilt, rounded at the edge, convex, raised eagle in the centre, with stars surrounding; large size, one inch in exterior diameter; small size, half an inch.

1479. For Officers of the Corps of Engineers, the same as for the General Staff, except that, in place of the eagle and stars, there will be a raised E in German text.

1480. For Officers of Artillery, Infantry, Riflemen and Cavalry—gilt, convex, plain, with large raised letter in the centre; A, for the Artillery; I, for the Infantry; R, for the Riflemen; C, for the Cavalry; large size, seven-eighths of an inch in exterior diameter; small size, half an inch.

1481. Aids-de-Camp may wear the button of the General Staff, or of their regiments or corps, at their option.

1482. For enlisted men of Artillery—yellow, convex, large raised letter A in the centre; three-quarters of an inch in exterior diameter.

1483. For all other enlisted men, the same as for the Artillery, except that the number of the regiment, in large figures, will be substituted for the letter A.

Trowsers.

1484. The uniform trowsers for both officers and enlisted men will be of cloth throughout the year; made loose, and to spread well over the foot; of light (or sky) blue color for regimental officers and enlisted men; and of dark blue cloth for all other officers; reinforced for the Cavalry.

1485. For General officers—two stripes of gold lace on the outer seam, one-eighth of an inch apart, and each five-eighths of an inch in width.

1486. For Officers of the Adjutant General's Department, the Quartermaster General's Department, the Commissary General's Department, and the Corps of Engineers—one stripe of gold lace on the outer seam, one inch and a quarter in width.

1487. For the Medical Department—a black velvet stripe; one inch and a quarter in width, with a gold cord on each edge of the stripe.

1488. For Regimental officers—a stripe of cloth on the outer seam, one inch and a quarter in width; color according to corps: for Artillery, red; Cavalry, yellow; Infantry, dark blue.

1489. For the non-commissioned staff of regiments and for all sergeants, a stripe of cotton webbing or braid on the outer seam, one and a quarter inch in width; color according to arm of service.

1490. For all other enlisted men—plain.

Cap.

1491. Pattern—Of the form known as the French *kepi;* to be made of cloth.

1492. For General Officers, and Officers of the General Staff and Engineers—Dark blue band, sides and crown.

1493. For the Artillery—Dark blue band; sides and crown red.

1494. For the Infantry—Dark blue band; sides and crown light blue.

1495. For the Cavalry—Dark blue band; sides and crown yellow.

Marks to distinguish Rank.

1496. Four gold braids for General Officers; three for Field Officers; two for Captains, and one for Lieutenants, to extend from the band on the front, back and both sides to the top of the cap—and the centre of the crown to be embroidered with the same number of braids.

1497. For enlisted men—the cap will be of the same pattern; the band to be dark blue, and, as in the case of officers, the several arms of service will be designated by the color of the sides and crown—Red for Artillery; light blue for Infantry, and yellow for Cavalry. The number of the Regiment will be worn in front, in yellow metal.

1498. In hot weather, a white duck, or linen cover, known as a havelock, will be worn—the apron to fall behind, so as to protect the ears and neck from the rays of the sun. In winter, in bad weather, an oil skin cover will be worn, with an apron to fall over the coat collar.

Cravat or Stock.

1499. For all officers—black. When a cravat is worn, the tie not to be visible at the opening of the collar.

1500. For enlisted men—black leather, according to pattern.

Boots.

1501. For all officers—ankle or Jefferson.

1502. For enlisted men of Cavalry—ankle and Jefferson, according to pattern.

1503. For other enlisted men—Jefferson, according to pattern.

Spurs.

1504. For all mounted officers—yellow metal or gilt.

1505. For enlisted mounted men—yellow metal, according to pattern.

Gloves.

1506. For General Officers, and officers of the General Staff and Staff Corps—buff or white.

1507. For officers of Artillery, Infantry and Cavalry—white.

Sash.

1508. For General Officers—buff silk net, with silk bullion fringe ends; sash to go twice around the waist, and to tie behind the left hip; pendent part not to extend more than eighteen inches below the tie.

1509. For officers of the General Staff and Engineers, and of the Artillery and Infantry—red silk net. For officers of the Cavalry—yellow silk net. For medical officers—green silk net. All with silk bullion fringe ends; to go around the waist, and to tie as for General Officers.

1510. For sergeants—of worsted, with worsted bullion fringe ends; red for Artillery and Infantry, and yellow for Cavalry. To go twice around the waist, and to tie as above specified.

Sword Belt.

1511. For all officers—a waist belt, not less than one and one-half inches, nor more than two inches wide; to be worn over the sash; the sword to be suspended from it by slings of the same material as the belt, with a hook attached to the belt upon which the sword may be hung.

1512. For General Officers—Russian leather, with three stripes of gold embroidery; the slings embroidered on both sides.

1513. For all other officers—black leather, plain.

1514. For all non-commissioned officers—black leather, plain.

Sword Belt Plate.

1515. For all officers and enlisted men—gilt, rectangular; two inches wide, with a raised bright rim; a silver wreath of laurel encircling the "arms of the Confederate States."

Sword and Scabbard.

1516. For all officers—according to patterns to be deposited in the Ordnance Bureau.

Sword Knot.

1517. For all officers—of plaited leather, with tassels.

Badges to distinguish Rank.

1518. On the sleeve of the coat, rank will be designated by an ornament of gold braid, (in form as represented in the drawing deposited in the Quartermaster General's Office,) extending around the seam of the cuff, and up the outside of the arm to the bend of the elbow. To be of one braid for lieutenants; two, for captains; three, for field officers; and four, for general officers. The braid to be one-eighth of an inch in width.

1519. On the front part of the collar of the coat, the rank of officers will be distinguished as follows:

1520. *General Officers*—A wreath, with three stars enclosed, embroidered in gold. The edge of the wreath to be three-fourths of an inch from the front edge of the collar; the stars to be arranged horizontally; the centre one to be one and one-fourth inches in exterior diameter, and the others three-fourths of an inch.

1521. *Colonel*—Three stars, embroidered in gold, arranged horizontally, and dividing equally the vertical space of the collar. Each star to be one and one-fourth inches in exterior diameter; the front star to be three fourths of an inch from the edge of the collar.

1522. *Lieutenant Colonel*—Two stars of same material, size and arrangement as for a colonel.

1523. *Major*—One star of same material and size as for a colonel; to be placed three-fourths of an inch from edge of collar, and dividing equally the vertical space.

1524. *Captain*—Three horizontal bars, embroidered in gold; each one half-inch in width; the upper bar to be three inches in length; the front edge of the bars to incline to correspond with the angle of the collar, and to be three fourths of an inch from the edge; the line of the back edges to the vertical.

1525. *First Lieutenant*—Two horizontal bars of same material and size as for captains, and dividing equally the vertical space of collar.

1526. *Second Lieutenant*—One horizontal bar of same material and size as for the centre bar of captain and dividing equally the vertical space of collar.

Overcoats for Enlisted Men.

1527. For mounted men—of cadet gray cloth; stand-up collar; double breasted; cape to reach to the cuff of the coat, when the arm is extended, and to button all the way up, (buttons, eighteen.)

1528. For footmen—of cadet gray cloth; stand-up collar; double breasted; cape to reach to the elbows, when the arm is extended, and to button all the way up, (buttons, eighteen.) For the present, to be a talma, with sleeves, of water proof material; black.

Chevrons.

1529. The rank of non commissioned officers will be marked by chevrons on both sleeves of the uniform coat and the overcoat, above the elbow, of silk or worsted binding, half an inch wide; color the same as the edging of the coat; points down, as follows:

1530. For a *Sergeant Major*—three bars and an arc in silk.

1531. For a *Quartermaster Sergeant*—three bars and a tie in silk.

1532. For an *Ordnance Sergeant*—three bars and a star in silk.

1533. For a *First* (or *Orderly*) *Sergeant*—three bars and a lozenge in worsted.

1534. For a *Sergeant*—three bars in worsted.

1535. For a *Corporal*—two bars in worsted.

Hair and Beard.

1536. The hair to be short: the beard to be worn at the pleasure of the individual; but, when worn, to be kept short and neatly trimmed.

ARTICLES OF WAR.

AN ACT FOR ESTABLISHING RULES AND ARTICLES FOR THE GOVERNMENT OF THE ARMIES OF THE CONFEDERATE STATES.

SECTION 1. *The Congress of the Confederate States of America do enact*, That, from and after the passage of this act, the following shall be the rules and articles by which the armies of the Confederate States shall be governed:

ARTICLE 1. Every officer now in the army of the Confederate States shall, in six months from the passing of this act, and every officer who shall hereafter be appointed, shall, before he enters on the duties of his office, subscribe these rules and regulations.

ART. 2. It is earnestly recommended to all officers and soldiers diligently to attend divine service; and all officers who shall behave indecently or irreverently at any place of divine worship shall, if commissioned officers, be brought before a general court-martial, there to be publicly and severely reprimanded by the President; if non-commissioned officers or soldiers, every person so offending shall, for his first offence, forfeit one-sixth of a dollar, to be deducted out of his next pay; for the second offence, he shall not only forfeit a like sum, but be confined twenty-four hours; and for every like offence, shall suffer and pay in like manner; which money so forfeited, shall be applied, by the captain or senior officer of the troop or company, to the use of the sick soldiers of the company or troop to which the offender belongs.

ART. 3. Any non-commissioned officer or soldier who shall use any profane oath or execration, shall incur the penalties expressed in the foregoing article; and a commissioned officer shall forfeit and pay, for each and every such offence, one dollar, to be applied as in the preceding article.

ART. 4. Every chaplain, commissioned in the army or armies of the Confederate States, who shall absent himself from the duties assigned him (excepting in cases of sickness or leave of absence,) shall, on conviction thereof before a court-martial, be fined not exceeding one month's pay, besides the loss of his pay during his absence: or be discharged, as the said court-martial shall judge proper.

ART. 5. Any officer or soldier who shall use contemptuous or disrespectful words against the President of the Confederate States, against the Vice President thereof, against the Congress of the Confederate States, or against the Chief Magistrate or Legislature of any of the Confederate States, in which he may be quartered, if a commissioned officer, shall be cashiered, or otherwise punished, as a court-martial shall direct; if a non-commissioned officer or soldier, he shall suffer such punishment as shall be inflicted on him by the sentence of a court-martial.

ART. 6. Any officer or soldier who shall behave himself with contempt or disrespect towards his commanding officer, shall be punished, according to the nature of his offence, by the judgment of a court-martial.

Art. 7. Any officer or soldier who shall begin, excite, cause, or join in any mutiny or sedition, in any troop or company in the service of the Confederate States, or in any party, post, detachment, or guard, shall suffer death, or such other punishment as by a court-martial shall be inflicted.

Art. 8. Any officer, non-commissioned officer, or soldier, who, being present at any mutiny or sedition, does not use his utmost endeavor to suppress the same, or, coming to the knowledge of any intended mutiny, does not, without delay, give information thereof to his commanding officer, shall be punished by the sentence of a court-martial with death, or otherwise, according to the nature of his offence.

Art. 9. Any officer or soldier who shall strike his superior officer, or draw or lift up any weapon, or offer any violence against him, being in the execution of his office, on any pretence whatsoever, or shall disobey any lawful command of his superior officer, shall suffer death, or such other punishment as shall, according to the nature of his offence, be inflicted upon him by the sentence of a court-martial.

Art. 10. Every non-commissioned officer or soldier, who shall enlist himself in the service of the Confederate States, shall, at the time of his so enlisting, or within six days afterward, have the articles for the government of the armies of the Confederate States read to him, and shall, by the officer who enlisted him, or by the commanding officer of the troop or company into which he was enlisted, be taken before the next justice of the peace, or chief magistrate of any city or town corporate, not being an officer of the army, or where recourse cannot be had to the civil magistrate, before the judge advocate, and in his presence shall take the following oath or affirmation: "I, A. B., do solemnly swear, or affirm, (as the case may be,) that I will bear true allegiance to the Confederate States of America, and that I will serve them honestly and faithfully against all their enemies or opposers whatsoever, and observe and obey the orders of the President of the Confederate States, and the orders of the officers appointed over me, according to the Rules and Articles for the government of the armies of the Confederate States." Which justice, magistrate, or judge advocate, is to give to the officer a certificate, signifying that the man enlisted did take the said oath or affirmation.

Art. 11. After a non-commissioned officer or soldier shall have been duly enlisted and sworn, he shall not be dismissed the service without a discharge in writing; and no discharge granted to him shall be sufficient which is not signed by a field officer of the regiment to which he belongs, or commanding officer, where no field officer of the regiment is present; and no discharge shall be given to a non-commissioned officer or soldier before his term of service has expired, but by order of the President, the Secretary of War, the commanding officer of a department, or the sentence of a general court-martial; nor shall a commissioned officer be discharged the service but by order of the President of the Confederate States, or by sentence of a general court-martial.

Art. 12. Every colonel, or other officer commanding a regiment, troop, or company, and actually quartered with it, may give furloughs to non-commissioned officers or soldiers, in such numbers, and for so long a time, as he shall judge to be most consistent with the good of the service; and a captain, or other inferior officer, commanding a troop or company, or in any garrison, fort or barrack of the Confederate States, (his field officer being absent,) may give furloughs to non-commissioned officers and soldiers, for a time not exceeding twenty days in six months, but not to more than two persons to be absent at the same time, excepting some extraordinary occasion should require it.

ART. 13. At every muster, the commanding officer of each regiment, troop, or company, there present, shall give to the commissary of musters, or other officer who musters the said regiment, troop, or company, certificates signed by himself, signifying how long such officers, as shall not appear at the said muster, have been absent, and the reason of their absence. In like manner, the commanding officer of every troop or company shall give certificates, signifying the reasons of the absence of the non-comissioned officers and private soldiers; which reasons and time of absence shall be inserted in the muster rolls, opposite the names of the respective absent officers and soldiers. The certificates shall, together with the muster rolls, be remitted by the commissary of musters, or other officer mustering, to the Department of War, as speedily as the distance of the place will admit.

ART. 14. Every officer who shall be convicted before a general court-martial of having signed a false certificate relating to the absence of either officer or private soldier, or relative to his or their pay, shall be cashiered.

ART. 15. Every officer who shall knowingly make a false muster of man or horse, and every officer or commissary of muster who shall willingly sign, direct, or allow the signing of muster-rolls wherein such false muster is contained, shall, upon proof made thereof, by two witnesses, before a general court-martial, be cashiered, and shall be thereby utterly disabled to have or hold any office or employment in the service of the Confederate States.

ART. 16. Any commissary of musters, or other officer, who shall be convicted of having taken money, or other thing, by way of gratification, on mustering any regiment, troop, or company, or on signing muster rolls, shall be displaced from his office, and shall be thereby utterly disabled to have or hold any office or employment in the service of the Confederate States.

ART. 17. Any officer who shall presume to muster a person as a soldier who is not a soldier, shall be deemed guilty of having made a false muster, and shall suffer accordingly.

ART 18. Every officer who shall knowingly make a false return to the Department of War, or to any of his superior officers, authorized to call for such returns, of the state of the regiment, troop, or company, or garrison, under his command; or of the arms, ammunition, clothing, or other stores thereunto belonging, shall, on conviction thereof before a court-martial, be cashiered.

ART. 19. The commanding officer of every regiment, troop, or independent company, or garrison, of the Confederate States, shall, in the beginning of every month, remit, through the proper channels to the Department of War, an exact return of the regiment, troop, independent company or garrison under his command, specifying the names of the officers then absent from their posts, with the reasons for and the time of their absence. And any officer who shall be convicted of having, through neglect or design, omitted sending such returns, shall be punished, according to the nature of his crime, by the judgment of a general court-martial.

Art. 20. All officers and soldiers who have received pay, or have been duly enlisted in the service of the Confederate States, and shall be convicted of having deserted the same, shall suffer death, or such other punishment as, by the sentence of a court-martial, shall be inflicted.

Art. 21. Any non-commissioned officer or soldier who shall, without leave from his commanding officer, absent himself from his troop, company, or detachment, shall, upon being convicted thereof, be punished according to the nature of his offence, at the discretion of a court-martial.

Art. 22. No non-commissioned officer or soldier shall enlist himself in any other regiment, troop, or company, without a regular discharge from the regiment, troop, or company in which he last served, on the penalty of being reputed a deserter, and suffering accordingly. And in case any officer shall knowingly receive and entertain such non-commissioned officer or soldier, or shall not, after his being discovered to be a deserter, immediately confine him and give notice thereof to the corps in which he last served, the said officer shall, by a court-martial, be cashiered.

Art. 23. Any officer or soldier who shall be convicted of having advised or persuaded any other officer or soldier to desert the service of the Confederate States, shall suffer death, or such other punishment as shall be inflicted upon him by the sentence of a court-martial.

Art. 24. No officer or soldier shall use any reproachful or provoking speeches or gestures to another, upon pain, if an officer, of being put in arrest; if a soldier, confined and of asking pardon of the party offended, in the presence of his commanding officer.

Art. 25. No officer or soldier shall send a challenge to another officer or soldier to fight a duel, or accept a challenge if sent, upon pain, if a commissioned officer, of being cashiered; if a non-commissioned officer or soldier, of suffering corporeal punishment, at the discretion of a court-martial.

Art. 26. If any commissioned or non-commissioned officer commanding a guard shall knowingly or willingly suffer any person whatsoever to go forth to fight a duel, he shall be punished as a challenger; and all seconds, promoters, and carriers of challenges, in order to duels, shall be deemed principals, and punished accordingly. And it shall be the duty of every officer commanding an army, regiment, company, post, or detachment, who is knowing to a challenge being given or accepted by any officer, non-commissioned officer, or soldier under his command, or has reason to believe the same to be the case, immediately to arrest and bring to trial such offenders.

Art. 27. All officers, of what condition soever, have power to part and quell all quarrels, frays, and disorders, though the persons concerned should belong to another regiment, troop, or company; and either to order officers into arrest, or non-commissioned officers or soldiers into confinement, until their proper superior officers shall be acquainted therewith; and whosoever shall refuse to obey such officer, (though of an inferior rank,) or shall draw his sword upon him, shall be punished at the discretion of a general court-martial.

Art. 28. Any officer or soldier who shall upbraid another for refusing a challenge, shall himself be punished as a challenger; and all officers and soldiers are hereby discharged from any disgrace or opinion of disadvantage which might arise from their having refused to accept of challenges, as they will only have acted in obedience to the laws, and done their duty as good soldiers who subject themselves to discipline.

ART. 29. No sutler shall be permitted to sell any kind of liquors or victuals, or to keep their houses or shops open for the entertainment of soldiers, after nine at night, or before the beating of the reveille, or upon Sundays, during divine service or sermon, on the penalty of being dismissed from all future sutling.

ART. 30. All officers commanding in the field, forts, barracks, or garrisons of the Confederate States, are hereby required to see that the persons permitted to suttle shall supply the soldiers with good and wholesome provisions, or other articles, at a reasonable price, as they shall be answerable for their neglect.

ART. 31. No officer commanding in any of the garrisons, forts, or barracks of the Confederate States, shall exact exorbitant prices for houses or stalls let out to sutlers, or connive at the like exactions in others; nor by his own authority, and for his private advantage, lay any duty or imposition upon, or be interested in, the sale of any victuals, liquors, or other necessaries of life brought into the garrison, fort or barracks, for the use of the soldiers, on the penalty of being discharged from the service.

ART. 32. Every officer commanding in quarters, garrisons, or on the march, shall keep good order, and, to the utmost of his power, redress all abuses or disorders which may be committed by any officer or soldier under his command; if, upon complaint made to him of officers or soldiers beating or otherwise ill-treating any person, or disturbing fairs or markets, or of committing any kind of riots, to the disquieting of the citizens of the Confederate States, he, the said commander, who shall refuse or omit to see justice done to the offender or offenders, and reparation made to the party or parties injured, as far as part of the offender's pay shall enable him or them, shall, upon proof thereof, be cashiered, or otherwise punished, as a general court-martial shall direct.

ART. 33. When any commissioned officer or soldier shall be accused of a capital crime, or of having used violence, or committed any offence against the person or property of any citizen of any of the C. S., such as is punishable by the known laws of the land, the commanding officer and officers of every regiment, troop, or company, to which the person or persons so accused shall belong, are hereby required, upon application duly made by, or in behalf of, the party or parties injured, to use their utmost endeavors to deliver over such accused person or persons to the civil magistrate, and likewise to be aiding and assisting to the officers of justice in apprehending and securing the person or persons so accused, in order to bring him or them to trial. If any commanding officer or officers shall wilfully neglect, or shall refuse, upon the application aforesaid, to deliver over such accused person or persons to the civil magistrates, or to be aiding and assisting to the officers of justice in apprehending such person or persons, the officer or officers so offending shall be cashiered.

ART. 34. If any officer shall think himself wronged by his colonel, or the commanding officer of the regiment, and shall, upon due application being made to him be refused redress, he may complain to the General commanding in the State or Territory where such regiment shall be stationed, in order to obtain justice; who is hereby required to examine into said complaint, and take proper measures for redressing the wrong complained of, and transmit, as soon as possible, to the Department of War, a true state of such complaint, with the proceedings had thereon.

ART. 35. If any inferior officer or soldier shall think himself wronged by his captain or other officer, he is to complain thereof to the commanding officer of the regiment, who is hereby required to summon a regimental court-martial, for the doing justice to the complainant; from which regimental court-martial either party may, if he think himself still aggrieved, appeal to a general court-martial. But if, upon a second hearing, the appeal shall appear vexatious and groundless, the person so appealing shall be punished at the discretion of said court-martial.

ART. 36. Any commissioned officer, store keeper, or commissary, who shall be convicted at a general court-martial of having sold, without a proper order for that purpose, embezzled, misapplied, or willfully, or through neglect, suffered any of the provisions, forage, arms, clothing, ammunition, or other military stores belonging to the Confederate States to be spoiled or damaged, shall, at his own expense, make good the loss or damage, and shall, moreover, forfeit all his pay, and be dismissed from the service.

ART. 37. Any non-commissioned officer or soldier who shall be convicted at a regimental court-martial of having sold, or designedly or through neglect, wasted the ammunition delivered out to him to be employed in the service of the Confederate States, shall be punished at the discretion of such court.

ART. 38. Every non-commissioned officer or soldier who shall be convicted before a court-martial of having sold, lost, or spoiled, through neglect, his horse, arms, clothes, or accoutrements, shall undergo such weekly stoppages (not exceeding the half of his pay,) as such court-martial shall judge sufficient for repairing the loss or damage; and shall suffer confinement, or such other corporeal punishment as his crime shall deserve.

ART. 39. Every officer who shall be convicted before a court-martial of having embezzled or misapplied any money with which he may have been intrusted, for the payment of the men under his command, or for enlisting men into the service, or for other purposes, if a commissioned officer, shall be cashiered and compelled to refund the money; if a non-commissioned officer, shall be reduced to the ranks, be put under stoppages until the money be made good, and suffer such corporeal punishment as such court-martial shall direct.

ART. 40. Every Captain of a troop or company is charged with the arms, accoutrements, ammunition, clothing, or other warlike stores belonging to the troop or company under his command, which he is to be accountable for to his colonel in case of their being lost, spoiled, or damaged, not by unavoidable accidents, or on actual service.

ART. 41. All non-commissioned officers and soldiers who shall be found one mile from the camp without leave, in writing, from their commanding officer, shall suffer such punishment as shall be inflicted upon them by the sentence of a court-martial.

ART. 42. No officer or soldier shall lie out of his quarters, garrison, or camp, without leave from his superior officer, upon penalty of being punished according to the nature of his offence, by the sentence of a court-martial.

ART. 43. Every non-commissioned officer and soldier shall retire to his quarters or tent at the beating of the retreat; in default of which he shall be punished according to the nature of his offence.

ART. 44. No officer, non-commissioned officer, or soldier shall fail in repairing, at the time fixed, to the place of parade, of exercise, or other rendezvous appointed by his commanding officer, if not prevented by sickness or some other evident necessity, or shall go from the said place of rendezvous, without leave from his commanding officer, before he shall be regularly dismissed or relieved, on the penalty of being punished, according to the nature of his offence, by the sentence of a court-martial.

ART. 45. Any commissioned officer who shall be found drunk on his guard, party, or other duty, shall be cashiered; any non-commissioned officer or soldier so offending shall suffer such corporeal punishment as shall be inflicted by the sentence of a court-martial.

ART. 46. Any sentinel who shall be found sleeping upon his post, or shall leave it before he shall be regularly relieved, shall suffer death, or such other punishment as shall be inflicted by the sentence of a court-martial.

ART. 47. No soldier belonging to any regiment, troop, or company, shall hire another to do his duty for him, or be excused from duty but in cases of sickness, disability, or leave of absence; and every such soldier found guilty of hiring his duty, as also the party so hired to do another's duty, shall be punished at the discretion of a regimental court-martial.

ART. 48. And every non-commissioned officer conniving at such hiring of duty aforesaid, shall be reduced; and every commissioned officer knowing and allowing such ill practices in the service, shall be punished by the judgment of a general court-martial,

ART. 49. Any officer belonging to the service of the Confederate States, who, by discharging of firearms, drawing of swords, beating of drums, or by any other means whatsoever shall occasion false alarms in camp, garrison, or quarters, shall suffer death, or such other punishment as shall be ordered by the sentence of a general court-martial.

ART. 50. Any officer or soldier who shall, without urgent necessity, or without the leave of his superior officer, quit his guard, platoon, or division, shall be punished, according to the nature of his offence, by the sentence of a court-martial.

ART. 51. No officer or soldier shall do violence to any person who brings provisions or other necessaries to the camp, garrison, or quarters of the forces of the Confederate States, employed in any parts out of the said States, upon pain of death, or such other punishment as a court-martial shall direct.

ART. 52. Any officer or soldier who shall misbehave himself before the enemy, run away, or shamefully abandon any fort, post, or guard which he or they may be commanded to defend, or speak words inducing others to do the like, or shall cast away his arms and ammunition, or who shall quit his post or colors to plunder and pillage, every such offender, being duly convicted thereof, shall suffer death; or such other punishment as shall be ordered by the sentence of a general court-martial.

ART. 53. Any person belonging to the armies of the Confederate States who shall make known the watchword to any person who is not entitled to receive it according to the rules and discipline of war, or shall presume to give a parole or watchword different from what he received, shall suffer death, or such other punishment as shall be ordered by the sentence of a general court-martial.

ART. 54. All officers and soldiers are to behave themselves orderly in quarters and on their march; and whoever shall commit any waste or spoil, either in walks or trees, parks, warrens, fish-ponds, houses or gardens, corn-fields, inclosures of meadows, or shall maliciously destroy any property whatsoever belonging to the inhabitants of the Confederate States, unless by order of the then commander-in-chief of the armies of the said States, shall (besides such penalties as they are liable to by law,) be punished, according to the nature and degree of the offence, by the judgment of a regimental or general court-martial.

ART. 55. Whosoever, belonging to the armies of the Confederate States in foreign parts, shall force a safeguard, shall suffer death.

ART. 56. Whosoever shall relieve the enemy with money, victuals, or ammunition, or shall knowingly harbor or protect an enemy, shall suffer death, or such other punishment as shall be ordered by the sentence of a court-martial.

ART. 57. Whosoever shall be convicted of holding correspondence with, or giving intelligence to, the enemy, either directly or indirectly, shall suffer death, or such other punishment as shall be ordered by the sentence of a court-martial.

ART. 58. All public stores taken in the enemy's camp, towns, forts, or magazines, whether of artillery, ammunition, clothing, forage, or provisions, shall be secured for the service of the Confederate States; for the neglect of which the commanding officer is to be answerable.

ART. 59. If any commander of any garrison, fortress, or post shall be compelled, by the officers and soldiers under his command, to give up to the enemy, or to abandon it, the commissioned officers, non-commissioned officers, or soldiers who shall be convicted of having so offended, shall suffer death, or such other punishment as shall be inflicted upon them by the sentence of a court-martial.

ART. 60. All sutlers and retainers to the camp, and all persons whatsoever, serving with the armies of the Confederate States in the field, though not enlisted soldiers, are to be subject to orders, according to the rules and discipline of war.

ART. 61. Officers having brevets or commissions of a prior date to those of the corps in which they serve, will take place on courts-martial or of inquiry, and on boards detailed for military purposes, when composed of different corps, according to the ranks given them in their brevets or former commissions; but in the regiment, corps or company to which such officers belong, they shall do duty and take rank, both in courts and on boards as aforesaid, which shall be composed of their own corps, according to the commissions by which they are there mustered.

ART. 62. If upon marches, guards, or in quarters, different corps shall happen to join, or do duty, together, the officer highest in rank, according to the commission by which he is mustered, in the army, navy, marine corps, or militia, there on duty by orders from competent authority, shall command the whole, and give orders for what is needful for the service, unless otherwise directed by the President of the Confederate States, in orders of special assignment providing for the case.

ART. 63. The functions of the engineers being generally confined to the most elevated branch of military science, they are not to assume, nor are they subject to be ordered on, any duty beyond the line of their immediate profession, except by the special order of the President of the Confederate States; but they are to receive every mark of respect to which their rank in the army may entitle them respectively, and are liable to be transferred, at the discretion of the President, from one corps to another, regard being paid to rank.

ART. 64. General courts-martial may consist of any number of commissioned officers; from five to thirteen inclusively; but they shall not consist of less than thirteen where that number can be convened without manifest injury to the service.

ART. 65. Any general officer commanding an army, or colonel commanding a separate department, may appoint general courts-martial whenever necessary. But no sentence of a court-martial shall be carried into execution until after the whole proceedings shall have been laid before the officer ordering the same, or the officer commanding the troops for the time being; neither shall any sentence of a general court-martial, in the time of peace, extending to the loss of life, or the dismission of a commissioned officer, or which shall either in time of peace or war, respect a general officer, be carried into execution, until after the whole proceedings shall have been transmitted to the Secretary of War, to be laid before the President of the Confederate States for his confirmation or disapproval, and orders in the case. All other sentences may be confirmed and executed by the officer ordering the court to assemble, or the commanding officer for the time being, as the case may be.

ART. 66. Every officer commanding a regiment or corps may appoint, for his own regiment or corps, courts-martial, to consist of three commissioned officers, for the trial and punishment of offences not capital, and decide upon their sentences. For the same purpose, all officers commanding any of the garrisons, forts, barracks, or other places where the troops consist of different corps, may assemble courts-martial to consist of three commissioned officers, and decide upon their sentences.

ART. 67. No garrison or regimental court-martial shall have the power to try capital cases or commissioned officers; neither shall they inflict a fine exceeding one month's pay, nor imprison, nor put to hard labor, any non-commissioned officer or soldier for a longer time than one month.

ART. 68. Whenever it may be found convenient and necessary to the public service, the officers of the marines shall be associated with the officers of the land forces, for the purpose of holding courts-martial, and trying offenders belonging to either; and, in such cases, the orders of the senior officer of either corps who may be present and duly authorized, shall be received and obeyed.

ART. 69. The judge advocate or some person deputed by him, or by the general, or officer commanding the army, detachment, or garrison, shall prosecute in the name of the Confederate States, but shall so far consider himself as counsel for the prisoner, after the said prisoner shall have made his plea, as to object to any leading question to any of the witnesses, or any question to the prisoner, the answer to which might tend to criminate himself, and administer to each member of the court, before they proceed upon any trial, the following oath, which shall also be taken by all members of the regimental and garrison courts-martial.

"You, A. B., do swear that you will well and truly try and determine, according to evidence, the matter now before you, between the Confederate States of America and the prisoner to be tried, and that you will duly administer justice, according to the provisions of 'An act establishing Rules and Articles for the government of the armies of the Confederate States,' without partiality, favor, or affection; and if any doubt should arise, not explained by said Articles, according to your conscience, the best of your understanding, and the custom of war in like cases; and you do further swear that you will not divulge the sentence of the court until it shall be published by the proper authority; neither will you disclose or discover the vote or opinion of any particular member of the court-martial, unless required to give evidence thereof, as a witness, by a court of justice, in a due course of law. So help you God."

And as soon as the said oath shall have been administered to the respective members, the president of the court shall administer to the judge advocate, or person officiating as such, an oath in the following words:

"You, A. B., do swear, that you will not disclose or discover the vote or opinion of any particular member of the court-martial, unless required to give evidence thereof, as a witness, by a court of justice, in due course of law; nor divulge the sentence of the court to any but the property authority, until it shall be duly disclosed by the same. So help you God."

Art. 70. When a prisoner, arraigned before a general court-martial, shall, from obstinacy and deliberate design, stand mute, or answer foreign to the purpose, the court may proceed to trial and judgment as if the prisoner had regularly pleaded not guilty.

Art. 71. When a member shall be challenged by a prisoner, he must state his cause of challenge, of which the court shall, after due deliberation, determine the relevancy or validity, and decide accordingly; and no challenge to more than one member at a time shall be received by the court.

Art. 72. All the members of a court-martial are to behave with decency and calmness; and in giving their votes are to begin with the youngest in commission.

Art. 73. All persons who give evidence before a court-martial are to be examined on oath or affirmation, in the following form:

"You swear, or affirm (as the case may be, the evidence you shall give in the cause, now in hearing shall be the truth, the whole truth, and nothing but the truth. So help you God."

Art. 74. On the trials of cases not capital, before court-martial, the deposition of witnesses, not in the line or staff of the army, may be taken before some justice of the peace, and read in evidence; provided the prosecutor and person accused are present at the taking the same, or are duly notified thereof.

ART. 75. No officer shall be tried but by a general court-martial, nor by officers of an inferior rank, if it can be avoided. Nor shall any proceedings of trials be carried on, excepting between the hours of eight in the morning and three in the afternoon; excepting in cases which, in the opinion of the officer appointing the court-martial, require immediate example.

ART. 76. No person whatsoever shall use any menacing words, signs, or gestures, in presence of a court-martial, or shall cause any disorder or riot, or disturb their proceedings, on the penalty of being punished at the discretion of the said court-martial.

ART. 77. Whenever any officer shall be charged with a crime, he shall be arrested and confined in his barracks, quarters, or tent, and deprived of his sword by the commanding officer. And any officer who shall leave his confinement before he shall be set at liberty by the commanding officer, or by a superior officer shall be cashiered.

ART. 78. Non-commissioned officers and soldiers, charged with crimes, shall be confined until tried by a court-martial, or released by proper authority.

ART. 79. No officer or soldier who shall be put in arrest shall continue in confinement more than eight days, or until such time as a court-martial can be assembled.

ART. 80. No officer commanding a guard, or provost marshal, shall refuse to receive or keep any prisoner committed to his charge by an officer belonging to the forces of the Confederate States; provided the officer committing shall, at the same time, deliver an account in writing, signed by himself, of the crime of which the said prisoner is charged.

ART. 81. No officer commanding a guard, or provost marshal, shall presume to release any person committed to his charge without proper authority for so doing, nor shall he suffer any person to escape, on the penalty of being punished for it by the sentence of a court-martial.

ART. 82. Every officer or provost marshal, to whose charge prisoners shall be committed, shall, within twenty-four hours after such commitment, or as soon as he shall be relieved from his guard, make report in writing, to the commanding officer, of their names, their crimes, and the names of the officers who committed them, on the penalty of being punished for disobedience or neglect, at the discretion of a court-martial.

ART. 83. Any commissioned officer convicted before a general court-martial of conduct unbecoming an officer and a gentleman, shall be dismissed the service.

ART. 84. In cases where a court-martial may think it proper to sentence a commissioned officer to be suspended from command, they shall have power also to suspend his pay and emoluments for the same time, according to the nature and heinousness of the offence.

ART. 85. In all cases where a commissioned officer is cashiered for cowardice or fraud, it shall be added in the sentence, that the crime, name, and place of abode and punishment of the delinquent, be published in the newspapers in and about the camp, and of the particular State from which the offender came, or where he usually resides; after which it shall be deemed scandalous for an officer to associate with him.

ART. 86. The commanding officer of any post or detachment, in which there shall not be a number of officers adequate to form a general court-martial, shall, in cases which require the cognizance of such a court, report to the commanding officer of the department, who shall order a court to be assembled at the nearest post or department, and the party accused, with necessary witnesses, to be transported to the place where the said court shall be assembled.

ART. 87. No person shall be sentenced to suffer death but by the concurrence of two-thirds of the members of a general court-martial, nor except in the cases herein expressly mentioned; and no officer, non-commissioned officer, soldier, or follower of the army, shall be tried a second time for the same offence.

ART. 88. No person shall be liable to be tried and punished by a general court-martial for any offence which shall appear to have been committed more than two years before the issuing of the order for such trial, unless the person, by reason of having absented himself or some other manifest impediment, shall not have been amenable to justice within that period.

ART. 89. Every officer authorized to order a general court-martial shall have power to pardon or mitigate any punishment ordered by such court, except the sentence of death, or of cashiering an officer; which, in the cases where he has authority (by Article 65) to carry them into execution, he may suspend, until the pleasure of the President of the Confederate States can be known; which suspension, together with copies of the proceedings of the court-martial, the said officer shall immediately transmit to the President for his determination. And the colonel or commanding officer of the regiment or garrison where any regimental or garrison court-martial shall be held, may pardon or mitigate any punishment ordered by such court to be inflicted.

ART. 90. Every judge advocate, or person officiating as such, at any general court-martial, shall transmit, with as much expedition as the opportunity of time and distance of place can admit, the original proceedings and sentence of such court-martial to the Secretary of War; which said original proceedings and sentence shall be carefully kept and preserved in the office of said Secretary, to the end that the persons entitled thereto may be enabled, upon application to the said officer, to obtain copies thereof.

The party tried by any general court-martial shall, upon demand thereof, made by himself, or by any person or persons in his behalf, be entitled to a copy of the sentence and proceedings of such court-martial.

ART. 91. In cases where the general, or commanding officer may order a court of inquiry to examine into the nature of any transaction, accusation, or imputation against any officer or soldier, the said court shall consist of one or more officers, not exceeding three, and a judge advocate, or other suitable person, as a recorder, to reduce the proceedings and evidence to writing; all of whom shall be sworn to the faithful performance of their duty. This court shall have the same power to summon witnesses as a court-martial, and to examine them on oath. But they shall not give their opinion on the merits of the case, excepting they shall be thereto specially required. The parties accused shall also be permitted to cross-examine and interrogate the witnesses, so as to investigate fully the circumstances in the question.

ART. 92. The proceedings of a court of inquiry must be authenticated by the signature of the recorder and the president, and delivered to the commanding officer, and the said proceedings may be admitted as evidence by a court-martial, in cases not capital, or extending to the dismission of an officer, provided, that the circumstances are such that oral testimony cannot be obtained. But as courts of inquiry may be perverted to dishonorable purposes, and may be considered as engines of destruction to military merit, in the hands of weak and envious commandants, they are hereby prohibited, unless directed by the President of the Confederate States, or demanded by the accused.

ART. 93. The judge advocate or recorder shall administer to the members the following oath:

"You shall well and truly examine and inquire, according to your evidence, into the matter now before you, without partiality, favor, affection, prejudice, or hope of reward. So help you God."

After which the president shall administer to the judge advocate or recorder, the following oath:

"You, A. B., do swear that you will, according to your best abilities, accurately and impartially record the proceedings of the court, and the evidence to be given in the case in hearing. So help you God."

The witnesses shall take the same oath as witnesses sworn before a court-martial.

ART. 94. When any commissioned officer shall die or be killed in the service of the Confederate States, the major of the regiment, or the officer doing the major's duty in his absence, or in any post or garrison, the second officer in command, or the assistant military agent, shall immediately secure all his effects or equipage, then in camp or quarters, and shall make an inventory thereof, and forthwith transmit the same to the office of the Department of War, to the end that his executors or administrators may receive the same.

ART. 95. When any non-commissioned officer or soldier shall die, or be killed in the service of the Confederate States, the then commanding officer of the troop or company shall, in the presence of two other commissioned officers, take an account of what effects he died possessed of, above his arms and accoutrements, and transmit the same to the office of the Department of War, which said effects are to be accounted for, and paid to the representatives of such deceased non-commissioned officer or soldier. And in case any of the officers, so authorized to take care of the effects of such deceased non-commissioned officers and soldiers, should, before they have accounted to their representatives for the same, have occasion to leave the regiment or post, by preferment or otherwise, they shall, before they be permitted to quit the same, deposit in the hands of the commanding officer, or of the assistant military agent, all the effects of such deceased non-commissioned officers and soldiers, in order that the same may be secured for, and paid to their respective representatives.

ART. 96. All officers, conductors, gunners, matrosses, drivers, or other persons whatsoever, receiving pay or hire in the service of the artillery, or corps of engineers of the Confederate States, shall be governed by the aforesaid rules and articles, and shall be subject to be tried by courts-martial, in like manner with the officers and soldiers of the other troops in the service of the Confederate States.

Art. 97. The officers and soldiers of any troops, whether militia or others, being mustered and in pay of the Confederate States, shall, at all times and in all places, when joined, or acting in conjunction with the regular forces of the Confederate States, be governed by these Rules and Articles of War, and shall be subject to be tried by courts-martial, in like manner with officers and soldiers in the regular forces; save only that such courts-martial shall be composed entirely of militia officers.

Art. 98. All officers serving by commission from the authority of any particular State, shall, on all detachments, courts-martial, or other duty, wherein they may be employed in conjunction with the regular forces of the Confederate States, take rank next after all officers of the like grade in said regular forces, notwithstanding the commissions of such militia or state officers may be older than the commissions of the officers of the regular forces of the Confederate States.

Art. 99. All crimes not capital, and all disorders and neglects, which officers and soldiers may be guilty of, to the prejudice of good order and military discipline, though not mentioned in the foregoing Articles of War, are to be taken cognizance of by a general or regimental court-martial, according to the nature and degree of the offence, and be punished at their discretion.

Art. 100. The President of the Confederate States shall have power to prescribe the uniform of the army.

Art. 101. The foregoing Articles are to be read and published, once in every six months, to every garrison, regiment, troop or company, mustered, or to be mustered, in the service of the Confederate States, and are to be duly observed and obeyed by all officers and soldiers who are, or shall be, in said service.

Sec. 2. *And be it further enacted*, That in time of war, all persons not citizens of, or owing allegiance to, the Confederate Stotes of America, who shall be found lurking as spies in and about the fortifications or encampments of the armies of the Confederate States, or any of them, shall suffer death, according to the law and usage of nations, by sentence of a general court-martial.

www.ingramcontent.com/pod-product-compliance
Lightning Source LLC
Chambersburg PA
CBHW031349290326
41932CB00044B/576
9783337184872